COLLECTED PLAYS
Volume One

Collected Plays

Volume One
*The Enemy Within · Philadelphia, Here I Come! ·
The Loves of Cass McGuire · Lovers: Winners and Losers ·
Crystal and Fox · The Gentle Island*

Volume Two
*The Freedom of the City · Volunteers · Living Quarters ·
Aristocrats · Faith Healer · Translations*

Volume Three
Three Sisters (after Chekhov) · *The Communication Cord ·
Fathers and Sons* (after Turgenev) · *Making History ·
Dancing at Lughnasa*

Volume Four
The London Vertigo (after Macklin) · *A Month in the Country*
(after Turgenev) · *Wonderful Tennessee · Molly Sweeney ·
Give Me Your Answer, Do!*

Volume Five
Uncle Vanya (after Chekhov) · *The Yalta Game* (after Chekhov) ·
The Bear (after Chekhov) · *Afterplay · Performances ·
The Home Place · Hedda Gabler* (after Ibsen)

Brian Friel

COLLECTED PLAYS

Volume One

Edited by Peter Fallon

ff

FABER & FABER

Gallery Books

Collected Plays: Volume One
is first published in paperback and in a clothbound edition
by The Gallery Press and in paperback by Faber and Faber Limited
in 2016. Originated at The Gallery Press.

The Gallery Press
Loughcrew
Oldcastle
County Meath
Ireland

Faber and Faber Limited
Bloomsbury House,
74–77 Great Russell Street,
London WCIB 3DA
England

ISBN 978–0–571–33174–1

MIX
Paper from
responsible sources
FSC® C013604

Contents

THE
ENEMY
WITHIN

Preface

The Enemy Within is neither a history nor a biography but an
imaginative account, told in dramatic form, of a short period
in St Columba's thirty-four years of voluntary exile. I have
avoided the two spectacular and better known aspects of the
saint — the builder of monasteries in Ireland and in Scotland,
and the prophet and miracle worker, both of which are described generously in St Adamnan's *Life* — and have concen-
trated instead on the private man.

When I have relied on specific events of the time I have tried
to be accurate. The scholar may object to many liberties I have
taken and particularly to my translation of old names into their
modern equivalents (e.g. Hy is here Iona, Dalraida is County
Antrim, Cinel Eoghain is split into County Derry and County
Tyrone, the Scotland and England in the text are the countries
as we know them), but I felt that once I put modern prose
into the mouths of the characters, geographical alterations were
necessary too.

When Columba first went to Iona he brought with him twelve
followers, among whom were Grillaan, Caornan, Dochonna and
Diarmuid. Little or nothing is recorded of these four so that my
treatment of them is purely speculative.

When considering these days one should remember that they
were violent and bloody, that Columba was reared 'among a
people whose Constitution and National Construction rendered
civil faction almost inseparable from their existence' (Reeves),
and that it was not until 804, over two hundred years after
Columba's death, that monastic communities were formally
exempted from military service.

Brian Friel

Characters

COLUMBA, Abbot of Iona
GRILLAAN, Prior
DOCHONNA, domestic manager
CAORNAN, copyist
DIARMUID, personal attendant to Abbot
All these five were founder members and priests

BRENDAN, farm manager
OSWALD, novice
BRIAN, messenger
EOGHAN, Columba's brother
AEDH, Eoghan's son

Time and place

The year 587 — autumn.
The island of Iona, off the west coast of Scotland.

Act One: Autumn afternoon.
Act Two: Three weeks later.
Act Three: Two weeks later.

Set and costume

The action throughout takes place in Columba's cell. It is an austere, comfortless apartment furnished with a few stools, a stone bed covered with straw, a stone pillow (right), a large wooden table (left). On the wall above the table hangs a collection of scrolls — the equivalent of a library.

Each monk wears a heavy woollen robe of natural colour. It has a hood. They wear sandals. Columba's robe is of the same rough texture but is white.

The Enemy Within was first produced by the Abbey Theatre, Dublin, at the Queen's Theatre, on 6 August 1962, with the following cast:

COLUMBA	Ray McAnally
GRILLAAN	Philip O'Flynn
DOCHONNA	Micheál Ó hAonghusa
CAORNAN	Micheál Ó Briain
DIARMUID	Geoff Golden
OSWALD	Vincent Dowling
BRIAN	Patrick Laffan
BRENDAN	Eóin Ó Suilleabháin
AEDH	T P McKenna
EOGHAN	Edward Golden

Produced by	Ria Mooney
Setting by	Tomás Mac Anna
Stage Management by	Bert Carroll

Music

The orchestra under the direction of Seán Ó Riada performed the following selections:
Overture: *Idomeneo* (Mozart)
First interval: *Lyric Suite* (Grieg)
Second interval: *Ceol Gaedhealach* (Ó Riada)

for Bobby Toland
in friendship

ACT ONE

An autumn afternoon in Columba's room. The monk CAORNAN, *who is a scribe, is working at the large wooden table. He is a frail old man of seventy-one years. His eyesight is weak. He stops occasionally to rub his eyes. He is pale and gentle and soft-spoken.* DOCHONNA *enters. He is sixty-six. His manner is brusque but there is a deep attachment between* CAORNAN *and himself. They look on themselves as the old fellows of the community. The monk* DOCHONNA *is domestic manager — in charge of the kitchen. He is deaf.*

DOCHONNA Where is he?

CAORNAN Out giving a hand with the corn. He said he wouldn't be long.

DOCHONNA *grunts and glances at Caornan's work.*

DOCHONNA When did you start working in his room?

CAORNAN The day before yesterday. My own room faces north. Too dark.

DOCHONNA More light here?

CAORNAN (*Nodding in agreement*) That's it. Yes.

DOCHONNA How are the eyes?

CAORNAN Grand, thanks, Dochonna. And your hearing?

DOCHONNA What's that?

CAORNAN (*Pointing to his own ears*) The hearing — how is it?

DOCHONNA Nothing wrong with my hearing. Whatever about the rest of you, thank God I have all my faculties about me.

CAORNAN We're getting no younger.

DOCHONNA I'll tell you something, Caornan: I'm younger than he is. Did you know that?

CAORNAN I thought you and he were both sixty-six?

DOCHONNA There's something you never knew before, eh?

CAORNAN (*Contents himself with nodding*) Yes, yes. (*It is a strain to keep shouting to Dochonna*)

DOCHONNA And if he thinks he's young enough at sixty-six to be out at the corn, then he should allow his juniors to be out at it too. There now.

> *He goes to the door as if he is about to leave, stops and comes back again.*

Of course I can understand him keeping you at your work, Caornan. You're a much older man.

CAORNAN You know very well I'm seventy-one.

DOCHONNA But me that's younger than him — you never knew that before, did you now?

> CAORNAN *shakes his head: No, no.*

He was born on the 7th of December, 521, and I was born on the 11th of December, 521. You see?

CAORNAN You're only a young fellow, Dochonna.

DOCHONNA Four days younger — much as he would like to forget it. Huh! Out there slogging like one of the novices!

CAORNAN He likes to be out and to be active.

DOCHONNA What's that?

CAORNAN He's very strong, very energetic.

DOCHONNA Four full days between us. I'm younger than either of you.

CAORNAN What are you preparing for next Sunday?

DOCHONNA Eh?

CAORNAN Next Sunday — the feast day of Finnian of Clonard.

DOCHONNA I know that.

CAORNAN What are you giving us? (*Points to his mouth*) Food.

DOCHONNA That's what I want to see him about — to get permission to go out to Tiree for a sheep.

CAORNAN Lovely.

DOCHONNA A sheep.

CAORNAN (*Nodding*) Yes. Very nice.

The young monk BRENDAN *bursts in. He is the farmer. He holds the skirts of his habit up around his knees because he has been running. He is a very powerful young man.*

BRENDAN Columba — where is he?

CAORNAN Out at the harvest, Brendan.

BRENDAN The cow — the cow — she's calved in the lower meadow. A wee beauty — strong as a horse —

BRENDAN *dashes off again.*

DOCHONNA Him and those bees of his! They're either swarming or stinging him!

CAORNAN It's the cow, Dochonna. She's calved at last.

DOCHONNA (*Recovering*) The cow has calved. I know that, Caornan. I'm not deaf. I just mentioned the bees in passing.

CAORNAN Yes, Dochonna.

DOCHONNA I'd better get back to my work. There are so many foreigners about the place these times that if you turn your back for five minutes they're slipping garlic or some other poison into the food.

As he is about to leave GRILLAAN *and* OSWALD *enter.* GRILLAAN *is Prior, second in command to* COLUMBA. *He is in his sixties but straight and well-preserved. He is a calm, balanced man and his opinions are respected by the other monks.* OSWALD *is new to Iona — a novice. He speaks with a pronounced English accent. He is very ardent, very tense, very eager to throw himself into his new life.* GRILLAAN *is showing him around.*

GRILLAAN And this is Columba's room – our Abbot.

CAORNAN *rises to greet the newcomer.*

A new novice, Oswald, all the way from the south

coast of England. (*Introducing him*) Dochonna, who is our house manager and sees that we get enough to eat —

DOCHONNA You're welcome, boy.

OSWALD Thank you very much.

GRILLAAN And Caornan, our scribe, and one of the best Greek scholars in Europe.

CAORNAN Don't listen to the Prior, son. I hope you're happy with us.

OSWALD Are all the monks old men?

GRILLAAN (*Laughs*) Heavens, no, boy! I've introduced you only to what's left of the founder members of Iona — Caornan and Dochonna here; and Columba and Diarmuid we met outside, and myself — yes, five survivors from the original twelve. But there are scores of young men from all over the world: French and German and Italian and Spanish and, of course, Irish — from all over the place. Don't worry; you'll have plenty of company.

OSWALD This is a comfortable room.

GRILLAAN (*Indulgently*) Yes — Columba insists on fresh straw on his stone bed.

CAORNAN How long have you been travelling, Oswald?

OSWALD About eight days. Father came with me the length of the mainland.

CAORNAN I'm sure he's lonely now whoever sees him. And your mother too.

OSWALD As a matter of fact he was very sensible about it all. (*To* GRILLAAN) When do I begin?

GRILLAAN Time enough, son. You'll spend a day or two just looking around, getting to know the island and our routine here. You have all your life before you.

CAORNAN Is there any particular work you like, Oswald?

OSWALD I hope to be a scribe.

CAORNAN I'm sure you'll be a good scribe.

DOCHONNA (*To* OSWALD) Did you ever hear tell of a place called Lough Conn, in Connaught?

OSWALD I am English — from the south of England.

DOCHONNA No, no, not England, Connaught, in the west of

Ireland. That's where I come from — Lough Conn.

OSWALD *looks to* GRILLAAN.

GRILLAAN (*To* OSWALD) He is deaf. (*To* DOCHONNA) This boy is from the south of England, Dochonna.

DOCHONNA Aw — another foreigner.

GRILLAAN (*To* OSWALD) He sounds gruff but he's really very kind.

> COLUMBA *enters, followed by* DIARMUID. COLUMBA *is sixty-six but looks a man sixteen years younger. There is vitality, verve, almost youthfulness in every gesture. He has an open healthy face. He looks for no subservience from his community; they are like brothers together. When he comes on the atmosphere is breezy and vital. He is followed by* DIARMUID, *fat and puffy, his personal attendant.* DIARMUID *is a crank; he is constantly worried about his health. He is panting behind his Abbot and trying helplessly to pick the straws off* COLUMBA'S *habit.*

COLUMBA (*To* OSWALD) I'm sorry for keeping you but we had to get the field stooked before the light fails. Have you met everybody?

> *From the moment* COLUMBA *comes on* OSWALD'S *eyes never leave him.*

OSWALD Only the old men, Columba.

COLUMBA (*Laughing heartily*) And that describes them all right! Aren't they a depressing sight? Grillaan here isn't so bad — although he's no fledgling either. But as for Caornan and Dochonna, it's near time they got their reward, the poor souls. And you can see yourself Diarmuid here is killed trying to keep up with me.

DOCHONNA Columba —

COLUMBA   What is it, Dochonna?

DOCHONNA   Have I your permission to go to Tiree for a sheep?

COLUMBA   Have we a feast this week?

CAORNAN   Next Sunday is the thirty-eighth anniversary of Finnian's death.

COLUMBA   Thirty-eight years — is it that length?

GRILLAAN   It seems like a year at most.

COLUMBA   The times we had there in Meath, do you remember? Brendan and Colman and Canice —

GRILLAAN   And Ciaran —

COLUMBA   And Ciaran. And do you remember young Comgall with the black eyes and the innocent face?

They have all been in Finnian's monastery together. This is an old joke of theirs.

GRILLAAN   'Why are you working in the forge, Comgall?'

COLUMBA   'Because I was picked, Finnian.'

GRILLAAN   'You are a Christian now, not a Pict. Get out!'

They all laugh at this — except OSWALD. DOCHONNA laughs too although he is not sure what he is laughing at.

COLUMBA   And the day Enda came from Aran, do you remember?

CAORNAN   With the cartload of dulse! I remember that!

DIARMUID   Don't mention it. I was sick for a week after.

GRILLAAN   'So thoughtful of you, Enda. A load of manure — the very thing we need.'

COLUMBA   I thought Enda would die laughing.

DIARMUID   They claimed they could hear him in Kildare, remember?

GRILLAAN   But old Finnian, the shrewd fox, he didn't bat an eye. 'Dulse? Oh, yes, I have heard of it. My mother used to give it to the young pigs.'

DIARMUID   Never stuck for an answer. Never.

DOCHONNA   Do you remember the day he found young Comgall in the forge?

COLUMBA We were just talking about that, Dochonna.

DOCHONNA What's this it was he said? 'Out you go, boy. I didn't choose you for iron work and you're a Christian now.' (*Chuckles*)

DIARMUID No. No, no, Dochonna. You've messed it all up.

DOCHONNA What's that? What's he saying?

COLUMBA It was a good one, wasn't it, Dochonna? And what was it he used to call you? 'The Hardy Trout' — wasn't that it?

DOCHONNA (*Delighted*) Aye, aye, aye. On account of Lough Conn. Aye, 'The Hardy Trout'. So well you remember, Columba, eh?

COLUMBA I remember everything. The beech trees and the chestnuts and the oaks and the flat, green plains and the silver of the Boyne water on a good summer's day. And the day he died, I remember too. I was in Derry at the time — you were there too, Grillaan — and I remember I was in the chapel saying a mouthful of prayers and —

> He breaks off because the memory embarrasses him.

He was a good man, Finnian; a good man.

OSWALD What happened in the chapel?

GRILLAAN He knew that Finnian had died. He told me when he came out. We didn't get word until two days later.

OSWALD (*Intensely to* COLUMBA) You had a vision? An angel appeared to you? What happened? How did you know he was dead?

COLUMBA Here! How did we get away back into the past like that? Do you know, Oswald, these old doters will soon have me as bad as themselves. Did you have anything to eat yet?

OSWALD I had a meal at noon. I don't want anything more today.

COLUMBA You'll eat when you're told to; and I'm telling you now. Take him off with you, Dochonna, and give him as much as he can hold.

DOCHONNA *does not understand.*

Food. Plenty.

OSWALD With your permission, Columba, I would prefer not to eat. The Prior tells me you allow yourself only one small meal each day. I wish to do exactly as you do.

COLUMBA I eat once a day for two very good reasons, son: Dochonna's cooking and my own stomach. You might as well know that both Diarmuid and myself are very bad stomach cases.

The others laugh at this.

DIARMUID That's not fair, Columba. Apart from the run at Mull last Friday I haven't been seasick for a week.

COLUMBA Argyll the day before yesterday?

DIARMUID There was a gale blowing then. Everyone was sick except yourself.

DOCHONNA Come on, lad. Come on.

COLUMBA (*To* OSWALD) And after you've eaten, come and see me. We'll have a chat then.

DOCHONNA Is it all right if I go to Tiree, Abbot?

COLUMBA By all means, Dochonna, and choose the fattest you can get. Yes, yes. Go, go.

As DOCHONNA *and* OSWALD *go towards the door,* BRENDAN *charges in as before.*

BRENDAN Columba! — Columba! — Another calf! — A second! — Twins! Two of them.

COLUMBA Another?

BRENDAN She's had one already — a regular bull —

COLUMBA Good for you, Brendan! You always said she was a good cow, that!

BRENDAN Give me a hand with them, Diarmuid. The men are all at the corn.

DIARMUID Me?

COLUMBA Go on, man. Let them see the fine substantial community they have joined.

> BRENDAN *and* DIARMUID *go off.* GRILLAAN *goes towards the door.*

GRILLAAN I've never seen twin calves in all my life.

COLUMBA And listen, Grillaan —

GRILLAAN Yes?

COLUMBA Tell Brendan he's to go to bed for the rest of the day. He's been up with the cow for the past two nights.

GRILLAAN He doesn't like the bed any more than yourself.

COLUMBA Whether he likes it or not. And Grillaan —

> GRILLAAN *halts at the door.*

Don't put that new novice into the end cell.

GRILLAAN Why not? The last in always uses it. That's the tradition.

COLUMBA He comes of wealthy people and was used to every luxury. We must wean him slowly.

GRILLAAN You're the Abbot.

> GRILLAAN *goes off.*

CAORNAN He will make a good monk, Columba.

> COLUMBA *stretches himself. Between* CAORNAN *and himself there is a special intimacy.*

COLUMBA Oswald? Too early to say yet.

CAORNAN No, he has clean eyes and the smell of courage about him.

COLUMBA If he's strong enough for the life here, Caornan.

CAORNAN He hopes to be a scribe.

COLUMBA We have a scribe — the best there is. How is it going?

COLUMBA *goes to the table to look at the work.*

CAORNAN   I'm at Chapter 10, Verse 37.
COLUMBA   You find it easier to work here?
CAORNAN   My eyes don't tire as easily. As long as I'm not in your way.
COLUMBA   I'm glad to have you, man. You're company for me. Let's see today's work.
CAORNAN   I got only four verses done today.

COLUMBA *picks up the scroll and looks at it.*

COLUMBA   Beautiful, beautiful, beautiful.
CAORNAN   (*Childishly pleased*) You like it?
COLUMBA   Exquisite, Caornan Mac Ua Soghain. Exquisite.
CAORNAN   I'm inclined to go off the lines now —
COLUMBA   (*Reading*) 'Do not think that I come to send peace upon earth; I come not to send peace but the sword. For I come to set a man at variance against his father and the daughter against her mother and the daughter-in-law against her mother-in-law. And a man's enemies shall be they of his own household. He that loveth father or mother more than Me is not worthy of Me — ' A man's enemies — they of his own household —
CAORNAN   That epsilon — I blotted it slightly.
COLUMBA   Caornan, you must pray for me, Caornan.

CAORNAN *looks at him.*

Because I need your prayers; because I am ringed with enemies.
CAORNAN   Enemies? You?
COLUMBA   Because I am not worthy of Him.
CAORNAN   Abbot!
COLUMBA   Out at the corn there, Cormac was cutting, and I was behind him tying, and the sun was warm on my back, and I was stooped over, so that this bare, black exile was shrunk to a circle around my feet.

And I was back in Tirconaill; and Cormac was Eoghan, my brother, humming to himself; and the dog that was barking was Ailbe, our sheepdog; and there were trees at the bottom of the field as long as I did not look; and the blue sky was quick with larks as long as I did not lift my head; and the white point of Errigal mountain was behind my shoulder as long as I kept my eyes on the ground. And when we got to the bottom of the field Cormac called to me, 'Look what I found! A horseshoe! That's for luck!' But I did not look up because he was still Eoghan, my brother, and the earth was still Gartan earth; and the sound of the sea was the water of Gartan Lough; and any minute Mother would come to the head of the hill and strike the iron triangle to summon us in for food. And when Cormac spoke I did not answer him because I could not leave them, Caornan. As God is above, I could not leave them!

CAORNAN There is a layman in every priest, Columba.

COLUMBA But I am old, Caornan. And virtue has not grown with the years. And when He sends for me He will find me as naked as I was when Etchen imposed hands on me in Clonfad.

CAORNAN Your monasteries — all over Ireland — at least a score of them. And here in Scotland, as many more. You are famous, Columba, all over the Christian world. Your name is spoken with reverence in Rome itself.

COLUMBA As a builder of churches! As a builder of schools! As an organizer! But the inner man — the soul — chained irrevocably to the earth, to the green wooded earth of Ireland!

He becomes conscious of his intensity and pretends to laugh.

I'll tell you a funny thing I heard the last time I was over there — when was it? Easter a year? Anyhow, I was visiting the Derry house and I was speaking to a young monk, a neighbour of our own, a young lad from Kilmacrenan, who was about to be sent to France on mission work. And in the course of conversation I said to him, 'You'll miss Derry and the Foyle and the hills?' and he blushed, this young lad, and he said to me, 'I won't, Patronus.' 'What?' I said. 'Not even a little?' And he became more and more confused and eventually he stammered, 'I've — I've taken the cure!' 'Cure?' 'Yes,' he said. 'Before I left home I spent a night on the Flag of Columba.'

CAORNAN   What's that?

COLUMBA   That's what I said. It appears that one night, years and years ago, on my way home from Slieve League, I slept on this great slab of rock. Needless to say, I don't remember doing it. But it seems that ever since a pious practice has grown round the spot and all the young Tirconaill emigrants spend their last night there. And this is the funny part — by doing this they are guaranteed to be freed from homesickness and longing for their native land! Ironical, isn't it?

CAORNAN   It could well be. I wouldn't mock at it.

COLUMBA   I'll tell you the explanation: the night on the rock paralyzes them with rheumatism and when they do remember Tirconaill afterwards they curse it to the depths of hell! (COLUMBA *laughs heartily at his joke*)

CAORNAN   Columba, there is something I wish to ask you. I have been trying to gather courage for the past six months —

COLUMBA   Anything that I can grant, Caornan.

CAORNAN   I know I have no right to ask you or to expect anything. You have always been like a father to all of us here, but this request I must make —

Enter GRILLAAN.

GRILLAAN   The second calf was dead-born; so I have still to see twin calves.

COLUMBA   Mm?

GRILLAAN The first one is quite sturdy though. And Brendan says with your permission he's going to call it Rufus.

COLUMBA A red one?

GRILLAAN Black as a raven. Did you not know? Brendan's colour blind!

COLUMBA He's not! Someone should tell him. The novices will make a terrible fool of him.

GRILLAAN Too late. They're finished in the cornfield and they're all gathered round it, stroking it and admiring it and saying it's the reddest calf they ever saw, my goodness such a red calf! And Brendan's standing there as proud as if he were the father!

They laugh. CAORNAN *rises, gathers his writing materials and prepares to leave.*

CAORNAN I think I'll do no more work today.

GRILLAAN It looks like a storm. The seagulls are settling below on the rocks.

COLUMBA It's well we got the corn cut.

CAORNAN If you'll excuse me —

COLUMBA You were asking me something, Caornan?

CAORNAN (*Confused*) Time enough, Columba. Time enough until tomorrow —

As he goes towards the door he walks into a stool, knocks it over and stumbles.

COLUMBA Are you all right?

CAORNAN Yes — yes — yes — I'm all right — I must have tripped on something.

COLUMBA *holds* CAORNAN's *arm.* GRILLAAN *picks up his pen and scrolls from the floor.*

GRILLAAN Your pen, Caornan. It's broken.

CAORNAN My pen! My good pen! It was my best pen!

COLUMBA *takes a pen from the wall.*

COLUMBA You can have mine, Caornan, the one King Brude gave me. Here you are — a royal pen for a royal scribe.

GRILLAAN It's my opinion he broke his own deliberately. He has always had his eye on that one.

CAORNAN (*To* COLUMBA) May I?

COLUMBA It's yours.

CAORNAN Thank you, thank you. It's a beautiful pen. Thank you.

COLUMBA You're welcome.

CAORNAN Thank you again. Thank you —

CAORNAN goes off. COLUMBA *stands looking after him.* GRILLAAN *looks at the floor where* CAORNAN *stumbled.*

GRILLAAN The floor is quite even.

COLUMBA I know.

GRILLAAN What are you thinking?

COLUMBA How privileged we are to live with him.

He turns and comes back to centre of stage.

Do you know, Grillaan, that he wears chains which have eaten into the flesh of his body?

GRILLAAN I am his spiritual director, too.

COLUMBA I am worried about Caornan. His sight is going and his health is poor. I have been thinking of sending him to Clonmore in Louth. He would be near his own county then when the end comes.

GRILLAAN Strangford Lough area, isn't he?

COLUMBA Near Downpatrick. He has never once been back in Ireland in our twenty-four years here.

GRILLAAN I don't suppose he cares much.

COLUMBA He cares, Grillaan — as much as I care myself.

GRILLAAN From the day I left, thank God, Ireland never gave me a second thought.

COLUMBA He used to talk to me years ago about his father and his mother and about a sister of his that was delicate

— he was very attached to her.

GRILLAAN He has got over that long ago.

COLUMBA I do know that originally he disliked Iona —

GRILLAAN Which of us liked it?

COLUMBA (*Briskly*) Anyhow, remind me to speak to him tomorrow about going home.

GRILLAAN You told me to remind you about the Picts in Cromarty.

COLUMBA You're quite right. Any further news?

GRILLAAN Just what we know already: that they are supposed to be reviving old Druidical practices in the mountains there.

COLUMBA I'll go myself and find out what's happening. Very often these stories lose nothing in the telling.

GRILLAAN You'll not get away tomorrow if I'm any judge of the weather.

COLUMBA The next day then. There's nothing very urgent about it.

GRILLAAN Will you want me with you?

COLUMBA No. Diarmuid will do. We'll be gone only a few nights.

GRILLAAN (*Going to door*) He won't be keen. He says he sinks in the bogs.

COLUMBA It will take some of the beef off him. See that I'm not disturbed, will you, Grillaan? I have some prayers to catch up with.

GRILLAAN I'll see to it.

> GRILLAAN *goes off.* COLUMBA *kneels beside his bed and begins to pray. It is getting dark. Occasional gusts of wind. Pause. Then:*

GRILLAAN (*Off*) Columba!

COLUMBA Yes?

GRILLAAN (*Off*) A traveller here to see you — a kinsman.

> COLUMBA *is irritated at being disturbed. But at the mention of kinsman his face lights up with delight.*

COLUMBA A kinsman? Bring him in! Bring him in!

Enter the messenger, BRIAN, followed by GRILLAAN. BRIAN is a young man, cool, calm, confident. He speaks quietly, never once raising his voice.

I don't know your face, kinsman, but I'll tell you something about yourself. You are from the Kingdom of O'Neill all right — from the north. Just hold your chin up — that's it — yes — and you were born between two loughs, Lough Foyle and Lough Swilly, and you are an Innishowen man. Am I right?

BRIAN You are uncanny, Columba.

COLUMBA I am observant, kinsman. You are welcome to Iona.

GRILLAAN is alert, watchful, uneasy.

GRILLAAN You know one another?

COLUMBA Not his name, Grillaan, but his bones and his eyes and his neck and his shoulders and his walk. He comes from a good land; and his mother has fed him often on salmon and lobster and wild duck, and he hears Mass in Iskaheen chapel. Am I right, Innishowen man?

BRIAN You are right, Columba. My name is Brian.

COLUMBA Brian? Brian? — More likely it's your father I would know, or your grandfather. Who was he?

BRIAN You wouldn't know him, Columba, because I told you a lie. I am no kinsman of yours.

GRILLAAN I thought it strange a man appearing at this time of evening —

BRIAN I told you a lie in case you wouldn't see me. I come with a message from a kinsman.

COLUMBA Well, out with the message. Who is it from?

BRIAN From your cousin, Hugh, son of Ainmire.

COLUMBA And what's troubling big Hugh?

BRIAN It is a — (*looks at GRILLAAN*) — a private message.

COLUMBA Grillaan, have a meal prepared for this messenger and his companions. And fix up some beds for them in the guest house, will you?

BRIAN We can't stay, Columba. Thank you all the same. We have got to return tonight. We haven't time even for a meal.

COLUMBA You're going back tonight?

BRIAN Those are Hugh's orders.

GRILLAAN You know there's a storm rising?

BRIAN Those are Hugh's orders.

COLUMBA You're not on Hugh's land now, messenger, and you take orders from me. You can risk your lives in the storm if you like but at least you'll drown on a full stomach. (*To* GRILLAAN) Tell Dochonna to get something ready.

GRILLAAN Very well, Abbot.

COLUMBA For friends, tell him, for Innishowen men.

GRILLAAN *goes off, reluctantly.*

Now Brian, what's the matter with big Hugh? He hasn't decided to get married, has he? Sit down, man, and have a rest.

GRILLAAN *is still at the door.*

What is it, Grillaan?

GRILLAAN Nothing — nothing, Abbot — nothing —

COLUMBA The best food in the house for the men of Tirconaill.

GRILLAAN *now leaves.* COLUMBA *and* BRIAN *are seated.*

Well, Brian.

BRIAN You know of Baedan's murder?

COLUMBA His father and mine were brothers. May they both rest in peace.

BRIAN You know who murdered him?

COLUMBA He was killed by Cumine, son of Colman Beg Mac Diarmada at Léim-an-Eich.

BRIAN Nine months ago. Now that same Cumine, son of

Colman Beg, and his cousin, Cumine, son of Libran, have vowed to kill Hugh —

COLUMBA *gets to his feet and begins to pace.*

COLUMBA Hugh is not an infant. He can look after himself.

BRIAN — because they see his pastures and his cattle and his horses and they have covetousness in their hearts.

COLUMBA They are all — Hugh, the two Cumines, Libran, Colman — they are all my cousins. Has Hugh forgotten that? Has he forgotten that Niall of the Nine Hostages was great-great-grandfather to all of us?

BRIAN He has not forgotten. Nor has he forgotten the Battle of Cúl-Dreimhne in the County Sligo twenty-six years ago —

COLUMBA He has a long memory, Hugh —

BRIAN — when his father fought for you against Colman's father.

COLUMBA Messenger, let me tell you a story. Once upon a time there was a monk whose father was one of the rulers of Tirconaill and whose mother was descended from the Kings of Leinster — with the result he had cousins and uncles and nephews all over the country. And every time these cousins or uncles or nephews got into a brawl — and that was very often — the first thing they said was, 'Send for our kinsman, the monk. He will settle this. He will see that *mine* is the good cause.' And invariably they sent for this monk and invariably he went because he loved them all, and maybe, too, because he was a foolish monk. Anyhow, during his life he got himself involved in a dozen small rows and in two battles, battles in which many people were killed. But at last this monk got sense — no credit to him, messenger — because by this time he was quite old and it was as much as he could do to say his prayers and look after his communities and visit his monasteries. Before the altar of God, seven years ago, when he returned to his exile after the battle of Coleraine, he took a vow never to become embroiled in bloody conflict again. And although he has been tempted to break that vow on many occasions since, although every native instinct and inclination tore at him to go to the aid of his friends, he kept his vow — by the grace of God — for these seven years . . . Had you a good crossing?

BRIAN *resumes as if* COLUMBA *had not spoken.*

BRIAN   The Kingdom of O'Neill will never be at rest as long as Columba Beg lives.

COLUMBA   We have a young novice here from Carndonagh. Perhaps you know him. His name is —

BRIAN   They have three cunning leaders on their side — Colman and the two Cumines — while Hugh, your cousin, is alone.

COLUMBA   His name is Kieran — he will be a fine preacher — a grand voice.

BRIAN   For months they have been gathering and inciting their supporters — as far south as Fermanagh and Leitrim and Sligo — the same mob that opposed you at Cúl-Dreimhne.

COLUMBA *is getting angry — at* BRIAN's *persistence and at his involuntary interest.*

COLUMBA   A vow has been taken, messenger. With the grace of God it will be kept.

BRIAN   If they are not opposed they will sweep through Tyrone and Tirconaill and up to Derry itself. Then all the Kingdom of O'Neill will be under the tyranny of Colman and his son, the murderers of Baedan, your uncle.

COLUMBA   Hugh is a wily fighter. He knows the terrain.

BRIAN   He cannot fight single-handed — against God.

COLUMBA   Against God?

BRIAN The priest, Sirinus, from the monastery of Bangor, is riding by the side of Colman while he musters his followers.

COLUMBA Sirinus? From Bangor?

BRIAN Comgall's monastery — the same Comgall against whom you battled at Coleraine seven years ago when Hugh stood by you like a man.

COLUMBA Comgall and I are friends now — (*there is doubt in his voice*) — and have been for the past two years — I have visited him —

BRIAN This Sirinus tells the people that Colman is leading an army to crush the irreligious Hugh, who, he says, is a sun worshipper —

COLUMBA Rubbish!

BRIAN — and in proof of his claim he says that Columba, the monk, hides in Iona out of shame and has denounced his cousin, Hugh, for his pagan practices.

COLUMBA That's a lie! Hugh is a good man!

BRIAN He points out that if it were not the truth, Columba, the monk, would be standing at his cousin's side, but Columba, he says, is ashamed of his cousin.

COLUMBA (*Now very angry*) That's a damned lie and you know it! I had meals with Hugh last Easter twelve months. I slept in his house. He gave me his best cow for my community here.

BRIAN Now he is alone.

COLUMBA What does Comgall say? Can he not silence this Sirinus of his?

BRIAN Comgall is at present in Aran Island, off Galway.

COLUMBA And Hugh? Hugh's no fool. Can he not speak up for himself?

BRIAN Against the word of a priest?

COLUMBA Priest? Some raving idiot who hopes to get land from Colman!

BRIAN If they are not opposed, Colman and the Cumines, they will take the land that was your father's and your grandfather's; they will drive up as far as Innishowen. And who can tell, Columba, how your fifteen churches in these areas will fare under the mad Sirinus?

COLUMBA I will write a letter — to Hugh and to my people —
to be read out to them — I will state that Hugh is
a Christian and a good one — that I have never
denounced him — that I am not ashamed —

BRIAN A letter is no good; they will say it is a forgery. We
need a priest to lead us. They have a priest.

COLUMBA They have a liar.

BRIAN A man of God leading an army against a sun
worshipper.

COLUMBA Our Hugh is no pagan!

BRIAN They murdered Baedan last year. They will murder
Hugh this year.

COLUMBA I took a vow, messenger. I told you I took a vow.

BRIAN Your fifteen churches will be in the kingdom of
murderers led by a priest.

COLUMBA *switches from anger to pleading.*

COLUMBA Next Sunday is a feast day here — Finnian of
Clonard, our old teacher. We — we always have a
great day —

BRIAN Your own people in Gartan say, 'Columba will not
disappoint us.'

COLUMBA There is a storm getting up. You could be marooned
here for weeks.

BRIAN They say, 'If he loves us as he says he does, he will
come.'

At the mention of Gartan COLUMBA's *full fury is
released. He catches* BRIAN *by the throat and shakes
him.*

COLUMBA Listen to me, silver-tongued Innishowen man!
Listen to me! I love them, yes, I love them; and
every hill and stream and river and mountain from
the top of Fanad down to the waters of blue Melvin.
And never a day passes but I see the clouds sit
down on Errigal or smell the wrack at Gweebarra

or hear the wood pigeons in the oaks of Derry. But I am a priest, messenger, a man of God, an *alter Christus* — a poor priest, but still a priest. For the sake of Christ, messenger, leave me alone! Don't wedge my frailties between my soul and its Maker!

> *He releases* BRIAN *and goes to the far side of the stage. There is a silence.* BRIAN *is as calm as ever.* DOCHONNA *enters.*

DOCHONNA Your meal is ready when you are.

BRIAN What is your answer?

COLUMBA Go and eat. You may yet be home before the storm breaks.

DOCHONNA What's that?

COLUMBA He's going, Dochonna. He's going now.

BRIAN What do I say to your cousin Hugh?

DOCHONNA This way, son. Your friends have started already.

BRIAN We have skins in the boat to keep you warm during the crossing and there are horses waiting for us in Derry to take us the rest of the journey.

> BRIAN *goes off.* DOCHONNA, *sensing that something is wrong, looks back at* COLUMBA.

COLUMBA Tell Caornan I want him.

DOCHONNA What's that, Columba?

COLUMBA (*Irritably*) Caornan! Caornan! Tell him I need him! Now!

DOCHONNA (*Not hearing but trying to understand*) Aye, Caornan — he's looking very poor, isn't he?

COLUMBA (*Helplessly*) It doesn't matter — (*Waves* DOCHONNA *off*) See to the visitors, Dochonna — see to the visitors.

> DOCHONNA *goes off irresolutely.* COLUMBA *holds his head in his hands, then goes on his knees below the crucifix and prays. After about thirty seconds* GRILLAAN *comes in.*

GRILLAAN That fellow distinctly told me he was a relation —

He sees COLUMBA *praying.*

I'm sorry —

COLUMBA *rises from his knees.*

What's the matter, Abbot? Bad news from home?
COLUMBA Home is a millstone round my neck, Grillaan.
GRILLAAN Something wrong in one of our houses?
COLUMBA No — no — not our houses —
GRILLAAN Thank God for that.
COLUMBA Yes. Thank God for that.

GRILLAAN *has seen this struggle before. He knows the symptoms.*

GRILLAAN Family again?
COLUMBA Again.

Pause.

GRILLAAN Columba, you are our founder, our patronus, our Abbot —
COLUMBA I know that introduction; and you are my spiritual director and you are about to lecture me —
GRILLAAN Advise you — remind you of the past — of the progress you have made in prudence and moderation —
COLUMBA Do you know what Colman Beg is saying? That Hugh, big, innocent, guileless, thick-headed, quick-tempered Hugh is a sun worshipper! Hugh!
GRILLAAN And he wants you to bless his men and pray over them and dignify his brawl with a crucifix?
COLUMBA Our churches in Tyrone and Tirconaill are in danger.
GRILLAAN They always are.
COLUMBA I mean it, Grillaan.
GRILLAAN And his enemies — whoever they are this time —

no doubt they have a churchman to bless their standards too, with the result that God is fighting for both causes. Isn't that the usual pattern?

COLUMBA A mad monk leading a gang of murderers!

GRILLAAN You are a priest — not a rallying cry!

COLUMBA (*Controlled*) Hugh is my cousin and a good man. We ate his barley bread for lunch today. It was his cow that calved in the meadow today.

> *Both tempers are now up. The two monks raise their voices.*

GRILLAAN And this is the payment he demands? That you kneel bare-headed on a hilltop, an old man with white hair, Columba the church builder, and pray aloud for victory for the drunken land grabbers fighting below your feet?

COLUMBA Easy, Prior, easy!

GRILLAAN Have you a better name for them? Do you absolve them before they reel into battle, their beery faces flushed with blood lust, or do you wait until 'right' has conquered and give the dead of both sides conditional absolution?

COLUMBA We come of kings, Prior. To lead is in our blood. We are not savages.

GRILLAAN You are a priest — with a priest's vows.

COLUMBA Royal blood that answers to the call of its people! Kings of Leinster and rulers of the land of Conall!

GRILLAAN (*Changing tactics*) Columba, listen to me, listen. You are a holy man, Columba. You haven't eaten a proper meal since we came to this place; you haven't slept for more than five hours any night. You pray longer and harder than any of us do. You do the most menial jobs in the monastery —

COLUMBA Please, Grillaan, please —

GRILLAAN You are kind and humble and generous and self-sacrificing and God has blessed your work a hundred, thousand fold. Everything, Columba, everything you have surrendered but this one. And now is your opportunity.

> BRIAN *appears suddenly at the door.*

BRIAN There is not time to eat. Let us get away before the wind rises.

> *He comes into the room.* COLUMBA *is in the centre,* GRILLAAN *on one side of him,* BRIAN *on the other. He is torn between the two.*

GRILLAAN The last tie, Columba. Cut it now. Cut it. Cut it.

BRIAN They are your people. It is your land.

GRILLAAN A priest or a politician — which?

BRIAN They rallied round you at Sligo and at Coleraine. All they ask is your blessing.

GRILLAAN He that loveth father or mother more than Me is not worthy of Me.

BRIAN Are they to die in their sins at the hands of murderers?

GRILLAAN You are a priest in voluntary exile for God — not a private chaplain to your family.

BRIAN Son of Fedhlimidh and Eithne.

GRILLAAN Abbot!

> COLUMBA *has been standing absolutely motionless. Now, as if he were demented, he comes alive, strides to the door and roars:*

COLUMBA Diarmuid! Diarmuid!

> GRILLAAN *knows that he has lost.* COLUMBA *knows he cannot afford to listen to him. He charges around the stage, barking instructions, gathering his belongings, consciously busying himself. He avoids* GRILLAAN'*s eyes.*

Hoist your sails, Innishowen man, and strip your oarsmen to the waist! Hurry! Hurry!

BRIAN *goes off.* COLUMBA *turns to* GRILLAAN:

You will be in charge, Prior, until I return. Travel to
Cromarty tomorrow — take Cormac with you —
and find out what's brewing there. And on Sunday
see that the feast's a worthy one.

DIARMUID, *puffing, enters.*

DIARMUID Yes, Columba?
COLUMBA Get into your travelling clothes! We are going home!
Now!

DIARMUID *stands aghast. He might even consider
trying to joke his way out of another sea journey.*

Are you deaf too? What have I here? A nunnery of
senile crones?
DIARMUID My stomach, Columba —
COLUMBA At once, I say, monk! Obedience!

DIARMUID *goes off quickly.* COLUMBA's *fury dies
suddenly.* GRILLAAN *is standing far off from him
with his back to him.* COLUMBA *looks at* GRILLAAN's
*back, hangs his head and slowly — very slowly —
goes towards him. Then he kneels behind the Prior.*

(*Softly*) Grillaan, your blessing.

GRILLAAN *does not move. Pause.*

(*Slightly louder*) Your blessing, Grillaan.

OSWALD *stands framed in the door.*

(*Still louder*) Grillaan — ?

He looks up at GRILLAAN, *sees the hard back to him,
waits for five seconds, then, his fury roused again,*

he jumps to his feet and charges towards the door.
As COLUMBA *comes towards him,* OSWALD *says:*

OSWALD You said you would talk to me after I had eaten,
Columba —

    COLUMBA *scarcely sees him. He brushes roughly*
past him, knocking him to the side as he goes out.
OSWALD *looks towards* GRILLAAN's *back, question-*
ingly. What has he done wrong, his look asks. Then
GRILLAAN *turns round slowly and looks beyond*
OSWALD *to the door. Now the storm breaks — thun-*
der, lightning, wind — a tremendous crash.
    Quick curtain.

ACT TWO
Scene One

There is an air of happy anticipation: COLUMBA *is home again; he is getting out of the boat at the harbour below.* GRILLAAN *is taking the straw off Columba's bed and putting things in order. He is happy but he hides his pleasure in working.* DOCHONNA *is standing at the door from where he can see the harbour. He reports to* GRILLAAN *all that is happening. He is beaming with joy and bouncing up and down on his toes in jerky, restless movements. Occasionally he breaks into a high-pitched giggle.*

DOCHONNA They have pulled her on the slip now and they're carrying stuff off her. And — aye — aye — aye — it's Diarmuid — it's Diarmuid all right — lying across the wall of the pier and vomiting his stomach out — (*Giggles*)

> BRENDAN *enters, carrying an armful of fresh straw.*

Get a move on, boy. He'll be here in a minute or two.

GRILLAAN (*To* DOCHONNA) Have you a meal ready for them? (*To* BRENDAN) Just throw it there. (*To* DOCHONNA) Have you a meal ready?

DOCHONNA What's that?

GRILLAAN Food. Have you food?

DOCHONNA Aye, aye. Aye. Food. In the oven. Waiting.

GRILLAAN (*To* BRENDAN) Take this straw away and clean up the floor.

DOCHONNA He's saying goodbye to the boatman. They mustn't be coming up.

BRENDAN (*To* GRILLAAN) Are you going to tell him this evening?

GRILLAAN I've got to. He's bound to ask.

DOCHONNA (*Laughs*) Diarmuid — he's pulled himself away from the wall and he's reeling up the path — and his face — it's the colour of pea soup —

BRENDAN *goes off with the old straw.*

He's coming now himself — he's coming — he's coming —

DOCHONNA *comes into the room and begins fussing about.*

GRILLAAN Shove that table over to the corner and clean up the floor.

DOCHONNA (*Not hearing*) The place feels different already, doesn't it, eh? Like — it's full again, isn't it?

GRILLAAN Bring the food in now. On a tray. The food.

DOCHONNA Oh, aye, aye, the food —

He goes towards the door, singing: 'The Abbot's back, the Abbot's back, the Abbot's back to Iona.'

GRILLAAN Dochonna!

DOCHONNA Eh? Eh? What? What?

GRILLAAN I'll break the news to him — later on.

DOCHONNA *looks blankly at him.*

About Caornan. We'll wait until he has settled in.

DOCHONNA (*Suddenly very old, dejected*) Caornan — aye — Caornan —

He shuffles out, an old, old man, mumbling 'Caornan . . . Caornan'. GRILLAAN *goes on working. Then* BRENDAN *returns.*

BRENDAN Diarmuid's outside and Columba's halfway up the path.

GRILLAAN I'm telling Dochonna — we'll wait until he has

settled in and has something to eat.

BRENDAN He's going to take it badly.

GRILLAAN I know, I know. We'll give him the best welcome we can.

BRENDAN Maybe you shouldn't tell him until tomorrow?

GRILLAAN Caornan will be the first he'll ask for.

Enter DIARMUID — *staggering, groaning. He has been sick during the crossing and is determined to make everybody aware of his reduced condition.*

DIARMUID Awwww — !

He reels across the stage and drops on to the bed.

GRILLAAN Diarmuid! How are you, man? How are you?

BRENDAN (*Solemnly*) Awwww — !

GRILLAAN What sort of crossing had you?

DIARMUID Crabs — in the bottom of the boat — I was going great until I smelt them —

BRENDAN Was Columba sick too?

DIARMUID All he could do was laugh. Aw, those boats — they'll kill me yet —

GRILLAAN Was there much bloodshed over there?

DIARMUID Please — please —

DOCHONNA, *happy again, comes in with a tray.*

DOCHONNA He made it, did he? Good man yourself, Diarmuid —

DIARMUID (*Faintest greeting*) Dochonna —

DOCHONNA You're ravenous, are you, eh? Look what I have here for you — mutton chops — just what you love!

DIARMUID *groans even louder and covers his eyes.*

GRILLAAN (*To* DOCHONNA) Seasick.

DOCHONNA But this is good for him. Something to get up again.

GRILLAAN Let him be. Let him be. Listen!

COLUMBA (*Off*) And it's good to see you, too. Yes — yes — I'll be over later — later.

BRENDAN   It's himself!

COLUMBA   (*Off*) I've got a new skin for the currach. I'll bring it over later. Right — right —

GRILLAAN   Remember — not a word until he has eaten!

> COLUMBA *enters. He is loaded with wooden boxes of all sizes. As with his entrance in Act One, he seems to charge the atmosphere with vigour and vitality. He is delighted at being back. The three monks gather round him,* DOCHONNA *almost frisking with joy at having the Abbot home again.*

COLUMBA   Grillaan! And Dochonna! And Brendan! It's good to see you.

DOCHONNA   Welcome home, Columba! Welcome! Welcome!

GRILLAAN   The change did you good.

COLUMBA   Good? I feel as fresh as a novice, Grillaan. And Dochonna? How are you, Dochonna!

> *The emotional stress —* CAORNAN's *death, the Abbot's return — is too much for the old man. He holds on to* COLUMBA's *arm and begins to cry.*

DOCHONNA   Don't go away again, Columba. Don't leave us.

COLUMBA   (*Pause — then briskly*) Here man, what sort of a welcome is this? Three weeks — that's all I was gone. And wait until you see what I've got for you here — and something for Caornan —

> DIARMUID *groans.* COLUMBA *starts.*

Is he — ? (*Sees that it is* DIARMUID) Oh, it's only the sailor. I thought for a moment —

GRILLAAN   (*Quickly*) You must be hungry, Columba. Dochonna has a meal here for you.

COLUMBA   Later. Later. But the news first! How did you get on without me?

BRENDAN   We got the last of the hay in today.

COLUMBA How's the calf doing, Brendan?

BRENDAN Thriving, Columba.

COLUMBA I've got something here for you, too.

He begins rooting through his boxes.

GRILLAAN Was there a battle, Columba?

COLUMBA Battle? No. There was no battle because the rats wouldn't stand for a battle. Ran like the hammers of Jericho down through Monaghan and Cavan and when we cornered them at a place called Cul-Fheadha on the banks of the Blackwater — Diarmuid can tell you — if they had half a hundred scamps behind them, that was the height of it. And Sirinus, the monk — we had a good name for him; we called him 'The Brave Beetle' because he was a black wart of a man. Led the retreat as hard as he could go! But a monk? He was no monk, yon fellow! Comgall himself never heard of him!

GRILLAAN Were many killed?

Pause.

COLUMBA (*Quietly*) Colman Beg, son of Diarmuid, and Libran, son of Illadhan, and a dozen or so slaves. God rest their souls.

GRILLAAN And Hugh?

COLUMBA (*Elated*) Hugh's married. The day before yesterday! In the Raphoe church!

GRILLAAN No!

COLUMBA We would have been back last Friday but for that. To a girl from near Aughnacloy. A fine girl she is, too. He saw her for the first time on our way south when we were chasing the MacDiarmuid mob and on the way home — not a whisper to any of us — didn't he take her back with him! You should have seen my face when he said to me, 'Columba, will you do a wee job for me?'

GRILLAAN Good for Hugh.

COLUMBA   They've been eating and drinking there for the past ten days. Don't think it was the crossing alone that set the sailor here off!

DOCHONNA   You weren't over by the west in your travels, were you?

COLUMBA   Where were we anyhow? We were in Derry and Kilmacrenan and Gartan and Raphoe for Hugh's wedding — when was that?

GRILLAAN   That would be last Tuesday.

COLUMBA   Tuesday — and the Saturday before that we were in Kilmore. They had the new chapel finished there now — a beautiful job. And Fedhlimidh himself was asking for you all. He wanted us to go to Kells with him the following day but we were anxious to get back. And then on the Monday we had lunch in Ballymagroarty and that night we stayed in Ballynascreen. I think that was everywhere. No, a night with Comgall in Bangor!

GRILLAAN   How are they all in Derry?

COLUMBA   Do you know who I met there? Old Fintan!

GRILLAAN   (*Parodying the Cork accent*) Fintan from Cork?

COLUMBA   No, not that Fintan. Do you remember a very tall lanky man in Clonard? Do you not remember they used to pull his leg about being able to reach up to the bell tower to ring the bell! (*To* DOCHONNA) You would remember him, Dochonna. Fintan — big, long Fintan.

DOCHONNA   Fintan, eh? Fintan Caol?

COLUMBA   Fintan Caol! The very name!

DOCHONNA   You met him again. How is he? He must be a right age now, eh?

COLUMBA   Ninety-six, he tells me.

DOCHONNA   And going strong?

COLUMBA   Like a boy.

DOCHONNA   (*Looking around*) There now! And he could be my father!

COLUMBA   As straight as a rush and as clear in the head as Brendan there. He gave me a present of a pen for Caornan because he said he never saw work to equal his in all his days. Where *is* Caornan? Go and tell him I'm back, Brendan.

> BRENDAN *looks at* GRILLAAN. GRILLAAN *signals to him to stay where he is.*

GRILLAAN What have you got in all these parcels?

COLUMBA What have I not got? The boat couldn't hold half the stuff Hugh gave us. What have we anyhow? (*Opening boxes*) Candles for the chapel from Comgall —

DOCHONNA (*Picking up the word*) Comgall, aye, that's Comgall of Bangor.

COLUMBA Talking fourteen to the dozen as usual. And a crate of honey from Hugh. And what's this? Yes, yes, a crucifix from the Derry house. The best of oak. And a side of bacon from Hugh too —

GRILLAAN We'll not starve this winter.

COLUMBA And for you, Grillaan — a present. (*Holds up a pair of sandals*) I heard you sniffing a lot before I left.

GRILLAAN That was the haymaking did that.

COLUMBA If they don't fit we can get them changed.

GRILLAAN Sandals! Beautiful soft sandals!

BRENDAN The novices will never hear you coming in those!

GRILLAAN Thanks, Columba. The very thing I needed.

> *He takes them to the other side of the stage to try them on. During the distribution of these presents there is a childlike simplicity and joy in the giving and receiving.*

COLUMBA And Dochonna — something for your hearing.

DOCHONNA What's that, Columba, eh?

COLUMBA A tip an old fellow in Raphoe gave me — for your hearing.

> *He produces the horn of a cow.*

DOCHONNA What — what is it?

COLUMBA It's the horn of a cow. When anyone wishes to speak to you, he speaks through this end here.

DOCHONNA *takes it and puts it up on his temple.*

DOCHONNA Eh? Eh? Like this here? Eh?

BRENDAN He's like the leader of the Vandals! Look, Grillaan.

COLUMBA No, no, no, no. This way. The small end *into* your ear.

DOCHONNA Aye?

COLUMBA You hold it there and I speak through here.

DOCHONNA (*Very pleased*) I hear — I hear the water of Lough Conn —

BRENDAN He thinks it's a sea shell.

COLUMBA (*Speaking into horn*) Does it sound better?

DOCHONNA Aye, water. That's what I'm telling you. Water — like home —

> *He wanders away smiling to himself.* GRILLAAN *struts across the stage with mock elegance, holding his habit up to his knees.*

GRILLAAN Well?

COLUMBA Are they comfortable?

GRILLAAN As fur.

COLUMBA Good. I took the biggest pair I could get.

GRILLAAN Your own aren't so small.

COLUMBA And Brendan — for the calf — a curry comb.

BRENDAN That was very thoughtful of you, Columba.

COLUMBA With a black handle to match his coat.

BRENDAN The calf is red — but that doesn't matter.

COLUMBA Stupid me! It was the black one that died, wasn't it?

BRENDAN It was white, Columba.

> COLUMBA *sees* GRILLAAN *laughing at him.*

COLUMBA Huh! Well — whatever colour it was —

BRENDAN Thank you again.

COLUMBA And now — Caornan. What's keeping him? Did you tell him I had come?

GRILLAAN The meat is getting cold, Columba. What about something to eat now?

COLUMBA *suddenly senses that something is wrong.*

COLUMBA Where is Caornan? Caornan, where is he?

> BRENDAN *and* GRILLAAN *look away.* DIARMUID *sits upright on the bed.*

BRENDAN — Grillaan — where is Caornan, the scholar?

> *There is a pause. Then suddenly* COLUMBA *impetuously goes to the door and roars:*

COLUMBA Caor-nan!

GRILLAAN It happened within twenty-four hours after you left —

COLUMBA (*Slightly softer*) Caor-nan!

GRILLAAN That night he got up in the small hours, as he always did, for his vigil. There was a high wind and no moon. We believe he tripped on a stone and struck his head on the old anvil at the door of the forge.

DIARMUID Dead?

COLUMBA (*Whisper*) Caor-nan —

GRILLAAN Brendan found him at dawn. He was alive then and conscious until he died a few hours later. He asked me to thank you for all your kindness to him. He said he would not forget you.

> *Enter* DOCHONNA.

DIARMUID He is with God now because he was a simple man.

GRILLAAN He spoke to each of us in turn — he lay there on your bed; this was the nearest room — but to Dochonna most of all. And although he spoke in a whisper, he heard every word he said. Then he got the Eucharist. Then he died.

DIARMUID What day was that?

GRILLAAN It was Thursday.

DIARMUID We were in Kilmacrenan on Thursday — feasting

before the battle.

COLUMBA *is standing looking down at his bed.*

GRILLAAN We thought of sending for you — Brendan volunteered to go and find you — but we had no idea where to look. You could have been in any of fifty places!

DIARMUID That's where we were. Singing and feasting and laughing.

COLUMBA Caornan, son of regal Ronan and the fair Maeve, clean child of Down with the wisdom of twelve men, monk and true man of God, my Caornan, my brother Caornan —

He buries his face in his hands and sobs.

GRILLAAN We buried him with his chains. They were part of the body in places.

DIARMUID (*To* DOCHONNA) What were his last words?

GRILLAAN He spoke to the novices and to the deacons and then to the monks —

COLUMBA I had a surprise for Caornan — to be kept secret until next week.

DIARMUID He arranged for him to have a large, well-lit room in the Clonmore house, a stone's throw from his birthplace. The boat was to call for him next Wednesday.

COLUMBA The day I left he said he had a request to make — I knew what it was: because of his health and years, to release him from his exile and allow him to die in Ireland — a big room and a big table and a small chair — they are waiting for him.

DIARMUID What did he say to you, Dochonna?

DOCHONNA Caornan?

DIARMUID His last words to you.

DOCHONNA He said — he said that if God should spare him, he was going to ask the Abbot to release him because he said that as the years had gone by, he had come to love Iona and he was too happy here with all his own friends. So he was going to ask the Abbot to let him go up to the Isles of Orkney and find a hermitage there —

COLUMBA Orkney?

DOCHONNA For there he would be all alone and there he could do penance for all the joy he found in the life here. And — and — and —

DOCHONNA goes to COLUMBA and holds on to him.

— and he called me 'The Hardy Trout' —

He breaks down. COLUMBA and he hold on to one another.

The old doter was five years older than me — that's one thing he could never deny — the old doter —

COLUMBA They call me Sanctus, Sanctus Pater, Sanctus Senior — Merciful Christ, give me the sight of Caornan, your scribe. Have pity on me.

Quick curtain.

ACT TWO

Scene Two

Later that day. COLUMBA *and* GRILLAAN *are seated at the table looking at a map.* COLUMBA *is very quiet, as if he were preoccupied.* GRILLAAN, *knowing this, talks on and on in the hope of interesting him.*

GRILLAAN We spent the first night in the north of Argyll and the following day we travelled along the banks of Lough Ness and slept that night in a shepherd's hut. The next night we crossed into Cromarty — somewhere around here — Cormac and the guide and myself.

COLUMBA Guide?

GRILLAAN I told you. We called with Gregory in Bracholy on the second day. He insisted we take a guide with us.

COLUMBA Yes — yes — yes —

GRILLAAN So we worked our way up the coast here — and right across the plain between Ben Wyvis and the sea. Then we doubled back, crossed into Inverness again, travelling this time down along the northern bank of the lough. The guide came with us all the way.

He pauses for COLUMBA *to comment.*

We discovered very little — apart from the fact that Druidism is as good as dead. The stories we heard were completely false. Not a trace of an organized revival. We did discover though that many families that had been Christian ten or fifteen years ago have fallen away because they never see a priest from one year to the next.

53

He looks at COLUMBA *to see if he is showing any interest.*

You have no idea how isolated some of those houses are. We even came across one old fellow who thought we were Romans! And Rome, he thought was one of the Shetland Islands. That sort of thing —

COLUMBA So there is no fear of a rebirth of Druidism.

He rises from the table and walks across the stage. GRILLAAN *looks after him and then goes on talking.*

GRILLAAN Gregory had some interesting stories. He was telling us about a young German who arrived at his monastery one night in the middle of last winter. They hadn't seen a soul for weeks — completely cut off with snowdrifts — when suddenly this night, as they were about to retire, there was a gentle tapping on the door. He must have been leaning against the door because when it was pulled back he fell into the room. They lifted him up and carried him to a bed. Gregory said that he mustn't have had a bite to eat for at least a week. Anyhow, they heard this story. His great-grandfather, he claimed, was helmsman on board the ship that brought Patrick back to Ireland with the faith. And —

COLUMBA *interrupts him. He has not heard a word that* GRILLAAN *has said.*

COLUMBA Grillaan, I want you, as my spiritual adviser, to impose on me the most severe penances you can think of: starvation, beating, weeks of unceasing prayer — anything, all of them, whatever you advise.

GRILLAAN I have advised you before, Columba.

COLUMBA I know. I know. Prudence, you say, and patience, and counsel — the virtues of old men with wet chins and shapeless feet. But I cannot *feel* my sixty-six years, Grillaan. I am burdened with this strong, active body that responds to the whistle of movement, the fight of the sail, the swing of the axe, the warm breadth of a horse beneath it, the challenge of a new territory. I try! I try! And it betrays me!

GRILLAAN We have talked of this often, Columba.

COLUMBA Let me fast. Give me Caornan's chains. Forbid me my bed for five years. But conquer me, Grillaan! Crush this violent Adam into subjection!

GRILLAAN I need your full obedience — your willing obedience.

COLUMBA You have it. You know that.

GRILLAAN To do exactly — *exactly* as I say.

COLUMBA Exactly, with God's grace.

GRILLAAN I believe your course is simple. You must live the Rule of Iona to the letter.

COLUMBA I try to —

GRILLAAN No. You exceed it, Columba. You eat less each day than a sparrow eats. You sleep only three hours at night. You pray longer and work harder than anyone else in the island. And those very excesses are surrenderings to this Adam you speak of.

COLUMBA Excesses?

GRILLAAN Columba, may I, the least worthy, advise you?

COLUMBA Whatever you say, I will do it.

GRILLAAN I say to you: subject yourself to the wise discipline of the monastery and to it alone; eat your two meals a day; sleep your five hours sleep; read your Office; celebrate your Mass; look after your administrative work. And beyond that — nothing. No more immersions in icy water, no more fasts or vigils or days of prayer. Only the Rule — but the Rule to the letter. Each man's cleansing, Columba, is of a different kind. Yours is in moderation in all things, in calm, reasoned moderation. This I advise.

COLUMBA And atonement for my past?

GRILLAAN In some men, Abbot — as it was with Caornan — sanctity is a progression, a building of stone upon stone, year after year, until the edifice is complete.

	In other men it is in the will and determination to start, and then to start again, and then to start again, so that their life is a series of beginnings. You are of the second kind, Columba.
COLUMBA	So I must begin again — like a novice!
GRILLAAN	The Rule is a wise rule.
COLUMBA	But at times when I need to do penance for all my violence —
GRILLAAN	Your greatest penance will be found in keeping the Rule.
COLUMBA	At sixty-six I am back where I began! It is a poor record!
GRILLAAN	You will take my guidance?
COLUMBA	With God's help, Grillaan. I am no leader for you.
GRILLAAN	We need no leader — but a father. And that we have. (*Changing the subject*) You told me nothing about the battle yet, Columba.
COLUMBA	It was no battle. I told you that. A shabby squabble between neighbours. I stood on a hill, as you said I would, prudent Grillaan, and watched them below me, hack at each other.
GRILLAAN	It's never any different.
COLUMBA	Never again — no, never. I know I've said that before, dozens of times. But there on the banks of the Blackwater I saw Colman Beg being split and fall from his horse. Although he was my enemy I ran as fast as I could. But when I got to him he was dead, his white hair loose about the grass, his eyes open, his strong face calm and at peace. (*Pause*) He had a look of my father, Grillaan.
GRILLAAN	(*Still trying to brighten him*) And Hugh is married! After all these years.

OSWALD *appears at the door. Stands there.*

COLUMBA	Time for him, too.
GRILLAAN	The honey is very sweet. Brendan says his bees are put to shame.
COLUMBA	(*To himself*) Prudence — that's what I need — and

calm, reasoned moderation.

Now GRILLAAN *sees* OSWALD *at the door.*

GRILLAAN   Oswald! Come in, boy! Come in!
COLUMBA   Yes — the young Englishman, isn't it?
OSWALD   I wish to speak to you, Columba.
COLUMBA   By all means, Oswald. Come on in.
GRILLAAN   I was about to leave anyhow.

OSWALD *enters.* GRILLAAN *goes to door.*

COLUMBA   Thank you, Grillaan. What was it you called it? — The will and determination to begin? It's there — it's there in plenty.

> GRILLAAN *smiles back. Then leaves.* OSWALD *has the same intense look as when we first saw him. It is clear that* COLUMBA *is a hero to him: he never takes his eyes off him. His body, his movements, his voice are stilled and hushed in the Abbot's presence.* COLUMBA — *the man of action — is not aware of this. He brightens considerably when* OSWALD *comes in.*

Now, Oswald, the Englishman, how does Iona suit you? Pull up a stool there and sit down.
OSWALD   You have been gone twenty-two days.
COLUMBA   And now I'm back again to start — with you. You and I together, Oswald. Are you happy here?
OSWALD   I am now, for the first time.
COLUMBA   Every novice is homesick. It's nothing to be ashamed of — provided it still isn't tugging at him when he's an old man.
OSWALD   I've never been so miserable in all my life.
COLUMBA   They tell me the south of England is a beautiful place.
OSWALD   I wasn't homesick, Abbot. Five minutes after I had left home I forgot what it looked like.

COLUMBA You are lucky then, young Oswald. Detachment is a precious thing. How are you getting on with the other novices?

OSWALD I hate them! I hate every single one of them! I dread the hours when we are permitted to talk!

COLUMBA No, no, you don't hate —

OSWALD Great, rustic louts who mock my accent and my table manners and the way I pronounce the Latin —

COLUMBA Your ways are new to them.

OSWALD And their endless joking and camaraderie and coarse humour so that if you make a serious comment they pounce on it and turn it to ridicule.

COLUMBA That is something you will discover always where men are cut off from the refining influence of women, Oswald. The same with soldiers, the same with sailors. I wouldn't let it upset me. Be — yes, be prudent in your judgement of them.

OSWALD I can forget about them now that you're back. They don't exist any more.

COLUMBA Tell me, Oswald, why did you choose Iona?

OSWALD Why?

COLUMBA When Aidan wrote to me to ask me to accept you he spoke so highly of you that I wondered at the time he hadn't persuaded you to join his own monastery.

OSWALD He did try.

COLUMBA And you preferred to come here?

OSWALD Yes.

COLUMBA I believe you were wise. It is not a good thing to be near home, Oswald.

OSWALD That did not influence me.

COLUMBA What did, then?

From here on OSWALD *is unable to contain himself. His boyish hero-worship of* COLUMBA *must be spoken. At first* COLUMBA *does not understand, is then amused, then irritated, finally — because of his own sense of guilt — infuriated.*

OSWALD You. I had to be with you.

COLUMBA Me?

OSWALD (*In a rush*) Everybody in the south of England knows of you and talks of you. From I was so high, when I first heard of you, I knew that one day I would join you here in Iona. I have always admired you more than anybody else in my whole life.

COLUMBA 'In your whole life!' Oswald, son, God has many strange ways of calling each of us. But we must not confuse the means with the end. You are here only because you wish above all things to be a monk.

OSWALD And to be with you, to see you, to watch you, to copy you, to do everything exactly as you do it.

COLUMBA Hold on! Hold on! Hold on! You are young, Oswald, and inexperienced —

OSWALD You eat practically nothing and you sleep only three hours each night —

COLUMBA (*Calmly*) Will you listen to me?

OSWALD Sorry.

COLUMBA Young boys need heroes, Oswald. When I was your age our hero was Niall of the Nine Hostages. We used to play Niall day in and day out; and we used to fight among ourselves who would be leader next, because each of us wanted to be Niall the King and none of us wanted to be the leader of the enemy. Then as I grew older I learned some things about Niall — that he was pig-headed, and blustering, and bloodthirsty, and his temper was violent, and he was a very, very imprudent ruler of his people.

OSWALD You have prophesied the future many times and —

COLUMBA In the same way, Oswald, you, too, may have had an idea of a man, built out of old women's tales and endowed with every possible virtue by simple pious folk. But you are not a child now —

OSWALD You have changed water into wine, and cast out devils, and calmed a stormy sea, and spoken with the angels —

COLUMBA (*Angrily*) You are not a child, I say. You are a man —

59

or at least the makings of a man. (*Calm again*) Now, Oswald, now together, you and I, we are going to try to become holy men because that is why we are here. Together we will start. And the first thing we have got to do is to keep the Rule of the monastery. At this moment you should be at your Scripture lessons and I should be in the chapel.

OSWALD You raised a boy from the dead. He was lying in his coffin and before dozens of witnesses you stretched out your hand —

COLUMBA And you must remember that I am Abbot here — to be obeyed.

OSWALD You knew when Finnian of Clonard died. You had a vision in the church in Derry. You must have known, too, when the old blind man here had died.

COLUMBA Get to your Scripture lesson.

OSWALD You knew he was dead. You had a vision over in Ireland. An angel told you. You are too humble to speak about it.

COLUMBA Get out of my way, boy! I am trying to start again!

OSWALD The others may say that you are too stern or too lenient or too mild or too quick; but I know the wonderful man you are, the man of heroic virtue —

COLUMBA Stop it! Stop it! Stop it!

OSWALD Because I know that you are a saint, Columba!

COLUMBA *slaps him across the face with his open hand.* OSWALD *looks at him in shock, in horror. Then turns and runs off.* COLUMBA *pauses for a second, trying to realize what he has done. Then he rushes to the door calling:*

COLUMBA Oswald — Oswald — I'm sorry, Oswald — Come back — come back — Oh God, I'm sorry —

Curtain.

ACT THREE

DIARMUID *is working at the table where* CAORNAN *used to work. When he dips his pen into the ink, which he keeps on the floor, he turns his face away so that he will not smell the ink.* BRENDAN *enters. He moves wearily. He is carrying a cloak.*

DIARMUID Any luck?

> BRENDAN *shakes his head.*

BRENDAN Where will I leave this?
DIARMUID Throw it on the bed there.

> BRENDAN *leaves the cloak on the bed.*

You're wasting your time. He has cleared off to the south of England. What does he say himself?
BRENDAN Nothing.
DIARMUID And I suppose he went straight from the boat to the chapel?

> BRENDAN *nods: Yes.*

All over a young, conceited brat of a novice! That was my opinion of him. A pup!
BRENDAN Everywhere we go he stumbles over the heather and through the rocks, calling 'Oswald — Oswald' as if it were his own child he was looking for.
DIARMUID Where were you today?
BRENDAN North end of Mull.
DIARMUID He's gone. Told him that myself. At this moment he's sitting in Daddy's best armchair and making his posh friends chuckle at his little escapade —

three weeks on an island monastery.

BRENDAN How's it going?

DIARMUID Rotten!

BRENDAN Mm. Mm. Mm. Fair. A bit spidery — but — quite good, everything considered.

DIARMUID It's very good.

BRENDAN That's what I say — apart from those smudges there — and the unevenness of the lines —

DIARMUID What lines?

BRENDAN Those and those. And those and those.

DIARMUID *looks more closely at the work.*

DIARMUID The ink is the cause of that.

BRENDAN And the pen and the rough table and the poor quality of the paper.

DIARMUID Not the ink itself but the smell of it. It goes for me here.

He indicates his stomach. BRENDAN *pretends to be very sympathetic.*

BRENDAN Where?

DIARMUID Here. Just there.

BRENDAN Tch, tch.

DIARMUID That's why I have to keep it on the floor. And every time I need a dip, I have to do it behind my back! That's why I have so little done.

BRENDAN Yes. Very awkward. Tch, tch.

DIARMUID Even if I hold it at my side — like this here — the very sight of the thing sets me off.

BRENDAN I know.

DIARMUID And if I get a whiff of the ink itself — ohhhhh! The searing pain shoots right up to the chest.

BRENDAN I wonder — still, no —

DIARMUID What?

BRENDAN I was going to suggest that you leave the inkwell outside the door altogether.

DIARMUID Eh?

BRENDAN   Then you would neither see it nor smell it.

DIARMUID   You may laugh! It's easily seen you were never doubled up with excruciating agonies!

BRENDAN *moves away, laughing.*

BRENDAN   You have no one to thank but yourself, Diarmuid. What have you tried so far? Sacristan, cook, smithy, carpenter, weaver, mason, silversmith, novice-master, personal attendant to the Abbot, and now scribe. No wonder we call you our 'all-round' man!

DIARMUID   When I was sacristan, it was the candles; when I was cook, it was the smell of fat; when I was smithy, it was the heat of the furnace; when I was —

BRENDAN   I'm not criticizing you, Diarmuid. I'm just pointing out that this is the only job you hadn't tried. If you ask me he's been more than patient with you.

DIARMUID   Brendan, I — I'm thinking of asking for another change.

BRENDAN   But you've been round them all!

DIARMUID   My old job back — I've been thinking about it here.

BRENDAN   Which of the ten, Diarmuid?

DIARMUID   Yours.

BRENDAN   Mine?

DIARMUID   You would like to get back to the farming again, wouldn't you?

BRENDAN   But your stomach and the boats and all the travel-ling —

DIARMUID   I have it all worked out. I'll wait until he gives up this mad search of his. It will soon be winter. He has been in Ireland a month ago so he won't be going there for a long time. He isn't due a visit to the Scottish houses for another nine months. And even if an emergency should arise it would prob-ably be too stormy to go anywhere.

BRENDAN   You're a crafty old fox!

DIARMUID   It's not for myself, Brendan, you know that. It's for my stomach.

BRENDAN   Of course, Diarmuid.

DIARMUID A good plan, eh?

BRENDAN Very good.

DIARMUID You don't mind being shifted around?

BRENDAN As long as it's for the good of your health.

DIARMUID Good man. I knew you would understand. Now you run along and get something to eat. I suppose you had nothing since yesterday.

BRENDAN A slice of bread.

DIARMUID Tch, tch, tch. That's the way I used to be — completely indifferent to myself. And now look at me. What I mean is, now I just have to take care of myself if I'm not to be a dead weight on the community.

BRENDAN Dochonna will scrape up something for me.

DIARMUID Poor Dochonna. Have you noticed, Brendan?

BRENDAN I have.

DIARMUID It must have been the shock of Caornan's death.

BRENDAN He seems happy enough, though.

DIARMUID Living in the past.

BRENDAN *is about to go off.*

BRENDAN Tell him his cloak's over there.

DIARMUID We had new roots today. Very nice they were, too.

BRENDAN I dug them this morning before we left.

DIARMUID Yes, I think I'll join you — I always find that I can work much better after a little break.

DIARMUID *rises from the table and joins* BRENDAN.

BRENDAN Too much concentration is bad for the stomach.

DIARMUID You find that too? Exactly the same with me. Concentration and long fasts — disastrous! The best cure I know is small quantities of food frequently —

At the door they meet GRILLAAN *coming in.*
DIARMUID *stands in the doorway.*

GRILLAAN The Abbot's not here?

BRENDAN He's around somewhere. Did you try the chapel?

GRILLAAN   I've just been there.

DIARMUID   Here he is.

BRENDAN   His clothes are wet. You should persuade him to change.

GRILLAAN   Persuade *him*?

> COLUMBA *enters. For the first time he looks his years. Tired, weary, apathetic. His face is drawn and worried. At last he is old. On his way past* DIARMUID *he pats him on the shoulder and says, 'Well, Diarmuid', and crosses the stage and drops into a seat.*

BRENDAN   Did you leave the rowlocks in the boat, Columba?

COLUMBA   I did. We'll be needing them again tomorrow.

BRENDAN   Right. Give me a call when you need me.

COLUMBA   Thank you, Brendan. Thank you.

> BRENDAN *and* DIARMUID *go off.* GRILLAAN *stands looking down at* COLUMBA *who fingers the bottom of his habit.*

GRILLAAN   This has got to stop, Columba.

COLUMBA   I had one foot in the boat and the other on dry land. When I jumped, the boat shot out from under me and down I went into the water. You should have heard Brendan laugh.

GRILLAAN   I said this can't go on.

COLUMBA   Luckily it was shallow water and I landed on my hands and knees.

GRILLAAN   The Bishop of Perth was here again today to see you — that's twice in one week — and I had to tell him you were still out on visitation.

> COLUMBA *does not speak.*

Somebody every day. And I have to invent excuses for you: you are gone to Tiree; you are visiting Colonsay; you're away to Arran.

COLUMBA We have searched Tiree and Colonsay and Arran.

GRILLAAN At this very moment there are two men waiting to see you.

COLUMBA (*Listlessly*) Who are they?

GRILLAAN I don't know who they are. Look, Columba, there are at least a dozen things to be discussed and we never even get mentioning them.

COLUMBA What's wrong, Grillaan?

GRILLAAN Two of the novices are ill, very ill, and Sillan says he has tried all the cures he knows of.

COLUMBA I must call on them.

GRILLAAN The roof of the refectory could fall any minute. We need to repair the choir seats. Another message from Gregory of Bracholy: their crops all failed and they have only enough food to last them until the middle of next week. Cormac says he needs new sails for the big boat. And Dochonna — he's a danger to himself in that kitchen; some of these days he'll set fire to himself. What are we going to do about him? And the farm — there's no one competent to look after it since you took Brendan off on this wild goose chase of yours.

COLUMBA I'll find him yet, Grillaan.

GRILLAAN And Brendan – that's another thing.

COLUMBA What's wrong with Brendan?

GRILLAAN Have you looked at him recently? Have you looked at anything for the past two weeks?

COLUMBA What's wrong with Brendan?

GRILLAAN He's not eating. He's not sleeping. He's failed away to sticks. He's not half the man he was.

COLUMBA I thought he enjoyed being out in the boat.

GRILLAAN If he's with you — anywhere — he's happy. He was always like you, but now he models himself completely on you. Last night, Columba — you were in the chapel at the time — the young Swiss student said something to Brendan that annoyed him. I don't know what it was. But Brendan flew into a wild temper and only that I was there he would have struck the Swiss boy. He could have been you — in the old days.

COLUMBA   I'm trying, Grillaan, as God's my judge. I'm trying.

GRILLAAN   (*Softly*) Give it up, Columba. Give it up. This obses-
sion — it's bad for your body, it's bad for your soul.
Oswald's gone. What matter? Not a month passes
but a new student arrives. Forget him. We need you
here, Columba. The monastery needs you. We all
need you.

COLUMBA   You gave me your advice, Grillaan, and I am trying
to follow that advice. I keep the Rule like the most
ardent youth on the island —

GRILLAAN   How blind can you be? He came here because of
you — because of your reputation —

COLUMBA   None of us knows that.

GRILLAAN   And out there in the study hall at the moment are
forty young students who need you, who have
heard of the life you have founded and have left all
to follow it. You have a duty to them — ordinary
sensible boys who need you.

COLUMBA   Give me one more day — that's all I ask — one
more day to search the Isle of Rhum.

GRILLAAN   It's always one more with you — one more visit to
Derry, one more night in the chapel, one more
appeal from the family, one more territory to open
up. Can you never say no?

COLUMBA   I could have started again with him. And instead of
that I was a scandal giver.

GRILLAAN   Tomorrow then and that's the end of it. (*Not un-
kindly*) You're shivering with cold. Go to the kitchen
and dry yourself.

COLUMBA   I'll see the two men who are sick first. Where are
they?

GRILLAAN   You'll dry yourself first. Then I'll tell you where
they are.

COLUMBA *rises and goes towards the door.*

COLUMBA   Iona would be lost without you, Grillaan.

GRILLAAN   No, it wouldn't. I'm busy over many things. Go on and dry yourself. We have enough patients in the place as it is.

> COLUMBA *goes off.* GRILLAAN *goes to the door to look at him. Then returns. Sees the cloak on the bed. Lifts it. It is wet, too. He is about to go off with it when* EOGHAN *and* AEDH *enter.* EOGHAN *is Columba's brother. They do not resemble each other in any way.* EOGHAN *is small, lean and carries himself carelessly. He has all the worst characteristics of a countryman: cunning, wary, watchful, smiling too easily. Yet he has a gauche dignity, a quiet power that marks him out as a leader. He is dressed in rough brown tweeds.* AEDH, *his son, a young man in his late twenties, is a finer figure. He is lightly built, holds himself well — almost arrogantly — and is obviously in a bad temper and anxious to be off. He has not much time for monks or monasteries.*

EOGHAN It's only us again. Did he come back since?

> GRILLAAN *treats them with courtesy — and no more.*

GRILLAAN Yes. He's here now. Come in and take a seat. I'll get him for you.
EOGHAN We had a stroll round there. Great place you have here. Powerful altogether.
GRILLAAN A lot of improvements are needed. Most of the buildings haven't been touched since the day we put them up. Here's a stool here.
EOGHAN It's a bed we need after that big meal you gave us.
GRILLAAN He shouldn't be long. Your names are — ?
EOGHAN This is Aedh, my son. And I'm his brother. Just tell him Ownie's here.
GRILLAAN Eoghan and Aedh.

> GRILLAAN *stops at the door.*

You've just come to see Columba and the island?

EOGHAN That's it. I missed him when he was home last month.

GRILLAAN There's nothing the matter at home, is there?

AEDH Are you going to get him or are you not? We can't hang around this godforsaken place all day!

EOGHAN That'll do you, boy!

GRILLAAN I'm not asking out of curiosity. And I would like to remind you that he is Columba of Iona and not Columba of Kilmacrenan.

GRILLAAN *goes off.*

AEDH Who the hell does he think he is?

EOGHAN Quiet. Quiet. Quiet.

AEDH Bloody cheek! Columba of Iona! You would think he was the Emperor of Rome or something!

AEDH *stands sullenly at the corner of the stage. His father moves about examining the room with all the curiosity and vague awe of a layman in a monastery. Occasionally, when he thinks he hears someone coming, he stands innocently looking at the table.* AEDH *takes no interest in what his father does.*

EOGHAN Draughty old place, isn't it? (*He feels the bed*) Stone, by God! If you slept on one of those things you wouldn't be so hard to get up in the morning.

He moves over to the table and looks up at the scrolls.

All them books! Powerful altogether. Powerful.

He takes one down, tries to read it and cannot. He puts it back, looks at the crucifix and taps it.

Just thought it was oak.

AEDH   We're wasting our time here.

EOGHAN *examines a stool.*

EOGHAN   Whoever made that was no craftsman.

AEDH   I said we're wasting our time here.

EOGHAN   I used to think when your mother died, may she
rest happy, I used to think it would be a good idea
to retire to a place like this.

AEDH   Why didn't you?

EOGHAN   And live on that stuff they gave us there now? What
was it? Seal? No wonder Columba likes to come
home now and again for his food. Still and all — no
women, that's a big advantage.

AEDH   That's good coming from you! Does your reverend
brother know about the Fermanagh tramp you have
living with you?

EOGHAN   (*Nastily*) We're here because of your slut, Aedh, and
don't forget it!

AEDH   Because she wouldn't live under the same roof as
a whore.

EOGHAN   She'll be gone when we get back. I told her to clear
out.

AEDH   Then it will be another one — won't it?

EOGHAN   Shut up! Here he is! And let me do all the talking!

AEDH   Talk to your heart's content.

COLUMBA *enters, followed by* GRILLAAN. *At the sight
of his brother and nephew,* COLUMBA *brightens
considerably. He is almost the old* COLUMBA *again.*
EOGHAN *wears his most pleasant smile.* GRILLAAN
stands watchfully at the side.

EOGHAN   Columba!

COLUMBA   Eoghan! You're welcome! And Aedh! The pair of
you — I'm delighted to see you! Have you been
here long?

EOGHAN   Only a wee while.

COLUMBA   Your first visit to the island and I would have to be away! Have you eaten?

EOGHAN Up to here (*indicating his neck*). Man, but you're looking well!

COLUMBA Why wouldn't I with nothing to do and two hundred men to look after me?

EOGHAN Powerful. Powerful.

COLUMBA And Aedh! You're welcome to Iona, Aedh. They say at home he's like me, Grillaan, do you think so?

GRILLAAN Perhaps in temperament, Abbot.

COLUMBA God forbid, Aedh. With your father's looks and my temperament you would be in a poor way. Sit down. Sit down. What sort of a crossing had you? Did you come alone?

>   COLUMBA *recovers his old form more strongly as time passes.*

EOGHAN We had no notion of coming here at all. The two of us were out after the pollock and when we found ourselves up round Malin Head we thought we might as well nip over to see you when we were that near.

COLUMBA Not that old tub with the warped beam!

EOGHAN A good man can handle her.

COLUMBA You should go down to the slip and see this thing, Grillaan. You wouldn't put a waterhen out in her.

EOGHAN She took us this length and she'll take us back.

COLUMBA And did you pull the whole way?

EOGHAN I'll grant you my arms are a wee bit tired.

COLUMBA Strong as horses, these Tirconaill men! But tell me, Aedh — how's the baby? (*He tries to remember the name*) Donnchadh, that's it. (*To* GRILLAAN) You didn't know I was a grand-uncle, did you?

EOGHAN Spoiled. Ruined. All it says is 'No, no.'

COLUMBA Well, we know whose fault that is. (*To* GRILLAAN) The last time I was there he wouldn't let it down off his knee for a minute. (*To* AEDH) Is it going to be a Tirconaill man or an Antrim man?

EOGHAN It's the spitting image of our father, God be good to him.

COLUMBA (*Very pleased*) How could it be? A great-grand-
father?

EOGHAN I'm telling you — its eyes and its laugh and the way
it holds its head to the side.

COLUMBA Donnchadh will be a good man then — which reminds me —

*He goes to the head of his bed and pulls out a box
from which he takes a ring.*

EOGHAN What is he at now?

COLUMBA Something I've always intended doing since
Donnchadh was born. I forget to bring it with me
each time I go over.

EOGHAN (*To* AEDH) Thank him for the wee silver cross he sent
the child.

AEDH Thank you for the wee silver cross you sent the child.

COLUMBA Don't mention it, Aedh. No, this is something different — something the heir to the family should
have —

EOGHAN What is it, Columba?

COLUMBA It is a ring that was given by Patrick to Conall
Culban, son of Niall Naoighiallach. And Conall
Culban passed it down to his son, Fergus Ceann-
fada. And he to his son, Fedhlimidh, my father. And
he to me. And now I to you, Aedh, for your son,
Donnchadh, who will one day come to power, and
rule strongly and justly and wisely, with God's help.

AEDH *takes the ring. He is embarrassed — by the
gift and because of his moody silence up to this.*

AEDH Columba — thank you —

EOGHAN I often wondered where that ring went to.

GRILLAAN *is assured that this is just a happy family
reunion. He goes to door.*

GRILLAAN If there is anything you need I'll be in the community room.

COLUMBA These men will be staying the night. Grillaan, will you look after them?

EOGHAN No, no, Columba, we can't stay the night. They would think at home we were drowned if we didn't turn up before dawn.

COLUMBA Who's to miss you? Ita's looking after the baby and you know very well she's glad to be rid of her cranky old father-in-law for a day or two.

EOGHAN We'll see then; we'll see.

COLUMBA *waves to* GRILLAAN *to go. The matter is settled.* AEDH *stands examining the ring.*

COLUMBA That's settled then. It's seldom enough I see either of you. And talking of Ita, how is she, Aedh?

AEDH She's —

EOGHAN Fine, Columb — just fine —

COLUMBA She made a good convert, Ita. She's a credit to both of you and to your good Christian home.

AEDH *looks at his father — defying him to speak.*

EOGHAN And you should see how she has taught the wee lad to bless himself.

COLUMBA Already?

EOGHAN And say the Our Father — after his own style, of course — grunting and blathering away yonder.

COLUMBA Her own people — they never forgave her, did they?

EOGHAN A thick crowd, them Antrim Picts. But they'll get over it. It will pass. (*Changing subject*) Man, this is a great place you've got here. Powerful altogether.

COLUMBA Had you a look around?

EOGHAN It would take you a week to see it right.

COLUMBA I'll show you over it in the morning. You're very quiet, Aedh. Have you the harvest in yet?

AEDH Most of it —

EOGHAN I see your own hay's all up.

COLUMBA For a change. We're always late here. Poor soil.

EOGHAN Where were you when we came?

COLUMBA I was out looking for one of the novices who — got lost.

EOGHAN On an island this size?

COLUMBA He was new here — about to begin. It's a beautiful ring, isn't it, Aedh?

AEDH is tired of his father's hedging.

AEDH Tell him the truth. Stop beating about the bush!

EOGHAN Aye — the truth — the truth —

COLUMBA What's this?

EOGHAN Well you see, Columb, it's like this here, you see, like this —

AEDH Ita's gone back to Antrim and taken the baby with her!

EOGHAN Let me tell it, let me tell it.

COLUMBA When did this happen?

EOGHAN Four or five days ago — nothing to worry about —

AEDH It was his idea that we come to you. I wanted to settle it my own way.

EOGHAN That's what I'm trying to avoid, Columb. His temper's as quick as your own. So what I says to him, I says, we'll do nothing hasty, I says. We'll go across to your uncle and he'll advise us what to do. You see yourself it's a tricky business like, her being a convert and now herself and the wee lad being held by them heathen Picts.

COLUMBA Held?

AEDH Give me half-a-dozen men and I'll get her back.

EOGHAN Do you see what I'm up against — rearing to fight the whole of Antrim single-handed.

COLUMBA Tell me what happened.

EOGHAN It all began with a bit of a row between the boy here and Ita — nothing much — just a bit of a tiff — you know what young couples are. So up she gets this night, takes a horse and trap, and off with herself and the baby back home.

COLUMBA She is a good wife and a good mother, Aedh?

AEDH There isn't better.

COLUMBA And you treated her properly?

AEDH It was his fault, the whole thing, if he were man enough to admit it, and this was his idea — dragging you into it.

COLUMBA Have you gone to bring her back?

AEDH I went the length of the River Bann and a brother of hers met me there. They're not letting her back — neither her nor the child.

EOGHAN So he came home to gather the clan and take her back by force and as soon as I heard that I said we would come and see you.

COLUMBA What can I do?

EOGHAN Well you know yourself the feeling there is at home when he had to go and marry a Pict in the first place.

AEDH She's better than many a Christian I could name!

EOGHAN And that feeling hasn't died down yet. Many of them are saying no son of a Pict will lead them.

COLUMBA If they respect Aedh they'll respect Aedh's son.

AEDH If they ever see him again.

COLUMBA You'll have to go back and try again.

AEDH I vowed I would — with an army.

EOGHAN Big talk. You know you wouldn't get a handful to follow you.

COLUMBA No, no, no, no. That's no solution. You'll have to go back alone, Aedh, and talk to them.

AEDH I don't even know where they're holding her — could be anywhere in the Antrim mountains.

COLUMBA It will be near Larne. Wasn't that her home place?

AEDH What do you want me to do? Search the whole of the north-east coast myself?

EOGHAN No. He'll never get her back that way. They have her now and they'll keep her.

COLUMBA There's no other way.

EOGHAN You could get her back, Columb.

COLUMBA Me? How? Wait a minute — yes. Comgall of Bangor — his men work right up through that area —

EOGHAN That's not what I had in mind — What I was think-
        ing was that you could — you know there — you
        could get the men together round Aedh and maybe
        you yourself would lead them over to —

COLUMBA You said you came for my advice, Eoghan.

AEDH   Come on. He's not interested.

COLUMBA I am interested! You are my nephew and Donnchadh
        is my grand-nephew and the heir to Kilmacrenan.
        He must be got back. There is no question about
        that. But as to the best course —

EOGHAN (*Quickly*) Forty men would do it — half that with
        you at their head.

COLUMBA That day is over for me — finished.

EOGHAN I sounded them myself and they said they'll go but
        only if Columba is leading them.

COLUMBA No — no — finished — finished.

EOGHAN There'll be no fighting. All we need is a show of
        strength. Give me twenty good men with you in
        front and I'll show you the backside of a full army
        of Picts.

COLUMBA It is no way — no way —

EOGHAN Nothing to do but walk in and take the woman and
        the baby home to Tirconaill. Not a blow struck. Two
        days going and two days coming back. You'll be
        home in Iona by Sunday night.

COLUMBA No — no — no —

EOGHAN I know you don't want to fight or to have anything
        to do with fighting, Columb; neither does Aedh nor
        myself, and there will be no fighting — I promise
        you that. All we need to do to get the heir back is to
        show our courage, to prove that we're not afraid of
        a breed of savages, to show that we're sons of kings
        and men of valour.

COLUMBA Valour has many meanings.

EOGHAN And it is in God's cause that you are going to lead
        us — to save Ita and the baby from the heathens.

COLUMBA I'll go to Comgall — myself — tonight —

EOGHAN My blood and yours and the blood of Fedhlimidh,
        our father, flows in the veins of that child, Columb.

What would he say if he were standing here now — leave it to the Picts? Let it grow up a heathen, a stranger to the soft lands of Gartan? Let them keep it? Is that what he would say?

AEDH I'm going home. I knew he didn't care.

COLUMBA I do care! I do care!

EOGHAN Hugh is waiting for us at home and Seán Bán and young Turlough and the seven sons of Brian Ceann Dubh and the Cumines —

COLUMBA (*Surprised*) The two Cumines?

EOGHAN This is family, Columb! Our family — his, yours, mine. And in a matter like this — a religious matter — all personal differences are forgotten. Yes, the Cumines that you routed a month ago, they are going to supply the horses and the food — provided you lead us.

COLUMBA Eoghan — Eoghan —

EOGHAN Is it a bad thing we are asking of you — that you save two souls for the Church of God, that you unite under the banner of Christ the cousins that have fought against one another for generations? Is that a bad thing? That you do your priestly work of peace and salvation for your own family? Is that a bad thing?

COLUMBA I don't know — I don't —

EOGHAN A young shepherd — a boy from Tory Island —lives on the slopes of Slemish mountain. We have been in touch with him. Three days from now he is to meet us at Coleraine to bring what news he can find out. He is a sharp lad and he will know exactly where they are being held. All we will have to do is bring them home in triumph.

> COLUMBA's *questions are half voluntary, half automatic.*

COLUMBA They will be strongly guarded. The Picts are cunning warriors.

EOGHAN They will expect us from the north. We can surprise

	them from the south.
COLUMBA	With twenty men?
EOGHAN	We'll rally a legion if you are leader.
COLUMBA	This Tory boy — can you trust him?
EOGHAN	He was baptised in your own church in Tory.
COLUMBA	His father's name?
EOGHAN	Canice, son of Colman.
COLUMBA	I knew him.
EOGHAN	We meet on Friday. If he says they are waiting for us you will lead us south to Antrim town and from there up to the foot of the mountains.
COLUMBA	And the Cumines — they have forgotten their defeat?
EOGHAN	Family, Columb, family!
COLUMBA	We need fifty horses and enough food for three days.
EOGHAN	If we go south it will take a week at least —
COLUMBA	In Tyrone we'll eat off the land. We need food only for the time in Antrim.
AEDH	He will wear the ring and be worthy of it, Columba!
EOGHAN	Like his grandfather and *his* grandfather and *his* grandfather!

> DOCHONNA *enters. He is doting. His habit is untidy. His expression strange, vacant.* COLUMBA *goes to him.*

DOCHONNA	It's Caornan, Columba — he's not about anywhere. I've gone right round the island and I can't find him —
COLUMBA	I want you to meet —
DOCHONNA	He's an old man, you see, and his sight's not so good and I'm afraid something might happen to him.
COLUMBA	He's in bed resting.
DOCHONNA	What's that?
COLUMBA	Caornan — he's asleep.
DOCHONNA	Asleep?
COLUMBA	In his room having a rest.
DOCHONNA	He's not as young as us, Columba. He tires easily.

COLUMBA You are the youngest of the three of us.

DOCHONNA Aye, aye, aye, funny thing that — I'm the youngest. Do you know what we're going to do tomorrow, Caornan and me? It was his suggestion — he came in there to me in the kitchen and whispered it to me.

COLUMBA What are you going to do, Dochonna?

DOCHONNA Build a room for you. The Abbot should have a room of his own, a big room, the size of Finnian's.

COLUMBA But I have a room, Dochonna.

DOCHONNA That's what he whispered to me. The pair of us — I'll carry the stones and he'll do the building — for I've got the strength and he's got the head —

COLUMBA Yes, Dochonna, yes, yes —

DOCHONNA He says we'll make a great room for the Abbot where he can work and pray with no one to interfere with him — that's what he says.

> DOCHONNA *fades out and looks around bewilderedly.* COLUMBA *catches him by the arm and steers him towards the door.*

COLUMBA You are tired too, Dochonna. You have worked too hard.

DOCHONNA He can work and pray with no one to interfere with him — that's what Caornan says —

> DOCHONNA *goes off.* COLUMBA *watches him go.*

EOGHAN They're not all like that, are they?

COLUMBA That is a holy priest.

> COLUMBA *comes back into the centre of the room.*

AEDH We'll cross tonight and be home by tomorrow morning.

EOGHAN Seán Bán wants until Monday. He has to go to Innishowen to gather the Disert Eigne men.

AEDH And meet in Derry.

EOGHAN At the ferry at noon.

AEDH (*To* COLUMBA) We'll have too many now that you're in front of us!

EOGHAN It will be a sight, man, a sight!

AEDH And Antrim is rich! The booty there'll be!

EOGHAN He'll lead us on his white horse and the road will open before him!

COLUMBA (*Softly*) I'm not going.

EOGHAN What?

AEDH What did he say?

COLUMBA I can't go! I can't go!

EOGHAN Columba, son of Fedhlimidh —

COLUMBA's *speech is a plea — a pathetic appeal. He cannot refuse his family. He begs them to release him.*

COLUMBA Look at me, brother, look at me. I am an old man. My arms are scarred by the wounds of battle. Look at them. And here — here is a heart that leaps when you call, and pounds against my ribs to join you and lead you and fight with you. But I have a soul, too, that whispers to me. I am small and puny, it says, because you have neglected me. And in a short time I will be standing before the King, it says, and I am pale and untried, it says. I am not reddened by blood, it says. Give me at least your failing years, it says, to battle with the flesh —

AEDH You said you would go! You said it yourself!

COLUMBA Leave me — please leave me —

AEDH If you are a priest you'll go!

EOGHAN *signals to his son to keep quiet. He is still confident.*

EOGHAN Columb, Columb, there are men there waiting for you, men who are straining for bloodshed. If you come with us you can prevent that bloodshed. But if you don't come no man can hold them, no man. And there will be killing and torture and death; and

men who have not confessed their sins for a twelve-
month will die in their guilt and be damned forever!

COLUMBA For God's sake, leave me —

AEDH Are you afraid? Is Columba a coward?

COLUMBA I am afraid to meet my God.

AEDH I told you he was no good! They're all old women
in this place!

EOGHAN Columb —

COLUMBA I can't go, Eoghan — I can't go — I can't go —

EOGHAN I have fought with you in every battle you have
ever fought.

COLUMBA Please —

EOGHAN At Culdrevny, at Coleraine, at Culfada last month.

COLUMBA *shakes his head: No, no, no.*

I never asked the why or wherefore but when the
call came from my brother Columb I answered it
like a man and ran my risk with the rest.

COLUMBA I'll go to Comgall — yes, I'll speak to Comgall —
today —

AEDH Come home, father! Can't you see he's a drivelling
old woman!

EOGHAN'*s façade of pleasantness is dropped.*

EOGHAN You deny us, Columb? And your father's great-
grandchild?

COLUMBA If Comgall can do anything —

EOGHAN And Gartan, your birthplace, and Kilmacrenan and
Churchill, all Tirconaill — you deny it all?

COLUMBA I can't — I can't —

EOGHAN You deny them? You spit on them?

COLUMBA I have a soul —

EOGHAN Then we deny you, monk!

AEDH Leave him to his dotage!

EOGHAN And we curse you! And Kilmacrenan curses you!
And Derry curses you! And Gartan that bred you
curses you! And Innishowen curses you! And the

whole of Tirconaill and Tyrone curse you for a traitor and a coward!

AEDH Leave him! Leave him!

EOGHAN And your father, Fedhlimidh, and your mother, Eithne, from their graves, they curse you, monk, for denying their own!

> EOGHAN *is white with fury.* AEDH *tries to pull him off stage.*

AEDH He's no good! He's no good! He has no time for anyone but himself!

EOGHAN May all your faculties fail you, monk. And may you end your days without food or friend on a barren rock without shade or shelter!

> AEDH *has pushed his father to the door. There he stops; takes the ring from his pocket and flings it across the stage.*

AEDH There! Take your ring and keep it!

EOGHAN And when you die may no grave ever cradle your ungrateful remains. May the hawks eat your flesh and the dogs gnaw at your white bones! And may your work wither and die with you! And may my grandchildren and my great-grandchildren curse you every day they draw breath!

> AEDH *gets him off.* EOGHAN's *voice comes to* COLUMBA *standing alone in the centre of the stage.*

Coward! Traitor! Traitor! Traitor! Traitor! Traitor!

COLUMBA Get out of my monastery! Get out of my island! Get out of my life! Go back to those damned mountains and seductive hills that have robbed me of my Christ! You soaked my sweat! You sucked my blood! You stole my manhood, my best years! What more do you demand of me, damned Ireland? My

soul? My immortal soul? Damned, damned, damned
Ireland! — (*His voice breaks*) Soft, green Ireland —
beautiful, green Ireland — my lovely green Ireland.
O my Ireland —

> *He staggers back, drops on to a stool and lies across*
> *the table. Long pause. Silence.* BRENDAN *comes*
> *running in.*

BRENDAN Columba! Abbot, are you all right? I'll tear him
asunder if he laid a hand on you. Are you hurt?
Who let him in here? Who was he? Where was he
from?

COLUMBA He was my brother — he was my brother from
Kilmacrenan.

BRENDAN Did he strike you? Did he touch you?

COLUMBA He came to save me, Brendan. To make me a real
exile.

BRENDAN If he ever puts his foot in this place again I'll catch
him by the back of his blue jacket and fling him into
the tide!

COLUMBA He won't be back — ever again —

> GRILLAAN *enters.*

GRILLAAN They're gone?

BRENDAN Lucky for them! Just let them come back here again!

GRILLAAN They made a lot of noise. (*To* COLUMBA) You wouldn't
go?

COLUMBA You knew?

GRILLAAN I had a good suspicion.

COLUMBA They cursed me, Grillaan. They cursed and dis-
owned me.

GRILLAAN I gathered the novices into the chapel to pray for
you.

COLUMBA Bring me there, too, because I am empty.

> COLUMBA *rises.* DOCHONNA *appears in the doorway.*

DOCHONNA Caornan! Caornan! I found him! I found him! In the cave on the east side!

GRILLAAN My God, what is he up to!

DOCHONNA Come in, Caornan! Come in!

OSWALD *enters, head down, emaciated, weary, ashamed of himself.*

Look at him, Columba, like something the sea washed up!

BRENDAN Oswald!

OSWALD I came back because I was hungry.

COLUMBA *breaks away from* GRILLAAN *and* BRENDAN *and runs to embrace the boy.*

COLUMBA Welcome — welcome home — welcome home, Oswald.

OSWALD There was nothing to eat but barnacles and dulse —

COLUMBA Oh, Oswald! Oswald! Oswald! Oswald!

DOCHONNA You said he was asleep, Columba, but I knew he wasn't. I knew he wasn't!

COLUMBA We were both asleep, Dochonna of Lough Conn! But we are awake now and ready to begin again — to begin again — to begin again!

Quick curtain.

PHILADELPHIA,
HERE I COME!

Characters

MADGE, housekeeper
GAR O'DONNELL (PUBLIC) ⎫ son of the house
GAR O'DONNELL (PRIVATE) ⎭
S.B. O'DONNELL, Gar's father
KATE DOOGAN / MRS KING, daughter of Senator Doogan
SENATOR DOOGAN
MASTER BOYLE, local teacher
LIZZY SWEENEY, Gar's aunt
CON SWEENEY, Lizzy's husband
BEN BURTON, friend of the Sweeneys
NED ⎫
TOM ⎬ the boys
JOE ⎭
CANON MICK O'BYRNE, the parish priest

Time and place

The present in the small village of Ballybeg in County Donegal, Ireland. The action takes place on the night before, and on the morning of, Gar's departure for Philadelphia.

Set

When the curtain rises the only part of the stage that is lit is the kitchen, i.e. the portion on the left (from the point of view of the audience). It is sparsely and comfortlessly furnished — a bachelor's kitchen. There are two doors; one left which leads to the shop, and one upstage leading to the scullery (off). Beside the shop door is a large deal table, now set for tea without cloth and with rough cups and saucers. Beside the scullery door is an old-fashioned dresser. On the scullery wall is a large school-type clock.

Stage right, now in darkness, is Gar's bedroom. Both bedroom and kitchen should be moved upstage, leaving a generous apron. Gar's bedroom is furnished with a single bed, a wash-hand basin (crockery jug and bowl), a table with a record player and records, and a small chest of drawers.

These two areas — kitchen and Gar's bedroom — occupy more than two-thirds of the stage. The remaining portion is fluid: in Episode One, for example, it represents a room in Senator Doogan's home.

The two Gars, Public Gar and Private Gar, are two views of the one man. Public Gar is the Gar that people see, talk to, talk about. Private Gar is the unseen man, the man within, the conscience, the alter ego, the secret thoughts, the id. Private Gar, the spirit, is invisible to everybody, always. Nobody except Public Gar hears him talk. But even Public Gar, although he talks to Private Gar occasionally, never sees him and never looks at him. One cannot look at one's alter ego.

Music

Mendelssohn's *Violin Concerto in E minor, Op. 64*.
Céilí music.
'All Round My Hat' — first verse.
'She Moved through the Fair' — second verse.
'California, Here I Come!'.
'Give the Woman in the Bed More Porter'.

Philadelphia, Here I Come! was first produced at the Gaiety Theatre, Dublin, on 28 September 1964, by Edwards-MacLiammoir: Dublin Gate Theatre Productions Ltd in association with the Dublin Theatre Festival and Oscar Lewenstein Ltd, with the following cast:

MADGE	Maureen O'Sullivan
GAR O'DONNELL (PUBLIC)	Patrick Bedford
GAR O'DONNELL (PRIVATE)	Donal Donnelly
S.B. O'DONNELL	Eamon Kelly
KATE DOOGAN / MRS KING	Máire Hastings
SENATOR DOOGAN	Cecil Barror
MASTER BOYLE	Dominic Roche
LIZZY SWEENEY	Ruby Head
CON SWEENEY	Tom Irwin
BEN BURTON	Michael Mara
NED	Eamon Morrissey
TOM	Brendan Sullivan
JOE	Emmet Bergin
CANON MICK O'BYRNE	Alex McDonald

Directed by	Hilton Edwards
Setting by	Alpho O'Reilly

for my mother and father

EPISODE ONE

Kitchen in the home of County Councillor S.B. O'Donnell who owns a general shop. As the curtain rises MADGE, *the housekeeper, enters from the scullery with a tray in her hands and finishes setting the table. She is a woman in her sixties. She walks as if her feet were precious. She pauses on her way past the shop door.*

MADGE Gar! Your tea!
PUBLIC (*Off*) Right!

> *She finishes setting the table and is about to go to the scullery door when* PUBLIC GAR *marches on stage. He is ecstatic with joy and excitement: tomorrow morning he leaves for Philadelphia.*

PUBLIC (*Singing*) 'Philadelphia, here I come, right back where I started from . . . ' (*Breaks off and catches* MADGE) Come on, Madge! What about an old time waltz!
MADGE Agh, will you leave me alone.

> *He holds on to her and forces her to do a few steps as he sings in waltz time.*

PUBLIC 'Where bowers of flowers bloom in the spring'—
MADGE (*Struggling*) Stop it! Stop it! You brat, you!
PUBLIC Madge, you dance like an angel.

> *Suddenly lets her go and springs away from her.*

  Oh, but you'd give a fella bad thoughts very quick!
MADGE And the smell of fish of you, you dirty thing!

> *He grabs her again and puts his face up to hers, very confidentially.*

PUBLIC   Will you miss me?

MADGE   Let me on with my work!

PUBLIC   The truth!

MADGE   Agh, will you quit it, will you?

PUBLIC   I'll tickle you till you squeal for mercy.

MADGE   Please, Gar —

PUBLIC   (*Tickling her*) Will you miss me, I said?

MADGE   I will — I will — I will — I —

PUBLIC   That's better. Now tell me: what time is it?

MADGE   Agh, Gar —

PUBLIC   What time is it?

MADGE   (*Looking at clock*) Ten-past-seven.

PUBLIC   And what time do I knock off at?

MADGE   At seven.

PUBLIC   Which means that on my last day with him he got
ten minutes overtime out of my hide. (*He releases
Madge*) Instead of saying to me: (*Grandly*) 'Gar, my
son, since you are leaving me forever, you may have
the entire day free,' what does he do? Lines up five
packs of flour and says: (*In flat dreary tones*) 'Make
them up into two-pound pokes.'

MADGE   He's losing a treasure, indeed!

PUBLIC   So d'you know what I said to him? I just drew myself up and looked him straight in the eye and said
to him: 'Two-pound pokes it will be' — just like that.

MADGE   That flattened him.

> *She goes off to the scullery. He stands at the door and
> talks in to her.*

PUBLIC   And that wasn't it all. At six o'clock he remembered
about the bloody pollock, and him in the middle of
the Angelus.

> *He stands in imitation of the father: head bowed,
> hands on chest. In flat tones:*

'Behold-the-handmaid-of-the-Lord-Gut-and-salt-
them-fish.' So by God I lashed so much salt on those

bloody fish that any poor bugger that eats them will die of thirst. But when the corpses are strewn all over Ballybeg, where will I be? In the little old USA! Yip-eeeeee!

He swings away from the scullery door and does a few exuberant steps as he sings —

'Philadelphia, here I come, rightah backah where Ah started from — '

He goes into his bedroom, flings himself down on his bed, rests his head on his hands, and looks at the ceiling. Sings alternate lines of 'Philadelphia' — first half — with PRIVATE *(off).*

PUBLIC It's all over.

PRIVATE *(Off, in echo-chamber voice)* And it's all about to begin. It's all over.

PUBLIC And it's all about to begin.

PRIVATE *(Now on)* Just think, Gar.

PUBLIC Think . . .

PRIVATE Think . . . Up in that big bugger of a jet, with its snout pointing straight for the States, and its tail belching smoke over Ireland; and you sitting up at the front (PUBLIC *acts this*) with your competent fingers poised over the controls; and then away down below in the Atlantic you see a bloody bugger of an Irish boat out fishing for bloody pollock and — (PUBLIC *nosedives, engines screaming, machine guns stuttering*)

PUBLIC Rat-tat-tat-tat-tat-tat-tat-tat-tat-tat.

PRIVATE Abandon ship! Make for the lifeboats! Send for Canon Mick O'Byrne! (PUBLIC *gains altitude and nosedives again*)

PUBLIC Rat-tat-tat-tat-tat-tat-tat-tat-tat.

PRIVATE To hell with women and children! Say an Act of Contrition!

PUBLIC Yip-eeeee!

PUBLIC *finishes taking off the shop coat, rolls it into a bundle, and places it carefully on the floor.*

PRIVATE It looks as if — I can't see very well from the distance — but it looks as if — yes! — yes! — the free is being taken by dashing Gar O'Donnell (PUBLIC *gets back from the coat, poises himself to kick it*), pride of the Ballybeg team. (*In commentator's hushed voice*) O'Donnell is now moving back, taking a slow, calculating look at the goal. I've never seen this boy in the brilliant form he's in today — absolute magic in his feet. He's now in position, running up, and —

PUBLIC *kicks the coat into the air.*

PUBLIC Ya-hoooo! (*Sings and gyrates at same time*) 'Philah-delph-yah, heah Ah come, rightah backah weah Ah stahted from, boom-boom-boom-boom — '

He breaks off suddenly when PRIVATE *addresses him in sombre tones of a judge.*

PRIVATE Gareth Mary O'Donnell.

PUBLIC *springs to attention, salutes, and holds this absurd military stance. He is immediately inside his bedroom door, facing it.*

PUBLIC Sir.
PRIVATE You are fully conscious of all the consequences of your decision?
PUBLIC Yessir.
PRIVATE Of leaving the country of your birth, the land of the curlew and the snipe, the Aran sweater and the Irish Sweepstakes?
PUBLIC (*With fitting hesitation*) I-I-I-I have considered all these, Sir.
PRIVATE Of going to a profane, irreligious, pagan country of gross materialism?

PUBLIC   I am fully sensitive to this, Sir.

PRIVATE   Where the devil himself holds sway, and lust — abhorrent lust — is everywhere indulged in shamelessly? (PUBLIC *winks extravagantly and nudges an imaginary man beside him*)

PUBLIC   Who are you tellin'? (*Poker-stiff again*) Shamelessly, Sir, shamelessly.

> MADGE *has entered from the scullery, carrying an old suitcase and a bundle of clothes.*

PRIVATE   And yet you persist in exposing yourself to these frightful dangers?

PUBLIC   I would submit, Sir, that these stories are slightly exaggerated, Sir. For every door that opens —

> MADGE *opens the bedroom door.*

MADGE   Oh! You put the heart across me there! Get out of my road, will you, and quit eejiting about!

PUBLIC   Madge, you're an aul' duck.

MADGE   Aye, so. There's the case. And there's a piece of rope for I see the clasp's all rusted. And there's your shirts and your winter vests and your heavy socks and you'll need to air them shirts before you — Don't put them smelly hands on them!

PUBLIC   Sorry!

MADGE   See that they're well aired before you put them on. He's said nothing since, I suppose?

PUBLIC   Not a word.

PRIVATE   The bugger.

MADGE   But he hasn't paid you your week's wages?

PUBLIC   £3 15s — that'll carry me far.

MADGE   He'll have something to say then, you'll see. And maybe he'll slip you a couple of extra pounds.

PUBLIC   Whether he says goodbye to me or not, or whether he slips me a few miserable quid or not, it's a matter of total indifference to me, Madge.

MADGE   Aye, so. Your tea's on the table — but that's a matter of total indifference to me.

PUBLIC Give me time to wash, will you?

MADGE And another thing: just because he doesn't say much doesn't mean that he hasn't feelings like the rest of us.

PUBLIC Say much? He's said nothing!

MADGE He said nothing either when your mother died. It must have been near daybreak when he got to sleep last night. I could hear his bed creaking.

PUBLIC Well to hell with him —

MADGE (*Leaving*) Don't come into your tea smelling like a lobster pot.

PUBLIC If he wants to speak to me he knows where to find me! But I'm damned if I'm going to speak to him first!

MADGE *goes off to the scullery.*

(*Calling after her*) And you can tell him I said that if you like!

PRIVATE What the hell do you care about him. Screwballs! Skinflint! Skittery Face! You're free of him and his stinking bloody shop. And tomorrow morning, boy, when that little ole plane gets up into the skies you'll stick your head out the window (PUBLIC *acts this*) and spit down on the lot of them!

S.B. *appears at the shop door. He is in his late sixties. Wears a hat, a good dark suit, collar and tie, black apron. He is a responsible, respectable citizen.*

S.B. Gar! (PUBLIC *reacts instinctively.* PRIVATE *keeps calm*)

PRIVATE Let the bugger call.

S.B. (*Louder*) Gar!

Instinct is stronger than reason: PUBLIC *rushes to his door and opens it. But as soon as he opens it and looks out at his father he assumes in speech and gesture a surly, taciturn gruffness. He always behaves in this way when he is in his father's company.*

PUBLIC   Aye?

S.B.   How many coils of barbed wire came in on the mail van this evening?

PUBLIC   Two. Or was it three?

S.B.   That's what I'm asking you. It was you that carried them into the yard.

PUBLIC   There were two — no, no, no, three — yes, three — or maybe it was — was it two?

S.B.   Agh!

> S.B. *retires to the shop.* PUBLIC *and* PRIVATE *come back into the bedroom.*

PRIVATE   What sort of a stupid bugger are you? Think, man! You went out and stood yarning to Joe the Post; then you carried one coil into the yard and came out with the sack of spuds for the parochial; then you carried in the second coil . . . and put it in the corner . . . and came out again to the van . . . and . . . (PUBLIC *skips into the air*) Ah, what the hell odds! That's his headache, old Nicodemus! After tomorrow a bloody roll of barbed wire will be a mere bagatelle to you. (*In cowboy accent*) Yeah, man. You see tham thar plains stretchin' 's far th'eye can see, man? Well, tham thar plains belongs to Garry the Kid. An' Garry the Kid he don't go in for none of your fancy fencin'. No siree. (*His eye lights on the fresh laundry* MADGE *brought in*) And what'll you wear on the plane tomorrow, old rooster, eh?

> PUBLIC *picks up a clean shirt, holds it to his chest, and surveys himself in the small mirror above his wash handbasin.*

Pretty smart, eh?

PUBLIC   Pretty smart.

PRIVATE   Pretty sharp?

PUBLIC   Pretty sharp.

PRIVATE   Pretty *oo-là-là*?

PUBLIC   *Mais oui.*

PRIVATE   And not a bad looker, if I may say so.

PUBLIC   You may. You may.

PRIVATE   (*In heavy US accent*) I'm Patrick Palinakis, president of the biggest chain of biggest hotels in the world. We're glad to have you, Mr O'Donnell.

PUBLIC   (*Sweet, demure*) And I'm glad to be here, Sir.

PRIVATE   Handsomely said, young man. I hope you'll be happy with us and work hard and one day maybe you'll be president of the biggest chain of biggest hotels in the world.

PUBLIC   That's my ambition, Sir.

PRIVATE   You are twenty-five years of age, Mr O'Donnell?

PUBLIC   Correct.

PRIVATE   And you spent one year at University College Dublin?

PUBLIC   Yes, Sir.

PRIVATE   Would you care to tell me why you abandoned your academic career, Mr O'Donnell?

PUBLIC   (*With disarming simplicity*) Well, just before I sat my First Arts exam, Sir, I did an old Irish *turas*, or pilgrimage, where I spent several nights in devout prayer, Sir.

PRIVATE   St Patrick's Pilgrimage — on Lough — ?

PUBLIC   St Harold's Cross, Sir. And it was there that I came to realize that a life of scholarship was not for me. So I returned to my father's business.

PRIVATE   Yeah. You mentioned that your father was a businessman. What's his line?

PUBLIC   Well, Sir, he has — what you would call — his finger in many pies — retail mostly — general dry goods — assorted patent drugs — hardware — ah — ah — dehydrated fish — men's king-size hose — snuffs from the exotic East . . . of Donegal — a confection for gourmets, known as Peggy's Leg — weedkiller — (*Suddenly breaking off: in his normal accent, rolling on the bed*) Yahoooooo! It is now sixteen or seventeen years since I saw the Queen of France, then the Dauphiness, at Versailles —

PRIVATE Let's git packin', boy. Let's git that li'l ole saddle bag
opened and let's git packin'. But first let's have a li'l
ole music on the li'l ole phonograph. Yeah, man. You
bet. Ah reckon. Yessir.

> PUBLIC *puts a record on the player: First Move-*
> *ment, Mendelssohn's* Violin Concerto. PUBLIC *is*
> *preening himself before his performance and, while*
> *he is flexing his fingers and adjusting his bow tie,*
> PRIVATE *announces in the reverential tones of a radio*
> *announcer:*

The main item in tonight's concert is the First Movement of the *Violin Concerto in E minor, Opus 64*, by
Jacob Ludwig Felix Mendelssohn. The orchestra is
conducted by Gareth O'Donnell and the soloist is
the Ballybeg half-back, Gareth O'Donnell. Music
critics throughout the world claim that O'Donnell's
simultaneous wielding of baton and bow is the
greatest thing since Leather Ass died. Mendelssohn's
Violin Concerto, First Movement.

> PRIVATE *sits demurely on the chair.* PUBLIC *clears his*
> *throat. Now* PUBLIC *plays the violin, conducts, plays*
> *the violin, conducts, etc. etc. This keeps up for some*
> *time. Then* PRIVATE *rises from his chair.*

Agh, come on, come on, come on! Less aul' foolin'.
To work, old rooster, to work.

> PUBLIC *stops. Turns player down low and changes*
> *from the First to the Second Movement. Takes a look*
> *at the case Madge brought in.*

Ah, hell, how can any bloody bugger head into a jet
plane with aul' cardboard rubbish like that! (PUBLIC
examines the surface) Dammit, maybe you could give
it a lick of paint! Or wash it! (PUBLIC *spits on the lid*
and rubs it with his finger) God, you'll rub a hole in

the damn thing if you're not careful! Maybe aul' Screwballs'll slip you a fiver tonight and you can get a new one in Dublin.

PUBLIC What a hope!

PUBLIC *opens the case and sniffs the inside.*

PRIVATE Oh! Stinks of cat's pee!

PUBLIC *lifts out a sheet of faded newspaper.*

PUBLIC (*Reads*) The *Clarion* — 1st January 1937.

PRIVATE Precious medieval manuscript . . . my God, was it? . . . By God it was — the day they were married — and it (*the case*) hasn't been opened since their honeymoon . . . She and old Screwballs off on a side-car to Bundoran for three days . . .

PUBLIC O God, the Creator and Redeemer of all the faithful, give to the soul of Maire, my mother, the remission of all her sins, that she may obtain . . .

PRIVATE She was small, Madge says, and wild, and young, Madge says, from a place called Bailtefree beyond the mountains; and her eyes were bright, and her hair was loose, and she carried her shoes under her arm until she came to the edge of the village, Madge says, and then she put them on . . .

PUBLIC Eternal rest grant unto her, O Lord, and let perpetual light shine . . .

PRIVATE She was nineteen and he was forty, and he owned a shop, and he wore a soft hat, and she thought he was the grandest gentleman that ever lived, Madge says; and he — he couldn't take his eyes off her, Madge says . . .

PUBLIC O God, O God the Creator and Redeemer . . .

PRIVATE And sometimes in that first year, when she was pregnant with you, laddybuck, the other young girls from Bailtefree would call in here to dress up on their way to a dance, Madge says, and her face would light up too, Madge says . . .

PUBLIC *puts the newspaper carefully inside the folds of a shirt . . .*

And he must have known, old Screwballs, he must have known, Madge says, for many a night he must have heard her crying herself to sleep . . . and maybe it was good of God to take her away three days after you were born . . . (*Suddenly boisterous*) Damn you, anyhow, for a bloody stupid bastard! It is now sixteen or seventeen years since I saw the Queen of France, then the Dauphiness, at Versailles! And to hell with that bloody mushy fiddler!

PUBLIC *goes quickly to the record player and sings boisterously as he goes:*

PUBLIC 'Philadelphia, here I come — '
PRIVATE Watch yourself, nut-head. If you let yourself slip that way you might find that —
PUBLIC '— right back where I started from.'

PUBLIC *has taken off the Mendelssohn and is now searching for another.*

PRIVATE Something lively! Something bloody animal! A bit of aul' thumpety-thump!

PUBLIC *puts on the record.*

An' you jist keep atalkin' to you'self all the time, Mistah, 'cos once you stop atalkin' to you'self ah reckon then you jist begin to think kinda crazy things — (*The record begins — Any lively piece of Céilí Band music*) Ahhhhh!
PUBLIC Yipeeeeeeeee!

PUBLIC *dances up and down the length of his bedroom. Occasionally he leaps high into the air or does a neat bit of footwork. Occasionally he lilts.*

Occasionally he talks to different people he meets on the dance floor.

Righ-too-del-loo-del-oo-del-oo-del-oo-del-oo-del-ah, Rum-ta-del-ah-del-ah-del-agh-del-ah-del-ah-del-agh. Hell of a crowd here the night, eh? Yah-ho! Man, you're looking powerful! Great!

> PRIVATE *sits on the chair and watches. When he speaks his voice is soft.* PUBLIC *pretends not to hear him.*

PRIVATE Remember — that was Katie's tune. You needn't pretend you have forgotten. And it reminds you of the night the two of you made all the plans, and you thought your heart would burst with happiness.

PUBLIC (*Louder*) Tigh-right-tigh-right-scal-del-de-da-del-ah. Come on! A dirty big swing! Yaaaaaaaaaaah!

PRIVATE (*Quietly, rapidly insisting*) Are you going to take her photograph to the States with you? When are you going to say goodbye to her? Will you write to her? Will you send her cards and photographs? You loved her once, old rooster; you wanted so much to marry her that it was a bloody sickness. Tell me, randy boy; tell me the truth: have you got over that sickness? Do you still love her? Do you still lust after her? Well, do you? Do you? Do you?

PUBLIC Bugger!

> PUBLIC *suddenly stops dancing, switches — almost knocks — off the record player, pulls a wallet out of his hip pocket and produces a snap. He sits and looks at it.*

PRIVATE Shhhhhhhhhhhhh . . .

PUBLIC (*Softly*) Kate . . . sweet Katie Doogan . . . my darling Kathy Doogan . . .

PRIVATE (*In same soft tone*) Aul' bitch. (*Loudly*) Rotten aul' snobby bitch! Just like her stinking rotten father and mother — a bugger and a buggeress — a buggeroo and a buggerette!

PUBLIC No, no; my fault — all my fault —

PRIVATE (*Remembering and recalling tauntingly*) By God, that was a night, boy, eh? By God, you made a right bloody cow's ass of yourself.

> PUBLIC *goes off right.*

Remember — when was it? — ten months ago? — you had just come back from a walk out the Mill Road, and the pair of you had the whole thing planned: engaged at Christmas, married at Easter, and fourteen of a family — seven boys and seven girls. Cripes, you make me laugh! You bloody-well make me die laughing. You were going to 'develop' the hardware lines and she was going to take charge of the 'drapery'! The drapery! The fishy socks and the shoebox of cotton spools and rusted needles! And you — you were to ask Screwballs for a rise in pay — 'in view of your increased responsibilities'! And you were so far gone that night, laddybuck —

> PUBLIC *and* KATE *enter from the left and walk very slowly across the front of the stage. They stop and kiss. Then they move on again.*

— so bloody-well astray in the head with 'love' that you went and blabbed about your secret egg deals that nobody knew anything about — not even Madge! Stupid bloody get! Oh my God, how you stick yourself I'll never know!

PUBLIC Kate — Kathy — I'm mad about you: I'll never last till Easter! I'll — I'll — I'll bloody-well burst!

> *He catches her again and kisses her.*

PRIVATE Steady, boy, steady. You know what the Canon says: long passionate kisses in lonely places . . .

PUBLIC Our daughters'll all be gentle and frail and silly, like you; and our sons — they'll be thick bloody louts, sexy goats, like me, and by God I'll beat the tar out of them!

KATE But £3 15s, Gar! We could never live on that.

PUBLIC (*Kissing her hair*) Mmmm.

KATE Gar! Listen! Be sensible.

PUBLIC Mmm?

KATE How will we *live*?

PRIVATE (*Imitating*) 'How will we *live*?'

PUBLIC Like lords — free house, free light, free fuel, free groceries! And every night at seven when we close — except Saturday; he stays open till damn near midnight on Saturdays, making out bloody bills; and sure God and the world knows that sending out bills here is as hopeless as peeing against the wind —

KATE Gar! No matter what you say we just couldn't live on that much money. It — it's not possible. We'll need to have more security than that.

PUBLIC Maybe he'll die — tonight — of galloping consumption!

KATE Gar . . .

PUBLIC What's troubling you?

He tries to kiss her again and she avoids him.

KATE Please. This is serious.

PRIVATE 'Please. This is serious.'

PUBLIC (*Irritably*) What is it?

KATE You'll have to see about getting more money.

PUBLIC Of course I'll see about getting more money! Haven't I told you I'm going to ask for a rise?

KATE But will he — ?

PUBLIC I'll get it; don't you worry; I'll get it. Besides, (*with dignity*) I have a — a — a source of income that he knows nothing about — that nobody knows nothing about — knows anything about.

KATE (*With joy*) Investments? Like Daddy?

PUBLIC Well . . . sort of . . . (*Quickly*) You know when I go round the country every Tuesday and Thursday in the lorry?

KATE Yes?

PUBLIC Well, I buy eggs direct from the farms and sell them privately to McLaughlin's Hotel — (*winks*) — for a handsome profit — (*quickly*) — but he knows nothing about it.

KATE And how much do you make?

PUBLIC It varies — depending on the time of year.

KATE Roughly.

PUBLIC Oh, anything from 12s 6d to £1.

KATE Every Tuesday and Thursday?

PUBLIC Every month. (*Grabs her again*) God, Kate, I can't even wait till Christmas!

KATE Shhhh.

PUBLIC But I can't. We'll have to get married sooner — next month — next week —

PRIVATE Steady, steady . . .

PUBLIC Kate . . . my sweet Katie . . . my darling Kathy . . .

They kiss. Suddenly KATE *breaks off. Her voice is urgent.*

KATE We'll go now, rightaway, and tell them.

PUBLIC Who?

KATE Mammy and Daddy. They're at home tonight.

She catches his arm and pulls him towards the left.

Come on. Quickly. Now, Gar, now.

PUBLIC (*Adjusting his tie*) God, Kathy, I'm in no — look at the shoes — the trousers —

KATE What matter. It must be now, Gar, now!

PUBLIC What — what — what'll I say?

KATE That you want their permission to marry me next week.

PUBLIC God, they'll wipe the bloody floor with me!

KATE Gar!

> *She kisses him passionately, quickly, then breaks off and goes.*
> *Stage right, now lit. A room in Doogan's house.*

PUBLIC God, my legs are trembling! Kathy . . .

KATE Anybody at home? Mammy! Daddy!

> PUBLIC *hesitates before entering Doogan's house.*
> PRIVATE *is at his elbow, prompting him desperately.*

PRIVATE Mr Doogan — Senator Doogan — I want to ask your permission . . . Oh my God . . . !

KATE Yo-ho!

PRIVATE Mrs Doogan, Kate and I have to get married right-away — Cripes, no — !

KATE Where is everybody! Yo-ho-yo-ho!

PRIVATE If the boys could see you now!

> KATE *comes back to him, gives him a quick kiss on the cheek.*

KATE Don't look so miserable. Here . . . (*Fixes his tie*)

PUBLIC Kathy, maybe we should wait until — until — until next Sunday —

KATE (*Earnestly*) Remember, it's up to you, entirely up to you.

DOOGAN (*Off*) That you, Kate?

KATE (*Rapidly*) You have £20 a week and £5,000 in the bank and your father's about to retire.

> *Turning and smiling at* DOOGAN *who has now entered.* DOOGAN *is a lawyer, senator, mid-forties.*

Just Gar and I, Daddy.

DOOGAN Hello, Gareth. You're a stranger.

PRIVATE Speak, you dummy, you!

KATE (*Filling in*) Where's Mammy?

DOOGAN She's watching TV. (*To* GAR) And how are things with you, Gareth?

PUBLIC Mr Doogan, I want —

PRIVATE Go on.

PUBLIC I won't be staying long.

DOOGAN (*To* KATE) Francis arrived when you were out. Took a few days off and decided to come north.

PRIVATE Cripes!

KATE He — he's — he's here — now?

DOOGAN Inside with your mother. Ask them to join us, will you?

> KATE *gives* PUBLIC *a last significant look.*

KATE You talk to Daddy, Gar.

PRIVATE God, I will, I will.

> KATE *goes off right.*

DOOGAN You've met Francis King, haven't you, Gareth?

PUBLIC Yes — yes —

PRIVATE King of the bloody fairies!

DOOGAN We don't want to raise Kate's hopes unduly, but strictly between ourselves there's a good chance that he'll get the new dispensary job here.

PUBLIC Kate's hopes?

DOOGAN Didn't she tell you? No, I can see she didn't. Of course there's nothing official yet; not even what you might call an understanding. But if this post does fall into his lap, well, her mother and I . . . let's say we're living in hope. A fine boy, Francis; and we've known the Kings, oh, since away back. As a matter of fact his father and I were class-fellows at school . . .

> DOOGAN *goes on and on. We catch an occasional word. Meantime* PRIVATE *has moved up to* PUBLIC's *elbow.*

PRIVATE Cripes, man!

DOOGAN . . . and then later at university when he did Medicine

	and I did Law we knocked about quite a bit . . .
PRIVATE	Oh God, the aul' bitch! Cripes, you look a right fool standing there — the father of fourteen children! Get out, you eejit, you! Get out! Get out quick before the others come in and die laughing at you! And all the time she must have known — the aul' bitch! And you promised to give her breakfast in bed every morning! And you told her about the egg money!
DOOGAN	. . . your father, Gareth?
PRIVATE	He's talking to you, thick-skull.
PUBLIC	What — what — what's that?
DOOGAN	Your father — how is he?
PUBLIC	Oh he — he — he's grand, thanks.
PRIVATE	Get out! Get out!
PUBLIC	Look, Mr Doogan, if you'll excuse me, I think I'd better move on —
DOOGAN	Aren't you waiting for supper? The others will be along in a moment for —
PUBLIC	No, I must run. I've got to make up half-a-hundred-weight of sugar bags.
PRIVATE	Brilliant!
PUBLIC	Say goodbye to —
DOOGAN	Certainly — certainly. Oh, Gareth — (PUBLIC *pauses. Awkwardly, with sincerity*) Kate is our only child, Gareth, and her happiness is all that is important to us —
PRIVATE	(*Sings*) 'Give the woman in the bed more porter — '
DOOGAN	What I'm trying to say is that any decision she makes will be her own —
PRIVATE	'— Give the man beside her water, / Give the woman in the bed more porter — '
DOOGAN	Just in case you should think that her mother or I were . . . in case you might have the idea . . .
PUBLIC	(*Rapidly*) Goodnight, Mr Doogan.

PUBLIC *rushes off.*

| DOOGAN | Goodbye . . . Gareth. |

DOOGAN *stands lighting his pipe.* KATE *enters down right of* DOOGAN *and sees that* GAR *is no longer there.*

KATE Where's Gar?
DOOGAN He didn't seem anxious to stay.
KATE But didn't he — did he — ?
DOOGAN No, he didn't.

He crosses KATE *to exit down right as light fades to blackout. Black out Doogan's room.* PUBLIC *and* PRIVATE *move back to the bedroom where* PUBLIC *is putting away the photograph and begins washing.*

PRIVATE (*Wearily*) Mrs Doctor Francis King. September 8th. In harvest sunshine. Red carpet and white lilies and Sean Horgan singing 'Bless This House' — and him whipped off to Sligo jail two days later for stealing turf. Honeymoon in Mallorca and you couldn't have afforded to take her to Malahide. By God, Gar, aul' sod, it was a sore hoke on the aul' prestige, eh? Between ourselves, aul' son, in the privacy of the bedroom, between you and me and the wall, as the fella says, has it left a deep scar on the aul' skitter of a soul, eh? What I mean to say, like, you took it sort of bad, between you and me and the wall, as the fella says —

PUBLIC (*Sings*) 'Philadelphia, here I come, right back — '

PRIVATE But then there's more fish in the sea, as the fella says, and they're all the same when they're upside down; and between you and me and the wall the first thing you would have had to do would have been to give the boot to Daddy Senator. And I'm thinking, Gar, aul' rooster, that wouldn't have made you his pet son-in-law, Mister Fair-play Lawyer Senator Doogan — 'her happiness is all that is important to us'! You know, of course, that he carries one of those wee black cards in the inside pocket of his jacket, privately printed for him: 'I am a Catholic. In case of accident send for a bishop.' And you know, too, that in his spare time he travels for maternity corsets; and that he's a double spy for the Knights and the Masons; and that he takes pornographic photographs of Mrs D and sends them anonymously to reverend mothers. And when you think of a bugger like that you want to get down on your knees and thank God for aul' Screwballs. (*Imitating his father's slow speech*) So you're going to America in the morning, son?

PUBLIC *carries on with his washing and dressing during this dialogue:*

PUBLIC Yes, Father.

PRIVATE Nothing like it to broaden the mind. Man, how I'd love to travel. But there's some it doesn't agree with — like me, there.

PUBLIC In what way, Father?

PRIVATE The bowels, son. Let me move an inch from the house here — and they stall.

PUBLIC No!

PRIVATE Like the time I went to Lough Derg, away back in '35. Not a budge. The bare feet were nothing to the agonies I went through. I was bound up for two full weeks afterwards.

PUBLIC It taught you a lesson.

PRIVATE Didn't it just? Now I wouldn't even think of travelling.

PUBLIC Anchored by the ass.

PRIVATE Bound by the bowels.

PUBLIC Tethered by the toilet. Tragic.

PUBLIC *has now finished dressing. He surveys himself in the mirror.*

PRIVATE Not bad. Not bad at all. And well preserved for a father of fourteen children.

PUBLIC (*In absurd Hollywood style*) Hi, gorgeous! You live in my block?

PRIVATE (*Matching the accent*) Yeah, big handsome boy. Sure
do.

PUBLIC Mind if I walk you past the incinerator, to the elevator?

PRIVATE You're welcome, slick operator.

> PUBLIC *is facing the door of his bedroom.* MADGE
> *enters the kitchen from the scullery.*

PUBLIC What'ya say, li'l chick, you and me — you know —
I'll spell it out for ya if ya like. (*Winks, and clicks his
tongue*)

PRIVATE You say the cutest things, big handsome boy!

PUBLIC A malted milk at the corner drugstore?

PRIVATE Wow!

PUBLIC A movie at the downtown drive-in?

PRIVATE Wow-wow!

PUBLIC Two hamburgers, two cokes, two slices of blueberry
pie?

PRIVATE: Wow-wow-wow.

PUBLIC And then afterwards in my apartment —

> MADGE *enters the bedroom.*

MADGE Gee, Mary, and Jay! Will you quit them antics!

PUBLIC Well, you should knock anyway before you enter a
man's room!

MADGE Man! I bathed you every Saturday night till you
were a big lout of fourteen! Your tea's cold waiting.

> *She makes towards door. She goes into the kitchen.*
> PUBLIC *and* PRIVATE *follow her.*

PUBLIC How was I to know that?

MADGE Amn't I hoarse calling you? Dear, but you're in for a
cooling when you go across!

> *As she passes through the shop door on way to
> scullery:*

Boss!

PRIVATE (*In imitation*) 'Boss!'

She pauses at the scullery door.

MADGE (*With shy delight*) I forgot to tell you. Nelly had a wee baby this morning.

PUBLIC Go on!

MADGE A wee girl — 7lb 4oz.

PUBLIC How many's that you have now?

MADGE Four grandnieces and three grandnephews. (*Pause*) And they're going to call this one Madge — at least so she *says*.

PUBLIC I'll send it a — a — a — an elephant out of my first wages! An elephant for wee Madge!

MADGE I had a feeling it would be a wee girl this time. Maybe I'll take a run over on Sunday and square the place up for her. She could do with some help, with seven of them.

PUBLIC You're a brick, Madge.

MADGE Aye, so.

As she goes to scullery:

Wee Madge, maybe . . .

PUBLIC *sits at the table.* PRIVATE *leans against the wall beside him.*

PRIVATE And now what are you sad about? Just because she lives for those Mulhern children, and gives them whatever few half-pence she has? Madge, Madge, I think I love you more than any of them. Give me a piece of your courage, Madge.

S.B. *enters from the shop and goes through his nightly routine. He hangs up the shop keys. He looks at his pocket watch and checks its time with the clock on the wall. He takes off his apron, folds it carefully, and leaves it on the back of his chair. Then he sits down to eat. During all these ponderous jobs* PRIVATE *keeps up the following chatter:*

And here comes your pleasure, your little ray of sunshine. Ladies and Gentlemen, I give you — the one and only — the inimitable — the irrepressible — the irresistible — County Councillor S — B — O'Donnell! (*Trumpet — hummed — fanfare. Continues in the smooth, unctuous tones of the commentator at a mannequin parade*) And this time Marie Celeste is wearing a cheeky little headdress by Pamela of Park Avenue, eminently suitable for cocktail parties, morning coffee, or just casual shopping. It is of brown Viennese felt, and contrasts boldly with the attractive beach ensemble, created by Simon. The pert little apron is detachable —

s.b. *removes apron.*

— thank you, Marie Celeste — and underneath we have the tapered Italian-line slacks in ocelot. I would draw your attention to the large collar stud which is highly decorative and can be purchased separately at our boutique. We call this seductive outfit 'Indiscretion'. It can be worn six days a week, in or out of bed. (*In polite tone*) Have a seat, Screwballs.

s.b. *sits down at the table.*

Thank you. Remove the hat.

s.b. *takes off the hat to say grace. He blesses himself.*

On again. (*Hat on*) Perfectly trained; the most obedient father I ever had. And now for our nightly lesson in the English language. Repeat slowly after me: Another day over.

s.b. Another day over.

PRIVATE Good. Next phrase: I suppose we can't complain.

s.b. I suppose we can't complain.

PRIVATE Not bad. Now for a little free conversation. But no obscenities, Father dear; the child is only twenty-five.

> s.b. *eats in silence. Pause.*

Well, come on, come on! Where's that old rapier wit of yours, the toast of the Ballybeg coffee houses?

s.b. Did you set the rat trap in the store?

PUBLIC Aye.

PRIVATE (*Hysterically*) Isn't he a riot! Oh my God, that father of yours just kills me! But wait — wait — shhh-shhh —

s.b. I didn't find as many about the year.

PRIVATE Oooooh God! Priceless! Beautiful! Delightful! 'I didn't find as many about the year!' Did you ever hear the beat of that? Wonderful! But isn't he in form tonight? But isn't he? You know, it's not every night that jewels like that, pearls of wisdom on rodent reproduction, drop from those lips! But hold it — hold it — !

> s.b. *takes out a handkerchief, removes his teeth, wraps them in the handkerchief, and puts them in his pocket.* PRIVATE *exhales with satisfaction.*

Ah! That's what we were waiting for; complete informality; total relaxation between intimates. Now we can carry on. Screwballs. (*Pause*) I'm addressing you, Screwballs. (s.b. *clears his throat*) Thank you.

> As the following speech goes on all trace of humour fades from PRIVATE's voice. He becomes more and more intense and it is with an effort that he keeps his voice under control.

Screwballs, we've eaten together like this for the

past twenty-odd years, and never once in all that time have you made as much as one unpredictable remark. Now, even though you refuse to acknowledge the fact, Screwballs, I'm leaving you forever. I'm going to Philadelphia, to work in an hotel. And you know why I'm going, Screwballs, don't you? Because I'm twenty-five, and you treat me as if I were five — I can't order even a dozen loaves without getting your permission. Because you pay me less than you pay Madge. But worse, far worse than that, Screwballs, because *we embarrass one another*. If one of us were to say, 'You're looking tired' or 'That's a bad cough you have', the other would fall over backways with embarrassment. So tonight d'you know what I want you to do? I want you to make one unpredictable remark, and even though I'll still be on that plane tomorrow morning, I'll have doubts: maybe I should have stuck it out; maybe the old codger did have feelings; maybe I have maligned the old bastard. So now, Screwballs, say . . . (*thinks*) . . . 'Once upon a time a rainbow ended in our garden' . . . say, 'I like to walk across the White Strand when there's a misty rain falling' . . . say, 'Gar, son — ' say, 'Gar, you bugger you, why don't you stick it out here with me for it's not such a bad aul' bugger of a place.' Go on. Say it! Say it! Say it!

S.B. True enough . . .

PUBLIC (*Almost inaudibly*) Aye?

S.B. I didn't find as many about the year.

PUBLIC (*Roars*) Madge! Madge!

S.B. No need to roar like that.

PUBLIC The — the — the — bread's done. We need more bread.

S.B. You know where it's kept, don't you?

MADGE *at scullery door.*

PUBLIC Can we have more bread, Madge . . . please . . . ?

MADGE Huh! Pity you lost the power of your legs.

PUBLIC   I'll — I'll get it myself — it doesn't matter . . .

> MADGE *comes over to the table and takes the plate from* PUBLIC. *She gives* S.B. *a hard look.*

MADGE   (*Irony*) The chatting in this place would deafen a body. Won't the house be quiet soon enough — long enough?

> *She shuffles off with the plate.*

PRIVATE   Tick-tock-tick-tock-tick-tock. It is now sixteen or seventeen years since I saw the Queen of France, then the Dauphiness, at Versailles . . . Go on! What's the next line?

> S.B. *produces a roll of money from his pocket and puts it on the table.*

S.B.   I suppose you'll be looking for your pay.

PUBLIC   I earned it.

S.B.   I'm not saying you didn't. It's all there — you needn't count it.

PUBLIC   I didn't say I was going to count it, did I?

PRIVATE   Tick-tock-tick-tock-tick-tock —

PUBLIC   More tea?

S.B.   Sure you know I never take a second cup.

PRIVATE   (*Imitating*) 'Sure you know I never take a second cup.' (*Brittle and bright again*) OK, OK, OK, it's better this way, Screwballs, isn't it? You can't teach new tricks to two old dogs like us. In the meantime there's a little matter I'd like to discuss with you, Screwballs . . . (*With exaggerated embarrassment*) It's — it's nothing really . . . it's just something I'm rather hesitant to bring up, but I'm advised by the very best Church authorities that you'll be only too glad to discuss it with your son. Admittedly we're both a bit late in attacking the issue now, but — ha — you see —

MADGE *enters with a plate of bread.* PRIVATE *makes a very obvious show of changing the subject.*

Oh marvellous weather — truly wonderful for the time of year — a real heat wave — all things considered —

MADGE A body couldn't get a word in edgeways with you two!

PRIVATE Madge has such a keen sense of humour, don't you agree? I love people with a sense of humour, don't you? It's the first thing I look for in a person. I seize them by the throat and say to them, 'Have you a sense of humour?' And then, if they have, I feel — I feel *at home* with them immediately . . . But where was I? Oh, yes — our little talk — I'm beginning to wonder, Screwballs — I suspect — I'm afraid — (*in a rush, ashamed*) — I think I'm a sex maniac! (*Throws his hands up*) Please, please don't cry, Screwballs; please don't say anything; and above all please don't stop eating. Just — just let me talk a bit more — let me communicate with someone — that's what they all advise — communicate — pour out your pent-up feelings into a sympathetic ear. So all I ask for the moment is that you listen — just listen to me. As I said, I suspect that I'm an S. M. (*Rapidly, in self-defence*) But I'm not the only one, Screwballs; oh, indeed I am not; all the boys around — some of them are far worse than I am. (*As if he had been asked the question*) Why? Why do I think we're all S. Ms? Well, because none of us is married. Because we're never done boasting about the number of hot courts we know — and the point is we're all virgins. Because — (*Voices off*) Shhhh! Someone's coming. Not a word to anybody. This is our secret. Scouts' honour.

Enter MASTER BOYLE *from the scullery. He is around sixty, white-haired, handsome, defiant. He is shabbily dressed; his eyes, head, hands, arms are constantly*

> *moving. He sits for a moment and rises again — he*
> *puts his hands in his pockets and takes them out*
> *again — his eyes roam around the room but see*
> *nothing.* s.b. *is barely courteous to him.*

s.b. Oh, goodnight, Master Boyle. How are you doing?

PUBLIC Master.

BOYLE Sean. Gar. No, no, don't stir. I only dropped in for a second.

PUBLIC Sit over and join us.

BOYLE No. I'm not stopping.

s.b. Here's a seat for you. I was about to go out to the shop anyway to square up a bit.

BOYLE Don't let me hold you back.

s.b. I'll be in again before you leave, Master.

BOYLE If you have work to do . . .

PRIVATE (*To* s.b.) Ignorant bastard! (*Looking at* BOYLE) On his way to the pub! God, but he's a sorry wreck too, arrogant and pathetic. And yet whatever it is about you . . .

BOYLE Tomorrow morning, isn't it?

PUBLIC Quarter-past-seven. I'm getting the mail van the length of Strabane.

BOYLE You're doing the right thing, of course. You'll never regret it. I gather it's a vast restless place that doesn't give a curse about the past; and that's the way things should be. Impermanence and anonymity — it offers great attractions. You've heard about the latest to-do?

PUBLIC Another row with the Canon? I really hadn't heard —

BOYLE But the point is he can't sack me! The organization's behind me and he can't budge me. Still, it's a . . . a bitter victory to hold on to a job when your manager wants rid of you.

PUBLIC Sure everybody knows the kind of the Canon, Master.

BOYLE I didn't tell you, did I, that I may be going out there myself?

PRIVATE Poor bastard.

BOYLE   I've been offered a big post in Boston, head of education in a reputable university there. They've given me three months to think it over. What are you going to do?

PUBLIC   Work in an hotel.

BOYLE   You have a job waiting for you?

PUBLIC   In Philadelphia.

BOYLE   You'll do all right. You're young and strong and of average intelligence.

PRIVATE   Good old Boyle. Get the dig in.

BOYLE   Yes, it was as ugly and as squalid as all the other to-dos — before the whole school — the priest and the teacher — dedicated moulders of the mind. You're going to stay with friends?

PUBLIC   With Aunt Lizzy.

BOYLE   Of course.

PRIVATE   Go on. Try him.

PUBLIC   You knew her, didn't you, Master?

BOYLE   Yes, I knew all the Gallagher girls: Lizzy, Una, Rose, Agnes . . .

PRIVATE   And Maire, my mother, did you love her?

BOYLE   A long, long time ago . . . in the past . . . He comes in to see your father every night, doesn't he?

PUBLIC   The Canon? Oh, it's usually much later than this —

BOYLE   I think so much about him that — ha — I feel a peculiar attachment for him. Funny, isn't it? Do you remember the Christmas you sent me the packet of cigarettes? And the day you brought me a pot of jam to the digs? It was you, wasn't it?

PRIVATE   Poor Boyle —

BOYLE   All children are born with generosity. Three months they gave me to make up my mind.

PUBLIC   I remember very well —

BOYLE   By the way — (*producing a small book*) a little something to remind you of your old teacher — my poems —

PUBLIC   Thank you very much.

BOYLE   I had them printed privately last month. Some of them are a bit mawkish but you'll not notice any

	distinction.
PUBLIC	I'm very grateful, Master.
BOYLE	I'm not going to give you advice, Gar. Is that clock right? Not that you would heed it even if I did; you were always obstinate —
PRIVATE	Tch, tch.
BOYLE	But I would suggest that you strike out on your own as soon as you find your feet out there. Don't keep looking back over your shoulder. Be one hundred per cent American.
PUBLIC	I'll do that.
BOYLE	There's an inscription on the flyleaf. By the way, Gar, you couldn't lend me 10s until — ha — I was going to say until next week but you'll be gone by then.
PUBLIC	Surely, surely.
BOYLE	I seem to have come out without my wallet . . .
PRIVATE	Give him the quid. . .

PUBLIC *gives over a note.* BOYLE *does not look at it.*

BOYLE	Fine. I'll move on now. Yes, I knew all the Gallagher girls from Bailtefree, long, long ago. Maire and Una and Rose and Lizzy and Agnes and Maire, your mother . . .
PRIVATE	You might have been my father.
BOYLE	Oh, another thing I meant to ask you: should you come across any newspapers or magazines over there that might be interested in an occasional poem, perhaps you would send me some addresses —
PUBLIC	I'll keep an eye out.
BOYLE	Not that I write as much as I should. You know how you get caught up in things. But you have your packing to do, and I'm talking too much as usual.

He holds out his hand and they shake hands. He does not release PUBLIC's *hand.*

	Good luck, Gareth.
PUBLIC	Thanks, Master.

BOYLE Forget Ballybeg and Ireland.

PUBLIC It's easier said.

BOYLE Perhaps you'll write me.

PUBLIC I will indeed.

BOYLE Yes, the first year. Maybe the second. I'll — I'll miss you, Gar.

PRIVATE For God's sake get a grip on yourself.

PUBLIC Thanks for the book and for —

BOYLE *embraces* PUBLIC *briefly.*

PRIVATE Stop it! Stop it! Stop it!

BOYLE *breaks away and goes quickly off through the scullery. He bumps into* MADGE *who is entering.*

MADGE Lord, the speed of him! His tongue out for a drink!

PRIVATE Quick! Into your room!

MADGE God knows I don't blame the Canon for wanting rid of that —

PUBLIC *rushes to the bedroom.* PRIVATE *follows.*

Well! The manners about this place!

She gathers up the tea things. PUBLIC *stands inside the bedroom door, his hands up to his face.* PRIVATE *stands at his elbow, speaking urgently into his ear.*

PRIVATE Remember — you're going! At 7.15. You're still going! He's nothing but a drunken aul' schoolmaster — a conceited, arrogant washout!

PUBLIC O God, the Creator and Redeemer of all the faithful —

PRIVATE Get a grip on yourself! Don't be a damned sentimental fool! (*Sings*) 'Philadelphia, here I come — '

PUBLIC Maire and Una and Rose and Agnes and Lizzy and Maire —

PRIVATE Yessir, you're going to cut a bit of a dash in them thar

States! Great big sexy dames and nightclubs and high living and films and dances and —

PUBLIC Kathy, my own darling Kathy —

PRIVATE (*Sings*) 'Where bowers of flowers bloom in the spring'

PUBLIC I don't — I can't —

PRIVATE (*Sings*) 'Each morning at dawning, everything is bright and gay / A sun-kissed miss says Don't be late —' Sing up, man!

PUBLIC I — I — I —

PRIVATE (*Sings*) 'That's why I can hardly wait.'

PUBLIC (*Sings limply*) 'Philadelphia, here I come.'

PRIVATE That's it, laddybuck!

TOGETHER 'Philadelphia, here I come.'

Curtain.

EPISODE TWO

A short time later. PUBLIC *is lying on the bed, his hands behind his head.* PRIVATE *is slumped in the chair, almost as if he were dozing.* PUBLIC *sings absently.*

PUBLIC   (*Sings*) 'Last night she came to me, she came softly in,
        So softly she came that her feet made no din,
        And she laid her hand on me, and this she did say,
        "It will not be long love till our wedding day."'

> *When the singing stops there is a moment of silence. Then, suddenly,* PRIVATE *springs to his feet.*

PRIVATE What the bloody hell are you at, O'Donnell? Snap out of it, man! Get up and keep active! The devil makes work for idle hands! It is now sixteen or seventeen years since I saw the Queen of France, then the Dauphiness, at Versailles.

> PUBLIC *gets off the bed and begins taking clothes from the chest of drawers and putting them into his case.*

PRIVATE (*Lilting to a mad air of his own making*) Ta-ra-del-oo-del-ah-dol-de-dol-de-dol-del-ah — (*Continuing as rapidly as he can speak*) Tell me this and tell me no more: Why does a hen cross the road?

PUBLIC Why?

PRIVATE To get to the other side. Ha-ha! Why does a hen lay an egg?

PUBLIC Why?

PRIVATE Because it can't lay a brick. Yo-ho. Why does a sailor wear a round hat?

PUBLIC   Why?

PRIVATE   To cover his head. Hee-hee-hee. Nought out of three;
          very bad for a man of average intelligence. That's the
          style. Keep working; keep the mind active and well
          stretched by knowing the best that is thought and
          written in the world, and you wouldn't call Daddy
          Senator your father-in-law. (*Sings*)

          'Give the woman in the bed more porter
              Give the man beside her water,
          Give the woman in the bed more porter
              More porter for the woman in the bed.'

          (*Confidentially*) D'you know what I think, laddie, I
          mean, just looking at you there.

PUBLIC   What?

PRIVATE   You'd make a hell of a fine President of the United
          States.

> PUBLIC *straightens up and for a second surveys the
> room with the keen eye of a politician. Relaxes again.*

PUBLIC   Agh!

PRIVATE   But you would!

PUBLIC   You need to be born an American citizen.

PRIVATE   True for you. What about Chairman of General
          Motors? (PUBLIC *shrugs indifferently*) Boss of the
          Teamsters' Union? (PUBLIC *shrugs his indifference*)

PRIVATE   Hollywood — what about Hollywood?

PUBLIC   Not what it was.

PRIVATE   Dammit but you're hard to please too. Still, there
          must be something great in store for you. (*Cracks
          his fingers at his brainwave*) The US Senate! Senator
          Gareth O'Donnell, Chairman of the Foreign Aid
          Committee!

> *He interviews* PUBLIC *who continues packing his
> clothes busily.*

Is there something you would like to say, Senator,
before you publish the findings of your committee?

PUBLIC Nothing to say.

PRIVATE Just a few words.

PUBLIC No comment.

PRIVATE Isn't it a fact that suspicion has fallen on Senator Doogan?

PUBLIC Nothing further to add.

PRIVATE Did your investigators not discover that Senator Doogan is the grandfather of fourteen unborn illegitimate children? That he sold his daughter to the king of the fairies for a crock of gold? That a Chinese spy known to the FBI as Screwballs —

PUBLIC Screwballs?

PRIVATE Screwballs.

PUBLIC Describe him.

PRIVATE Tall, blond, athletic-looking —

PUBLIC Military moustache?

PRIVATE — very handsome; uses a diamond-studded cigarette holder.

PUBLIC Usually accompanied by a dark seductive woman in a low-cut evening gown?

PRIVATE — wears a monocle, fluent command of languages —

PUBLIC But seldom speaks? A man of few words?

PRIVATE — drives a cream convertible, villas in Istanbul, Cairo and Budapest —

PUBLIC (*Declaims*) Merchant Prince, licensed to deal in tobacco —

PRIVATE An' sowl! That's me man! To a T! The point is — what'll we do with him?

PUBLIC Sell him to a harem?

PRIVATE Hide his cascara sagrada?

MADGE *comes into the kitchen to lift the tablecloth.*

PUBLIC (*Serious*) Shhh!

PRIVATE The boys? Is it the boys? To say goodbye?

PUBLIC Shhhh!

PRIVATE It's Madge — aul' fluke-feet Madge.

They both stand listening to the sound of MADGE

flapping across the kitchen and out to the scullery.

PUBLIC (*Calls softly*) Madge.

>PRIVATE *drops into the armchair.* PUBLIC *stands listening until the sound has died away.*

PRIVATE (*Wearily*) Off again! You know what you're doing, don't you, laddybuck? Collecting memories and images and impressions that are going to make you bloody miserable; and in a way that's what you want, isn't it?

PUBLIC Bugger!

>PRIVATE *springs to his feet again. With forced animation:*

PRIVATE Bugger's right! Bugger's absolutely correct! Back to the job! Keep occupied. Be methodical.
'Eeny-meeny-miny-moe
Catch-the-baby-by-the-toe.'
Will all passengers holding immigration visas please come this way.

>PUBLIC *produces documents from a drawer. He checks them.*

PRIVATE Passport?
PUBLIC Passport.
PRIVATE Visa?
PUBLIC Visa.
PRIVATE Vaccination cert?
PUBLIC Vaccination cert.
PRIVATE Currency?
PUBLIC Eighty dollars.
PRIVATE Sponsorship papers?
PUBLIC Signed by Mr Conal Sweeney.
PRIVATE Uncle Con and Aunt Lizzy. Who made the whole thing possible. Read her letter again — strictly for

belly laughs.

PUBLIC (*Reads*) Dear Nephew Gar, just a line to let you know that your Uncle Con and me have finalized all the plans —

PRIVATE Uncle Con and I.

PUBLIC — and we will meet you at the airport and welcome you and bring you to our apartment which you will see is located in a pretty nice locality and you will have the spare room which has TV and air conditioning and window meshes and your own bathroom with a shower —

PRIVATE Adjacent to RC church. No children. Other help kept.

PUBLIC You will begin at the Emperor Hotel on Monday 23rd which is only about twenty minutes away.

PRIVATE Monsieur, madam.

PUBLIC Con says it is a fine place for to work in and the owner is Mr Patrick Palinakis who is half-Irish —

PRIVATE Patrick.

PUBLIC — and half-Greek.

PRIVATE Palinakis.

PUBLIC His grandfather came from County Mayo.

PRIVATE By the hokey! The Greek from Belmullet!

PUBLIC We know you will like it here and work hard.

PRIVATE (*Rapidly*) Monsieur-madam-monsieur-madam-monsieur-madam —

PUBLIC We remember our short trip to Ireland last September with happy thoughts and look forward to seeing you again. Sorry we missed your father that day. We had Ben Burton in to dinner last evening. He sends his regards.

PRIVATE Right sort, Ben.

PUBLIC Until we see you at the airport, all love, Elise.

PRIVATE 'Elise'! Dammit, Lizzy Gallagher, but you came up in the world.

PUBLIC PS About paying back the passage money which you mentioned in your last letter — desist! — no one's crying about it.

PRIVATE Aye, Ben Burton was a right skin.

PUBLIC (*Remembering*) September 8th.

PRIVATE By God Lizzy was in right talking form that day —

PUBLIC 'You are invited to attend the wedding of Miss Kathleen Doogan of Gortmore House —'

PRIVATE (*Snaps*) Shut up, O'Donnell! You've got to quit this moody drivelling! (*Coaxing*) They arrived in the afternoon; remember? A beautiful quiet harvest day, the sun shining, not a breath of wind; and you were on your best behaviour. And Madge — remember? Madge was as huffy as hell with the carry-on of them, and you couldn't take your eyes off Aunt Lizzy, your mother's sister — so this was your mother's sister — remember?

> *Three people have moved into the kitchen:* CON SWEENEY, LIZZY SWEENEY *and* BEN BURTON. *All three are in the fifty-five to sixty region.* BURTON *is American, the* SWEENEYS *Irish-American.* CON SWEENEY *sits at the kitchen table with* BEN BURTON. LIZZY *moves around in the centre of the kitchen.* PUBLIC *stands at the door of his bedroom.* PRIVATE *hovers around close to* PUBLIC. *The three guests have glasses in their hands. None of them is drunk, but* LIZZY *is more than usually garrulous. She is a small energetic woman, heavily made-up, impulsive.* CON, *her husband, is a quiet, patient man.* BURTON, *their friend, sits smiling at his glass most of the time. As she talks* LIZZY *moves from one to the other and she has the habit of putting her arm around, or catching the elbow of, the person she is addressing. This constant physical touching is new and disquieting to* PUBLIC. *A long laugh from* LIZZY.

LIZZY Anyhow, there we are, all sitting like stuffed ducks in the front seat — Una and Agnes and Rose and Mother and me — you know — and mother dickied up in her good black shawl and everything — and up at the altar rails there's Maire all by herself and her shoulders are sorta working — you know — and you couldn't tell whether she was crying or giggling

— she was a helluva one for giggling — but maybe
she was crying that morning — I don't know —

CON Get on with the story, honey.

LIZZY (*With dignity*) Would you please desist from bustin'
in on me?

CON *spreads his hands in resignation.*

LIZZY But listen to this — this'll kill you — Mother's here,
see? And Agnes is here and I'm here. And Agnes
leans across Mother to me — you know — and she
says in this helluva loud voice — she says — (*laughs*)
this really does kill me — she says — in this whisper
of hers — and you know the size of Bailtefree chapel;
couldn't swing a cat in that place — (*Suddenly
anxious*) That chapel's still there, isn't it? It hasn't fell
down or nothing, has it?

CON (*Dryly*) Unless it fell down within the last couple of
hours. We drove up there this morning. Remember?

LIZZY (*Relieved*) Yeah. So we did. Fine place. Made me feel
kinda — you know — what the hell was I talking
about?

BEN Agnes leaned over to you and said —

LIZZY *puts her arm around him and kisses the crown
of his head.*

LIZZY Thanks, Ben. A great friend with a great memory! I'll
tell you, Gar, Ben Burton's one hundred per cent.
The first and best friend we made when we went
out. (*To* CON) Right, honey?

CON Right.

LIZZY Way back in '37.

CON '38.

LIZZY (*Loudly*) October 23rd, 19 and 37 we sailed for the
United States of America. (CON *spreads his hands*)
Nothing in our pockets. No job to go to. And what
does Ben do?

CON A guy in a million.

LIZZY He gives us this apartment. He gives us dough. He gives us three meals a day — until Bonzo (*Con*) finally gets himself this job. Looks after us like we were his own skin and bone. Right, honey?

CON Right.

LIZZY So don't let nobody say nothing against Ben Burton. Then when he (*Con*) gets this job in this downtown store —

CON First job was with the construction company.

LIZZY Would you please desist? (CON *spreads hands*) His first job was with Young and Pecks, hauling out them packing cases and things; and then he moved to the construction company, and *then* we got a place of our own.

PUBLIC You were telling us about that morning.

LIZZY What's he talking about?

PUBLIC The day my father and mother got married.

LIZZY That day! Wasn't that something? With the wind howling and the rain slashing about! And Mother, poor Mother, may God be good to her, she thought that just because Maire got this guy with a big store we should all of got guys with big stores. And poor Maire — we were so alike in every way, Maire and me. But he was good to her. I'll say that for S.B. O'Donnell — real good to her. Where the hell is he anyhow? Why will S.B. O'Donnell, my brother-in-law, not meet me?

CON He (*Public*) told you — he's away at a wedding.

LIZZY What wedding?

CON Some local girl and some Dublin doc.

LIZZY What local girl? You think I'm a stranger here or something?

CON (*To* PUBLIC) What local girl?

PUBLIC Senator Doogan's daughter.

PRIVATE Kathy.

LIZZY Never heard of him. Some Johnny-hop-up. When did they start having senators about this place for Gawd's sakes?

BEN (*To* PUBLIC) You have a Senate in Dublin, just like our

Senate, don't you?

LIZZY Don't you start telling me nothing about my own country, Ben. You got your own problems to look after. Just you leave me to manage this place, OK?

BEN Sorry, Elise.

LIZZY Ben! (*She kisses the top of his head*) Only that I'm a good Irish-American Catholic — (*To* PUBLIC) and believe me, they don't come much better than that — and only that I'm stuck with Rudolph Valentino (*Con*) I'd take a chance with Ben Burton any day (*kisses him again*), black Lutheran and all that he is.

> MADGE *appears at the door of the shop. She refuses to look at the visitors. Her face is tight with disapproval. Her accent is very precise.*

MADGE Are there any *Clarions* to spare or are they all ordered?

PUBLIC They're all ordered, Madge.

LIZZY Doing big deals out there, honey, huh?

MADGE Thank you, Gareth.

> MADGE *withdraws.*

LIZZY 'Thank you, Gareth!' (*She giggles to herself*)

CON Honey! (*To* PUBLIC) You'll think about what we were discussing?

PUBLIC I will, Uncle Con.

CON The job's as good as you'll get and we'd be proud to have you.

LIZZY Don't force him.

CON I'm not forcing him. I'm only telling him.

LIZZY Well now you've told him — a dozen times. So now desist, will you? (CON *spreads his hands*)

PUBLIC I will think about it. Really.

LIZZY Sure! Sure! Typical Irish! He will think about it! And while he's thinking about it the store falls in about his head! What age are you? Twenty-four? Twenty-five? What are you waiting for? For S.B. to run away

	to sea? Until the weather gets better?
CON	Honey!
LIZZY	I'm talking straight to the kid! He's Maire's boy and I've got an interest in him — the only nephew I have. (*To* BEN) Am I right or am I wrong?
BEN	I'm still up in Bailtefree chapel.
LIZZY	Where? (*Confidentially to* CON) Give him no more to drink. (*Patiently to* BEN) You're sitting in the home of S.B. O'Donnell and my deceased sister, Maire, Ben.
CON	You were telling us a story about the morning they got married, honey, in Bailtefree chapel.
LIZZY	Yeah, I know, I know, but you keep busting in on me.
PUBLIC	You were about to tell us what Agnes whispered to you.
LIZZY	(*Crying*) Poor Aggie — dead. Maire — dead. Rose, Una, Lizzy — dead — all gone — all dead and gone.
CON	Honey, you're Lizzy.
LIZZY	So what?
CON	Honey, you're not dead.
LIZZY	(*Regarding* CON *cautiously*) You gone senile all of a sudden? (*Confidentially to* BEN) Give him no more to drink. (*To* CON) For Gawd's sakes, who says I'm dead?
BEN	You're very much alive, Elise.

She goes to him and gives him another kiss.

LIZZY	Thank you, Ben. A great friend with a great intellect. Only one thing wrong with Ben Burton: he's a black Baptist.
BEN	Just for the record, Gar, I'm Episcopalian.
LIZZY	Episcopalian — Lutheran — Baptist — what's the difference? As our pastor, Father O'Flaherty, says — 'My dear brethren,' he says, 'let the whole cart-load of them, and the whole zoo of them, be to thee as the Pharisee and the publican.'
CON	Honey!
LIZZY	But he's still the best friend we have. And we have many good, dear, kind friends in the US. Right, honey?

CON Right.

LIZZY But when it comes to holding a candle to Ben Burton — look — comparisons are — he's not in the half-penny place with them!

BEN (*Laughing*) Bang on, Elise!

LIZZY Am I right or am I wrong?

CON Honey!

LIZZY (*To* PUBLIC) And that's why I say to you: America's Gawd's own country. Ben?

BEN Don't ask me. I was born there.

LIZZY What d'ya mean — 'Don't ask me?' I am asking you. He should come out or he should not — which is it?

BEN It's just another place to live, Elise: Ireland — America — what's the difference?

LIZZY You tell him, honey. You tell him the set-up we have. (*Now with growing urgency, to* PUBLIC) We have this ground-floor apartment, see, and a car that's air-conditioned, and colour TV, and this big collection of all the Irish records you ever heard, and fifteen thousand bucks in Federal Bonds —

CON Honey.

LIZZY — and a deep freezer and — and — and a backyard with this great big cherry tree, and squirrels and night owls and the smell of lavender in the spring and long summer evenings and snow at Christmas and a Christmas tree in the parlour and — and — and —

CON Elise . . .

LIZZY And it's all so Gawd-awful because we have no one to share it with us . . . (*She begins to sob*)

CON (*Softly*) It's OK, honey, OK . . .

LIZZY He's my sister's boy — the only child of five girls of us —

BEN I'll get the car round the front.

BEN *goes off through the scullery.*

LIZZY — and we spent a fortune on doctors, didn't we, Connie, but it was no good, and then I says to him

(*Con*), 'We'll go home to Ireland,' I says, 'and Maire's boy, we'll offer him everything we have — '

PRIVATE   (*Terrified*) No. No.

LIZZY   '— everything, and maybe we could coax him — you know — ' Maybe it was sorta bribery — I dunno — but he would have everything we ever gathered —

PRIVATE   Keep it! Keep it!

LIZZY   — and all the love we had in us —

PRIVATE   No! No!

CON   Honey, we've a long drive back to the hotel.

LIZZY   (*Trying to control herself*) That was always the kind of us Gallagher girls, wasn't it . . . either laughing or crying . . . you know, sorta silly and impetuous, shooting our big mouths off, talking too much, not like the O'Donnells — you know — kinda cold —

PRIVATE   Don't man, don't.

CON   Your gloves, honey. It's been a heavy day.

LIZZY   (*To* PUBLIC, *with uncertain dignity*) Tell your father that we regret we did not have the opportunity for to make his acquaintance again after all these —

PUBLIC   (*Impetuously*) I want to go to America — if you'll have me —

PRIVATE   Laddy!

CON   Sure. You think about it, son. You think about it.

PUBLIC   Now — as soon as I can, Aunt Lizzy — I mean it —

LIZZY   Gar? (*To* CON, *as if for confirmation*) Honey?

CON   Look, son —

LIZZY   To us, Gar? To come to us? To our home?

CON   Ben's waiting, Elise.

PUBLIC   If you'll have me . . .

LIZZY   If we'll have him, he says; he says if we'll have him! That's why I'm here! That's why I'm half-shot-up!

She opens her arms and approaches him.

Oh, Gar, my son —

PRIVATE   Not yet! Don't touch me yet!

LIZZY *throws her arms around him and cries happily.*

LIZZY My son, Gar, Gar, Gar . . .

PRIVATE (*Softly, with happy anguish*) God . . . my God . . . Oh, my God . . .

> *Blackout. When the bedroom light goes up* PUBLIC
> *and* PRIVATE *are there. The kitchen is empty.* PUBLIC
> *bangs the lid of his case shut and* PRIVATE *stands
> beside him, jeering at him. While this taunting goes
> on* PUBLIC *tries to escape by fussing about the room.*

PRIVATE September 8th, the sun shining, not a breath of wind
— and this was your mother's sister — remember?
And that's how you were got! Right, honey? Silly
and impetuous like a Gallagher! Regrets?

PUBLIC None.

PRIVATE Uncertainties?

PUBLIC None.

PRIVATE Little tiny niggling reservations?

PUBLIC None.

PRIVATE Her grammar?

PUBLIC Shut up!

PRIVATE But, honey, wasn't it something?

PUBLIC Go to hell.

PRIVATE Her vulgarity?

PUBLIC Bugger off.

PRIVATE She'll tuck you into your air-conditioned cot every
night.

> PUBLIC, *so that he won't hear, begins to whistle
> 'Philadelphia, Here I Come!'*

And croon, 'Sleep well, my li'l honey child.' (PUBLIC
whistles determinedly) She got you soft on account of
the day it was, didn't she? (PUBLIC *whistles louder*)
And because she said you were an O'Donnell —
'cold, like'.

PUBLIC It is now sixteen or seventeen years since I saw the
Queen of France —

PRIVATE But of course when she threw her arms around you

— well, well, well!

PUBLIC — then the Dauphiness, at Versailles —

PRIVATE Poor little orphan boy!

PUBLIC Shut up! Shut up!

PRIVATE (*In child's voice*) Ma-ma . . . Ma-ma.

> PUBLIC *flings open the bedroom door and dashes into the kitchen.* PRIVATE *follows behind.*

PUBLIC Madge!

PRIVATE: (*Quietly, deliberately*) You don't want to go, laddy-buck. Admit it. You don't want to go.

> MADGE *enters from the scullery.*

PUBLIC (*Searching for an excuse*) I can't find my coat. I left it in my room.

> MADGE *gives him a long, patient look, goes to the nail below the school clock, lifts down the coat, and hands it to him. He takes it from her and goes towards the scullery door.*

If you would only learn to leave things where you find them you wouldn't be such a bad aul' nuisance.

> PUBLIC *and* PRIVATE *go off.*

MADGE (*Calls*) Don't you dare come home drunk!

> PUBLIC's *head appears round the door.*

PUBLIC (*Softly*) I'm going to say goodbye to the boys over a quiet drink or two. And how I spend my nights is a matter entirely for myself.

MADGE 'The boys!' Couldn't even come here to say goodbye to you on your last night.

PRIVATE Straight to the bone!

PUBLIC Just you mind your business and I'll mind mine.

MADGE How many of them are getting the pension now?

PUBLIC And in case you're in bed when I get back I want a call at half-six.

MADGE The clock'll be set. If you hear it well and good.

> PUBLIC *disappears.* MADGE *fusses about the kitchen until* S.B. *enters from the shop. He has a newspaper in his hand and sits at the top of the table. She watches him as he reads. She adjusts a few things. She looks back at him, then suddenly, on the point of tears, she accuses him.*

MADGE You sit there, night after night, year after year, reading that aul' paper, and not a tooth in your head! If you had any decency in you at all you would keep them plates in while there's a lady in your presence!

S.B. (*Puzzled*) Eh?

MADGE I mean it. It — it — it — it just drives me mad, the sight of you! (*The tears begin to come*) And I have that much work to do: the stairs have to be washed down, and the store's to be swept, and your room has to be done out — and — and — I'm telling you I'll be that busy for the next couple of weeks that I won't have time to lift my head!

> *She dashes off.* S.B. *stares after her, then out at the audience. Then, very slowly, he looks down at the paper again — it has been upside down — and turns it right side up. But he can't read. He looks across at Gar's bedroom, sighs, rises, and exits very slowly to the shop. Silence for a second after* S.B. *leaves. The silence is suddenly shattered by the boisterous arrival of the* BOYS *and* GAR. *We hear their exaggerated laughter and talk outside before they burst in. When they enter they take over the kitchen, sprawling on chairs, hunting for tumblers for the stout they produce from their pockets, taking long, deep pulls on their cigarettes, giving the impression that they are busy, purposeful, randy gents about*

to embark on some exciting adventure. But their bluster is not altogether convincing. There is something false about it. Tranquillity is their enemy: they fight it valiantly. At the beginning of this scene GAR is flattered that the BOYS have come to him. When they consistently refuse to acknowledge his leaving — or perhaps because he is already spiritually gone from them — his good humour deserts him. He becomes apart from the others. NED is the leader of the group. TOM is his feed-man, subserviently watching for every cue. JOE, the youngest of the trio and not yet fully committed to the boys' way of life, is torn between fealty to NED and TOM and a spontaneous and simple loneliness over Gar's departure. Nothing would suit him better than a grand loud send-off party. But he cannot manage this, and his loyalty is divided. He is patently gauche, innocent, obvious.

NED There's only one way to put the fear of God up them bastards — (*points to his boot*) every time — you know where.

JOE Who's the ref, Ned?

TOM Jimmy Pat Barney from Bunmornan. (*Guardedly to* PUBLIC) Where's the aul' fella?

PUBLIC Haven't a bloody clue. Probably in the shop. Relax, man.

NED That (*the boot*) or the knee — it's the only game them gets can play; and we can play it too.

TOM (*Relaxing*) They've a hell of a forward line all the same, Ned.

NED They'll be on crutches this day week. By God, I can hardly wait to get the studs planted in wee Bagser Doran's face! (*He crashes his fist into the palm of his hand*)

TOM All the same, Jimmy Pat Barney's the get would put you off very quick.

NED He won't say a word to me. He knows his match when he meets it.

TOM *laughs appreciatively.* MADGE *appears at the scullery door.*

MADGE (*Coldly*) Just thought I heard somebody whispering. So yous finally made it.

JOE (*Holding up glass*) True to our word, Madge, that's us!

PUBLIC (*Happily*) They were on their way here when I ran into them.

MADGE Aye, so. (NED *belches*) Mister Sweeney, too; gentlemanly as ever.

NED (*Slapping his knee*) Come on away over here and I'll take some of the starch out of you, Madge Mulhern. How long is it since a fella gripped your knee? Haaaaaaaaaaaa!

MADGE None of your smutty talk here, Mister Sweeney. And if the boss comes in and finds them bottles —

PUBLIC I'll keep them in order, Madge.

MADGE 'Boys'! How are you!

She goes out.

TOM (*Calling*) You're jealous because you're past it — that's what's wrong with you. Right, Ned?

PUBLIC (*Raising glass*) Well, boys, when you're lining out on the pitch you can think of me, because I'll be thinking of you.

JOE (*Earnestly*) Lucky bloody man, Gar. God, I wish I was in your —

NED (*Quickly*) By the way, lads, who's the blondie thing I seen at the last Mass on Sunday?

TOM A big redhead?

NED Are you bloody-well deaf! A blondie! She wouldn't be Maggie Hanna's niece, would she?

TOM There was two of them, sitting over near the box?

NED I seen one.

TOM Cos they're English. Staying at the hotel. But the big red thing — she's one of Neil McFadden's girls.

NED Annie? Is Annie home?

141

JOE Aye, she is. So I heard the Mammy saying.

NED Bloody great! That's me fixed up for the next two weeks! Were any of yous ever on that job?

JOE No, I wasn't, Ned.

TOM For God's sake, she wouldn't spit on you!

NED Game as they're going, big Annie. But you need the constitution of a horse. I had her for the fortnight she was home last year and she damned near killed me.

PUBLIC Big Annie from up beyond the quarry?

JOE You know, Gar — the one with the squint.

NED (*With dignity*) Annie McFadden has no squint.

PUBLIC Away and take a running race to yourself, Ned.

NED (*With quiet threat*) What do you mean?

PUBLIC You were never out with Big Annie McFadden in your puff, man.

NED Are you calling me a liar?

PRIVATE (*Wearily*) What's the point.

TOM (*Quickly*) Oh, by God, Ned was there, Gar, many's and many's the time. Weren't you, Ned?

PUBLIC Have it your own way.

JOE (*Nervously*) And maybe she got the squint straightened out since I saw her last. All the women get the squints straightened out nowadays. Dammit, you could walk from here to Cork nowadays and you wouldn't see a woman with a —

NED I just don't like fellas getting snottery with me, that's all.

There follows an uneasy silence during which PRIVATE surveys the group.

PRIVATE The boys . . . They weren't always like this, were they? There was a hell of a lot of crack, wasn't there? There was a hell of a lot of laughing, wasn't there?

TOM (*Briskly*) Bit of life about the place next week, lads — the Carnival. Too bad you'll miss it, Gar. By God, it was a holy fright last year, night after night. (*To NED*) Remember?

NED (*Sulkily*) Bloody cows, the whole bloody lot of them!

TOM Mind the night with the two wee Greenock pieces?

NED (*Thawing*) Aw, stop, stop!

TOM Talk about hot things!

NED Liveliest wee tramps I ever laid!

TOM And the fat one from Dublin you picked up at the dance that night — the one that hauled you down into the ditch!

NED I was never the same since.

TOM (*To* PUBLIC) Whatever it is about him (*Ned*), if there's a fast woman in the country, she'll go for Ned first thing. Lucky bugger! (*Pause*) Aye, lucky bugger!

> *Another brief silence. These silences occur like regular cadences. To defeat them someone always introduces a fresh theme.*

PUBLIC I'm for off tomorrow, boys.

NED (*Indifferently*) Aye, so, so . . .

TOM Brooklyn, isn't it?

PUBLIC Philadelphia.

TOM Philadelphia. That's where Jimmy Crerand went to, isn't it? Philadelphia . . .

NED (*Quickly*) Mind the night Jimmy and us went down to the caves with them Dublin skivvies that was working up at the Lodge? (*To* PUBLIC) Were you — ? No, you weren't with us that night.

JOE Was I there, Ned?

NED You mind the size of Jimmy? — five foot nothing and scared of his shadow.

PUBLIC Best goalie we ever had.

NED One of the women was Gladys and the other was Emmy or something —

TOM Dammit, I mind now! Gladys and Emmy — that was it, Ned!

NED Anyhow the rest of us went in for a swim —

TOM In the bloody pelt!

NED — and your man Jimmy was left in the cave with the women; and what the hell do they do but whip the trousers off him!

JOE No, I wasn't there that night.

NED And the next thing we see is wee Jimmy coming shouting across the White Strand and the two Dublin cows haring after him.

TOM Not a stab on him!

NED — and him squealing at the top of his voice, 'Save me, boys, save me!'

TOM Never drew breath till he reached home!

NED You (*Gar*) missed that night.

TOM 'Save me, boys, save me!'

NED I don't think we went to bed that night at all.

TOM You may be sure we didn't.

NED Powerful.

Another silence descends. After a few seconds PRIVATE *speaks.*

PRIVATE We were all there that night, Ned. And the girls' names were Gladys and Susan. And they sat on the the rocks dangling their feet in the water. And we sat in the cave peeping out at them. And then Jimmy Crerand suggested that we go in for a swim; and we all ran to the far end of the shore; and we splashed about like schoolboys. Then we came back to the cave and wrestled with one another. And then out of sheer boredom, Tom, you suggested that we take the trousers off Crerand — just to prove how manly we all were. But when Ned started towards Jimmy — five foot nothing, remember? — wee Jimmy squared up and defied not only the brave Ned but the whole lot of us. So we straggled back home, one behind the other, and left the girls dangling their feet in the water. And that was that night.

PUBLIC If the ground's not too hard you'll do well on Sunday.

NED Hard or soft — (*examining his boot*) I've a couple of aul' scores to settle.

PUBLIC You'll never get as good a half-back as the one you're losing.

NED (*Quickly, with pretended interest*) D'you know what I'm thinking? We'd better see about transport.

TOM Dammit, you're right. I'll get the aul' fella's van easy enough. Can you get your Charlie's lorry?

NED Just maybe. I'd better try him the night.

JOE What about a song from Gar, boys, before we break up?

NED What time is it?

JOE It's early in the night yet.

TOM Twenty-past-nine.

NED We'd better move then; Charlie was talking about going to a dance in Ardmore.

TOM Dammit, that's an idea!

JOE We'll all go — a big last night for Gar!

NED Ardmore? Are you mad? Bloody women in that place don't know what they're for!

TOM True for you. Scream their heads off if you laid a hand on them.

NED But I'll tell you what we'll do — call in home first to see Charlie and then go on to the hotel for a dirty big booze-up.

JOE I don't like drinking in that place.

NED Them two English bits — what's their name?

TOM Them strangers? Agh, you wouldn't have a chance there. They do nothing but walk and look at weeds and stuff —

NED Who wouldn't have a chance?

TOM I know, Ned. But them two — they're sort of stiff-looking — like — like they worked in a post office or something.

NED They're women, aren't they?

TOM Dammit, we might! . . . Still I don't know . . . They knit a lot . . . (*To* PUBLIC) What d'you think?

JOE I vote we stay here.

PUBLIC And you can count me out. I've an early start.

NED £10 to a shilling I click with one or other of them!

PUBLIC I won't be here to collect my winnings.

NED Come on! Any takers? Never clapped eyes on them and I'm offering ten notes to a bob!

TOM Cripes, I know that look in his eyes!

NED Wise bloody men! The blood's up, lads! Off to the front! Any volunteers for a big booze-up and a couple of women?

TOM Did he say women? Sign me on!

JOE I don't think I'm in form the night, boys —

NED We'll show them a weed or two, eh?

TOM Out to the sandbanks! Get them in the bloody bent!

NED We're away — Wait! Wait! — How much money have you?

They both produce their money — a fistful of small coins.

TOM 2s 6d . . . 2s 11d . . . 3s 3d. . . 3s 5½d.

NED And I have 6s 2d. It'll have to do. Say a prayer they're fast and thrifty.

TOM Dirty aul' brute! Lead the way, Bull!

NED I'm telling you — the blood's up!

TOM Coming, lads?

PUBLIC I'm getting up at half-six.

NED (*Casually from the door*) So long, Gar. You know the aul' rule — if you can't be good . . .

TOM Send us a pack of them playing cards — the ones with the dirty pictures on the back!

NED And if the women are as easy as the money out there we might think of joining you. (*To* TOM) Right, old cock?

TOM Bull on regardless! Yaaaaaaaaaaaah!

They open the door. NED *hesitates and begins taking off the broad leather belt with the huge brass buckle that supports his trousers.*

NED (*Shyly, awkwardly*) By the way, Gar, since I'll not see you again before you go —

TOM Hi! What are you at? At least wait till you're sure of the women!

NED (*Impatiently to* TOM) Agh, shut up! (*To* PUBLIC) If any

of them Yankee scuts try to beat you up some dark
night you can . . . (*Now he is very confused and flings
the belt across the room to* PUBLIC) . . . you know . . .
there's a bloody big buckle on it . . . many's a get I
scutched with it . . .

TOM Safe enough, lads: he has braces on as well!

NED I meant to buy you something good but the aul' fella
didn't sell the calf to the jobbers last Friday . . . and
he could have, the stupid bastard, such a bloody
stupid bastard of an aul' fella!

PUBLIC (*Moved*) Thanks, Ned . . . thanks . . .

JOE Dammit, I have nothing for you, Gar.

TOM (*Quickly*) Are we for the sandbanks or are we not?

NED You'll make out all right over there . . . have a . . .

TOM I know that look in his eyes!

> NED *wheels rapidly on* TOM, *gives him a more than
> playful punch, and says savagely:*

Christ, if there's one get I hate, it's you!

> *He goes off quickly.* TOM *looks uncertainly after him,
> looks back at* PUBLIC, *and says with dying con-
> viction:*

TOM The blood's up . . . Oh, by God, when he goes on like
that, the . . . the blood's up all right . . .

> TOM *looks after* NED, *then back to* JOE *and* GAR, *as if
> he can't decide which to join, then impetuously he
> dashes off after* NED, *calling:*

Hi! Ned, Ned, wait for me . . .

> *There is a silence.* PUBLIC *is looking at the belt.* JOE
> *begins to fidget. Now* PUBLIC *becomes aware of him.*

PUBLIC What the hell are you waiting for?

JOE Dammit, man, like it's your last night and all, and I

thought —

PUBLIC Get to hell and run after them.

JOE Sure you know yourself they'll hang about the gable of the hotel and chat and do nothing.

PUBLIC For God's sake, man, those English women will be swept off their feet!

JOE (*Uncertainly*) You're taking a hand at me now.

PUBLIC I'm telling you, you're missing the chance of a lifetime.

JOE Maybe — eh? — what d'you think?

PUBLIC Go on! Go on!

JOE God, maybe you're right. You never know what'll happen, eh? You finish that (*drink*) for me! God, maybe we'll click the night! Say a wee prayer we do! Cripes, my blood's up too! Where's my cap?

He grabs the cap, dashes to the door, remembers he won't see GAR again.

Send us a card, Gar, sometimes, eh?

PUBLIC Surely, Joe.

JOE Lucky bloody man. I wish I was you.

PUBLIC There's nothing stopping you, is there?

JOE Only that the Mammy planted sycamore trees last year and she says I can't go till they're tall enough to shelter the house.

PUBLIC You're stuck for another couple of days, then. Away off with you, man.

JOE Good luck, Gar. And tell Madge that the next time she asks us up for tea we'd bloody-well better get it.

PUBLIC She *asked* you?

JOE That's why I was joking her about us keeping our word. As if we wanted tea, for God's sake! But I'd better catch up with the stirks before they do damage . . . So long, aul' cock!

He runs off.

PUBLIC Madge . . . Oh God . . .

*PRIVATE moves over beside him. He speaks quickly,
savagely at first, spitting out the first three lines.
Gradually he softens, until the speech ends almost in
a whisper.*

PRIVATE They're louts, ignorant bloody louts and you've
always known it! And don't pretend you're surprised; because you're not. And you know what
they'll do tonight, don't you? They'll shuffle around
the gable of the hotel and take an odd furtive peep
into the lounge at those English women who won't
even look up from their frigid knitting! Many a
time you did it yourself, bucko! Aye, and but for
Aunt Lizzy and the grace of God, you'd be there
tonight, too, watching the lights go out over the
village, and hearing the front doors being bolted,
and seeing the blinds being raised; and you stamp-
ing your feet to keep the numbness from spreading,
not wanting to go home, not yet for another while,
wanting to hold on to the night although nothing
can happen now, nothing at all . . . Joe and Tom and
big, thick, generous Ned . . . No one will ever know
or understand the fun there was; for there *was* fun
and there *was* laughing — foolish, silly fun and
foolish, silly laughing; but what it was all about you
can't remember, can you? Just the memory of it —
that's all you have now — just the memory; and
even now, even so soon, it is being distilled of all its
coarseness; and what's left is going to be precious,
precious gold . . .

There is a knock at the door. PUBLIC *goes off to
answer it.*

KATE (*Off*) Hello, Gar.
PRIVATE Kate!
KATE (*On*) This isn't a healthy sign, drinking by yourself.
PRIVATE Talk! Talk!
PUBLIC What — what are you doing here?

KATE I hear you're off to America.

PUBLIC First thing in the morning.

KATE You wouldn't think of calling to say goodbye to your friends, I suppose?

PUBLIC I was going to, but I —

PRIVATE Careful!

PUBLIC — it went clean out of my mind. You know how it is, getting ready . . .

KATE I understand, Gar.

PRIVATE She's a married woman, you bugger!

KATE Philadelphia?

PUBLIC Yes. Take a seat.

KATE To an aunt, isn't it?

PUBLIC That's right. A sister of Mother's.

KATE And you're going to work in a hotel.

PUBLIC You know as much about it as I do.

KATE You know Baile Beag — Small Town.

PUBLIC I'll probably go to night school as well — you know, at night —

PRIVATE Brilliant.

PUBLIC — do Law or Medicine or something —

PRIVATE Like hell! First Arts stumped you!

KATE You'll do well, Gar; make a lot of money, and come back here in twenty years' time, and buy the whole village.

PUBLIC Very likely. That's my plan anyhow.

PRIVATE Kate . . . Kathy . . .

PUBLIC How's your father and mother?

KATE Fine, thanks. And Mr O'Donnell?

PUBLIC Grand, grand. Is Dr King well?

KATE I hear no complaints.

PRIVATE Then the Dauphiness of Versailles. And surely never lighted on this orb, which she hardly seemed to touch, a more delightful vision. I saw her just above the horizon, decorating and cheering the elevated sphere she just began to move in —

PUBLIC (*A shade louder than necessary*) I'll come home when I make my first million, driving a Cadillac and smoking cigars and taking movie-films.

KATE   I hope you're very happy there and that life will be good to you.

PUBLIC   (*Slightly louder*) I'll make sure life's good to me from now on.

KATE   Your father'll miss you.

PUBLIC   (*Rapidly, aggressively*) That's his lookout! D'you know something? If I had to spend another week in Ballybeg I'd go off my bloody head! This place would drive anybody crazy! Look around you, for God's sake! Look at Master Boyle! Look at my father! Look at the Canon! Look at the boys! Asylum cases, the whole bloody lot of them!

PRIVATE   (*Pained*) Shhhhhhh!

PUBLIC   Listen, if someone were to come along to me tonight and say, 'Ballybeg's yours — lock, stock, and barrel,' it wouldn't make that (*cracks his fingers*) much difference to me. If you're not happy and content in a place — then — then — then you're not happy and content in a place! It's as simple as that. I've stuck around this hole far too long. I'm telling you: it's a bloody quagmire, a backwater, a dead end! And everybody in it goes crazy sooner or later! Everybody!

PRIVATE   Shhhhhhhh . . .

PUBLIC   There's nothing about Ballybeg that I don't know already. I hate the place, and every stone, and every rock, and every piece of heather around it! Hate it! Hate it! And the sooner that plane whips me away the better I'll like it!

KATE   It isn't as bad as that, Gar.

PUBLIC   You're stuck here! What else can you say!

PRIVATE   That'll do!

PUBLIC   And you'll die here! But I'm not stuck! I'm free! Free as the bloody wind!

KATE   All I meant was —

PUBLIC   Answerable to nobody! All this bloody yap about father and son and all this sentimental rubbish about 'homeland' and 'birthplace' — yap! Bloody yap! Impermanence — anonymity — that's what I'm looking for; a vast restless place that doesn't give a damn about the past. To hell with Ballybeg, that's what I say!

PRIVATE Oh, man . . .

KATE I'd better go. Francis'll be wondering what's keeping me.

PUBLIC (*Recklessly*) Tell him I was asking for him.

KATE Goodbye, Gar.

PUBLIC (*In same tone*) Enjoy yourself, Kate. And if you can't be good — you know?

PUBLIC *goes with* KATE.

(*Off*) Be sure to call the first one after me.

She is gone. PUBLIC *returns and immediately buries his face in his hands.*

PRIVATE Kate . . . sweet Katie Doogan . . . my darling Kathy Doogan . . .

PUBLIC *uncovers his face and with trembling fingers lights a cigarette and takes a drink. As he does:*

PRIVATE (*Very softly*) Oh my God, steady man, steady — it is now sixteen or seventeen years since I saw the Queen of France, then the Dauphiness, at Versailles, and surely never lighted on this orb — Oh God. Oh my God, those thoughts are sinful — (*Sings*) 'As beautiful Kitty one morning was tripping with a pitcher of milk — '

PUBLIC *attempts to whistle his song 'Philadelphia, Here I Come!' He whistles the first phrase and the notes die away.* PRIVATE *keeps on talking while* PUBLIC *attempts to whistle.*

We'll go now, right away, and tell them — Mammy

and Daddy — they're at home tonight — now, Gar, now — it must be now — remember, it's up to you, entirely up to you — gut and salt them fish — and they're going to call this one Madge, at least so she *says* — (PUBLIC *makes another attempt to whistle*) a little something to remind you of your old teacher — don't keep looking back over your shoulder, be one hundred per cent American — a packet of ciga-rettes and a pot of jam — seven boys and seven girls — and our daughters'll all be gentle and frail and silly like you — and I'll never wait till Christmas — I'll burst, I'll bloody-well burst — goodbye, Gar, it isn't as bad as that — Goodbye, Gar, it isn't as bad as that — goodbye, Gar, it isn't as bad as that —

PUBLIC (*In whispered shout*) Screwballs, say something! Say something, Father!

Quick curtain.

EPISODE THREE

Part One

A short time later. The Rosary is being said. PUBLIC *is kneeling with his back to the audience.* S.B. *is kneeling facing the audience.* MADGE *is facing the shop door.* PRIVATE *kneels beside* PUBLIC. MADGE *is saying her decade, and the other three —* S.B., PUBLIC *and* PRIVATE *— are answering. The words are barely distinct, a monotonous, somnolent drone. After a few moments* PRIVATE *lowers his body until his rear is resting on the backs of his legs. We cannot see* PUBLIC'S *face. While* PRIVATE *talks, the Rosary goes on.*

PRIVATE   (*Relaxing, yawning*) Ah-ho-ho-ho-ho-ho. This time tomorrow night, bucko, you'll be saying the Rosary all by yourself — unless Lizzy and Con say it (*joins in a response in American accent*) — Holy Mairy, Mother of Gawd, pray for us sinners now and at the hour . . . (*He tails off as his mind wanders again*) No, not this time tomorrow. It's only about half-four in Philadelphia now, and when it's half-nine there it'll be the wee hours of the morning here; and Screwballs'll be curled up and fast asleep in his wee cot — (*To* S.B.) right, honey? And when he's dreaming you'll be swaggering down 56th Street on Third at the junction of 29th and Seventh at 81st with this big blonde nuzzling up to you —

> *Suddenly kneels erect again and responds in unison with* PUBLIC. *Keeps this up for two or three responses and slowly subsides again.*

You'd need to be careful out there, boy; some of those Yankee women are dynamite. But you'll never marry;

never; bachelor's written all over you. Fated to be
alone, a man without intimates; something of an
enigma. Who is he, this silent one? Where is he from?
Where does he go? Every night we see him walking
beneath the trees along the bank of the canal, his black
cloak swinging behind him, his eyes lost in thought,
his servant following him at a respectful distance. (*In
reply*) Who is he? I'll tell you who he is: The Bachelor.
All the same, laddybuck, there are compensations in
being a bachelor. You'll age slowly and graciously,
and then, perhaps, when you're quite old — about
forty-three — you'll meet this beautiful girl of nineteen, and you'll fall madly in love. Karin — that's her
name — no — ah — ah — Tamara — (*caressing the
word*) Tamara — granddaughter of an exiled Russian
prince, and you'll be consumed by a magnificent
passion; and this night you'll invite her to dinner in
your penthouse, and you'll be dressed in a deep blue
velvet jacket, and the candles will discover magic
fairy lights in her hair, and you'll say to her, 'Tamara',
and she'll incline her face towards you, and close her
eyes, and whisper —

> *From a few seconds back the droning prayers have
> stopped. Now* MADGE *leans over to* PUBLIC *and gives
> him a rough punch.*

MADGE Your decade!

> PRIVATE *and* PUBLIC *jump erect again and in perfect
> unison give out their decade. Gradually, as the prayers
> continue, they relax into their slumped position.*

PRIVATE When you're curled up in your wee cot, Screwballs,
do you dream? Do you ever dream of the past,
Screwballs, of that wintry morning in Bailtefree, and
the three days in Bundoran . . . ?

> PUBLIC *stays as he is.* PRIVATE *gets slowly to his feet*

and moves over to S.B. *He stands looking down at him.*

. . . and of the young, gay girl from beyond the mountains who sometimes cried herself to sleep? (*Softly, nervously, with growing excitement*) God — maybe — Screwballs — behind those dead eyes and that flat face are there memories of precious moments in the past? My God, have I been unfair to you? Is it possible that you have hoarded in the back of that mind of yours — do you remember — it was an afternoon in May — oh, fifteen years ago — I don't remember every detail but some things are as vivid as can be: the boat was blue and the paint was peeling and there was an empty cigarette packet floating in the water at the bottom between two trout and the left rowlock kept slipping and you had given me your hat and had put your jacket round my shoulders because there had been a shower of rain. And you had the rod in your left hand — I can see the cork nibbled away from the butt of the rod — and maybe we had been chatting — I don't remember — it doesn't matter — but between us at that moment there was this great happiness, this great joy — you must have felt it too — although nothing was being said — just the two of us fishing on a lake on a showery day — and young as I was I felt, I knew, that this was precious, and your hat was soft on the top of my ears — I can feel it — and I shrank down into your coat — and then, then for no reason at all except that you were happy too, you began to sing: (*Sings*)
    'All round my hat I'll wear a green coloured
        ribbon-o,
    All round my hat for a twelve month and a day.
    And if anybody asks me the reason why I wear it,
    It's all because my true love is far, far away.'

The Rosary is over. MADGE *and* S.B. *get slowly to*

156

their feet. PUBLIC *and* PRIVATE *are not aware that the prayers are finished.* S.B. *does the nightly job of winding the clock.*

MADGE Will you take your supper now?
S.B. Any time suits you.

MADGE goes to PUBLIC, *still kneeling.*

MADGE And what about St Martin de Porres?
PUBLIC Mm?

He blesses himself hurriedly, in confusion, and gets to his feet.

MADGE Supper.
PUBLIC Yes — yes — please, Madge —
MADGE (*Going off*) I suppose even the saints must eat now and again, too.

Pause. S.B. *consults his pocket watch.*

S.B. What time do you make it?
PUBLIC Quarter-to-ten.
S.B. It's that anyhow.
PRIVATE Go on! Ask him! He must remember!
S.B. The days are shortening already. Before we know we'll be burning light before closing time.
PRIVATE Go on! Go on!
PUBLIC (*In the churlish, offhand tone he uses to* S.B.) What ever happened to that aul' boat on Lough na Cloc Cor?
S.B. What's that?
PRIVATE Again!
PUBLIC That aul' boat that used to be up on Lough na Cloc Cor — an aul' blue thing — d'you remember it?
S.B. A boat? Eh? (*Voices off*) The Canon!
PRIVATE Bugger the Canon!

The CANON *enters; a lean, white-haired man with*

alert eyes and a thin mouth. He is talking back to
MADGE *in the scullery.*

CANON   Hee-hee-hee — you're a terrible woman.

S.B.   Well, Canon!

CANON   That Madge . . . hee-hee-hee.

PUBLIC   Goodnight, Canon.

CANON   She says I wait till the Rosary's over and the kettle's on . . . hee-hee-hee.

S.B.   She's a sharp one, Madge.

CANON   'You wait,' says she, 'till the Rosary's over and the kettle's on!'

PRIVATE   Hee-hee-hee.

S.B.   Pay no heed to Madge, Canon.

PRIVATE   And how's the O'Donnell family tonight?

CANON   And how's the O'Donnell family tonight?

PUBLIC *sits when the* CANON *sits.*

S.B.   Living away as usual. Not a thing happening.

PRIVATE   Liar!

CANON   Just so, now, just so.

S.B.   Will we have a game now or will we wait till the supper comes in?

CANON   We may as well commence, Sean. I see no reason why we shouldn't commence.

S.B.   (*Setting the board*) Whatever you say, Canon.

CANON   Hee-hee-hee. 'You wait,' says she, 'till the Rosary's over and the kettle's on.'

PRIVATE   She's a sharp one, Madge.

S.B.   She's a sharp one, Madge.

CANON   It'll be getting near your time, Gareth.

PUBLIC   Tomorrow morning, Canon.

CANON   Just so, now. Tomorrow morning.

PRIVATE   Tomorrow morning.

CANON   Tomorrow morning.

S.B.   Here we are.

CANON   Powerful the way time passes, too.

S.B.   Black or white, Canon?

CANON (*Considering the problem*) Black or white . . .

PRIVATE Black for the crows and white for the swans.

CANON Black for the crows and white for the swans.

PRIVATE Ha-ha! (*He preens himself at his skill in prophecy*)

S.B. Have a shot at the black the night.

CANON Maybe I will then.

PRIVATE Can't take the money off you every night.

CANON Can't take the trousers off you every night. Hee-hee-hee.

PRIVATE (*Shocked*) Canon O'Byrne!

S.B. You had a great streak of luck last night, I'll grant you that.

CANON (*A major announcement*) D'you know what?

S.B. What's that, Canon?

CANON You'll have rain before morning.

S.B. D'you think so?

CANON It's in the bones. The leg's giving me the odd jab.

S.B. We could do without the rain then.

CANON Before the morning you'll have it.

S.B. Tch tch tch. We get our fill of it here.

CANON The best barometer I know.

S.B. Aye. No want of rain.

CANON Before the morning.

S.B. As if we don't get enough of it.

CANON The jabs are never wrong.

PRIVATE (*Wildly excited*) Stop press! News flash! Sensation! We interrupt our programmes to bring you the news that Canon Mick O'Byrne, of Ballybeg, Ireland, has made the confident prediction that *you'll* have rain before the morning! Stand by for further bulletins!

CANON 'You wait,' says she, 'till the Rosary's over and the kettle's on!'

S.B. Usual stakes, Canon?

CANON I see no reason to alter them.

S.B. What about putting them up — just for the first game?

CANON The thin end of the wedge, eh, as the Bishop says? No, Sean, the way I see it, a halfpenny a game'll neither make nor break either of us.

Enter MADGE *with cups of tea and a plate of biscuits.*

MADGE Have you begun already?

S.B. Shh!

MADGE If it was turkeys or marble clocks they were playing for they couldn't be more serious!

S.B. Quiet!

MADGE Agh!

She leaves their tea beside them and brings a cup over to PUBLIC. *They talk in undertones.*

MADGE Wouldn't you love to throw it round them!

PUBLIC Scalding hot!

MADGE And raise blisters on their aul' bald pates! — God forgive me!

PUBLIC Madge.

MADGE What?

PUBLIC Why don't you take a run over to see the new baby?

MADGE I've more on my mind than that.

PUBLIC I'll put up the jars and wash up these few things.

MADGE And this the last night we'll have you to torment us?

PUBLIC Go on. Go on. We won't start swopping the dirty stories till we get you out of the road.

S.B. Shhhhhhh!

PUBLIC Hurry up. Nelly'll be wondering why you didn't show up.

MADGE Aye, so.

PUBLIC Your own namesake, isn't it?

MADGE So she *says*.

PUBLIC Get a move on. You'll be back before bedtime.

MADGE What d'you think?

PUBLIC Quick!

MADGE I'm away!

She takes a few steps away and comes back.

Don't forget: them shirts isn't right aired.

Just when she is at the scullery door:

PUBLIC   Madge.

MADGE   What is it?

PRIVATE   Don't! Don't!

PUBLIC   Why did my mother marry him (S.B.) instead of Master Boyle?

MADGE   What?

PUBLIC   She went with both of them, didn't she?

MADGE   She married the better man by far.

PUBLIC   But she went with Boyle first, didn't she?

MADGE   I've told you before: she went with a dozen — that was the kind of her — she couldn't help herself.

PUBLIC   But is that what started Boyle drinking?

MADGE   If it was, more fool he. And any other nosing about you want to do, ask the Boss. For you're not going to pump me.

She goes off.

PRIVATE   What the hell had you to go and ask that for! Snap, boy, snap! We want no scenes tonight. Get up and clear out of this because you're liable to get over-excited watching these two daredevils dicing with death.

PUBLIC *takes his cup and goes towards his bedroom.*

Into your survival shelter and brood, brood, brood. (*As if replying to the draught players who have not noticed his exit*) No, no, I'm not leaving. Just going in here to have a wee chat with my Chinese mistress.

PUBLIC *goes into his bedroom leaving the door open.* PRIVATE *stays in the kitchen.* PUBLIC *in the bedroom mimes the actions of* PRIVATE *in the following sequence.* PRIVATE *stands at the table between* S.B. *and* CANON.

PRIVATE   Canon battling tooth and nail for another half-
           penny; Screwballs fighting valiantly to retain his
           trousers! Gripped in mortal combat! County Coun-
           cillor versus Canon! Screwballs versus Canonballs!
           (*Stares intently at them*) Hi, kids! Having fun, kids?

> PRIVATE *gets to his feet, leans his elbow on the table,
> and talks confidentially into their faces.*

Any chance of a game, huh? Tell me, boys, strictly
between ourselves, will you miss me? You will? You
really will? But now I want you both to close your
eyes — please, my darlings — don't, don't argue —
just do as I say — just close your eyes and think of
all the truly wonderful times we've had together.
Now! What'll we chat about, eh? Let's — chat —
about — what? No, Screwballs, not women; not before you-know-who. (*Looking at the* CANON) Money?
Agh, sure, Canon, what interest have you in money?
Sure as long as you get to Tenerife for five weeks
every winter what interest have you in money? But
I'm wasting my time with you, Canon — Screwballs
here is different; there's an affinity between Screwballs and me that no one, literally no one could
understand — except you, Canon (*deadly serious*),
because you're warm and kind and soft and sympathetic — all things to all men — because you could
translate all this loneliness, this groping, this dread-
ful bloody buffoonery into Christian terms that will
make life bearable for us all. And yet you don't say
a word. Why, Canon? Why, arid Canon? Isn't this
your job? — to translate? Why don't you speak,
then? Prudence, arid Canon? Prudence be damned!
Christianity isn't prudent — it's insane! Or maybe
this just happens to be one of your bad nights —
(*Suddenly bright and brittle again*) A pound to a
shilling I make you laugh! (*Dancing around, singing
to the tune of 'Daisy':*) 'Screwballs, Screwballs, give
me your answer, do. I'm half crazy all for the love

of you. I'm off to Philadelphey, and I'll leave you on the shelfey — '

s.b. *gives a short dry laugh.*

PRIVATE A pound you owe me! Money for aul' rope! And you, Canon, what about giving us a bar or two?

CANON Aye.

PRIVATE You will? Wonderful! What'll it be? A pop number? An aul' Gregorian come-all-ye? A whack of an aul' aria?

CANON I had you cornered.

PRIVATE 'I had you cornered' — I know it! I know it! I know it! (*Sings in the style of a modern crooner*) 'I had you cornered / That night in Casablanca / That night you said you loved me' — all set? Boys and girls, that top, pop recording star, Kenny O'Byrne and the Ballybeg Buggers in their latest fabulous release, 'I Had You Cornered'.

> PRIVATE *stands with head lowered, his foot tapping, his fingers clicking in syncopated rhythm, waiting for the* CANON *to begin. He keeps this up for a few seconds. Then in time to his own beat he sings very softly, as he goes to the bedroom:*

'Should aul' acquaintance be forgot
And never brought to min'?
Should aul' acquaintance be forgot
And days o' lang-syne?'
Yah — ooooo.

> PUBLIC *suddenly sits up in bed.*

Mendelssohn! That's the bugger'll tear the guts out of you!

> PUBLIC *puts on a recording of the Second Movement of the* Violin Concerto. PRIVATE, *now almost*

frenzied, dashes back to the kitchen.

Give us a bar or two, Mendelssohn, aul' fella. Come on, lad; resin the aul' bow and spit on your hands and give us an aul' bar!

The record begins. PRIVATE *runs to the table and thrusts his face between the players.*

Listen! Listen! Listen! D'you hear it? D'you know what the music says? (*To* S.B.) It says that once upon a time a boy and his father sat in a blue boat on a lake on an afternoon in May, and on that afternoon a great beauty happened, a beauty that has haunted the boy ever since, because he wonders now did it really take place or did he imagine it. There are only the two of us, he says; each of us is all the other has; and why can we not even look at each other? Have pity on us, he says; have goddam pity on every goddam bloody man jack of us.

He comes away from the table and walks limply back to the bedroom. When he gets to the bedroom door he turns, surveys the men.

To hell with all strong silent men!

He goes into the bedroom, drops into the chair, and sits motionless. PUBLIC *sinks back on to the bed again. Silence.*

CANON What's that noise?
 S.B. What's that, Canon?
CANON A noise of some sort.
 S.B. Is there?

They listen.

I don't hear —

CANON Wait.

   s.b. Is it —

CANON It's music — is it?

   s.b. Music?

CANON Aye. It's music.

   s.b. That'll be Gar then.

CANON Oh.

   s.b. Playing them records of his.

CANON Thought I heard something.

   s.b. All he asks is to sit in there and play them records all day.

CANON It makes him happy.

   s.b. Terrible man for the records.

CANON Just so, now. It'll be getting near his time, he tells me.

   s.b. Tomorrow morning.

CANON Tomorrow morning.

   s.b. Aye, tomorrow morning. Powerful the way time passes, too.

CANON 'You wait,' says she, 'till the Rosary's over and the kettle's on.'

   s.b. A sharp one, Madge.

CANON Ah-hah. There's hope for you yet.

   s.b. I don't know is there.

CANON No. You're not too late yet.

   s.b. Maybe . . . maybe . . .

CANON No, I wouldn't say die yet — not yet I wouldn't.

Slow curtain.

EPISODE THREE

Part Two

The small hours of the morning. The kitchen is dimly lit. In the kitchen, just outside the bedroom door, are Gar's cases, and lying across them are his coat, his cap, and a large envelope containing his X-ray and visa. The bedroom is in darkness: just enough light to see PUBLIC *on the bed and* PRIVATE *in the chair.* S.B. *comes in from the scullery carrying a cup of tea in his hand. He is dressed in long trousers, a vest, a hat, socks. He moves slowly towards the table, sees the cases, goes over to them, touches the coat, goes back towards the table, and sits there, staring at the bedroom door. He coughs. Immediately* PRIVATE *is awake and* PUBLIC *sits up sleepily in bed.*

PRIVATE What — what — what's that? (*Relaxing*) Madge probably. Looking to see is the door bolted.

> PUBLIC *gets out of bed and switches on the light. Looks at his watch.*

You'll not sleep again tonight, laddo.
PUBLIC Bugger.

> PUBLIC *looks at himself in the mirror and then sits on edge of bed.*

PRIVATE Four more hours. This is the last time you'll lie in this bed, the last time you'll look at that pattern on the wallpaper, the last time you'll listen to the silence of Ballybeg, the last time you'll —
PUBLIC Agh, shut up!
PRIVATE It is now sixteen or seventeen years since I saw the Queen of France. Go into the shop, man, and get

yourself a packet of aspirin; that'll do the trick. (*Looking up at ceiling*) Mind if I take a packet of aspirin, Screwballs? Send the bill to the USA, OK? Out you go, boy, and get a clatter of pills!

They both go into the kitchen. PUBLIC *stops dead when he sees* S.B. *staring at him.*

PUBLIC My God! Lady Godiva!
PRIVATE Is this where you are?
    S.B. Aye — I — I — I — I wasn't sleeping. What has you up?

PUBLIC *goes to where the key of the shop is hung up.*

PUBLIC I — I wasn't sleeping either. I'll get some aspirins inside.
    S.B. It's hard to sleep sometimes . . .
PUBLIC It is, aye . . . sometimes . . .
    S.B. There's tea in the pot.
PUBLIC Aye?
    S.B. If it's a headache you have.
PUBLIC It'll make me no worse anyway.

PUBLIC *goes into the scullery.* PRIVATE *stands at the door and talks into him.*

PRIVATE Now's your time, boy. The small hours of the morning. Put your head on his shoulder and say, 'How's my wee darling Daddy?'

PUBLIC *puts his head round the door.*

PUBLIC You take some?
    S.B. Sure you know I never take a second cup.
PRIVATE Playing hard to get. Come on, bucko; it's your place to make the move — the younger man. Say — say — say — say, 'Screwballs, with two magnificent legs like that, how is it you were never in show biz?' Say,

'It is now sixteen or seventeen — Say — oh, my God
— say — say something.

PUBLIC *enters with a cup of tea.*

PUBLIC You'll need a new tyre for the van.

S.B. What one's that?

PUBLIC The back left-hand one. I told you. It's done.

S.B. Aye. So you did.

PUBLIC And — and —

PRIVATE What else?

PUBLIC — and don't forget the fencing posts for McGuire
next Wednesday.

S.B. Fencing posts.

PUBLIC Twelve dozen. The milk lorry'll take them. I spoke
to Packey.

S.B. Aye . . . right . . .

PRIVATE Go on! Keep talking!

PUBLIC And if you're looking for the pliers I threw them into
the tea chest under the counter.

S.B. Which tea chest?

PUBLIC The one near the window.

S.B. Oh, I see — I see.

PRIVATE You're doing grand. Keep at it. It's the silence that's
the enemy.

PUBLIC You'll be wanting more plug tobacco. The traveller'll
be here this week.

S.B. More plug.

PUBLIC It's finished. The last of it went up to Curran's wake.

S.B. I'll — I'll see about that.

PUBLIC And you'll need to put a new clasp on the lower
window — the tinkers are about again.

S.B. Aye?

PUBLIC They were in at dinner time. I got some cans off
them.

S.B. I just thought I noticed something shining from the
ceiling.

PUBLIC It's the cans then.

S.B. Aye.

PUBLIC That's what it is. I bought six off them.

S.B. They'll not go to loss.

PUBLIC They wanted me to take a dozen but I said six would do us.

S.B. Six is plenty. They don't go as quick as they used to — them cans.

PUBLIC They've all got cookers and ranges and things.

S.B. What's that?

PUBLIC I say they don't buy them now because the open fires are nearly all gone.

S.B. That's it. All cookers and ranges and things these times.

PUBLIC That's why I wouldn't take the dozen.

S.B. You were right, too. Although I mind the time when I got through a couple of dozen a week.

PUBLIC Aye?

S.B. All cans it was then. Maybe you'd sell a kettle at turf-cutting or if there'd be a Yank coming home . . .

Pause.

PUBLIC Better get these pills and then try to get a couple of hours sleep —

S.B. You're getting the mail van to Strabane?

PUBLIC *gives him a quick, watchful look.*

PUBLIC At a-quarter-past-seven.

S.B. (*Awkwardly*) I was listening to the weather forecast there . . . moderate westerly winds and occasional showers, it said.

PUBLIC Aye?

S.B. I was thinking it — it — it — it would be a fair enough day for going up in thon plane.

PUBLIC It should be, then.

S.B. Showers — just like the Canon said . . . And I was meaning to tell you that you should sit at the back . . .

PRIVATE It is now sixteen or seventeen years — the longest way round's the shortest way home —

s.b.   So *he* was saying, too . . . you know there — if there
         was an accident or anything — it's the front gets it
         hardest —

PUBLIC   I suppose that's true enough.

s.b.   So *he* was saying . . . not that I would know — just
         that he was saying it there . . .

PRIVATE (*Urgently, rapidly*) Now! Now! He might remember
         — he might. But if he does, my God, laddo — what
         if he does?

PUBLIC   (*With pretended carelessness*) D'you know what kept
         coming into my mind the day?

s.b.   Eh?

PUBLIC   The fishing we used to do on Lough na Cloc Cor.

s.b.   (*Confused, on guard*) Oh, aye, Lough na Cloc Cor —
         aye — aye —

PUBLIC   We had a throw on it every Sunday during the
         season.

s.b.   That's not the day nor yesterday.

PUBLIC   (*More quickly*) There used to be a blue boat on it —
         d'you remember it?

s.b.   Many's the fish we took off that same lake.

PUBLIC   D'you remember the blue boat?

s.b.   A blue one, eh?

PUBLIC   I don't know who owned it. But it was blue. And the
         paint was peeling.

s.b.   (*Remembering*) I mind a brown one the doctor brought
         from somewhere up in the —

PUBLIC   (*Quickly*) It doesn't matter who owned it. It doesn't
         even matter that it was blue. But d'you remember
         one afternoon in May — we were up there — the
         two of us — and it must have rained because you
         put your jacket round my shoulders and gave me
         your hat —

s.b.   Aye?

PUBLIC   — and it wasn't that we were talking or anything —
         but suddenly — suddenly you sang 'All round my
         hat I'll wear a green coloured ribbon-o' —

s.b.   Me?

PUBLIC   — for no reason at all except that we — that you

were happy. D'you remember? D'you remember?

There is a pause while s.b. *tries to recall.*

s.b. No . . . no, then, I don't . . .

PRIVATE *claps his hands in nervous mockery.*

PRIVATE (*Quickly*) There! There! There!
s.b. 'All Round My Hat'? No, I don't think I ever knew that one. It wasn't 'The Flower of Sweet Strabane', was it? That was my song.
PUBLIC It could have been. It doesn't matter.
PRIVATE So now you know: it never happened! Ha-ha-ha-ha-ha.
s.b. 'All Round My Hat'? — that was never one of mine. What does it go like?
PUBLIC I couldn't tell you. I don't know it either.
PRIVATE Ha-ha-ha-ha-ha-ha-ha-ha.
s.b. And you say the boat was blue?
PUBLIC It doesn't matter. Forget it.
s.b. (*Justly, reasonably*) There was a brown one belonging to the doctor, and before that there was a wee flat-bottom — but it was green — or was it white? I'll tell you, you wouldn't be thinking of a punt — it could have been blue — one that the curate had down at the pier last summer —

PRIVATE'S *mocking laughter increases.* PUBLIC *rushes quickly into the shop.* PRIVATE, *still mocking, follows.*

A fine sturdy wee punt it was, too, and it could well have been the . . .

s.b. *sees that he is alone and tails off. Slowly he gets to his feet and goes towards the scullery door. He meets* MADGE *entering. She is dressed in outside clothes. She is very weary.*

MADGE What has you up?

S.B. Me? Aw, I took medicine and the cramps wouldn't let me sleep. I thought you were in bed?

MADGE I was over at Nelly's. The place was upside down.

S.B. There's nothing wrong, is there?

MADGE Not a thing.

S.B. The baby's strong and healthy?

MADGE Grand — grand.

S.B. That's all that matters.

MADGE They're going to call it Brigid.

S.B. Brigid — that's a grand name . . . Patrick, Brigid, and Colmcille . . .

She takes off her hat and coat.

Madge . . .

MADGE You'll get a cold padding about in yon rig.

S.B. Madge, I'll manage rightly, Madge, eh?

MADGE Surely you will.

S.B. I'll get one of Charley Bonner's boys to do the van on Tuesdays and Thursdays and I'll manage rightly?

MADGE This place is cold. Away off to bed.

S.B. It's not like in the old days when the whole countryside did with me; I needed the help then. But it's different now. I'll manage by myself now. Eh? I'll manage fine, eh?

MADGE Fine.

S.B. D'you mind the trouble we had keeping him at school just after he turned ten. D'you mind nothing would do him but he'd get behind the counter. And he had this wee sailor suit on him this morning —

MADGE A sailor suit? He never had a sailor suit.

S.B. Oh, he had, Madge. Oh, Madge, he had. I can see him, with his shoulders back, and the wee head up straight, and the mouth, aw, man, as set, and says he this morning, I can hear him saying it, says he, 'I'm not going to school. I'm going into my Daddy's business' — you know — all important — and, d'you mind, you tried to coax him to go to school, and not a move you could get out of him, and him as manly looking, and this wee sailor suit as smart looking on him, and — and — and at the heel of the hunt I had to go with him myself, the two of us, hand in hand, as happy as larks — we were that happy, Madge — and him dancing and chatting beside me — mind? — you couldn't get a word in edgeways with all the chatting he used to go through . . . Maybe, Madge, maybe it's because I could have been his grandfather, eh?

MADGE I don't know.

S.B. I was too old for her, Madge, eh?

MADGE I don't know. They're a new race — a new world.

S.B. (*Leaving*) In the wee sailor suit — all the chatting he used to go through . . . I don't know either . . .

MADGE (*Looking at case*) Tomorrow'll be sore on him (*Gar*): his heart'll break tomorrow, and all next week, and the week after maybe . . . Brigid — aye, it's all right — (*Trying out the sound of the name*) Brigid — Biddy — Biddy Mulhern — Brigid Mulhern — aye — like Madge Mulhern doesn't sound right — (*Trying it out*) — Madge Mulhern — Madge Mulhern — I don't know — It's too aul'-fashioned or something . . . Has he his cap? (*Finds it in the pocket of the coat. Also finds an apple*) . . . Aye, he has. And an apple, if you don't mind — for all his grief. He'll be all right. That Lizzy one'll look after him well, I suppose, if she can take time off from blatherin'. Garden front and back, and a TV in the house of lords — I'll believe them things when I see them! Never had much time for blatherin' women . . . (*Remembering*) An envelope . . .

> She takes two notes from her pocket, goes to the dresser, and finds an envelope. She puts the money into the envelope and slips the envelope into the coat pocket.

That'll get him a cup of tea on the plane. I had put

them two pounds by me to get my feet done on the fair day. But I can wait till next month. From what I hear there's no big dances between now and then ... (*She stands looking at the bedroom door*) So. I think that's everything ...

She raises her hand in a sort of vague benediction, then shuffles towards the scullery.

When the boss was his (*Gar's*) age, he was the very same as him: leppin', and eejitin' about and actin' the clown; as like as two peas. And when he's (*Gar*) the age the boss is now he'll turn out just the same. And although I won't be here to see it you'll find that he's learned nothin' in between times. That's people for you — they'd put you astray in the head if you thought long enough about them.

PUBLIC *and* PRIVATE *enter from the shop.*

PUBLIC You down too? Turning into a nightclub, this place.
MADGE I'm only getting back.
PUBLIC Well, how's the new Madge?
MADGE Strong and healthy — and that's all that matters. Were you and the boss chatting there?
PUBLIC When's the christening?
MADGE Sunday. After last Mass.
PUBLIC Madge Mulhern. Are you proud?
MADGE I'm just tired, son. Very tired.
PUBLIC You're sure there's nothing wrong, Madge?
MADGE If there was something wrong, wouldn't I tell you?
PRIVATE Of course she would. Who else has she?
PUBLIC Did you tell her she's getting an elephant out of my first wages?
MADGE Aye, so. The jars are up?
PUBLIC They are.
MADGE And the dishes washed?
PUBLIC All done.
MADGE I'll give you a call at half-six then.

PUBLIC   Madge — Madge, you'd let me know if — if he got sick or anything?

MADGE   Who else would there be?

PUBLIC   Just in case . . . not that it's likely — he'll outlive the whole of us . . .

MADGE   Goodnight.

PUBLIC   Sleep well, Madge.

MADGE   Sleep well, yourself.

> MADGE *goes off.* PUBLIC *and* PRIVATE *watch her shuffle off.*

PRIVATE   Watch her carefully, every movement, every gesture, every little peculiarity: keep the camera whirring; for this is a film you'll run over and over again — Madge Going to Bed On My Last Night At Home . . . Madge . . .

> PUBLIC *and* PRIVATE *go into bedroom.*

         God, boy, why do you have to leave? Why? Why?

PUBLIC   I don't know. I — I — I don't know.

> *Quick curtain.*

THE LOVES OF
CASS McGUIRE

Preface

In my description of the set I mention that the winged chair is never used throughout the play except during the three rhapsodies. These occur, one in each Act, as part of the formal pattern or ritual of the action; and the musical term, rhapsody, seemed to me to be the most accurate description of them. Each of the three characters who rhapsodize — Trilbe, Ingram and Cass — takes the shabby and unpromising threads of his or her past life and weaves it into a hymn of joy, a gay and rapturous and exaggerated celebration of a beauty that might have been. (And to pursue the musical imagery a stage further and, as a signpost for future productions, I consider this play to be a concerto in which Cass McGuire is the soloist.)

When I wrote the play I envisaged these rhapsodies being played against a musical background; and I chose Wagner because his *Tristan Und Isolde* legend has parallels of sorts in Cass McGuire's story. But during rehearsals I discovered that two of the actors spoke their rhapsodies with such grace and dignity, invested their soliloquies with such cantabile magic, that any background music would have been a distraction. So Wagner was dropped. But I have left the directions for the music in the text because subsequent companies may not be so fortunate in their rhapsodists and they may be grateful for the potent crutch that the 'Liebestod', for example, affords.

Brian Friel

Characters

HARRY McGUIRE
MOTHER, his mother
ALICE, his wife
DOM McGUIRE, his youngest son
CASS, his sister
TESSA, maid in Eden House
PAT QUINN
TRILBE COSTELLO
MR INGRAM
MRS BUTCHER
} all residents in Eden House

Time and place

The present in Ireland.
Act One: Two weeks before Christmas. Morning.
Act Two: One week before Christmas. Afternoon.
Act Three: Christmas Eve. Evening.

Set

A spacious, high-ceilinged room, somewhere between elegance
and austerity, which serves as the common room in Eden House,
a home for old people, and also as the living room in the home
of Harry McGuire, a wealthy Irish businessman/accountant.

The back wall consists of glass and French windows which
open out to a formal garden where a Cupid statue (illuminated)
is frozen in an absurd and impossible contortion.

A large marble fireplace on wall right (from the point of view
of the audience). Round mahogany table centre stage. Two fireside chairs and several upright chairs.

Downstage right, conspicuous in its isolation, is a big, winged
armchair. This is never used throughout the play except during
the three rhapsodies.

Upstage left, on a raised platform, is a bed, bedside table, and a
chair. This area will be Cass's bedroom in Eden House. It will
be black when the curtain first rises.

The Loves of Cass McGuire was first produced at the Helen Hayes Theater, New York, on 6 October 1966, by the David Merrick Arts Foundation, with the following cast:

MOTHER	Frances Brandt
DOM	Don Scardino
ALICE	Sylvia O'Brien
HARRY	Liam Redmond
CASS	Ruth Gordon
TESSA	Mary Greaney
PAT QUINN	Arthur O'Sullivan
TRILBE COSTELLO	Brenda Forbes
MR INGRAM	Dennis King
MRS BUTCHER	Dorothy Blackburn
Directed by	Hilton Edwards
Setting by	Lloyd Burlingame

It was first produced in Europe at the Abbey Theatre, Dublin, on 10 April 1967, with the following cast:

MOTHER	May Craig
DOM	Desmond Cave
ALICE	Máire Ní Néill
HARRY	Patrick Layde
CASS	Siobhán McKenna
TESSA	Máire Ní Ghráinne
PAT QUINN	Micheál Ó hAonghusa
TRILBE COSTELLO	Joan O'Hara
MR INGRAM	Bill Foley
MRS BUTCHER	Peggy Hayes
Directed by	Tomás Mac Anna

for Nano and Mary

ACT ONE

When the curtain rises Harry McGuire's MOTHER, *is sitting in her wheelchair and young* DOM *is huddled over the fire reading a* True Detective *comic.* MOTHER *is eighty-nine and almost totally deaf. Black satin blouse, a rug around her knees, and a black shawl which has fallen from her shoulders. Were she able to walk around she would have the authority and self-possession of a queen; but because she is invalided she just looks monumental. The serene, superior expression on her face never varies because nothing can touch her now. Her speech is slow and dignified.*

DOM, *aged seventeen, wears flannels and a school blazer. He is too big physically to be a schoolboy and not yet a young man, and is conscious of his gaucheness.*

He looks furtively at the door, takes a cigarette from his pocket, lights it, and inhales ostentatiously. Then goes on reading.

MOTHER   The next question is an easy one. Hands up any child who can tell me the name of the new cardinal. Anyone in the class know?

DOM   Captain Mike O'Shea, Vice-Squad Headquarters, 47th Precinct.

MOTHER   I beg your pardon?

DOM   'O'Shea flung his men around the building and dashed inside. The startled Samoan girls in varying forms of undress ran screaming into Madam Lulana's.' Wow-wow-wow-wow!

MOTHER   I'm afraid you'll have to raise your voice a little.

DOM   You're a deaf and doting old bag of guts. D'you know why Madam Lulana kept only Samoan girls? Because all they think of is sex, Gran — just like you and me. And no matter what climate they're in they never wear underclothes.

MOTHER   And I'm told that Cardinal Logue is a brilliant classical scholar, too.

DOM I'll tell you a secret, Gran: when I leave school I'm going to set up a business of my own, right here in town — a kip house. And I'll make you the madam. And anyone that tries to get too smart you'll give them the old knee in the groin — one-two-three — Gorgeous Gran McGuire, The Sailors' Terror!

MOTHER I want everyone to repeat that ten times.

DOM Gorgeous Gran McGuire, The Sailors' Terror; Gorgeous Gran McGuire, The Sailors' Terror; Gorgeous Gran McGuire, The Sailors' . . .

He breaks off when he hears his mother approach left. Throws the cigarette into the fire, after a desperate effort to nick it, and dashes back to the table where his school books are impressively arrayed. Sticks the True Detective *into his jacket pocket. He is studying when his mother enters.*

ALICE *is in her fifties. She is expensively, but not attractively, dressed. She notices* DOM's *scramble to get a school book opened. She is carrying chairbacks for the fireside chairs.*

ALICE I thought you were studying.

DOM Gran and I were discussing the hierarchy.

ALICE I hear your father's car. Put your books away and take your grandmother with you into the dining room.

DOM Lunch ready?

ALICE Yours is. We aren't eating until later.

DOM What about Auntie Cass?

ALICE Still asleep.

DOM Can I bring up her tray?

ALICE No.

DOM I've bought a bar of chocolate for her.

ALICE I said she's asleep.

DOM No wonder. I could hear her singing at the top of her voice half the night.

ALICE That'll do, Dom.

DOM She must be feeling terrible today. Just as well Madam

184

Gran is deaf. (*Articulating into* GRAN's *ear*) She called you, her own mother, a Big Cow!

ALICE Dom, please!

MOTHER You'll not forget this day.

DOM (*Solemnly*) It's engraved on our hearts in letters of gold.

> *Enter* HARRY *left. Good black coat, soft hat, carrying a paper. He is sixty but looks younger. A measured middle-of-the-road man, well in control of himself. He has his mother's soft attractive voice. He gives* ALICE *a perfunctory kiss, hands her the coat and hat, and sits at the fire.*

ALICE You're late, aren't you?

HARRY I had a few calls to make. How are you today, Mother? Dom?

ALICE Will you have a drink?

HARRY Brandy, please. And nothing in it.

ALICE You and I are having a light lunch.

HARRY ?

ALICE The Traynors are coming to dinner tonight.

HARRY Hell.

ALICE (*Leaving*) They're your friends.

HARRY (*To* DOM) How's the work going?

DOM All right.

HARRY I phoned the college and told them you had a cold. (*Pause*) How is it?

DOM All right.

HARRY You're sure you don't want a grind during the Christmas holidays?

DOM No . . . no . . .

HARRY I can get young Coyle to come to the house, you know.

DOM No, it's . . . all right.

HARRY A matter for yourself. (*Nods and smiles at* GRAN) Mother.

MOTHER They tell me the beaches are crowded.

HARRY It's freezing outside.

MOTHER I'm thinking seriously of investing in a parasol.

ALICE *enters with a drink and a letter. She hands both to* HARRY.

ALICE A letter from Betty. They bought that house after all.

HARRY How much?

ALICE Seventeen thousand.

HARRY Very nice.

ALICE And they're coming for Christmas . . . with the baby.

HARRY That's good news. We'll have a full house. (*Opening letter*) Mother seems to think it's summer.

ALICE She has been teaching me Latin roots all morning. Anything fresh downtown?

HARRY Not a thing. Here?

ALICE All quiet so far.

HARRY She hasn't appeared yet?

ALICE Not a sound. Did you find out where she was? What happened?

HARRY Where was she not. I called in Sweeney's pub on the way home and paid for the breakages. Apparently every table in the lounge was an antique.

ALICE And the police?

HARRY The sergeant was with me. I squared that. Dom!

ALICE And the clay on her shoes — how did she get it?

HARRY Bring my briefcase in from the car, son, please.

ALICE You've got to do something, Harry.

The subdued domestic atmosphere is suddenly and violently shattered by CASS's *shouts. She charges on stage (either from the wings or from the auditorium) shouting in her raucous Irish-American voice. Everyone on stage freezes.*

CASS *is a tall, bulky woman of seventy. She wears a gaudy jacket (because of the cold weather) over gaudy clothes; rings; earrings; two voluminous handbags which never leave her. She smokes incessantly and talks loudly and coarsely (deliberately at times). Ugly is too strong a word to describe her, and plain not nearly strong enough. If she ever had good features there is no trace of them now. A life of hard*

> *physical work has ravaged her. Only her spirit is strong and resilient.*

CASS What the hell goes on here?

ALICE Cass — !

HARRY Cass, you can't break in, Cass, at — !

> CASS *addresses the audience directly. They are her friends, her intimates. The other people on stage are interlopers.*

CASS Cass! Cass! Cass! I go to the ur-eye-nal for five minutes and they try to pull a quick one on me!

HARRY The story has begun, Cass.

CASS The story begins where I say it begins, and I say it begins with me stuck in the gawddam workhouse! So you can all get the hell outa here!

HARRY The story begins in the living room of my home, a week after your return to Ireland. This is my living room and we're going to show bit by bit how you came —

CASS (*Looking around set*) Sure! Real nice and cosy! (*Directly to audience*) The home of my brother, Mister Harold McGuire, accountant, brick manufacturer, big-deal Irish businessman. Married to Alice, only child of Joe Connor, the lawyer, who couldn't keep his hands off young girls.

HARRY That's enough, Cass!

CASS Four kids: one a lady doctor; one an architect; one a clergyman; and one a student — if I may say so. What else do they (*audience*) need to know?

ALICE Harry, for heaven's sake — !

CASS (*Looking around*) Yeah, this'll do for the workhouse. We have swank windows, too, opening out on to a garden, only we don't have a nekked kid holding his hands in front of his rice crispies all day.

HARRY This isn't fair to us, Cass. It must be shown slowly and in sequence why you went to Eden House.

CASS I didn't go, Harry boy, I was stuck in! Oh, sure, sure, go back and show them how patient you all were with the terrible woman that appeared out of the blue after fifty-two years! — how her Momma doesn't reconnize her, and how her brother is embarrassed by her, and how Alice — Jeeze, yes — I think poor Alice is afraid of her! You afraid of me, Alice?

ALICE   Harry — !

HARRY   Cass, I insist we unfold the story in proper sequence!

CASS   And then this day she goes and visits her father's grave — that's how she got the clay on her shoes, sweetie — and then gets plastered and kicks up a bit of a shindy in a downtown bar, and someone calls the cops, and someone keeps screaming, 'It's Mr McGuire's sister, the returned Yankee!' and then her folks have this big solemn meeting — I just saved you all that — and decide to stick her into the workhouse and —

HARRY   Eden House is a rest home for elderly people.

CASS   Listen to him! He could sell fur coats to chow dawgs in the Sahara. So we're going to skip all that early stuff, all the explanations, all the excuses, and we'll start off later in the story — from here. (*Light up bed area*) My suite in the workhouse, folks. Drop in and see me sometime, OK? Where the hell was I? (*Remembering*) Yeah — the homecoming — back to the little green isle. Well, that's all over and done with — history; and in my book yesterday's dead and gone and forgotten. So let's pick it up from there, with me in the . . . rest home. (*To* HARRY *who is about to go offstage*) Go ahead and call out the National Guard if you like; but you're not going to move me! What's this goddam play called? *The Loves of Cass McGuire*. Who's Cass McGuire? Me! Me! And they'll see what happens in the order *I* want them to see it; and there will be no going back into the past!

MOTHER   The present Chief Justice is a past pupil of mine.

CASS   And I'm Garibaldi's mistress. And this ain't no visiting day in Eden House. So get the hell outa here, all of you. Go on, go on; clear. You, too, professor (*Dom*). The less you see of your old Auntie Cass the better, because she ain't got no money, and we suspect she doesn't go to church, and we're not too sure if she's a maiden aunt at all. (ALICE *quickly signals to her family to leave*)

HARRY You'll regret this, Cass.

CASS I regret nuthin'.

HARRY You may think you can seal off your mind like this, but you can't. The past will keep coming back to you.

CASS I live in the present, Harry boy! Right here and now!

HARRY We have a point of view, too, and in fairness to all of us — (*At the word 'fairness' she makes an extravagant dismissing gesture with her hand*)

CASS Aaaaaaaaagh!

> *She moves into her bedroom and sits on the bed.* HARRY *holds a brief consultation with his family and apparently they decide to go away because they move off. Now that she is alone with the audience, her friends,* CASS *is more subdued. She talks to them almost confidentially. But the past scene has disturbed her more than she would like to admit: her hands are shaking. She fumbles for a cigarette and lights it. Then she makes up. During all this business she addresses the audience.*

Well, that stirred things up a bit, dinnit? The past . . . poof! (*To herself in the hand mirror*) Ugh! It's not like whiskey, beautiful; the years don't improve it. (*Remembering*) Like there was this bum used to come in for breakfast every morning into this joint on the Lower East Side I worked in. Boy, you should ov seen his hands! Joe Balowski, that was his name; they said he was a concert pianist or something before he messed hisself up. Anyways, Joe would look at me like I was the blazing July sun or something, and he would say, 'Honey, I pulled the chain on better-looking things.' Asked me to marry him, too. Every Friday night. When he was drunk. (*Producing half-bottle of whiskey from one of the bags*) Hellova guy, Joe. (*Drinks straight from bottle*) To the future . . . Shhhh.

> INGRAM *appears outside French windows. After a few
> seconds he is joined by* COSTELLO.

See that? That's old Ingram. She's probably there with
him — Trilbe Costello. Trilbe — now there's a name
for you! I sez to her the first day, 'You some kind of
hat or something?' They're gooks, OK, real gooks,
phew . . . He played the organ in some swank English
cathedral, he tells me; and she was — you know — a
professor of speech and elocution and all that crap.
Real swank. Always talking about poetry and music
and stuff. And as Pat Quinn sez — you'll see him
around, too; a good guy, Pat — as he sez, you'd think
they'd be past all that now, wouldn't you? Kinda
sweet though, aren't they? And there's something
about old Ingram, I dunno, maybe it's the quiet way
he talks but he reminds me of Harry.

> *In the gloom immediately beyond Cass's bed* HARRY
> *appears in his dressing gown and slippers. He talks
> softly, gently, and* CASS *answers him in a remote tone
> at first. He looks at her but she stares straight down
> into the auditorium. This is the first of the memory
> sequences that haunt Cass. Some of them she keeps at
> bay by talking resolutely to the audience. But some
> are so potent that she is seduced into reliving them.*

HARRY You should have let me run you out in the car, Cass.

CASS I wanted to be alone.

HARRY The grave's nice. And the flowers. Alice planted them.

CASS Pretty flowers.

HARRY We got a stonemason up from Cork to do the head-
stone.

CASS I sent ten dollars. All I had at the time.

HARRY Apparently Father had been living for over twenty
years in a . . . sort of dosshouse, right in the centre
of Glasgow. They lived in a two-roomed flat on the

ground floor.

CASS Three weeks buried before I even knew.

HARRY He must have told this woman he was a widower because she asked me how long Mother was dead. I didn't . . . tell Alice that.

CASS (*Briskly to audience*) There was this guy owned the joint I worked in . . .

HARRY He looked much older than seventy-six. The woman said he had been invalided for the last five years.

CASS — I told you about it — a breakfast counter . . .

HARRY Oh, yes, I forgot: she said Father talked a lot about his daughter, Cass.

CASS Jeff Olsen was his name. And he had this dawg, see, this bitch, and we lived in this two-roomed apartment . . .

HARRY What age were you when he went away, Cass? Fifteen? Sixteen?

CASS — and when that bitch would get high she would yap-yap-yap, and all the dawgs in the block they would yap-yap-yap back — Oh Jeeze — until everyone was screaming murder.

HARRY I was only five when he left. I have no memory of him at all.

CASS So, Jeff, first he got that bitch de-sexed; and then when that done no good he got it de-barked — you know, so that it couldn't bark no more; and there was this bum, Slinger, from down South, sometimes he took coffee in our joint, and when Jeff told him about the dawg being de-sexed and de-barked, Slinger said, 'Nothin' left for it but to dee-cease, Jeff.' Real funny guy, you know . . .

HARRY She knew all about his job on the old railway, and how you would hide in the signal box with him when you should have been at school with Mother.

CASS (*Brutally*) That's finished! All over!

HARRY *drifts into the darkness of the wings.*

And I don't go in for the fond memory racket! For

fifty-two years I work one block away from Skid Row
— deadbeats, drags, washouts, living in the past!
Washing, scrubbing, fixing sandwiches — work so
that you don't have no time to think, and if you did
you thought of the future. (*Fumbling greedily for the
bottle*) The past's gone. Good luck to it. And Gawd
bless it.

> CASS *drinks. Then lights another cigarette.*
> TESSA, *the maid, enters from the right. She is dis-
> tributing clean pillowslips for the beds. The boredom
> and drudgery of working with old people have made
> her weary at eighteen. She is untidy (until Act Three)
> and protects herself from the senility around her by
> an acquired casualness of manner. When she sees her
> CASS hides the bottle.*

TESSA You're almost a week in the house now and you know
fine well you're not allowed in your bedroom between
breakfast and teatime.

CASS Sweet little Tessa.

TESSA And another thing: unless you're sick you're supposed to be down in the oratory for Mass in the
morning.

CASS What time's that at?

TESSA Seven.

CASS I'm always in the DTs till ten at least.

TESSA Will you move? How can I fix the bed with you on it?

CASS You've got a point there.

> *While* TESSA *changes the pillowslip* CASS *gathers her
> things to go to the common room.*

TESSA Are you a bed wetter?

CASS Only when I'm waiting to be raped, sweetie.

> TESSA *goes off left.* CASS *goes upstage. At the same
> time* PAT QUINN *enters right. A small, plump man.
> Assured, confident, cunning. The know-all of the*

institution. Anxious to please. In his early sixties.

    Hi, Pat.

PAT How are you, Miss McGuire?

CASS Where is everybody?

PAT All in bed, pretending they're sick, on account of the cold weather.

CASS Ain't they got no peat around here now?

PAT The boiler's busted. But by the time they get round to fixing it I'll be gone — back to the nephew's farm.

CASS (*Not listening, searching bag*) You bet.

PAT He has 500 acres and 350 head of cattle. I'm only temporary here, you know, until himself and the missus move into the new house.

CASS Same here. I'm temporary, too.

PAT He's chairman of the Young Farmers' League.

CASS Big deal.

PAT And I keep an eye on the men when he's away at the meetings.

CASS You going downtown today, Pat?

PAT I'm on my way out now for the papers.

CASS You know that store right next the post office?

PAT What place is that now?

CASS The first store below the post office on the same side.

PAT Is it Sweeney's pub you're talking about?

CASS You go in there and ask the bartender — Tommy's his name — you ask him for the same again for Miss McGuire.

PAT The same again . . . ?

CASS And have one on me outa the change.

PAT Is it . . . drink . . . for you?

CASS It's not baby powder I'm looking for!

PAT Holy God, if the matron caught me at that game!

CASS (*Taking back money*) Gimme. Someone else'll get it for me.

PAT No, no, it's all right. A wee drop now and again is good for the health.

CASS That's it, Pat. Look at the woman it made of me.

TRILBE COSTELLO *bursts in, followed by* MR INGRAM. *She is in her early seventies but is full of energy. She has been an elocution teacher all her life — but without the necessary qualifications and consequently never recognized by the education department — and her speech and manner both reflect this: she articulates fanatically and is inclined to domineer. At the same time one is conscious of an insecurity behind the extravagant exterior.* MR INGRAM *is a small, withered, testy, nervous old man. He is English. He is so frail and hesitant that he seldom finishes a sentence. He carries large volumes with him everywhere he goes. Now, as they enter,* TRILBE *is consulting some sheets of paper and at the same time addressing an imaginary group of people.* CASS *is still new to* TRILBE *and views her with open wonder.* PAT *knows* TRILBE *well and humours her.*

TRILBE Before I announce the results of the competition I would like to take this opportunity to thank all those young boys and girls who came up here so bravely and spoke their test piece with such courage and gusto. A very sincere thank you to you, indeed.

PAT There you are, now.

CASS Hi.

TRILBE (*Softly*) Morning. Morning. I'm adjudicating at a speech festival for junior schools next week. Just a little rehearsal.

CASS Sure, sure — you just blast ahead.

TRILBE You know 'The Highwayman', don't you?

CASS Which one? Where I worked they were all —

TRILBE 'The wind was a torrent of darkness among the gusty trees,

The moon was a ghostly galleon tossed upon cloudy seas . . . '

PAT There's speaking for you!

TRILBE Noyes.

CASS Well, maybe just a little —

TRILBE Alfred J Noyes. Not his best but it fires the young

194

imagination. Next Thursday. You're welcome if you choose to come. (*Adjudicating again and moving slowly off*) I liked in particular competitors number 7, 8 and 13 whose sense of rhythm stirred me. 'Tlot-tlot in the empty silence, tlot-tlot in the echoing night.' Thrilling.

INGRAM   It is our experience . . . we find . . . we find that one doesn't feel the cold so . . . so . . . if one keeps on the move and doesn't . . .

TRILBE   Mr Ingram!

INGRAM   Coming, Miss Costello. We walk round past the refectory and along the . . . it's a very pleasant little . . . good morning . . .

> CASS *looks after them as they exit right.*

CASS   Boy, would Ed Sullivan eat them up!

PAT   Adjudicating! That one — sure she wasn't even qualified to teach that elocution stuff! Running about the countryside from the nuns to the brothers, scrounging meals and picking up an odd shilling here and there. A tramp with notions — that's what that one is!

CASS   (*Mopping her face*) Can she spit!

PAT   The Costellos from Ardbeg — didn't I know them all in my day. All high-falutin' chat and not a penny to scratch themselves with. Your mother there could tell you all about them.

CASS   I'm sure *she* could. You going downtown, Pat, or are you not?

PAT   (*Leaving*) I'll be back in ten minutes. The same again for Miss McGuire. And no one'll know a word about it. By the way, boiled bacon for dinner, and stewed apples after.

> *He exits.* CASS *sits down in the common room, lights a cigarette, and addresses the audience.*

CASS   Wonderful! And prunes for breakfast. All I need now is to go on a rum bash. Funny title, too, innit? *The Loves of Cass McGuire* — like I was Mata Hari or something. I'm seventy, by the way. And Harry, he's pushing sixty. And Momma, she's . . . gee, Momma must be eighty-nine now . . . yeah . . . 'cos Father he was three years older than her. He sailed off when I was a kid — just to fill you in on the background — 'cos Momma and him didn't hit it off too well when he took a drop. Never wrote nor nothing. Just got hisself lost in Scotland. So, when I was eighteen I kinda got the same idea, you know; not that Momma and me didn't hit it off; we got on OK, I guess, but . . . Well, what the hell was there to do around here, I mean. Oh boy, she raised Cain, I'll tell you; real school teacher stuff; sent for Father O'Neill to speak to me and all . . . (*Remembering*) Now, whatever happened to him? Dead, I guess. He was some guy, you know: big and heavy and this voice like a foghorn. Should ov been in the marines. (*Laughs gently*) The night he caught Connie Crowley guzzling the hell outa me below the crooked bridge! 'You bastard,' he sez — well, mebbe he didn't use that word — 'Are you comfortable in your sinning?' And poor Connie, Jeeze, I could feel his knees going, he sez, 'Please, no, Father. The grass's damp.' Anyways, I saved up and gathered the passage money and left a note for Momma and one for Connie . . . and off I blew . . . (*looks around the room*) and back I come home to my own people — and they have this big solemn meeting — and decide to kick me out!

> HARRY *strides on from right, his coat across his arm.*
> *He is very stern but tries to control himself.* CASS *is*
> *aware of what he is saying to her but talks on*
> *resolutely to the audience.*

HARRY I've just been told what happened this morning, Cass.
CASS So now you know it all.
HARRY And I will not have you insult Alice about her father.
CASS Harry's four kids, boy, they got on good: Betty, she's a doc in London , and Tom's a priest, and Aidan's an architect, and Dom —

HARRY But this is only the last of many, many insults.

CASS Fine kids — I haven't met them yet — but you'll see, they'll be along one of these days to meet their Auntie Cass —

HARRY And before I say any more I want you to know that the decision I've made is entirely my own. Alice had nothing to do with it.

CASS Betty, she has a baby — fourteen months — I seen pictures of it.

HARRY In fact she has just asked me not to mention this until after Christmas.

CASS (*Unable to hold her own line*) So I left a note for Momma and one for Connie . . .

HARRY But I said no, definitely no.

CASS They tell me Connie's a big-shot in Dublin now — two department stores and married and all and a chauffeur-driven car . . .

HARRY And I can tell you that Dom is missing none of your antics, and at his impressionable age, too.

CASS So I left a note for him, see; one for him and one for Momma; but he must never have gotten his.

HARRY But that's all finished, all finished. And to get back to my decision —

> CASS *cannot fight the memory any longer. She suddenly wheels wildly round to him. She almost screams her lines.*

CASS Say out what you're trying to say, Harry! Speak up and say it out straight!

HARRY Cass, I've come to the decision —

CASS Well?

> ALICE *appears at the door left,* DOM *and* MOTHER *at the door right.* CASS's *volume drops rapidly.*

HARRY I've arranged for you to go into Eden House next Monday.

CASS Where?

HARRY   It's a rest home for elderly people, at the end of the town, near the black church.

ALICE   Harry, I asked you to wait until —

CASS   That the workhouse?

HARRY   It's where the workhouse used to be.

ALICE   There's no urgency, Cass. You can stay with us — over Christmas.

CASS   (*Incredulous*) Jeeze, the work—

HARRY   It's not the workhouse. It's a rest home.

CASS   (*Totally broken*) I'm not going.

HARRY   Every week the bank will pay your board and send you an allowance.

CASS   I'm not going.

ALICE   They're very particular about who they take in there, Cass.

HARRY   And you're under no obligation whatever to me. You're entirely independent.

CASS   I haven't a dime.

HARRY   Your own money will support you adequately.

CASS   I haven't a dime.

HARRY   It's all intact.

CASS   I'm not going.

ALICE   Any time you feel like coming out to visit us . . .

CASS   (*In desperation*) Momma . . . ?

MOTHER You'll remember this day.

CASS   Dommie boy . . . ?

DOM   I'll call on my way from school every —

HARRY   Dom! You're too sensible to make a scene, Cass.

She surveys them slowly. Pause.

CASS   Next Monday?

ALICE   I think we should wait until after —

HARRY   Next Monday. It's all settled.

CASS *turns her back on them and talks to the audience. She is still very, very subdued. The brashness has vanished.*

CASS (*Searching for any words*) Monday for wealth, Tuesday for health, Wednesday the best day of all; Thursday for crosses, Friday for losses. (*Driving herself into a sort of gaiety*) I wear sneakers, you know, with the toes cut out 'cos my feet, boy, they sure give me hell standing behind that counter. Fine on a Monday morning, and not too bad on Tuesday, but by Wednesday — Jeeze — way up like this; and for the rest of the week they're throbbing like they had the neuralgia.

> *The others drift out quietly.*

And this doc I go to, boy, is he a comedian, he sez: You gotta spend the mosta the day in a recumbent posture. No filthy cracks, Mister, I sez, in case you haven't noticed, I'm a lady, 'cos I thought he was making his move. But Jeff he told me what the doc meant, and when I knew what it was I just laughed — you know — serving coffee in a recumbent posture! . . . Hell, this is no fun for you, huh? No way to make friends and influence people. *The Loves of Cass McGuire* — huh! Where did he get that title from anyways? (*Rising to her feet. As if confused*) Where have all the real people gone?

INGRAM (*Off, reading*) 'At that time young Tristan lived at the court of his uncle, King Mark.'

> *Immediately* CASS *hears* TRILBE *and* INGRAM *approaching, she pulls open her bag, takes out a compact, and powders herself rapidly.*

CASS Abbott and Costello again! Maybe they'll give us a laugh.

> *They enter.* INGRAM *is reading from one of the books he always carries and* TRILBE *is listening to him attentively.*

TRILBE We've been round three times. I feel positively intoxicated.

CASS   Boy, you're lucky.

INGRAM 'And there he captivated everybody with his good looks and his minstrelsy . . .'

CASS   Don't he get tired doing the mobile library act?

TRILBE (*Confidentially*) His Wagner, m'dear. Won't trust them with anyone.

CASS   Wagner?

INGRAM You know Wagner?

CASS   Do I know Wagner! Voted for him every election.

INGRAM Elect— ?

CASS   Best mayor New York ever had.

TRILBE There you are. It's a small world, isn't it. By the way, m'dear, what *is* your Christian name?

CASS   Cass.

TRILBE Cass? Cass? It's certainly not Cass. (*To* INGRAM) Did you ever hear of anyone being christened Cass?

CASS   I was baptized Catherine.

TRILBE Agh, Catherine! Now we have it! I'll call you Catherine and I insist you call me Trilbe. (*Softly*) His Christian name is Meurice. He is convinced his father did it to him on purpose.

CASS   Couldn't we call him Buster or something?

TRILBE (*Seriously assessing the name*) Buster . . .

CASS   Or what about . . . yeah, Pop! Huh?

TRILBE I don't think he'd like that, m'dear. He has been Mr Ingram for so long now. (*Aloud*) Continue reading, Mr Ingram. (*Softly*) His explosives are very vital —

CASS   Gee . . .

TRILBE — but his vowels are inclined to be flabby.

CASS   Oh, I'm sorry to hear —

INGRAM (*Irritably*) If you would only keep quiet.

TRILBE Nobody's saying a word. (*Softly*) I've my adjudication almost ready.

CASS   Yeah?

TRILBE It should be quite impressive. Shhhhhh.

INGRAM 'But in a duel with the warrior Morhol he was seriously wounded and went to Ireland to recuperate.'

TRILBE I can't hear you. Catherine can't hear you. More chest. More lungs.

INGRAM 'And there he met Isolde, the daughter of the Queen — '

TRILBE Better.

INGRAM '— who ministered to him and tended him and restored him to former vigour.'

CASS (*To audience*) Jeeze, didn't I tell you!

INGRAM 'But when his uncle, King Mark, was told of the beauty of Isolde, he dispatched Tristan to fetch Isolde for himself, and Tristan reluctantly set out to do the king's bidding. As he was bringing her back by boat both he and Isolde drank by mistake the potion which was to make them inseparable lovers.'

CASS (*To audience*) What the hell's keeping Pat Quinn with my potion of hooch!

TRILBE (*Cosily*) It's the part about the exile I like best.

INGRAM 'The king married Isolde, and although his spies were constantly on the lookout, she and Tristan met frequently in secret. But finally the king learned of their trysts and exiled Tristan to the coast of Brittany.'

TRILBE Ah!

INGRAM 'And there he married another Isolde but his love was always for the first, the Irish, Isolde. Eventually, having been wounded again . . . '

CASS (*To audience*) That guy should ov bought hisself accident insurance.

> *At this* TRILBE *gets to her feet and comes over to* CASS. *She has got to play the following sequence on two levels at once: she is her normal, vital self, inquisitive and anxious to help; and at the same time she must convey the first inklings of an 'otherness', of the private world she and* INGRAM *have created and take refuge in occasionally.*

TRILBE M'dear, who are you addressing?

CASS You just carry on. I'm sorta — you know — having an odd word with the folks out there. (*Indicates audience*)

TRILBE Who?

CASS The folks.

TRILBE *shades her eyes against the footlights and searches the auditorium. She looks back at* CASS *and again at the auditorium. She sees no one out there.*

TRILBE Catherine, m'dear, we are your only world now. We have the truth for you.

CASS Yeah?

TRILBE Join with us, Catherine, for we have the truth.

CASS Sure . . . sure . . .

INGRAM May I?

TRILBE We know what is real, Catherine.

INGRAM Does anybody wish to listen?

TRILBE Mr Ingram, I'm going to sit in the winged chair.

INGRAM It's almost lunchtime and —

TRILBE I haven't sat in it for three whole weeks, and now I wish to remember.

INGRAM I really think you ought to wait until —

TRILBE The past, and all the riches I have, and all that nourishes me.

INGRAM Very well, Miss Costello.

TRILBE Mr Ingram knows my story. And I know his. And we tell our stories to one another occasionally when we're alone . . .

> *She sits in the winged chair. Very gently bring up Wagner's 'Venusberg' music (omit first two minutes of it).* TRILBE *and* INGRAM *relax into the mood and respond to one another.* CASS *is not in their sphere. She watches and listens alertly, cautiously, nervously.*

I was called Trilbe because I was born the year the book was published; and Father loved it so much — he was so romantic — and he was so fond of Paris. And it was springtime, and he and I were travelling in Provence —

INGRAM In the south of France.

TRILBE — and we were spending a few days in Arles when I met him, Gordon —

INGRAM Gordon McClelland.

TRILBE — from Edinburgh. And Father was so proper, you know; so proper and so stern, poor Father.

INGRAM And what is your profession, young man?

TRILBE I love your daughter, sir; I love your daughter, Trilbe.

INGRAM I see. I see.

TRILBE Father always said that when he was puzzled. And in the afternoons, when he would go to his room to rest, Gordon and I would walk hand in hand along the country roads —

INGRAM Between the poplars.

TRILBE — in the shafts of golden sun; and every so often we would stop, and he would touch my face with his fingertips and whisper to me —

INGRAM My little golden Trilbe.

TRILBE And I would tremble with delight at his gentleness and his beauty and his love for me. And when we married we bought a chateau —

INGRAM On the banks of the Rhône.

TRILBE — and had servants and music and wine and still days of sun and children with golden hair, named after princes and princesses; and we travelled and travelled and travelled — Russia, India, Persia, Palestine — never stopping, always moving —

INGRAM My little golden Trilbe.

TRILBE — sleeping in strange beds, eating strange food . . .

INGRAM Goodbye . . . goodbye . . .

TRILBE Travelling, moving, visiting strange places, meeting new people, with Gordon beside me.

INGRAM My little golden Trilbe.

TRILBE And the servants and the music and the wine and the travel and the poetry and his love for me and my love for him . . . all so real. My Gordon from Arles on the Rhône, my prince from Edinburgh in Provence . . . my father resting in the afternoon, my journeys to the Nile and the Volga, the road to Samarkand, the road, the traveller's road . . .

INGRAM Trilbe.

TRILBE Gordon McClelland.

INGRAM Golden Trilbe.

TRILBE My highland prince.

INGRAM My little golden Trilbe.

TRILBE Say it slowly after me: 'But I, being poor, have only my dreams . . .'

INGRAM Our truth.

TRILBE — 'I have spread my dreams under your feet.
Tread softly because you tread on my dreams.'

INGRAM Our truth.

TRILBE Love was his profession. And Father was such a sensible man.

She rises slowly to her feet and offers her arm to INGRAM.

You may lead me to the dining room, Mr Ingram.

INGRAM My pleasure.

He takes her arm and they exit like a king and his queen. The music fades with them. CASS *stares in naked astonishment after them. She is still gaping at the exit left when* DOM *appears in the shadows right. She does not turn to face him but answers him automatically: she is still thinking of what has happened.*

DOM Psst! Auntie Cass!

CASS Hi . . .

DOM Did you live with Jeff Olsen, the man that owned the place you worked in, Auntie Cass?

CASS (*Nodding: Yes*) Poor good Jeff . . . lost a leg in the Great War. . .

DOM Were you ever married to him?

CASS Had a wife somewhere on the west coast . . .

DOM Did you sleep with him?

CASS And when the pain in the missing leg got real bad I stroked his forehead . . . (*At this* DOM *laughs coarsely and darts into the wings.* CASS *turns round front. Calling softly, vaguely*) Jeff? . . . Jeff? . . . Connie?

Enter PAT *left.*

PAT I could smell the bacon on the street. Boys, but I could eat a horse.

CASS Hi, Pat . . .

PAT Are you all right? There's nothing wrong with you, is there?

CASS Pat, tell me, Pat, what did her father do?

PAT Whose father?

CASS Trilbe Costello's.

PAT He was a French polisher by trade but he couldn't hold a job. Never sober. Ended up as a sort of caretaker out at the greyhound track. Always wore wellingtons and a greasy bowler hat. Your mother could tell you all about —

CASS Did she travel?

PAT Didn't I tell you! Never lit — running from one school to the next, and hoping for a square meal.

CASS Or married — was she ever married to a guy from Scotland?

PAT For God's sake, woman, she wouldn't know the difference between a bull and a clucking hen! What the hell's come over you?

CASS I dunno, Pat. Jeeze, I dunno.

PAT You're foundered with the cold. Here's the stuff'll put some life into you. (*Produces bottle*)

CASS Yeah . . . yeah . . . phew!

PAT Have you a glass in your bag?

CASS I don't need a glass. Boy, is this a gook joint! Jeeze, a girl would want to have her wits about her here! (*To audience*) Gordon! What d'you know! Almost had me fooled, too. (*To* PAT) But I can handle gooks — spent a lifetime handling gooks. Skid Row, I'll tell you, it was full of them, full of them . . . (*She drinks from the bottle*) . . . And I'll handle this, too, Pat, huh?

> PAT *is watching her cautiously. He decides it is best to humour her, just as he did earlier with* TRILBE.

PAT Here's your change.

CASS Keep it. You bet, they'll not wear Cass McGuire down,

huh?

PAT You're looking better already.

CASS No, siree. I'll ride this gook joint.

PAT Now you're talking.

CASS By Jeeze, I'll ride it, Pat, huh.

PAT That's fighting language!

CASS And I'll beat it, too, Pat.

PAT I'm with you there.

CASS We'll beat it together, Pat!

PAT Up the Republic!

CASS Together, Pat, we'll beat it, boy! It'll not get us down. No, siree!

Quick curtain.

ACT TWO

When the curtain rises CASS *is sitting on her bed, making up Christmas parcels. A miniature Christmas tree sits on the pillow. She is smoking and has a bottle at hand. She talks directly to the audience.*

CASS Hi. I made damn sure to be in possession this time.
I'll tell you. And I hope you don't get the 'flu from
me 'cos nearly everybody in this joint got it — even
matron; and, boy, the bug that put her on her back
deserves a citation. Buster Ingram, he got it too, and
Pat, and most of the folks in the upper wing. Me —
I took precautions. (*Drinks*) But the whole house is
kinda depressed, you know. That's why I fixed this
(*tree*) up for the common room and bought a couple
of presents. Not that I ever went in for this Christmas
schmaltz. Hell, we open Christmas morning at 5.30
same as usual; probably the busiest morning in the
whole year; and the stream of poor bastards coming
howling for black coffee — you should ov seen them!
Happy Christmas — Jeeze! (*Softly*) But one Christmas
night, 19 and 42 it was, Jeff and me were sitting listening to the radio or something, and Jeff he jumps
up and sez, 'Hell, Cass, I almost forgot!', and he
hobbles into the kitchen and comes back with this
tiny box, and he sez, 'Here', like it was burning him;
and I opens it, and there's this brooch, made like it
was a shamrock with three leaves and all, and with
green and white and orange diamonds plastered all
over it — only they were glass, I guess. And, hell, I
dunno what happened to me; maybe I was drunk or
something; but I began to cry. And poor Jeff he didn't
know where to look, and he shouted, 'Jeeze, Cass, I
gave some Irish bum a ham and cheese sandwich for

it day before yesterday. You don't think I bought it?'
And, Gawd, I cried all the more then . . . must ov been
real drunk . . . you know, he was so kind to me . . .
(*Raucously*) Hell, I hate Sundays!

Enter TESSA *with a brush and dustpan.* CASS *hides the
bottle.*

TESSA Look at the mess the floor's in!
CASS I'll clean it up.
TESSA Some people were reared in a byre. (*Picks up one of the
presents, a spray of artificial flowers*) Aw, isn't that lovely!
CASS Like it?
TESSA They're nicer than real.
CASS Yeah.
TESSA And I have a pink dress, too.
CASS Well . . .
TESSA Would you ever?
CASS What?
TESSA Give them to me.
CASS (*Gently*) Sweetie, I wouldn't give you the time of day.
TESSA You dirty, mean aul' pagan! (*So refined*) Thanks be to
God *I* was at Mass this morning.

She swaggers off and CASS *watches her with amusement.*

CASS There goes a walking saint. It's (*the flowers*) for Trilbe;
and these gloves are for Buster Ingram; and I got
socks (*holds one up*) for Pat. I thought they went in
pairs, these things. (*She finds the other*) They do. Poor
guy, always talking about that nephew of his taking
him away. Some nephew, I'll tell you. Which reminds
me of something he was telling me the other day:
Ingram's married! What d'you know about that! (*Looks
around before she continues*) He was only a young guy,
see, slashing away at the organ in his swank English
cathedral, and this day in comes this hoofer from a
nearby music hall — you know — a dancer, flinging

her legs up and making guys sweat. Anyways, Buster he sees her and falls hard for her and can't let her outa his sight, not even for a second . . . (*Checking mentally: this has not occurred to her before*) But I ask you, what the hell was the hoofer doing in the swank cathedral in the first place? Mebbe her feet was hurting her. Anyways, old hot-rod Ingram he throws up the organ-bashing and follows the variety troupe she's in all over England! And his father — he was a judge or something — he goes chasing after Buster; and his Momma she goes chasing after his father. Must ov been like the Keystone Cops. But finally in some hick town on the coast he gets her to marry him. And two days after the wedding what does she do? Sails off with some German Count that has a yacht there! Never seen her again. How about that! (*Tailing off vaguely*) I guess it was the title tickled her . . . and the yacht . . . Count and Countess . . . Countess Connie . . . The Bastard! Anyways, she sailed away, and forgot everything and never came back again, and maybe that's what I should ov done. But I came back to Ireland and got such a welcome that, Jeeze, I thought for ten minutes I was Santa Claus!

> HARRY *enters. He is wearing slippers and is dressed in a cardigan. He has just had his evening meal and is relaxed. He sits beside the fire.* CASS *continues to address the audience.*

HARRY Lord, it really is wonderful, Cass, to have you back. I — I just can't believe it!

CASS She was a hoofer, but what the hell was her name . . . ?

HARRY The trouble is I've so much to tell you and so much to ask you that I don't know where to begin.

CASS Anyways, she sailed away for ever . . .

HARRY Fifty-one years — my God, it's a lifetime.

CASS Fifty-two.

HARRY And yet I distinctly remember the morning you went away. I ran up to the back attic — remember the back attic with the window you pushed open with the iron bar?

CASS Six slots in it . . .

HARRY And I threw myself across your bed and cried my heart out.

CASS Harry . . . I don't want to remember.

HARRY D'you know, I was convinced my heart was literally crushed!

CASS Please . . . please, Harry, let me forget.

HARRY We were always so close to one another, Cass. Always. I thought the sun rose and set on you. Welcome home a thousand times.

Now, for the first time, CASS wheels round and almost runs into the common room. She is ecstatic with joy. She wanders about the common room, looking at it, looking at HARRY, laughing foolishly.

CASS Home! I can't even begin to tell you what this means to me, Harry. This is what it was all for — to come home again. You and Alice and the kids — Jeeze, Harry, I hope it's not too much for me — you know — like a highball on an empty stomach.

HARRY We'll make up for all the lost years, Cass.

CASS And what a home. I'm so glad for you, Harry, I can't tell you.

Enter ALICE with a tray of drinks.

And Alice! You know you're just like you are in all those pictures. Hell, you were only — what! — a pollywog in a cot when I left, but I knew your father OK.

ALICE Everybody knew Father.

CASS Joe Connor? For Gawd's sakes every evening we'd be coming home from school we'd meet him at the courthouse steps and he'd call one of us over and . . . (*suddenly realizing*) and . . . he'd say, 'How are yous, girls?' . . . Oh, a real gentleman, Mr Connor, with his gold chain across here and his butterfly collar —

ALICE You must be exhausted after the flight. Would you try a little sherry?

CASS I'll try anything — whiskey for preference. Tell me, how's the kids?

ALICE Great.

CASS When am I going to see them?

ALICE We don't see a lot of them ourselves, but they'll all come flocking now.

CASS Father Tom still teaching away at the high school?

ALICE Didn't you know? He's left the seculars. In the Jays now.

CASS Yeah?

ALICE For the past three and a half years.

CASS Gawd! Can't the docs do nothing for him?

HARRY The Jays — the Jesuits, Cass.

CASS Jeeze, I thought she said the jakes!

HARRY I'm going to propose a toast.

CASS Lovely!

HARRY To Cass and to the future.

CASS I'll drink to that.

HARRY And I want to say this, too: this is your home now, Cass; look on yourself as one of the family.

ALICE Come and go as you wish.

CASS And I want to propose a toast. (*Recalling*) Hold on now — *Sliocht sleacht ar shliocht do shleachta.*

ALICE German?

CASS Hell, it's supposed to be gawddam Gaelic, and it means . . . I forget — May your offspring have offspring — or something.

HARRY Why did you never marry out there?

CASS Me?

ALICE We often thought you might have married the proprietor of the restaurant you were manageress in.

CASS The rest- ? Oh, Jeff Olsen! Hell, Jeff and me were too pally to get married, you know. A sweet guy, but as I used to say to him: 'Jeff , boy, I want a man with his two feet on the ground.'

HARRY He was a successful businessman, wasn't he?

CASS Sure. But he had only one leg. Who's for more swill?

(She pours herself another drink)

ALICE Did you mention the party to her?

HARRY I didn't have a chance yet.

CASS What's that?

HARRY We were talking of having a welcome-home party for you.

CASS Wonderful! I can still dance.

> *She lifts her skirt and does a few steps of an old-time waltz as she hums her own accompaniment.*

And I'll sing, by Gawd, if the neighbours don't object!
(*Sings*) 'Oft in the stilly night ere slumber's chains have bound me
Sad memory brings the light . . . '
Aw, hell, I haven't sang since the night James Michael Curley was buried!

ALICE You're a caution, Cass.

CASS This party — who's coming?

HARRY We'll have the Traynors and the Kirks and the Grahams and Tom and Mary —

CASS Do I know any of these folk?

HARRY Course you do. Remember old Jack Kirk out at the end of the town?

CASS Yeah, sure.

HARRY Well, this is his son and his wife. And d'you remember Goldpark Lodge?

CASS Colonel Johnson's place? He's not alive, is — ?

HARRY No, no; the Grahams bought it.

CASS The whole estate? Boy, they must be swank, huh?

ALICE They own a dancehall here. (*To* HARRY) Is that swank?

HARRY And the Dohertys and the Tobins and the Wallaces —

CASS (*Too casually*) I don't know none of them. But I'll pitch in. Any of the Crowleys knocking about still?

ALICE I don't think so.

HARRY Crowleys? No, moved to Dublin — oh, years ago. Con married a girl from there. Did very well for himself, too. And we'll have the Doyles and Bill Morgan and —

CASS *is moving around the room again, staring in admiration.*

CASS   Boy, Harry, you made out good, huh?

HARRY   Not bad, Cass.

CASS   And you tell me you don't work at the accountancy no more?

HARRY   Not for fifteen, twenty years. I didn't have the time.

CASS   Gee, I'm so glad for you. I was always worried in case — you know — with Momma living with you and all the kids getting education — like I thought you mebbe didn't have much to fling around. But this! Boy! (ALICE *whispers to* HARRY)

HARRY   I wasn't much of a letter writer, Cass.

CASS   You were just great, Harry. (*To* ALICE) You know he actually wrote me when Father died. Wasn't that something?

HARRY   I know, I know, I know, and I apologize.

CASS   If it hadn't ov been for you (*Alice*) the whole family might ov been — in the Jays.

HARRY   And I should have written to thank you for all the money you sent; every month without fail.

CASS   Forget it.

HARRY   No, I won't forget it. And I want to talk to you about it now.

ALICE   We never really thanked you properly.

CASS   I had no use for it.

HARRY   Only this morning I was checking up: ten dollars every month for fifty-two years —

ALICE   Not to talk of the children's birthdays and Christmas presents and —

CASS   I couldn't help making it. Honest. It just kept dropping into my lap.

HARRY   There would have been no point in telling you we really didn't need it: you would have sent it all the same.

CASS   Not now, Harry. (*Looking round again*) It's — it's elegant, that's what it is.

HARRY   Thank God we were never in want. In the beginning

	Mother's salary was adequate, and then I qualified and went into practice, and I had a few lucky ventures.
CASS	I would only have scattered it anyways.
HARRY	What troubles me now, though, is that perhaps you were the one who needed it, and not us.
CASS	It got candy for the kids, didn't it?
ALICE	Don't keep her in suspense. Tell her what you did.
CASS	I sent a few bucks 'cos I wanted to. So forget it. OK?
HARRY	I checked this morning. And over all the years — including birthdays, anniversaries, Christmas and all — you sent 7,419 dollars — something over two-and-a-half thousand pounds. And that's not counting interest.

Enter DOM *and* MOTHER. *They stay upstage.*

CASS	Boy, that would ov bought me one hellova head! Momma, how are you, Momma? Kid.
HARRY	Don't think we don't appreciate the sacrifices you made. We do, all of us —
CASS	(*To* MOTHER) Tell him to shut up, will you? He's boring the hell outa me.
HARRY	No, this must be said. When you went out there first ten dollars must have been a lot of money.
CASS	(*Getting really tired*) Harry —
HARRY	However, to get back to what I was saying: we saved it for you, Cass.
CASS	?
HARRY	It was all banked, every penny of it from the very beginning. As I said, we never really needed it. And now it's all intact, for you to use as you wish.
ALICE	It's a nice little nest egg.
HARRY	And it makes you independent of everyone.
ALICE	We've been planning this as a surprise.
HARRY	How you're fixed financially is your own affair, but this will provide a nice supplement to whatever you have. I'll give you the pass book tomorrow morning.
ALICE	And I'm warning you to keep an eye on this scrounger (*Dom*). Don't let him wheedle a halfpenny from you!

CASS (*Almost whispering*) None of it . . . never bought nothing?

HARRY If we had needed it. But, thank God, we never did. The important thing is not the money itself, Cass — it's not all that much — but the knowledge that you are not dependent on anyone. That's what it gives you.

CASS Dependent?

HARRY You can crack your fingers at all of us!

CASS The kids' birthdays . . . and the doc's bills . . . and Father Tom's education . . . ?

HARRY I assure you, Cass, we never wanted for anything. And we're as grateful as if we had used it.

> CASS *walks away from them. She is slowly trying to take in what she has been told. Pause.*

ALICE Cass . . . ?

CASS I could ov bought myself a mink coat! So! I could ov put a fan in the bedroom in the summer! Yeah! Another thing — I could ov eaten prime beef every Sunday!

ALICE We thought you'd be delighted.

> CASS *wheels round on them, madly, desperately elated. She speaks almost at full voice.*

CASS There was only one story would make Jeff laugh — you know? Brave as a lion but, Jeeze, that leg of his gave him hell at times; and when he would get away down there he would say to me, 'Tell me the story about the Irish Mick, Cass.' And I would stroke his forehead and tell him, see, and he would laugh and laugh even though he heard that story hundreds — millions of times —

MOTHER This is indeed a festive occasion.

CASS Boy, is she psychic! You know the story, Alice? About the Irish kid comes over to the States, see, and after three months he writes back to the folks: 'I've been made floor manager of this store. This is a feather in my cap.' And the folks back home they're thrilled, see, even though there's no dough in the envelope. And three months later he writes again: 'I've been made manager of the whole plant. This is a feather in my cap.' Again no dough, but the folks is pleased for him, see. And three months later another letter: 'I've been made president of the company. This is a feather in my cap.' (HARRY *laughs — an attempt at normality.* CASS *almost spits her anger at him*) You haven't heard the punch line yet! What the hell are you laughing at?

HARRY I just thought — president after nine months —

CASS And then they don't hear from the kid for months and months, see, not a line; until finally they get this air letter, very urgent, and written inside is: 'I'm broke. Please send fare home.' And the kid's pop, he gets pen and paper, and he clears the kitchen table, and he writes back, 'Stick the three feathers up your ass and fly home!' (*Only* DOM *laughs.* ALICE *turns to him rapidly*)

ALICE Take Mother to her room at once!

Exit DOM *and* MOTHER.

HARRY Cass, this sort of —

CASS When you planning to have this party? I'll supply the champagne — I got money, haven't I? And I'll sing and dance and I'll tell stories and I'll have all the Kirks and Colonel Johnson and all the Crowleys and all of them rolling in the aisles. (*To* ALICE *who is about to leave with the tray of drinks*) Come back with that hooch, honey! I'm only warming up!

ALICE *leaves.*

HARRY Cass —

CASS I got more stories than Bennett Cerf ever heard of — about cannibals and girls with Chinese tattoos on their bellies and about elephants and marooned sailors — hell, that's all Slinger ever done was tell me stories. He was a bum, OK, but he had lovely teeth.

Like the one about this guy that comes home drunk
every night and his wife she's about sick of him. You
know that one, Harry?

HARRY Cass, this sort of talk —

CASS So sick that she can't stick it no more. Anyways, this
night the guy comes home plastered again and falls
across the bed and starts snoring. And the wife she
has this empty candy box with a great big blue satin
rosette on the lid, and she takes the rosette off the box
and goes over to the bed and takes the guy's trousers
off and ties the bow to his rice crispies. And the next
morning when he wakes up first thing he sees is this
big blue rosette. And the wife she says to him, 'Where
were you last night?' And the guy he scratches his
head and he says, 'Jeeze, honey, I don't know. But
wherever I was I got first prize.'

HARRY I'll speak to you later, Cass.

He marches off. CASS, *left alone, suddenly slumps
into a chair. The false elation is all gone, the anger all
dead. She is on the verge of tears.*

CASS I never wanted no gawddam mink coat! And I hate
prime beef! And fans they give me the sinus! As for
air conditioning — Gawd — you can keep it, keep it
. . . I don't want it . . . not a cent of it! . . . (*Fumbles for
cigarettes, her hands shaking*) Some guy, Slinger, I'll tell
you, some hellova guy . . .

*Lights cigarette. Shades her eyes against the lights and
searches the auditorium.*

You still out there? Stick around and we'll have fun
together. You'll see, lots of fun . . . (*Looking around set*)
Where the hell *is* everybody? (*To audience*) You wanta
know why I never got married? 'Cos I hadn't time —
that's the why — working — and then I sorta fell in
with Jeff, and we had our own arrangement. He was
no sweet guy but he liked me — know he did — he

217

never said it but I know he did. And when he died, well what d'you do but come home . . . That's what it's all about, isn't it — coming home? Why the hell does he call it *The Loves of Cass McGuire*? A gook title, I'll tell you!

She hears TRILBE *approach and takes out her compact and makes up. While she does this she keeps her back to* TRILBE.

CASS Hi.

TRILBE Catherine, m'dear, what are you doing?

CASS (*Brisk, busy*) Getting ready for the ball.

TRILBE Are we having a ball?

CASS Why not. Where's Fred Astaire?

TRILBE I beg your pardon?

CASS Mr Ingram — he not about?

TRILBE He's in the chapel.

CASS Got religion all of a sudden?

TRILBE Catherine, I think you should know: today is the anniversary of his wife's death.

This shocks CASS *into normality. Pause.*

CASS Gee, I didn't know she was *dead*.

TRILBE Very tragic. Very, very tragic.

CASS When did it happen to her?

Enter INGRAM. CASS *stares at him.*

TRILBE Some other time . . . (*Briskly*) Tell us about the catering business in America, Catherine.

CASS (*Watching* INGRAM) Sure, sure, it was something . . . you bet . . . I worked in this . . . this downtown restaurant . . . you know, all big shots; and I was . . . sort of like a head waiter only I was a woman, you know . . . Hi, Mr Ingram.

TRILBE That must have been fascinating employment.

CASS You bet . . . yeah . . . Mr Ingram . . .

INGRAM Good afternoon.

CASS Mr Ingram, it has just come to my knowledge that you are bereaved of your spouse . . .

INGRAM Yes. Yes.

CASS And I would like you to understand that I am deeply grieved on your behalf.

INGRAM It was a long time ago.

CASS Was it TB or the cancer, Mr Ingram? Jeeze, the number of women I know that went down with the cancer — boy, you could ov packed Radio City with them.

TRILBE I think it is milder today, don't you?

INGRAM Stella was drowned, Miss McGuire.

CASS Gawd.

INGRAM Forty-six years ago. I will tell you about it.

He moves towards the winged chair and sits.

TRILBE Mr Ingram —

INGRAM On our honeymoon.

TRILBE Mr Ingram, dear, should you . . . today . . . ?

INGRAM I will tell you about it.

TRILBE Very well then.

Gently fade in Wagner's 'Magic Fire' music. Then, after a few seconds, INGRAM continues.

INGRAM I was twenty and she was eighteen, with hair golden as ripe wheat —

TRILBE A ballet dancer.

INGRAM And after the wedding we went to Salcombe —

TRILBE In Devon, in the south of England.

INGRAM And every night in the hotel I played the piano and she danced and danced and danced —

TRILBE Her hair swinging behind her.

INGRAM And I played and played, faster and faster —

TRILBE For her dancing, dancing.

INGRAM — until her eyes shone with happiness and the room swam with delight and my heart sang with joy —

TRILBE Oh, the dancing, dancing.

INGRAM And during the day we walked across the moors —
TRILBE Hand in hand.
INGRAM — and kissed and loved and ran and danced —
TRILBE Across the windy moors.
INGRAM — because my prize was a young prize, with hair golden as ripe wheat; and there was music in my ears, throbbing, heady, godly music . . .
TRILBE Away, away to the end of the promontory.
INGRAM Where we kissed and danced and loved . . .
TRILBE Poised above the waves.
INGRAM And then —
TRILBE And then —
INGRAM And then, one day, running before me, calling to me, she slipped . . .
TRILBE His Stella —
INGRAM And there was no sound.
TRILBE His star.
INGRAM No sound but the sound of the sea. And for nine days they searched —
TRILBE Probing with long poles.
INGRAM — from a German yacht that was fishing there; he was a prince.
TRILBE His dancing Stella.
INGRAM Swirling in the water, loose, being nosed by fish, her hair loose, her limbs loose . . .
TRILBE His dancing star.
INGRAM But they never found her. And the German yacht sailed away —
TRILBE On a spring morning.
INGRAM — away to the Mediterranean, to the sun . . . with hair golden as ripe wheat.
TRILBE Leaving them together, in Salcombe, in the south of England.
INGRAM My prize, my bride . . .
TRILBE His dancing bride.
INGRAM My dancing, swirling bride.
TRILBE Our truth.
INGRAM 'But I, being poor, have only my dreams —'
TRILBE 'I have spread my dreams under your feet —'

INGRAM 'Tread softly because you tread on my dreams.'
TRILBE Our truth.

> *They hold their positions for a few seconds; then*
> INGRAM *rises.*

INGRAM It is such a mild afternoon . . . I . . . I think we'll walk
past the refectory and along . . . it's a very pleasant
little . . .

> *He goes towards the door.*

TRILBE A splendid idea. Wait for me, Mr Ingram.

> *She goes with him, but hesitates before she exits and
> turns to* CASS.

Join with us, Catherine. Join with *us*.

> *They go off. Fade out music.* CASS *stares after them.
> Her reaction this time is not too violent. She is more
> perplexed, more puzzled. She talks to herself.*

CASS Jee-sus! What d'you know about that! (*Fumbling for a
cigarette*) As if those Germans couldn't find a needle
in a haystack, for Gawd's sake! (*To audience: far from
confident*) Hi! . . . Stick . . . stick around . . . This'll be
OK, you'll see; this'll all sort itself out . . . I dunno
. . . this gawddam going back into the past! Who the
hell knows what happened in the past! Joe Bolowski,
he thought he was a gawddam pianist! . . . Jeeze, how
do I know . . . maybe he was . . .

> ALICE *appears in the shadows upstage.* CASS *does not
> look at her and her answers are automatic.*

ALICE My father was always a gentleman, Cass, wasn't he?
CASS Sure . . . sure . . .
ALICE There were rumours, malicious rumours, about him;

but they weren't true, Cass, were they?

CASS A gentleman, honey. That was Joe Connor.

ALICE But there were whispers, and they were carried to me after his death.

CASS One of the most respected men in town.

ALICE He was, wasn't he?

CASS Sure.

ALICE And dignified, and scholarly, and courteous?

CASS You can say that again.

ALICE (*Grandly*) Yes, of course he was. One of the old families.

CASS Old as the Hudson.

ALICE Yes, the old gentility. They may not have had wealth but they had background. And background's so important.

She disappears into the wings.

CASS (*Turns, appealing*) Alice, honey . . . Momma? Harry? . . . Father? . . . Connie, Connie?

She is about to wander into her bedroom when PAT QUINN *makes his usual brisk entrance.*

PAT Wonderful! Wonderful! Wonderful!

CASS Pat! Gee, am I glad to see you, Pat! Where have you been?

PAT I told you all along but you never believed me!

CASS We'll have a party, Pat; and I've got presents to hand out; and I'll get Buster Ingram to play the piano and —

PAT He's coming for me this day week — him and the wife.

CASS Sure, Pat; you're only temporary —

PAT You won't believe me. You never did. But he's just after leaving the door. He took my trunk away with him. Look — the receipt from the matron! 'Paid with thanks.' A split new house with a room and all for me. In a week, on his way home from the monthly meeting.

CASS (*Totally deflated*) On the level?

PAT I knew you never believed me. You thought I was only blathering like yourself. But there it is in black and white. Ask Tessa. She helped me out with the trunk.

CASS (*With quiet venom*) You dirty bastard!

PAT Ha-ha-ha-ha-ha, we see the true colours now! The big swank American lady, Mr McGuire's sister! Aha, but you never fooled me, McGuire! A skivvy — that's what you were — written all over you! And a drunken aul' skivvy, living in sin with a dirty aul' Yank that kicked you out in the end!

CASS Shut up!

PAT But what else would you expect. Didn't your aul' fella do the same in Scotland. And we all know your stuck-up aul' mother that never paid a bill in her life. Oho, I know yous all right — tramps turned respectable! Respectable, how are you!

CASS Shut up!

PAT Who'll carry in your drink now? Aul' raving Costello? Aul' mad Ingram? Cripes, you'll be a prize trio. The people'll be paying to come and look at yous!

CASS Shut up, you bastard! Shut up!

PAT Oh, the ladylike Miss McGuire! Oh, the sweet lady! Good luck to you! It won't be long till you start raving, too! Rave away, woman! You'll be in good company!

> *He skips off.* CASS, *angry, sobbing, rushes into her room, takes the bottle from under the mattress and drinks. Throughout all this business she is mumbling incoherently to herself. She lights a cigarette and then makes up.*

CASS Jeeze, the fun Jeff and me had that day we went to Coney Island . . . Lincoln's Birthday, 19 and 27 . . . that's when it was . . . we laughed and laughed and laughed, that day on Coney Island . . . Connie . . . Connie . . .

The room is too lonely. She rushes back to the common room. Through the French windows we can see TRILBE: *she beckons to* CASS. CASS, *too, sees her, and swings round to the audience.*

TRILBE Catherine!

CASS shades her eyes and searches the auditorium.

Catherine!

CASS (*To* TRILBE) Leave me alone, will you? (*To audience*) They think they're going to run me back into the past but by Gawd they're not . . . I live in the present, Harry boy, right here and now. Where are you? Stick with me.

TRILBE Catherine!

CASS Go away! Go away! Gooks . . . real gooks living in the past, but not Cass McGuire. (*To audience*) If things get too rough I can go and hide in the signal box. I've always got places I can go to . . . always . . . you bet . . . a dozen of them . . . out to the crooked bridge . . . at the back of the mill . . . But the signal box . . . it's the safest . . . no one ever looks there . . . Where are you? Jeeze, where are you?

TRILBE Catherine!

She now stands strained between the calling voice and the audience. Her mouth forms words but no sound comes. We wait for her to break down. Then, in a voice that is firm and clear, she calls:

CASS One black coffee and one salad sandwich? You bet. Coming right up, sir. Coming right up.

Quick curtain.

ACT THREE

The evening of Christmas Eve. CASS *is lying asleep on her bed. She is partially dressed.* TRILBE *and* INGRAM *are sitting at the table. He is writing a letter and she is reading the paper. Silence.*

TRILBE   You are concentrating too deeply on that letter. You'll end up with a headache.

INGRAM   If I could only have a little quiet . . .

TRILBE   I used to suffer from migraine once. (*She reads*) Imagine that!

INGRAM   Mm?

TRILBE   The temperature in Sydney yesterday was 97 degrees.

INGRAM   Really.

TRILBE   I had a brother in Sydney. Peter.

INGRAM   Yes?

TRILBE   A diver.

INGRAM   What did he dive for? (*This has never occurred to* TRILBE *before*)

TRILBE   I beg your pardon?

INGRAM   What did he dive for?

TRILBE   How would I know what he dived for, Mr Ingram? He was a diver — a diver — a diver. And a professional diver — just dives, doesn't he?

INGRAM   I . . . I . . . I suppose so . . .

> *She goes on reading. He goes on writing.* CASS, *without opening her eyes, stretches out a hand, feels under the mattress, finds a bottle, puts it to her mouth. The bottle is empty. The hand throws it away. She drops off again.*

TRILBE   A report of Brother O'Rourke's funeral. Two bishops and three ministers of state.

INGRAM   Who's that?

TRILBE   I told you about him yesterday. Principal of Fairhill Secondary School. A Kerryman. A very . . . athletic principal.

INGRAM   I remember.

TRILBE   'He is survived by three sisters and three broth—' Surely that's a misprint!

INGRAM   Hm?

TRILBE   I presume it should read three sisters and three brothers. He would never have left three brothels, would he?

Enter TESSA *with a notebook and pencil. She is looking very much more alive and quite smart.*

TESSA   Matron says would yous rather a concert or a fillim tomorrow night?

INGRAM   I . . . I really don't . . .

TRILBE   A concert or a film; let us analyze this. Who would be the artists in the concert?

TESSA   How would I know? The fillim is called —

TRILBE   Film, child. One syllable. Film.

TESSA   — *General Custer's Last Stand.*

TRILBE   That sounds familiar. (*To* INGRAM) Who was General Custer?

INGRAM   Wasn't he one of the leaders of your Easter Rebellion?

TRILBE   I do believe you're right. (*To* TESSA) Yes, I vote for the film.

INGRAM   So do I.

TESSA   (*Holding out her left hand*) And none of yous noticed.

TRILBE   What?

TESSA   Look.

TRILBE   Chilblains, m'dear?

TESSA   I'm engaged. He gave it to me last night.

TRILBE   Well, I'm delighted. I wish you every happiness.

INGRAM *rises from the table, goes over to* TESSA, *takes her hand, and kisses her fingers. Throughout this brief ceremony* TESSA *is at first embarrassed, then giggles, and then is oddly moved. As he does this:*

INGRAM   May I (*kiss*)? A long and contented life to both of you.

TESSA   He's a building contractor by trade.

TRILBE   A very practical profession, too.

TESSA   Well, he's not a real contractor, yet.

TRILBE   But he's a fully fledged tradesman?

TESSA   He will be when he finishes his apprenticeship, and until he sets up on his own he's working as a brick-layer for Harvey and Todd. But he's going to go out on his own in the spring . . . after we're married.

INGRAM   That will be very . . . he'll do well, I'm . . .

TESSA   And the first thing he's going to do is build a bunga-low for us, with bay windows and venetian blinds, and a big garage and a red-tiled roof. I think a red roof's nice.

TRILBE   Indeed.

TESSA   We have a site and all in our head but we're not telling anybody where it is in case the price would be stuck up. And as soon as we're settled in comfortable I want yous two and Miss McGuire to come out and have high afternoon tea with us.

TRILBE   That will be something to look forward to.

TESSA   We're going to do all the entertaining before the babies start coming. I'll put Miss McGuire down for the fillim, too. (*At door*) The aul' woman to fill Pat Quinn's place has just arrived. Her name's Lizzie Butcher. She's crying her eyes out. Wouldn't you think at her age she wouldn't mind where she'd be?

She goes swinging off. There is a flatness after her departure, the first of a series that drain the atmos-phere of all life and buoyancy. INGRAM and TRILBE return without interest to their tasks.

TRILBE   Bungalows are all very well if you are positioned on a rise. Otherwise there is no privacy.

INGRAM   They'll have venetian blinds, she said.

TRILBE   You're quite right. (*Pause*) She must be resting. Haven't seen her all day. Have you?

INGRAM Have I what?

TRILBE You can be so stupid at times! Have you seen Catherine?

INGRAM No . . . no . . . I haven't.

TRILBE (*Hesitantly*) Did you get the impression last night, Mr Ingram, did it occur to you that Catherine was slashed?

INGRAM Good heavens! Slashed?

TRILBE Inebriated. Did that occur to you?

INGRAM Miss McGuire? Certainly not. I would be very shocked. (*Pause*) What made you think so?

TRILBE Nothing. Nothing at all. Probably I imagined it.

INGRAM I'm certain you did.

TRILBE Very well. I did. Let's not discuss it any further.

They continue reading and writing. Then suddenly TRILBE *has a revelation.*

Pearls!

INGRAM ?

TRILBE That's what people dive for! That's what Peter dived for! Peter dived for pearls. Round the rugged rocks the ragged rascals ran. My brother Peter dived for precious pearls. Little Tessa should practise on that type of exercise.

HARRY, ALICE *and* DOM *enter, dressed for an outing. They carry presents.*

HARRY We're looking for Miss McGuire. Matron said she would be here. (TRILBE *and* INGRAM *pay no attention*) Excuse me . . .

TRILBE Good evening. Very cold, isn't it?

ALICE Where could we find Miss McGuire?

TRILBE We haven't seen Miss McGuire all day, have we, Mr Ingram?

INGRAM That's . . . that's what we were just saying.

HARRY Would she be in her bedroom? I'm her brother.

INGRAM Her bedroom is just down the passage.
HARRY (*To* ALICE) I'll see if she's awake first.

HARRY *goes down front.* DOM *follows him at a distance.*

ALICE We brought a few chocolates for all the inma— for all the residents.
TRILBE Do you know Brother O'Rourke, m'dear?
ALICE I've heard my sons talk of him.
INGRAM Thank you for the —
TRILBE Well, he's dead, and we're puzzled by the report of his funeral. He had three sisters; that we know; but what we wish to establish is this: had he any brothers?

ALICE, INGRAM *and* TRILBE *go into mute conversation.* HARRY *stands beside Cass's bed. He speaks to her in a quiet, tender voice.* DOM *stands at a distance, tense, alert.*

HARRY Cass. Cass. It's me, Cass. Harry.

CASS *stirs slowly. Then sits up. Automatically gropes for cigarettes. Lights one with shaking hands. She looks and feels a wreck. Stares vaguely at her immediate surroundings on stage. Talks listlessly to herself.*

CASS Where the hell is everyone?
HARRY Cass . . .
CASS Gone . . . gone . . .
HARRY It's Harry, Cass. Alice is outside. We brought a few things for you. Slippers. Fruit.
CASS Boy, what a dream. Like it kinda went on and on every time I closed my eyes . . .
HARRY You're very comfortable here. And it's so cold outside. Snow's forecast.
CASS We're on this big ship, sailing home to Ireland, see . . . all laughing and singing and dancing and drinking . . . all the gang of us that used to get up the concerts for the White Cross and the boys on the run and the

church building and the prisoners' fund back home
... and we're having that much fun, all sailing for
home ...

HARRY Cass ...

CASS And they're all milling about; and there in the middle
of them — Jeeze and was I glad to see them! — there's
Joe Bolowski and Slinger having a ball to theirselves;
and Joe, he sees me standing up there in this big long
white wedding dress, and he shouts up to me, 'Cass,'
he shouts, 'I'd pull no chain on that.' And everyone
laughs and laughs and laughs, even Father O'Neill.
Boy, he should ov been in the marines.

HARRY We're going to have a quiet Christmas after all, Cass.
The children, it seems ... it seems they can't come.
Betty sent a telegram and Tom phoned this morning.
Naturally they're very disappointed. So I suggested
to Alice —

CASS Gawd, am I hung over!

HARRY I was wondering would you like to come out to us for
tomorrow ... and Boxing Day ... and perhaps for a
day or two more ...

CASS Jeff, he never has a head 'cos he drinks four pints of
iced water before he goes to bed. Sez it makes the
alcohol float to the top. Hell, I dunno; but a head's
better than running to the ur-eye-nal all night.

HARRY I'd give everything I have, Cass, anything, just to be
able to put a coat around you and drive you home
with me. But when a man gets married ... and we've
had Mother for so long ... although Alice couldn't
have been kinder to her ...

CASS *swings her feet out of the bed. The effort sets her
head throbbing.*

CASS Oooooh ... oh-oh-oh ... Gawd ...!

HARRY I don't suppose you know about them, Cass, but
she has her worries ... we both have ... we haven't
heard from Aidan for seven years, not since he went
to Switzerland; she worries a lot about that. And then

Betty's marriage isn't just as happy as . . . as . . . Even Tom at times . . . the seculars didn't suit him and we gather that he's restless again even though . . . You really are better off here, Cass.

CASS During Prohibition there was this hooch called Tiger's Piss. One swig of that stuff and you thought you were Anna May Wong. Oooooooooooh . . . !

HARRY I'll call again tomorrow. And every week. I promise.

He takes a half-bottle of whiskey from his pocket and leaves it at the foot of the bed.

CASS I dunno what I drunk last night. But I guess that tiger's still operating.

HARRY Goodbye, Cass. A happy Christmas.

He goes reluctantly back to the common room. After he has gone CASS *finds the bottle he left.*

CASS Well , I didn't know I had that much foresight.

As she is drinking DOM *darts forward and sticks his face up to* CASS's *right ear. His eyes are burning with disgust.*

DOM You're nothing but a dirty, rotten aul' — aul' — aul' — !

He cannot finish. He runs into the common room and then off.

HARRY Dom? (*Sternly*) Dom!
ALICE What happened to him?
HARRY He's probably — Where are you going?
ALICE I'll only be a minute.
HARRY There's no point in disturbing her.
ALICE I'll meet you at the car.
HARRY For heaven's sake, Alice, she's not —
ALICE I said I'll only be a minute. See where Dom has

gone to.

> HARRY *does not want a scene before* TRILBE *and* INGRAM. *He smiles blankly at them, apologetically, and mumbles:*

HARRY The compliments of the season to you. I'll be in again tomorrow or the next . . .

TRILBE And a very merry Christmas to you, sir.

> HARRY *looks uneasily after* ALICE *and then goes off to find* DOM. ALICE *has moved into Cass's bedroom and stands beside her.* CASS *is totally unaware that she is there.*

ALICE (*Warmly, leaning over*) It's me, Cass . . . I know Harry has told you: none of the children . . .

> *She checks herself in time; straightens up; continues with a control that is touching in its rigidity. She is on the point of tears.*

The children are all coming — all of them — Betty and Tom and Aidan — arriving tonight — late — a real family gathering. You'll like Aidan; he's — you know — unorthodox — his artistic temperament — always moving from job to job — always getting into little scrapes. Oh, you'll love him. And Tom. People say he's like my father; remember? But then Father was a more sort of scholarly man, wasn't he? He'll make an excellent bishop; great administrative ability. And Betty and the baby. We haven't seen it either, you know; our only grandchild. They turned out well, didn't they, Cass? And Harry worked so hard for them. (CASS *makes a quick movement and her head explodes*)

CASS Jeezus!

ALICE They're a consolation to us, Cass, aren't they?

CASS (*Sings*) 'Oft in the stilly night 'ere slumber's chains have bound me

Fond memory brings the light of other days around me.'

ALICE *makes a tentative gesture towards* CASS *again.*

ALICE Cass . . .
CASS Best mayor New York ever had.

> ALICE *withdraws. She dabs at her nose, straightens herself, and dashes out of the bedroom and through the common room.*

TRILBE And a very happy Christmas to you, too.
ALICE (*Vaguely*) Oh, yes . . . yes . . .

> *She goes off.*

TRILBE That was Catherine's brother and his wife and their youngest child. They also have a son an architect in UNO and a daughter a doctor, married to a London specialist, and a son a Jesuit.
INGRAM I'm not deaf, you know.
TRILBE A very satisfactory family. (*She opens the paper again. Then stops*) It's coming back to me now: he led a flying column in Tipperary!
INGRAM The Jesuit?
TRILBE General Custer.

> CASS *puts on her shoes. She takes a drink and feels better. Completes her dressing. She gets to her feet and is about to go into the common room when she hesitates, takes a few steps towards the footlights, shades her eyes, searches the auditorium. She sees nobody.*

CASS And I could ov swore there were folks out there. (*Shrugs*) What the hell.

> *She shuffles into the common room.* TRILBE*'s vigour*

makes her feel even more sour.

TRILBE Ah! There you are!

CASS Hi.

TRILBE We've missed you all day. (*Quietly*) He's very upset with the income tax people. They have confused him with some other Meurice Ingram, a professional wrestler.

INGRAM Good evening. (CASS *waves casually to him*)

TRILBE And now, Catherine, I want your advice. Where would be the best place to display my Christmas cards? (*Delving into bag*) I didn't want to keep them selfishly in my room. I was thinking of the walls —

CASS Sure.

TRILBE — or the mantelpiece. Or what about stringing them across the window? I've got some green tape here, too.

CASS Yeah, that's fine, fine.

TRILBE You Americans have such novel ideas about decoration. Here we are! Some of them are so pretty this year. (CASS *takes them listlessly*)

CASS Five?

TRILBE There are certainly more than that. (*Searches bag again*) Two more. And I'll get another from Mother Benignus of Loreto. She never has time to do hers until after the Christmas rush. What do you think?

CASS Well, as the broad said to the senator, you can't — (*Recovering quickly*) — I think mebbe we'll just be old-fashioned and set them up along here (*the mantelpiece*). OK?

TRILBE Yes. Yes, perhaps you're right.

> CASS *goes downstage and searches for the audience again. Finds no one.*

CASS No one. Must have been dreaming.

TRILBE What's that, m'dear?

CASS The folks — I guess you were right.

TRILBE Never mind, Catherine, you have us. Our world is

real, too.

INGRAM Our world is just as real.

> PAT *comes on, singing. He is carrying two cases. He is at the top of his form.*

PAT 'Adieu, adieu, kind friends adieu, adieu, adieu,
I can no longer stay with you, stay with you ... '

> *The other three go absolutely flat. They watch his antics with dead eyes, almost as if he weren't there.*

(*Rapidly*) It has been a pleasure knowing you all. And only that the nephew can't manage without me — he's outside in the car there with the missus, waiting for me — you'd never drag Pat Quinn away from Eden House and the good company and the grand food. Miss Costello, a very happy Christmas to you and the very best of good luck. Mister Ingram, sir, it has been an honour knowing you and being educated by your fine talk. Good luck to you. Miss Mac, we had our differences, Miss Mac, but that's all over and done with. (*Softer*) And if you want me to make an arrangement with Sweeney — you know where — I'm your man, d'you understand?

TESSA (*At door*) He says if you want to stay that suits him.

PAT Coming, darling, coming. The season of goodwill and forgiveness and all; and if ever you want anything done for you outside in the great big world just drop a note to Mister Patrick Joseph Quinn, Esquire, care of Mister John Quinn, Esquire, Cloughmore, and I'll see you right. A happy Christmas, one and all, and a bright and prosperous New Year, and may all your dreams come true. (*At door*) By the way, you're getting a slice of ham each for tea.

> *He exits. The silence now is total, the depression complete.* INGRAM *takes off his glasses and polishes them.* CASS, *her back to the audience, fingers the*

cards. TRILBE *gets a handkerchief and blows her nose*
vigorously. Pause. Then high unnatural talk bursts.

TRILBE I think perhaps my favourite piece for children is a
little poem I once came across in a magazine during
my travels. It is called 'Clickety-clack', and I have
recommended it to dozens of pupils:
'Clickety-clack, clickety-clack, goes the puffing train
on the railway track;
Bearing us off on a mystery tour,
And when we'll arrive we're never quite sure . . . '

INGRAM When he was a young barrister my father published
a pamphlet attacking capital punishment, and that
was . . . oh, fifty years ago . . . or more . . .

TRILBE 'We puff over meadows and rivers and streams
Till we come, puffing gaily, to the land of our dreams;
And there we are happy to wander and roam
For we feel so content in this land that is Home . . . '

INGRAM Long, long before the movement ever became popular. He was a stern man but I think he was a just man
. . . in his own way . . .

TRILBE We're having ham for tea.

INGRAM Snow is forecast.

TRILBE And turkey tomorrow.

INGRAM I don't suppose it'll lie.

TRILBE And a film at night.

They cannot sustain talk any longer. Silence flows
in and fills the room. Then, suddenly, CASS *with*
great effort and courage springs into activity.

CASS Hello! It's Christmas Eve, isn't it? I almost forgot!
What are we all moping for? (*Begins searching in one*
of her bags) I got some things in here. Sometimes I
think I carry the whole of Macy's around with me!
Yeah, yeah, here we are. (*Formally*) Mr Ingram, a very
merry Christmas to you. (*Gives him a parcel*)

INGRAM Is it — ?

CASS Sure, sure, go ahead. It ain't a Cadillac nor nothing

like that. But you might like it.

INGRAM I haven't had a Christmas present, Miss McGuire, since . . . oh, for . . . for . . .

CASS Agh, it's nothing; only a pair of — (*She suddenly realizes that she has given him the wrong present. She snatches it back from him again*) Jeeze, gimme that back! It's OK, OK, keep calm, keep calm, Father Christmas is still coming; I still got something for you, only I was giving you the wrong thing, see! (*Produces another packet*) And that wouldn't ov been real smart, huh? This is more like it. Yeah, this is it, OK.

INGRAM I'm deeply moved, Miss McGuire.

CASS How the hell can you be moved till you see what you got? It ain't no Cadillac neither, I can tell you. 'Cos they didn't have the colour I liked. (*To* TRILBE) I got something for you, too; an accessory for to match along with your pink sweater. Pretty nice.

INGRAM (*Displaying socks*) Thank you very, very much. They're . . . they're . . .

CASS Yeah, they're a couple of socks. Health to wear. You know like I kinda figured you do a lot of walking past the refectory and along the . . . you know. Only don't bring them back to me to mend. I'm not the sewing type.

> *The new resident,* MRS BUTCHER, *enters left and walks across stage to the exit right. She is small and old and perky. She is carrying a tiny cardboard case in one hand and a handkerchief in the other. She walks with hesitant courage because she is confused, unsure, timorous, and yet defiant. Because of her uncertainty her manner appears to be challenging. Immediately at her heels is* TESSA *carrying her bedclothes.*

TRILBE Good evening to you.

> *She looks at* TRILBE *and quickly at the others but does not answer and does not slacken her pace. When she*

goes off TESSA *puts her head back again.*

TESSA   Mrs Butcher, a bed-wetter if ever I seen one!

CASS   (*Impetuously*) Hi. Kid.

TRILBE   I would hazard a guess that our friend is not of a jovial disposition.

CASS   You kinda liked these, I think. Catch. Go on. Take it. It ain't rat poison.

TESSA   It's not the flowers, is it?

CASS   Take them away before I get mean again. And a happy Christmas to you.

TESSA   And the same to you, Miss McGuire. And thanks very much. No matter what the matron says, I knew you were a lady.

She exits.

CASS   Well, you can tell the matron from me that if she was on fire I wouldn't — Agh! Now what did I do that for!

TRILBE   She's engaged, you know.

CASS   Matron?

TRILBE   Tessa. She's going to be married in the spring.

CASS   Yeah? . . . In the spring? . . .

INGRAM   They're an excellent match for my new suit.

TRILBE   The Christmas atmosphere is really building up. (CASS *has nothing for* TRILBE *now except the gloves*)

CASS   (*Busily*) Yeah, and I got something for you, too, Trilbe, like I said . . . you bet . . . and I gave it some thought . . . and finally I came to the conclusion that what you needed most —

TRILBE   An accessory.

CASS   A pair of warm gloves — that's what it is — 'cos this place, hell, it would freeze the hair off a bald man. So that's what I went and got you — a pair of woollen gloves — mebbe a bit on the big side, but they'll shrink, won't they? Warm — woollen — gloves — and a happy Christmas to you.

TRILBE   Like Mr Ingram, Catherine, I'm speechless, I really am.

CASS That's a change.

TRILBE I'm deeply grateful to you. Thank you.

CASS Forget it. (*An awkwardness descends. The brief elation dies*) And that's about it. Everything's gone. All my worldly goods. (*Looking into bag*) Nothing left.

> CASS *returns to the mantelpiece. The silence flows in. To stop it:*

INGRAM Mr Quinn was a . . . a . . . he was a light-hearted man.

TRILBE He has gone, Mr Ingram.

INGRAM I know. I know.

TRILBE To a nephew who owns a substantial farm.

INGRAM He told me.

TRILBE He never really belonged, you know.

INGRAM In a way.

TRILBE Oh, no; he was never fully one of us.

INGRAM I suppose not.

TRILBE A willing little man, I'll grant you, but never one of us. Don't you agree, Catherine?

> CASS *moves away from the mantelpiece. She is looking at one of the cards. For the first time she is vague, dreamy, remote. And when she speaks all brashness is gone from her voice.*

CASS One Christmas I saw a man in a green sledge in Central Park, and he was being pulled along by two beautiful chestnuts. He must ov been a very rich man to keep two chestnuts in Manhattan, I'll tell you. And the horses they had these bells on their harness, you know, like music . . .

> *She goes forward to the winged chair and stands beside it.*

And as he was passing me he happened to look over. And do you know what he done? He lifted his black hat to me . . .

TRILBE (*Softly*) Tell us, Catherine.

CASS There's nothing to tell, really . . . just a man with a kind face and two chestnuts and a green sledge and the white of the snow and the music of the bells . . . and he looked at me and he lifted his black hat to me, that gentleman in Central Park did . . .

TRILBE Tell us.

INGRAM Tell us.

TRILBE Tell us.

> CASS *suddenly bursts into tears and drops into the winged chair. There she cries and groans, covering her face with her hands while the spasm lasts. Then, emerging from it, she sits up straight, almost with nobility, and very slowly lets her head come to rest on the back of the chair.*

TRILBE Perhaps you should read to us, Mr Ingram.

INGRAM I never get a chance to finish.

TRILBE Tell us the end of one of your stories, then.

INGRAM I'll finish the Tristan story. I know it by heart.

> *Fade in slowly and with growing volume the 'Liebestod' from* Tristan and Isolde. *After a few seconds of the music* CASS *begins to speak. She becomes more and more assured, as if the recounting of the events made their memory and their accuracy more vivid.*

CASS I stood at the stern of the ship, and two white and green lines spread out and out and out before me. And the gentleman I worked for, Mr Olsen, he was only a few years older than me, tall and straight and manly, with golden hair and kind soft patient eyes. And I had two dimples . . . (*Very rapidly: suddenly agitated*) What — what — where — what am I — ?

TRILBE No, no, go on, go on. Golden hair and patient eyes. And you had two dimples . . .

CASS (*Relaxing*) Yeah — yeah — two dimples . . . And he

would make me laugh and put his fingers into the dimples and say, 'Hooked you, Baby'. And the morning we got married my father he stood up and sung 'Oft In The Stilly Nights 'Ere Slumber's Chains Have Bound Me', and people there said if he had ov been a younger man he would ov made the big time, he was that good, my father; and Mr Joseph Bolowski, he played classical tunes on the piano; and Mr Slinger, he was the toastmaster; and everyone was so gay, so gay . . .

INGRAM 'But even though they were separated by exile Tristan's love for Isolde grew; and finally he sent for her.'

CASS And we moved into this great ten-roomed apartment on the West side, and from our bedroom window we could see the ships sailing off to South America and the Bahamas . . . and Ireland . . . and Glasgow . . . And all round the walls were pictures of Harry's kids; I was their Auntie Cass, you see; and regular as the clock came their letters — I have them all — fine kids . . .

TRILBE A doctor, a priest, an architect, a student.

CASS And when I came back home they were all down at Cork to meet me; and Harry and Alice and Momma; and Connie, he wanted us to stay over with his folks in Dublin but Harry wouldn't hear of that; and all the cars drove up, one behind the other, like it was a parade or something, some of them with chauffeurs and all, right up Harry's big wide avenue, underneath all them golden chestnuts, and all our friends came in and we had such a party . . .

INGRAM 'And at his bidding she came to him on a ship. But he, wounded on his couch, was too weak to meet her. And she got off the ship and rushed to his side and embraced him. And he died in her arms.'

CASS And Connie and me we slipped out by the back and went for a walk out to the crooked bridge and he said to me, 'Do you remember, Cass? Do you remember?', as if I ever forgot, even for a second. And we must ov spent so long out there that Harry, he got worried and went searching for us, and the police they were searching, too. And when we got back the party was over, and the house was quiet, and Momma, she and I had a long chat together, private, confidential, my Momma and me. And then I told Harry that I was going to move out 'cos I wanted to be independent; but he wouldn't listen to me, not Harry, he's too stubborn. But I insisted. So we bought this place close to the sea and we fixed it up, and Harry's kids, they come to see us all the time and play around on the beach; and we work and work and don't have no time to think . . .

INGRAM 'And she died, too, of love. And from their grave two rose trees grew up and intertwined so that they could never be separated again.'

CASS Connie and Father and Harry and Jeff and the four kids and Joe and Slinger . . . and I love them all so much, and they love me so much; we're so lucky, so lucky in our love. (*To* TRILBE) What is it you say?

TRILBE 'But I, being poor —'

CASS '— have only dreams.
I have spread my dreams under your feet.'

INGRAM 'Tread softly —'

CASS '— because you tread on my dreams.'

TRILBE Our truth.

INGRAM Our truth.

CASS Our truth.

The music fades. Enter MRS BUTCHER.

MRS BUTCHER (*Too loudly*) Good evening to you.

She goes immediately down front and sits on an upright chair, her back resolutely to the others. She opens a magazine and pretends she is reading. She addresses the audience confidentially.

My God, would you just look at them! If you met

them on a dark night you would think you were
doting.

The gong goes.

TRILBE Ah! Teatime! And how are you, m'dear? (MRS
BUTCHER *realizes she is being addressed*)
MRS BUTCHER What — what's that?
TRILBE You're well, I trust.
MRS BUTCHER Nothing wrong with me. Thanks be to God I was
never a burden to anybody.

INGRAM *and* TRILBE *get their things together to
go off for tea.*

TRILBE (*To* MRS BUTCHER) We're having cold ham for tea
this evening. Sometimes rather tasty. And General
Custer tomorrow night.
MRS BUTCHER (*Directly to audience*) Our Lady of the Seven Snows!
TRILBE A film of the '98 Rebellion.
MRS BUTCHER (*To audience*) Lunatics is sane compared with
these ones!
INGRAM (*To* TRILBE) Would the lady . . . is she . . . d'you
think she would care to . . . to . . . to . . . to join us?
TRILBE (*To* MRS BUTCHER) The dining room's along here,
m'dear.
MRS BUTCHER Carry on. I can look after myself.
INGRAM (*To* TRILBE) Perhaps I should . . . should I . . . ?
TRILBE Much too soon. She's still at *that* stage. Catherine?
CASS Yeah — yeah — coming — sure.
TRILBE (*To* INGRAM) I do believe I'm getting the Christ-
mas spirit fully now. (*Sings*) 'Good King Wenceslas
looked out . . .'

INGRAM *joins her and they exit, singing.* CASS
sees MRS BUTCHER *sitting alone and crosses to
her.*

CASS You gotta eat, you know. You can't go without

your vittles.

MRS BUTCHER I can look after myself, thank you very much. (*To audience*) Has she a drink on her?

CASS My name's Olsen, by the way. My late husband — mebbe you heard of him — General Cornelius Olsen — he made quite a name for himself in the last war. But you just call me Catherine.

MRS BUTCHER (*To audience*) Full!

CASS I dunno, but I think it's better to get into the routine here right away. (*Coaxing*) You'll like the tea they make. It looks like horse's — it looks like it was treacle, but it sure has a kick.

MRS BUTCHER You just run along now and have your meal.

CASS hesitates. She is conscious that she has some intelligence she could communicate, if only she knew what that intelligence were.

CASS When I first came here —

TESSA *appears at the door.*

TESSA (*To* MRS BUTCHER) You! You're wanted in the matron's office to sign some forms.

MRS BUTCHER If you're addressing me, my name happens to be Mrs Elizabeth Butcher, and I'm accustomed to —

TESSA And she says be quick about it.

MRS BUTCHER (*Directly to audience*) Maybe I should keep on the right side of that matron one. Not that I'll be here for long. (*Rises to leave*) Stay where you are. I'll be back in a minute.

She goes off right with pathetic dignity.

TESSA You! You're going the wrong way. Matron's office is back.

MRS BUTCHER *leaves.*

CASS   She'll learn, sweetie. She'll learn.

TESSA   Huh! And the airs of her! You'd think she was some-body! (*Suddenly coy: drawing* CASS*'s attention to the artificial flowers she was given as a preliminary to showing off her ring*) Nice?

CASS   Elegant.

TESSA   And what about that (*ring*)?

CASS   What?

TESSA   Engaged.

CASS   Well, well, well!

TESSA   (*By rote*) It's a solitaire diamond surrounded by a cluster of dazzling rubies and mounted on plat-ig-num and gold.

CASS *catches her hand and searches earnestly.*

CASS   Where's the diamond?

TESSA   God, are you blind, too? There!

CASS   Oh yeah — yeah — so it is. Gee, that's nice, sweetie.

TESSA *moves away, lost in contemplation of her ring.*

  Would you do me a favour?

TESSA   (*Not listening*) What?

CASS   I got this only brother, see, Harry, and I expect he'll drop in to see me sometime this evening, you know, for Christmas and all; and I want you to tell me as soon as he comes, sweetie, 'cos I don't want that matron to turn him away or nuthin'. That would hurt him. And make a big fuss about him, honey, will you? All his days he's been kicked around. Treat him like he was important, you know.

TESSA   He old, too?

CASS   Harry? No, Harry's not old. But he's one of those guys — you know — he never got nuthin' much outa life. Just the two of us, and I guess he didn't have it good. I was the one that made it.

TESSA   We're going to spend our honeymoon in Glasgow.

CASS   You'll keep an eye out for him, sweetie?

TESSA All right. (*Leaving*) Come on. Your tea's ready.
CASS (*To herself*) Poor, poor Harry . . .

> *She sighs at Harry's bad luck. Then brightens, looks around the common room with calm satisfaction.*

Home at last. Gee, but it's a good thing to be home.

> *She lifts her bags that she always carries, takes another contented look around, and goes off singing her own version of 'Good King Wenceslas'.*
> *Curtain.*

LOVERS
WINNERS · LOSERS

Characters

Winners

MAN
WOMAN
MAG
JOE

Losers

ANDY TRACEY
HANNA WILSON/TRACEY
MRS WILSON
CISSY CASSIDY

Time and place

The present in Ireland.

Lovers was first produced by the Gate Theatre, Dublin, on 18 July 1967, with the following cast:

Winners

MAN	Niall Toibin
WOMAN	Anna Manahan
MAG	Fionnula Flanagan
JOE	Eamon Morrissey

Losers

ANDY	Niall Toibin
HANNA	Anna Manahan
MRS WILSON	Ruth Durley
CISSY CASSIDY	Cathleen Delany

Directed by	Hilton Edwards
Setting by	Robert Heade

In memory of
Tyrone Guthrie

WINNERS

Episode One

When the curtain rises a MAN *and a* WOMAN *are seated on two high-backed chairs, one down left and one down right, at the edge of the stage. They are the Commentators. They are in their late fifties and carefully dressed in good dark clothes. Each has a book on his knee — not a volume, preferably a bound manuscript — and they read from this every so often. Their reading is impersonal, completely without emotion: their function is to give information. At no time must they reveal an attitude to their material.*

Between them and slightly upstage is Ardnageeha, the hill that overlooks the town of Ballymore. For this I would suggest a large pentagonal platform, approached by four or five shallow steps all round. This is the only stage furniture.

MAG *is seventeen, bubbling with life, inclined to be extreme in her enthusiasms. Although she is not really very beautiful her vivacity gives her a distinct attraction. Whatever she likes she loves; whatever she dislikes she hates — momentarily. She is either very elated or very depressed, but no emotion is ever permanent. She wears a blue school blazer, white blouse, grey skirt.*

JOE *is seventeen and a half. He is a serious boy, a good student, interested in his books. He is at the age when he is earnest about life; and he has a total and touching belief in the value and importance of education.*

MAN At approximately 9:45 on the morning of Saturday, June 4, 1966, Margaret Mary Enright set out from her home, a detached red-brick house on the outskirts of the town of Ballymore, County Tyrone, Northern Ireland. Before she left she brought breakfast to her mother who was still in bed; and as she passed her father's surgery, which is built as an annex to the house, she tapped with the back of her fingers on the frosted glass panel of the door. In a small attaché case she had her schoolbooks and sandwiches for lunch. She cycled through the town and at High Street she met two friends and stopped to talk to them: Joan O'Hara, a classmate, and Philip Moran. They told her they planned to go boating on Lough Gorm that afternoon and asked her to join them. She said that perhaps she would. Then she cycled out the Mill Road until she came to Whelan's Brae. There she left the road and pushed her bicycle —

MAG *enters at this point.*

— across the fields until she came to the foot of Ardnageeha, the hill that overlooks the town of Bally-more. She left her bicycle at the bottom of Ardnageeha and climbed to the top. It was a glorious summer's morning. Temperatures were in the lower seventies. And there was no wind.

When MAG *gets to the top of the hill she looks around for* JOE. *He has not arrived yet. She lights a cigarette, squats on the ground, and waits for him.*

WOMAN At roughly the same time as Margaret Enright set out, Joseph Michael Brennan left his home at 37 Railway Terrace. His mother had gone to work two hours previously and had left his breakfast ready for him. His father was still in bed and asleep.

He went out through the backyard, down the mews lane, and across the waste ground between the rear of Railway Terrace and the railway line. On his way across the waste ground he met some children who were throwing stones at rats. He followed the line out past the marshalling yard, under the iron bridge, and for a mile out into the country. He carried his schoolbooks in a leather satchel. When he got to the level crossing he cut across the fields until he came to the

foot of Ardnageeha, the hill that overlooks the town of
Ballymore.

> JOE *enters here.*

Then he climbed to the top.

> MAG *sees him coming up the hill. She goes down the*
> *far side, i.e., upstage, until she is out of sight. There*
> *she hides.*

MAN Margaret Enright was a pupil of St Mary's Grammar
School, run by the Sisters of Mercy. And Joseph Brennan
was a pupil of St Kevin's College, a grammar school for
boys run by the clergy of the diocese. She was seventeen; he seventeen and a half. And they had their books
with them because school was officially over for the
year and they planned to spend the day studying for
their final examinations at the end of their grammar
school course. The examinations began the following
Wednesday.

JOE Maggie! Maggie! (*Shouts*) Maaaaaag!

> *When he gets no response he squats on the ground,*
> *opens his bag, takes out a book, and begins to work.*

WOMAN They stayed on top of Ardnageeha, that overlooks the
town of Ballymore, from ten until two. They had their
lunch up there. We can assume that they did some
work because Joseph was an excellent student, not
brilliant, but very keen and very industrious. Margaret
was no scholar. She was intelligent but scattered. And
we can assume that they talked some and perhaps
dreamed some, because they were young and the day
was beautiful. And even though the examinations were
imminent they cannot have been all that important to
the young pair who were to be married in exactly three
weeks' time, on Saturday, June 25, because Margaret
was pregnant.

JOE glances up from his work and scans the land below him. No sign of MAGGIE. *He returns to his book. Now* MAGGIE *creeps up behind him and pounces on his back, trying to push him to the edge of the hill so that he will roll down. They wrestle for a few seconds.*

JOE Come on! Cut it out, will you! That'll do!

MAG Ha! You leaped like a rabbit!

JOE I was looking for you. Where were you?

MAG Waiting for you. You're late.

JOE I was here at ten exactly .

MAG I've been here for at least half-an-hour.

She throws herself on the ground in exaggerated exhaustion, produces cigarettes, and begins talking. During most of this episode JOE *is studying, or trying to study. But occasionally he tunes in to her prattle. By throwing in an occasional word he gives her the impression he is conversing with her.*

JOE Did you walk it?

MAG The bike's lying at the foot of the hill.

JOE I didn't see it.

MAG Sure you're half blind! God, my tongue's hanging out for a week after that! (*Inhales and exhales with satisfaction*) Aaah, bliss! Sister Pascal says: you may search the lists of the canonized but you will search in vain for the saint that smoked. Maybe you'll be a saint, Joe.

JOE Let's get started.

MAG I read in a book that there are one million two hundred thousand nuns in the world. Isn't that fierce? Imagine if they were all gathered in one place — on an island, say — and the Chinese navy was let loose at them — cripes, you'd hear the squeals in Tobermore! I have a wicked mind, too. D'you ever think things like that, Joe? I'm sure you don't. I think that women have far more corrupt minds than men, but I think that men are more easily corrupted than women.

JOE We'll get a couple of hours done before we eat.

MAG (*With excessive disgust*) Food! — I don't care if I never
see another bite ever again. My God, I thought I was
going to vomit my guts out this morning! And this
could keep up for the next seven months, according
to Dr Watson. The only consolation is that you're all
right. It would be wild altogether if you were at it too.
Sympathetic sickness, they call it. But it's only husbands
get it. Maybe you'll get it this day three weeks — the
minute we get married — God, wouldn't that be a
scream! D'you know what Joan O'Hara told me? That
all the time her mother was expecting Oliver Plunkett
her father never lifted his head out of the kitchen
sink. Isn't it crazy! And for the last three days he lay
squealing on the floor like a stuck pig and her mother
had to get the police for him in the end. I love this
view of Ballymore: the town and the fields and the
lake; and the people. When I'm up here and look
down on them I want to run down and hug them all
and kiss them. But then when I'm down among them
I feel like doing that (*she cocks a snook into* JOE's *face*)
into their faces. I bet you that's how God feels at times,
too. Wouldn't you think so?

JOE I don't know how God feels.

MAG Why not?

JOE Because I'm not God.

MAG Oh, you're so clever! Well, I'll tell you something: there
are occasions in my life when *I* know how God feels.

JOE Good for you.

MAG And one of those occasions is now. (*Puffing her cigarette
regally*) At this moment God feels . . . expansive . . . and
beneficent . . . and philanthropy.

JOE Philanthropic.

MAG (*After momentary setback*) And we will not be put into
bad humour by grubby little pedants.

JOE Look, Mag: we came up here to study. What are you
going to do first?

MAG French. And then maths. And then Spanish. And then
English language and literature. After lunch geography
and history of the world. I have planned a programme

for myself. The important thing about revising for an
examination is to have a method. What are you start-
ing with?

JOE Maths.

MAG Then what?

JOE That's all.

MAG Only maths?

JOE Huh-huh.

*She considers this absurd idea for a second. Then,
because* JOE *is wiser in these things than she, she
readily agrees with him.*

MAG Then that's what I'll do, too. (*Really worried*) My God, if
the volume of a cone doesn't come up, I'm scootrified!
Not that I care — I can afford to go down in one subject.
(*Pause*) Joe . . .

JOE What?

MAG What's the real difference between language and literature?

JOE You're not serious, Maggie!

MAG Don't — don't — don't tell me . . . I remember now . . .
One is talking and the other is . . . books!

JOE Talking . . . ?

MAG That's it.

JOE That's no definition! Language is —

MAG Don't say another word. I have it in my head. But if you
start lecturing I'll lose it again. I have my own way of
remembering things. Joe, last night again Papa asked
me to let him get the flat painted for us before we move
in.

JOE (*Doggedly*) I said I'll paint the flat.

MAG That's what I told him. And I was thinking, Joe . . .

JOE What?

MAG If we put a lace curtain across the kitchen window we
wouldn't actually *see* down into the slaughterhouse yard.

JOE And if we wore earplugs all the time we wouldn't
actually hear the mooing and the shooting!

MAG (*Softly to herself*) And even if a curtain did make the room darker it'd still be lovely.

JOE I signed the lease yesterday evening.

MAG (*Absolutely thrilled*) It's ours now? We own it?

JOE Old Kerrigan was so busy working he wouldn't take time off to go into the office; so we put the document on the back of a cow that was about to be shot and that's where we signed it. Cockeyed old miser!

MAG He's not!

JOE What?

MAG Cockeyed.

JOE I'm telling you. And crazy, too. In a big rubber apron and him dripping with blood. And cows and sheep and bullocks dropping dead all around him.

MAG Oh God, my stomach!

> JOE *realizes that his tale is successful. He gets up on his feet to enact the scene.* MAG *listens with delight and soon gets drawn into the pantomime.*

JOE 'Drive them up there! Another beast. Come on! Come on! I haven't all day. And what's bothering you, young Brennan? Steady, there! Steady! Bang! Bang! Drag it away! Slit its throat! Slice it open! Skin it!'

MAG Stop — stop!

JOE 'Another beast! Get a move on! What am I paying you fellas for?' You told me to call about the flat, Mr Kerrigan. 'Steady — bang! Bang! Dammit, I nearly missed — bang! — that's it. Drag him off. What are you saying, young Brennan? The lease? Oh, the lease! Oh, aye. Here we are.' (JOE *produces an imaginary document from his hip pocket*) 'Best flat in town. Hell, it's all blood now.' (JOE *wipes the imaginary document on his leg*) 'Come on! Another animal! There's a fine beast for you, young Brennan! Look at those shanks! Bang! Bang! Never knew what hit him! I sign here, son, don't I?' (JOE *pretends to write: but the pen does not work and he flings it away*) 'Hell, that doesn't write.'

MAG Bang! Bang!

JOE 'Keep behind me, young Brennan. This is a dangerous

job.'

MAG Let's sign it in blood, young Brennan.

JOE 'Finest view in town. And the noise down here's great company.' Bang! Bang!

MAG Like living in Dead Man's Creek.

JOE There's a bullock that looks like the president of St Kevin's. Bang! Bang!

MAG A sheep the image of Sister Paul. Bang! Bang!

JOE Drag 'em away!

MAG Slice 'em open!

JOE Joan O'Hara's white poodle, Tweeny.

MAG Bang! And Philip Moran's mother.

JOE Bang! Bang! Dr Watson.

MAG A friend. Pass, friend, pass.

JOE Skinny Skeehan, the solicitor.

MAG Bang-bang-bang-bang! Look — Reverend Mother!

JOE Where?

MAG To the right — behind the rocks!

JOE (*Calling sweetly*) Mother Dolores.

MAG (*Answering sweetly*) Yes, Joseph?

JOE (*Viciously*) Bang-bang-bang!

MAG *grabs her stomach and falls slowly.*

MAG Into Thy hands, O Lord —

JOE Bang!

The final bullet enters her shoulder.

MAG Oh shite — !

MAG *rolls on the ground, helpless with laughter.*

JOE The town clerk — bang! All the teachers — bang!

MAG The church choir —

JOE Bang! Everyone that lives along snobby, snotty Melville Road — bang-bang-bang-bang-bang!

MAG A holy-cost, by God.

JOE *listens attentively. Silence.*

JOE Everything's quiet. Now we'll have peace to study. Back to the books.

MAG I'm sore all over. (*Searching*) Give us a fag, quick.

JOE (*Bashfully*) I'm afraid — I — sort of — sort of lost my head there, ma'am.

MAG Does your mother know you act the clown like that?

JOE Does your father know you smoke? Look at the time it is! I came here to work.

He goes back to his books. He is immediately immersed.

MAG Joe . . .

JOE What?

MAG The flat's ours now?

JOE Isn't that what I'm telling you.

MAG You're sure you wouldn't like the top floor in our house?

JOE Positive.

MAG (*After a moment's hesitation*) So am I. I just wanted to know if you were, too.

JOE Goodbye.

MAG It's only that Papa'll be lonely without me. For his sake, really. But he'll get over that. And it's just that this is the first time he'll ever have been separated from me, even for a night. But he'll get over it. All parents have to face it sooner or later. (*Happily*) Besides, I can wheel the pram over every afternoon. (*She looks at* JOE, *lost in his books: and again she has the momentary dread of the exam*) I'm like you, Joe. When I concentrate you could yell at me and I wouldn't hear you. (*She opens a book — almost at random. Looks at the sky*) It's going to be very warm . . .

She takes off her school blazer, rolls up the sleeves of her blouse, and stretches out under the sun.

If we didn't have to work we could sunbathe. (*Pause*)

That Easter we were in Florence I kept thinking about your father and how good the sun there would have been for his asthma. I read in a book that asthma is purely psychosomatic and that a man with asthma has a mother fixation. Crazy the things they dig up, too. I'm glad Papa's not a doctor or he'd be watching me for symptoms all the time. Your parents are such wonderful people, Joe. I'm crazy about them. And I'm going to model myself on your mother. And from now on I'm going to treat my own parents with . . . with a certain dignity. My God, the things they said to me — they seared my soul forever —

And without drawing a breath she hums a few bars of a popular song. She has a book before her eyes — but her eyes are closed.

MAN   Joseph Brennan was the only child of Mick and Nora Brennan. Because of his asthma Mick Brennan has not had a job for over twenty years. He receives unemployment benefit and this is supplemented by the earnings of his wife who works as a charwoman from 8.00 a.m. until 8.00 p.m., six days a week, for two-and-six an hour. In a good week her wages come to around nine pounds. She has one hundred and thirteen pounds ten shillings and sixpence in post-office savings and three pounds five shillings and sevenpence in an ornate tea caddy in the kitchen. She is a quiet woman and all her dreams and love and hope and delight were centred unashamedly in Joe. Mick Brennan — or Mick the Moocher, as he is known in Ballymore — is keenly interested in horses, greyhounds, ferrets and pigeons. He spends most of his day at the greyhound track. To his friends he talked a lot about Joe, always referring to him in a casual, disparaging way as The Lad. Nora Brennan has no hobbies.

WOMAN   Margaret Enright was the daughter of Walter and Beth Enright. Walter is a dentist. When he married he was the only dentist in Ballymore. Now there are three;

and his practice is the smallest. As a young man he was interested in books and travel and music. Now, after his work, he sits at home, and drinks, and reads thrillers. Beth, his wife, has been under Dr Watson's care for seventeen years, ever since the death of her infant son. She gave birth to twins — Margaret and Peter — and five days after the birth Peter was discovered in his cot, smothered by a pillow. She never fully recovered from this. In her good days she is carefree — almost reckless. In her bad days she wears dark glasses and lies in bed. Walter looks after her constantly.

> MAG *is drowsy with the heat. Her head is propped against her case. Through slitted eyes she surveys the scene below in Ballymore. She is addressing* JOE *but knows that he is not listening to her.*

MAG I can see the boarders out on the tennis courts. They should be studying. And there's a funeral going up High Street; nine cars, and a petrol lorry, and an ambulance. Maybe the deceased was run over by the petrol lorry — the father of a large family — and the driver is paying his respects and crying his eyes out. If he doesn't stop blubbering he'll run over someone else. And the widow is in the ambulance, all in plaster, crippled for life.

> *She tries out a mime of this — both arms and legs cast in awkward shapes.*

And the children are going to be farmed out to cruel aunts with squints and moustaches. Sister Michael has a beard. Joan O'Hara says she shaves with a cut-throat every first Friday and uses an aftershave lotion called Virility. God, nuns are screams if you don't take them seriously. I think I'd rather be a widow than a widower; but I'd rather be a bachelor than a spinster. And I'd rather be deaf than dumb; but I'd rather be dumb than blind. And if I had to choose between lung cancer, a coronary and multiple sclerosis, I'd take the coronary. Papa's family all died of coronaries, long before they were commonplace. (*She sits up to tell the following piece of family history*) He had a sister, Nan, who used to sing at the parochial concert every Christmas; and one year, when she was singing 'Jerusalem' — you know, just before the chorus, when the piano is panting Huh-huh-huh-huh-huh-huh, she opened her mouth and dropped like a log . . .

Joe, d'you think (*quoting something she has read*) my legs have got thick, my body gross, my facial expression passive to dull, and my eyes lacklustre? I hope it's a boy, and that it'll be like you — with a great big bursting brain. Or maybe it'll be twins — like me. I wonder what Peter would have been like? Sometimes when she's very ill Mother calls me Peter. If it were going to be twins I'd rather have a boy and a girl than two boys or two girls; but if it were going to be triplets I'd rather have two boys and a girl or two girls and a boy than three boys or three girls. (*Very wisely and directed to* JOE) And I have a feeling it's going to be premature.

> JOE *is alerted. His eyes move away from his book but his head does not move.*

Mothers have intuitions about these things. We were premature. Five weeks. Very tricky.

JOE Tricky?

MAG Caesarean, as a matter of fact.

> JOE *has never heard the term.*

JOE (*Too casually*) That — sure — sure that's — so was I, too.

MAG (*Delighted*) Were you? Isn't that marvellous! We really have everything in common! Oh, Joe, wait till you hear: I was doing my hair this morning, and d'you know what I found in the comb? A grey hair! I'm old! Two months pregnant and I'm as grey as a badger! Isn't it a scream! I think a young face and silver hair is more attractive than an old face and black hair. But if I had to choose between a young face and black hair and an old face and silver hair I think I'd prefer the young face. (*Gently*) You have a young face. You're only a boy. You're only a baby really. I'll have two babies to take care of. (*She touches his shoe*) Joe, we'll be happy, Joe, won't we? It's such a beautiful morning. So still. I think this is the most important moment in my life. And I think (*she laughs with embarrassment*), I think sometimes that happiness, real happiness, was never discovered until we discovered it. Isn't that silly? And I want to share it with everyone — everywhere.

JOE Stupid.

MAG What?

JOE A fat lot you have to give.

MAG I didn't say give!

JOE You did!

MAG I did not!

JOE I heard you!

MAG Liar! I said 'share'!

JOE Share what?

MAG You wouldn't understand!

JOE Understand what?

MAG *has lost the thread of the argument.*

MAG Anything! 'Cos you're just a selfish, cold, horrible, priggish, conceited donkey! Stuck in your old books as if they were the most important thing in the world; and your — your — your intended waiting like a dog for you to toss her a kind word!

JOE I only asked.

MAG You hate me — that's it — you're going to marry me just to crush me! I've heard of men like you — sadicists! I've read about them in books! But I never thought for a second —

She breaks off suddenly and clasps her stomach in terrified agony. At the same time she is pleasantly aware of JOE's *mounting panic.*

MAG Oh, my God — !

JOE What?

MAG Ooooooooooh — !

JOE What — what — what is it, Maggie?

MAG Joe — !

JOE Mag, are you sick? Are you sick, Mag?

MAG (*Formally*) Labour has commenced.

JOE (*In panic*) Sweet God! How d'you know? What's happening? I'll get help! Don't move! Dr Watson warned you to stop cycling! How d'you feel? I'll carry you. Don't move — don't move!

In total consternation he searches her face, noting every flicker of every feature. She is gratified at his anxiety. She acts the brave sufferer.

MAG I . . . think —

JOE Don't talk! Don't move! Where did you leave your bike?

MAG Stay with me, Joe, please. Hold my hand.

JOE God, this is fierce! On top of a bloody hill! You're all right, Mag, aren't you? Aren't you all right?

MAG (*She gives him a brave smile*) Dear Joe. I'm fine, thank you, Joe.

JOE What's happening? Tell me.

MAG Nothing to be alarmed about. False pains.

JOE False . . . ?

MAG (*Cheerily*) Gone again. For the time being.

JOE They'll be back?

MAG Oh, yes. But maybe not for a month.

JOE God, I'm not worth tuppence.

MAG I'm sorry for calling you names.

JOE Maybe you should go home, Mag, eh?

MAG I'm fine. Really. Go on with your work.

JOE God, I don't know.

MAG (*Smiling reassuringly*) Please. I'll just rest.

> JOE *gropes for something tender to say. But he is too embarrassed.*

JOE Maggie, I'll . . . I'll try . . . I'll try to be —
MAG (*A revelation*) I know now!
JOE Huh?
MAG No breakfast!
JOE What are you — ?
MAG Hunger pangs! That's what it was! I'm ravenous!
JOE Hunger — ?
MAG I could eat the side of a horse!
JOE But you said you didn't care — ?
MAG Don't be always quoting what I said. There's nothing as detestable as being quoted. I change my mind every two minutes. Or would you rather it was labour?
JOE (*Totally baffled*) I . . . I . . . (*Resolutely*) I'm going to work.

> *He begins to study again.* MAG *opens her case and takes out a packet of sandwiches.*

MAG All the same, if I eat now I'll have nothing left for later. I'll do with two small sandwiches. Three. (*Eats vigorously*) My big regret now is that I dropped domestic science in Junior. Can't even remember how to make rock buns. And poor old Dorothy Quilty was so sweet to us all. Did I ever tell you what happened to her, Joe? (*She waits for a reply, gets none, and goes on anyhow*) She was from Dublin. And one afternoon, during the Christmas holidays, she went to the pictures. And this man sat in the seat beside her — gospel truth — Joan O'Hara heard it from a cousin of hers who's a guard in Dundalk. And anyhow during the film this fellow gave her an injection in the arm. Of course no one saw him. And when she passed out he carried her out to the street, and his accomplice was waiting there in a car, and they drove off with her. (*Waits again for* JOE's *reaction. Then goes on*) And four days later she was found in the Wicklow mountains — up a sycamore tree.

JOE *turns round slowly to face her.*

JOE What d'you mean — up a sycamore tree?
MAG Hiding.
JOE Hiding what?
MAG Herself. In the leaves.
JOE (*Deliberately*) You really are crazy.
MAG She was hiding in the leaves, stupid, because they had taken her clothes away — that's the way. And for your knowledge and information she had to give up teaching after that experience. Nervous . . . Nervosity; that's what the doctor said she had. And she's now a stitcher in a Belfast shirt factory — of all girls.
JOE For a woman that's going to be married in four weeks' time —
MAG Three.
JOE Honest to God, the stories that you come out with — juvenile, that's the only word for them. And I'm trying to work at integration. So, will you shut up?
MAG (*With dignity*) I will. I certainly will. And the next time I break breath with you you'll be a chastened man. (*Brief pause*) But before I go silent for the rest of the day there's something I want to get clear between us, Joseph Brennan. (*Pause*) Joe.
JOE What?
MAG You never proposed to me.
JOE Huh?
MAG You haven't *asked* me to marry you.
JOE What are you raving about?
MAG Propose to me.
JOE God!
MAG Now.
JOE You really are — !
MAG Ask me.
JOE Will-you-marry-me. Now!
MAG Thank you, Joseph. I will.

He goes back to his books.

JOE Bats! Raving bloody bats!

MAG The children will want to know. Especially the girls. And I'll tell them it was a beautiful morning in June, a Saturday, four days before the exams began, on top of Ardnageeha, the Hill of the Wind. And everything was still. And their father said, 'Maggie,' very shyly, 'Maggie Enright, will you make me the proudest and happiest man in the whole world? Will you be my spouse?' And I said, 'Joe' — nothing more. And I think that was the most important moment in my life. (*She looks at* JOE, *sees him engrossed in his work, has a sudden stab of anxiety and grabs a book*) I really am scootrified this time! Integration — that's on my course, too — I think. What in the name of God does it mean?

She buries her head in her hands and studies furiously.

MAN It is estimated that Joe Brennan and Maggie Enright came down from the top of Ardnageeha around two o'clock that afternoon. They were seen walking hand-in-hand along the Mill Road at about ten-past-two; and ten minutes later they were seen going in the direction of Lough Gorm which lies to the east of Ballymore. Both were on foot. Joe was wheeling Maggie's bicycle. The recorded temperature at 3.00 p.m. on that Saturday afternoon, June 4, 1966, was 77 degrees. And there was no wind.

WOMAN Lough Gorm is three miles long and half a mile broad and there are forty-nine islands of various sizes scattered over it. There are seven boats on the lake. And on that afternoon two of them were out. Philip Moran and Joan O'Hara were out in Mr O'Hara's boat. They went out at noon and returned at 1.30. The other boat was William Anthony Clerkin's, an accountant in the local bank. He fished from eleven that morning until two that afternoon. Then he pulled in on the south shore, beside the old limekiln, and went home for his lunch. He left the oars and rowlocks lying in the boat. When he returned an hour and twenty minutes later the boat was gone; and a girl's bicycle was lying at the edge of the water.

MAG I'll tell you a tip. (*Pause*) Joe. (*Pause*) D'you want to know a clever trick I have, Joe? In all exams the smart thing to do is to write down everything you know — no matter what the question is. *Les oiseaux qui en sont dehors désespèrent d'y entrer; et d'un pareil soin en sortir, ceux qui sont au-dedans;* if the moving line is at right angles to the plane figure the prism is a right prism; in 1586 Sir Philip Sidney met his death at Zutphen from a wound in the nether regions of the body; the volume of a cone is $\frac{1}{3}\pi$ dh multiplied by — my God, and that's the one thing I know! Shakespeare, the Bard of Avon, besides writing thirty-four extant plays, was married to a woman eight years his senior, and was the father of twins. Like Papa. As flies to wanton boys are we to the gods; they kill us for their sport. Sister Pascal says that you always know Protestants by their yellow faces and Catholics by their dirty fingernails.

She rises, moves away from JOE, *who is lost in his books, and stands at the edge of the hilltop. She looks down over the town.*

Nuns are screams — if you don't take them seriously . . . I don't know what things I take seriously . . . Never books or school or things like that . . . Maybe God sometimes, when I'm in trouble . . . and Papa . . . and being a good wife to you . . . It's so quiet, with the whole world before me . . . Joe (*she turns to face him*), Joe, you'll have to talk a lot more to me, Joe. I don't care if it's not sensible talk; it's just that — you know — I feel lonely at times . . . Of course I'll have Joan; she'll visit us; Phil and herself. And you'll like her better when you get to know her. All that's wrong with her is that she's not mature yet; and she can be cruel at times . . .

    After we're married we'll have lots of laughs together, Joe, won't we? We'll laugh a lot, won't we? (*She begins to cry inaudibly*) Joe, I'm nervous; I'm frightened, Joe; I'm terrified . . .

MAN At 6.20 William Anthony Clerkin reported to Sergeant Finlay that his boat had been stolen. The Sergeant and Mr Finlay returned to Lough Gorm and walked around a portion of the south shore. They sighted the upturned boat floating about fifty yards west of the biggest island, Oileán na gCrann.

WOMAN As a result of inquiries the Sergeant learned that the bicycle belonged to Margaret Mary Enright. He phoned the Enright home and discovered that the girl had left there early in the morning. He then called at the Brennan home and Mr Brennan informed him that he had not seen his son all day.

MAG I will tell my secrets to my baby.

MAN It was then 7.45 pm.

WOMAN At 8.10 a search party of twenty-three local men set out to search the forty-nine islands.

> MAG *has another twinge of conscience; she plunges into her book again.*

MAG (*Reads*) LP, MQ, and NR are ordinates perpendicular to the axis ox such that $LP = 8''$, $MQ = 7''$, and $NR = 4''$. Find the lengths of the ordinates at the midpoints of LM and MN of the circular arc through P, Q, and R, and by means of Simpson's rule and the five ordinates estimate . . . (*Her concentration fails*) Everything's so still. That's what I love. At a time like this, if I close my eyes and scarcely breathe, I sometimes have very important philosophic thoughts — about existence and life and et cetera. That's what people mean when they talk of a woman's intuitions. Every woman has intuitions but I think that pregnant women have more important intuitions than non-pregnant women. And another thing, too: a woman's intuitions are more important while she's pregnant than after she's had her baby. So when you see a pregnant woman sitting at the fire, knitting, not talking, you can be sure she's having very important philosophic thoughts about things. I wish to God I could knit. Years and years ago in primary school I began a pair of gloves; but the fingers scootrified me and I turned them into ankle socks . . .

I think your father's a highly intellectual man, really; a born naturalist. And your mother — she's so practical and so unassuming. That's what I want to be. One of these days I'm going to stop talking altogether — for good — and people will say: Didn't Mrs Joseph Brennan become dignified all of a sudden? Since the baby arrived, I suppose. I think now, Joe, it's going to be nineteen days overdue. And in desperation they'll bring me into the hospital and put me on the treadmill — that's a new yoke they have to bring on labour; Joan told me about it. An aunt of a second cousin of hers was on it non-stop for thirteen hours. They keep you climbing up this big wheel that keeps giving way under you. Just like the slaves in olden times. And after the baby's born they'll keep it in an oxygen tent for a fortnight. And when we get it home it'll have to be fed with an eye dropper every forty-nine minutes and we'll get no sleep at all and — (*Sudden alarming thought*) My God, you won't get asthma like your father when you get old, will you?

JOE . . . equals 2.8 x t x p — all over pv — to the power of 1.4 x v . . .

MAG Even if you do I'll rub your chest with menthol and give you the kiss of life.

JOE Shhhhhh.

> *She watches him for a moment in silence. He is unaware of her existence.*

MAG There's something I want to tell you, Joe, and there's something I want to ask you as well. And I think I'll ask you the thing I want to ask you before I tell you the thing I want to tell you. (*Pause*) Joe.

JOE (*Very irritable*) What-what-what?

MAG My parents sleep in separate rooms. Do yours?

JOE In our house there are two bedrooms. I'm in one of them.

MAG And do they — have a single bed or a double bed?

JOE Double. Satisfied, Nosy?

MAG (*Fully gratified*) I knew that was a real marriage. That's what I want. Like your parents. Joe, there's something I want to try to explain to you, too.

JOE Look — five minutes more — that's all I ask. (*He does not listen to her*)

MAG I look at Papa and Mother, and Mr and Mrs O'Hara, and all the other parents and I think — I think — none of them knows what being in love really is. And that's why I think we're different. God, doesn't that sound stupid when you say it! But that's the way I feel, Joe. At this moment — here — now — I'm crazy about you — and mad and reckless, so that I want to shout to the whole town: I love Joe Brennan! I'm mad about him! I'd do anything for him! D'you hear me, Mother Dolores? I love him so much — so much — that I want to — to become him! Isn't that stupid? And when I look around me — at Papa and Mother and the O'Haras — I think: by God we'll never become like that, because — don't laugh at me, Joe — because I think we're unique! Is that how you feel, too?

> JOE *flings his book from him in exasperation. Speaks very articulately.*

JOE You-are-a-bloody-pain-in-the-neck! (*Quickly*) You haven't shut up for five consecutive minutes since we got here! You have done no work yourself and you have wasted my morning, too! And if anyone should be working it's you, because you haven't a clue about anything! In fact, you're the stupidest person I ever met!

MAG Stewbag!

JOE Sticks and stones — go ahead!

MAG And you can't kick a football the length of yourself!

JOE What has that got to do with it?

MAG That's what everybody calls you 'cos that's all you can do is stew — stew — stew!

JOE Born stupid.

MAG (*Crying*) Stewbag! Stewbag!

JOE Bawl away. Bawl your head off. But if you think I'm going to waste my life in Skinny Skeehan's smelly office that's where you're mistaken. You trapped me into marrying you — that's all right — I'll marry you. But I'll lead my own life. And somehow — somehow I'll get a degree and be a maths teacher. And nobody, neither you nor your precious baby nor anyone else, is going to stop me! So put that in your pipe and smoke it!

He opens his book and pretends to work, but he is too agitated. MAG *covers her face and cries.*

MAN The search was continued without interruption for three days. An SOS was broadcast, and ports and airports were watched. It was reported to the police that a young couple answering to the description were seen in Liverpool and later in the Waterford area. But an investigation proved both reports to be false. Margaret Mary Enright and Joseph Michael Brennan had disappeared.

WOMAN On Wednesday, June 8, the search was called off.

Curtain.

WINNERS

Episode Two

The sun is warmer because it is early afternoon. JOE *and* MAG *have had their lunch: papers and paper cups are lying around.* MAG *is stretched out on the ground, her head pillowed on her case; the essence of sloth. Her eyes are closed.* JOE *is working at a calculation with total concentration.*

WOMAN The months of June and July 1966 were the warmest and driest Ballymore has had since records have been kept. The water supply to the town had to be cut off for three hours each morning because the level of Lough Gorm dropped by almost two feet.

MAN Beth Enright, Margaret's mother, spent the greater portion of these months in the County Psychiatric Clinic. She was visited daily by Walter, her husband, and on two occasions by Nora Brennan, Joseph's mother, who brought her grapes and magazines.

>   JOE *has finished his calculations. He closes his books with a satisfied flourish.*

JOE Maths done! They can do their damnedest now — I'm ready for them! I'll tell you something, Mag: you know when you're sitting in the exam hall and the papers have just been given out and your eye runs down the questions? Well, those are the happiest moments in my life. There's always that tiny uncertainty that maybe this time they'll come up with something that's going to throw you; but that only adds to the thrill because you know in your heart you're . . . invincible. (*He begins to put his books away:*

because he is on top of his work he is in an expansive mood) I didn't tell you; I met old Skinny Skeehan: 'I'll start you in my office, lad, as soon as your exams are over. On your mother's account I hope you're a good timekeeper and that your writing is legible.' I never looked at him right before: his eyelids are purple and his ears are all hairy. So I just said to him: 'Stick your clerkship up your legal ass and get a lawnmower at those ears of yours' — like hell. But that's what I should have said, the hungry get. (*Mentally ticking off*) About another hour to French and the same at history and I'll leave the English to tomorrow. Remember I was telling you how George Simpson got an extra degree at London University? Well, I wrote to them last night for a syllabus. Three years; that's all it takes. Joseph Brennan, Bachelor of Science. Then, by God, the world's our oyster. You asleep, Mag?

MAG (*She neither moves nor opens her eyes*) No.

JOE Nothing wrong with you, is there?

MAG No.

JOE Are you in bad form or something?

MAG No.

JOE Did I do anything, Mag?

MAG No.

JOE As long as those false pains don't come back. (*Going on gaily*) Pity we hadn't our togs. Be a great day for a swim, wouldn't it? — if we could swim!

MAG I trapped you into marrying me — that's what you said.

JOE Huh?

MAG That's what you said. Put that in your pipe and smoke it — that's what you said.

JOE Ah, come on, Mag. You're not huffing still.

MAG And you meant it, too.

JOE But you ate your lunch and all. You ate more than I did.

MAG There was hate in your eyes.

JOE I'm sorry.

MAG It's no good.

> *Pause. Then* JOE *decides to win her round by clowning.*

JOE Mag —

MAG I'm not looking.

JOE *Mag —*

MAG No.

JOE Who's this, Mag?

MAG I'm going asleep.

JOE (*In mincing voice*) 'Tweeny — Tweeny — Tweeny — Tweeny! Come on, Tweeny girl. Atta girl. Come on. Come on.'

MAG That's not one bit like Mr O'Hara.

JOE (*In excessive nasal tones*) 'Good example is something we should all practise, my dear people. Put one bad apple into a barrel of good apples, and all the good apples become corrupt.'

MAG I'm not listening.

JOE 'But put one good apple into a barrel of bad apples, and then — and then — '

MAG You're not one bit funny.

JOE ' — and then' — (*rapidly*) 'Devotions this evening at six o'clock in the name of the father son holy ghost.'

MAG (*In matching tone*) Ha-men.

JOE (*East London*) 'So sorry, Joseph, but my Phil 'e's not at 'ome at present.'

> MAG *suddenly giggles.*

''E's out on 'is bi-cycle on one of 'is solitary nature rambles.'

> MAG *sits up. She laughs out loud.*

'Like 'is poor dad used to. I'll tell 'im you called. Bye-bye.'

MAG 'Ta-ta.'

JOE 'Ta-ta.'

MAG No. 'Ta-ta for now.'

JOE 'Ta-ta for now.'

MAG 'Call again soon, Joseph.'

JOE 'I like my Phil to 'ave chum boys.'

> *They both howl with spontaneous, helpless laughter. When they try to speak they cannot finish.*

MAG Sister Pascal —

JOE Wha —

MAG Sister Pascal —

JOE — is a rascal!

MAG She says that for every five minutes you laugh you —

JOE You what — ?

MAG — you cry for ten!

> *This seems the crowning absurdity. They roll on the ground.*

JOE Oooooooh . . . !

MAG God, I'm sore!

JOE Cruel!

MAG We'll cry for weeks!

JOE Nuns — bloody nuts!

MAG Give me a handkerchief.

> *He throws her one. She wipes her eyes. They sober up — and wonder what set them off. She lights a cigarette.*

JOE What started that?

MAG I don't know.

JOE Give me (*handkerchief*). Oh, my God.

MAG Leave you weak.

JOE This whole town's nuts.

> MAG *is stretched out under the sun again. A wistful mood creeps over them now that the laughter is forgotten.*

MAG D'you think they'll get married?

JOE Who?

MAG Joan and Philip.

JOE How would I know? They're only seventeen.

MAG They say they're both going to be architects.

JOE How long does that take?

MAG Seven years. Maybe then.

> JOE *busies himself with gathering up the remains of the lunch.*

JOE Maybe then what?

MAG Maybe then they'll marry, after they qualify.

JOE Maybe. Who cares.

MAG I don't.

JOE Neither do I.

MAG Why talk about them then?

JOE You mentioned them first.

MAG You did. You imitated Mr O'Hara and Phil's mother.

JOE Maggie, I did not mention Joan O'Hara's name. As a matter of fact I can't stick the girl.

MAG Sister Pascal was right.

JOE What about?

MAG We *will* cry for twice the length.

JOE For God's sake, woman!

> *He heads off down the far side of the hill to get rid of the old papers he has gathered.*

MAG (*Quickly*) Where are you going?

JOE I am going to dispose of this stuff — if I have your permission.

MAG You don't have to have my permission for anything. And I don't have to have yours either. 'Cos I'm not married to you yet, Mr Brennan, in case you have forgotten.

JOE No, I haven't forgotten.

> *He disappears. She calls after him.*

MAG Well, just in case you should! (*She settles back and closes her eyes resolutely*)

MAN On Tuesday, June 21, a local boy was driving his father's cows down to the edge of Lough Gorm for a drink when he saw what he described as 'bundles of clothes' floating just off the north shore. He ran home and told his mother.

WOMAN The police were informed, and Sergeant Finlay accompanied by two constables went to investigate. The 'bundles' were the bodies of Mary Margaret Enright and Joseph Michael Brennan. They were floating, fully clothed, face down, in twenty-seven inches of water.

MAN A post-mortem was held in the parochial hall at 7.00 p.m. that evening.

JOE has returned. He speaks with a dignified sincerity.

JOE Mag, there is something I never told you. And since you are going to be my wife I don't want there to be any secrets between us. I have a post-office book. I have had it since I was ten and there is twenty-three pounds and fifteen shillings in it now. I intend spending that money on a new suit, new shoes, and an electric razor. And I'm mentioning this to you now in case you suspect I have other hidden resources. I haven't. (*He cannot maintain this tone. He continues naturally*) And I was working out our finances. The rent of the flat's two-ten. That'll leave us with about four-ten. And if I could get some private pupils, that would bring in another — say — thirty bob. We can manage fine on that, can't we? I mean, I can. What about you? (*Looks down at her*) Mag? You asleep, Mag? How the hell can you sleep when you have no work done? Maggie . . . ?

He kneels beside her and looks into her face. He gently puts her hair away from her eyes. He straightens up as he remembers the word 'Caesarean'.

Dictionary . . . (*He gets his own dictionary and searches for the word*) Cadet . . . cadge . . . Caesar . . . Caesarean, pertaining to Caesar or the Caesars — section — an operation by which the walls of the stomach are cut open and . . . (*Shocked and frightened*) . . . Cripes! (*Reads*) As with Julius — oh, my God! If I see you on that bike again I'll break your bloody neck! As with Julius — good God! Maggie, are you all right, Maggie? Oh God, that's wild, wild! Sleep, Mag; that's bound to be good for you. (*He lifts her blazer and spreads it over her*) There. God almighty! Cut open. (*Takes the blazer off*) Maybe you'll be too warm. God, I'd sit ten exams every day sooner than this! Don't say a word, Maggie; just sleep and rest! That twenty-three pound fifteen — it's for you, Maggie. And I want you to — to — to squander it just as you wish: fur coats, dresses, perfumes, make-up, all that stuff — anything in the world you want — don't even tell me what you spend it on; I don't want to know. It's yours. And curtains for the window — whatever you like. God, Mag, I never thought for a minute it was that sort of thing! (*He looks closely at her*) Mag . . . (*Whispers*) Mag, I'm not half good enough for you. I'm jealous and mean and spiteful and cruel. But I'll try to be tender to you and good to you; and that won't be hard because even when I'm not with you — just when I think of you — I go all sort of silly and I say to myself over and over again: *I'm crazy about Maggie Enright*; and so I am — crazy about you. You're a thousand times too good for me. But I'll try to be good to you; honest to God, I'll try.

He kisses her hand and replaces it carefully across her body. Then with sudden venom:

Those Caesars were all gets!

He takes an apple from one of the lunch bags, gets out his penknife, and peels it. As he does, he talks to MAG *even though he knows she is asleep.*

I hope it's a girl, like you; with blond hair like yours. 'Cos if it's a boy it'll be a bloody hash, like me. And every night when I come home from Skeehan's office I'll teach her maths and she'll grow up to be a prodigy. I saw a programme on TV once about an American professor who spoke to his year-old daughter in her cot in four different languages for an hour every day; and when the child began to talk she could converse in German, French, Spanish, and Italian. Imagine if my aul' fella looked down into our wee girl's cot and she shouted up to him: 'Buenos dias!' Cripes, he'd think she was giving him a tip for a horse! I hope to God it's a girl. But if it's twins I'd rather have two boys or two girls than . . . (*He glances shyly at* MAGGIE *and tails off sheepishly when he realizes he has fallen into her speech pattern*) . . . D'you hear me? That's the way married people go. They even begin to look alike. Wonder is old Skinny Skeehan married? I bet she looks like a gatepost . . . Your father, Mag, my God he's such a fine man. And your mother — I mean, she's such a fine woman. I remember — oh, I was only a boy at the time — I remember seeing them walking together out the Dublin Road; and I thought they were so — you know — so dignified looking. I'd like to be like him. God, such a fine man. And so friendly to everyone. You're lucky to have parents like that . . .

My aul' fella — lifting the dole on a Friday — that's what he lives for. She laughs and calls him her Man Friday; but I don't know how she can laugh at it. And to listen to him talking — cripes, you'd think he was bloody Solomon. How he can sit on his backside and watch her go out every morning with her apron wrapped in a newspaper under her arm — honest to God, I don't know how he does it. I said it to her once, you know; called him a loafer or something. And you should have seen her face! I thought she was going to hit me! 'Don't you ever — ever — say the likes of that again. You'll never be half the man he is.' Loyalty, I suppose; 'cos when you're that age, you hardly — you know — really love your husband or wife anymore . . . Did I ever tell you what he does when there's no racing? He has this tin trunk under his bed; he keeps all my old school reports in it. And he sits up there in the cold and takes out the trunk and pores over all those old papers — term reports and all, away back to my primary-school days! Real nut! I know damn well when he's at it, 'cos I can hear the noise of the trunk on the lino. And once when I went into the room he tried to stuff all the papers out of sight. Strange, too, isn't it . . . You know, we never speak at all, except maybe 'Is the tea ready?' or 'Bring in some coal.' . . . Sitting up there in that freezing attic, going over my old marks . . .

Maybe when I'm older, maybe we'll go to football matches together, like Peadar Donnelly and his aul' fella . . . I don't like football matches, but he does; and we shouldn't have to speak to each other — except going and coming back . . . Three years is no length for a degree. And I think myself I'd be a good teacher.

MAG *speaks but does not move or open her eyes. Her voice is sleepy.*

MAG What time is it?

JOE Quarter-to-two.

MAG Call me at half-past, will you? I have a bit of revision to do.

JOE A bit! You've done nothing!

MAG *has dropped off again.*

JOE Mag!

MAG Mm?

JOE That's all right! You go ahead and sleep! But I'm telling you: if I die of a heart attack and leave you with a dozen kids you'll be damned sorry you haven't your GCE Ordinary Levels!

She sits up and stares at him. He goes on defiantly.

I'm just being practical. Nowadays you're fit for nothing unless you have an education. And you needn't stare at me like that: any qualification is better than nothing. You'll always get some sort of a job. Hennigan that teaches us PT — that's all he has — is GCE. And I'm telling you: I wouldn't give a shilling for your chances at the moment!

MAG And the children?

JOE What children?

MAG Who's going to look after the dozen children when I'm up at St Kevin's teaching physical jerks?

JOE Oh, you're very smart.

MAG And where, may I ask, did the round dozen come from all of a sudden?

JOE Cut it out, will you? You know what I meant.

MAG Indeed I do. And if you think I'm going to spend my days like Big Bridie Brogan —

JOE Who's she supposed to be?

MAG She's married to a second cousin once removed of Joan O'Hara's —

JOE God, I might have known! If there's anyone I hate —

MAG — *and* after her third baby the doctor told her she'd die if she had any more; but her husband was an Irish brute and she had a fourth baby —

JOE And she died.

MAG She didn't die, smartie. But she lost her sight. And then she had a fifth baby —

JOE And she died.

MAG — and she went deaf. And she couldn't walk after the sixth. And after the seventh she had to get all her teeth out —

JOE Sounds like the Rose of Tralee.

MAG And by the time she had ten —

JOE Her husband died laughing at her.

MAG — she developed pernicious micropia.

JOE Pernicious what?

MAG I'm not in the habit of repeating myself. Anyhow, she's

thirty-three now and —

JOE You made that word up.

MAG I did not.

JOE You did, Maggie.

MAG I did not.

JOE Say it again, then.

MAG I told you — I'm not in —

JOE Pernicious what?

MAG You're too ignorant to have heard of it. My father came across frequent cases of it. I don't suppose your parents ever heard of it.

As soon as she has said this she regrets it. But she cannot retract now. JOE's *banter is suddenly ended. He is quietly furious.*

JOE Just what do you mean by that?

MAG What I say.

JOE I said: What do you mean by that remark?

MAG You heard me.

JOE You insulted my parents — deliberately.

MAG I was talking about a disease.

JOE You think they're nobody, don't you?

MAG You were mocking me.

JOE And you think your parents are somebody, don't you?

MAG *picks a book, opens it at random, turns her back to him and begins to read.*

MAG I have revision to do.

JOE Well, let me tell you, madam, that my father may be temporarily unemployed, but he pays his bills; and *my* mother may be a charwoman but she isn't running out to the mental hospital for treatment every couple of months. And if you think the Brennans aren't swanky enough for you, then by God you shouldn't be in such a hurry to marry one of them! (*As soon as he has said this he regrets it. But he cannot retract now*) You dragged that out of me. But it happens to be the truth.

And it's better that it should come out now than *after* we're married. At least we know where we stand . . . (*His anger is dead*) Margaret? . . . Maggie? . . . (*Stiff again*) Well, it was you that started it. And if you're going into another of your huffs I swear to you I'm not going to be the first to speak this time.

> *He picks a book, opens it at random, turns his back to her and begins to read.*

WOMAN At the post-mortem on the evening of June 21 evidence of identification was given by Walter Enright. He said that the body recovered from Lough Gorm was the body of his daughter, Margaret Mary Enright.

MAN Michael Brennan identified the male body as that of his son, Joseph Michael Brennan.

WOMAN Dr Watson said that he examined the bodies of both the deceased. There were no marks of violence on either, he said. And in his opinion — which, he submitted, was given after a hasty examination — death in both cases was due to asphyxiation.

MAN Mr Skeehan, the coroner, asked was there any evidence as to how both deceased fell into the water. Sergeant Finlay replied that there was no evidence.

WOMAN A verdict in accordance with the medical evidence was returned. Mr Skeehan and Sergeant Finlay expressed their grief and the grief of the community to the parents. And it was agreed that the inquest should be held as soon as possible because the coroner took his annual vacation in the month of July.

> JOE *looks up from his book and surveys the country-side with studied intelligence. When he speaks he tries to sound as matter-of-fact as possible — as if he were continuing a conversation: but his voice is strained.*

JOE We're about 450 feet above sea level here; isn't that interesting? (*Pause*) And all that area out there was covered with fir trees once. (*Pause*) Willie O'Rourke

did a survey of the whole area for his geography
practical last term and he found out all sorts of
fascinating things. (*Pause*) The average rainfall in
Ballymore is 17.4 percent above the county average
and 23.9 percent above the national average. (*Pause*)
That's because we get a lot of rain here. (*Quoting*)
And the moist climate determines the type and extent
of our husbandry: we are low in milk cattle and
high in mountain sheep. (*Pause*) And since a ring of
hills cuts us off from other community centres we
are traditionally inclined to be independent and self-
supporting — or so he claims. (*Pause*) It's an interesting hypothesis. (*Pause*) Busy? (*No answer. Formally*)
I'm sorry for losing my temper. (*Opens another book*)
If you have anything to say to me you'll find me here.
(*No answer. He looks at her*) You're crying? . . . Mag? . . .
(*Still no answer. He rises and stands behind her*) What the
hell are you crying about, Mag? . . . Mag . . . (*He goes
in front of her. She turns her back to him*) I said I'm sorry.
What more can I do . . . ? (*Pause*) It's going to be just
great if you're going to spend your life weeping all
the time! (*He casts around wretchedly for something to
entertain her. Decides on mimicry. As Mrs Moran:*) 'Well,
I mean to say — smoking at 'is age! I just says to 'im,
"Phil," I says, "if your poor daddy was alive 'e'd be so
vexed," I says. 'Ta-ta for now, Joe. Ta-ta for now.' (*No
response from* MAG. *As Kerrigan:*) 'What about that for a
bit of beef, eh? Bang. Best flat in town, lad. I could
have let it a dozen times over. Bang. Bang. Bang.' (*No
response*) Mag . . . Mag, is it true that in bed at night
the nuns wear their bloomers over their heads to keep
them warm? (*No response. Sings*)

'So I gave her kisses one, kisses one;
So I gave her kisses one, kisses one;
So I gave her kisses one — now the fun has just
   begun
So I settled down to give her kisses more.'

(*Says*) I'd be great on TV, wouldn't I? (*No response*)
When Father Kelly sent for me last Friday fortnight

I knew I was done for, and I pretended I was so frightened I had a stammer — did I tell you that part of it? (*Pompous*) 'You know, of course, Brennan, that we are going to expel you.'

(*Abject*) 'Yes, F-f-f-father.'

(*Pompous*) 'Because of your mother's pleadings on your behalf, however, we have decided to allow you to return to sit for your examinations. But in the meantime I must insist that you remove all your belongings from the college and that you don't set foot within the grounds until the morning of the first examination.'

(*Abject*) 'T-t-t-thank you, Father.'

(*Pompous*) 'I will not talk again about the dishonour you have brought to your school, your family and yourself. And I trust you have made your peace with God. Goodbye, Brennan.'

(*Abject*) 'Goodbye, Father.'

(*Pompous*) 'Incidentally, Brennan, when did you develop the stammer?'

(*Abject*) 'W-w-w-when Maggie told me she was in trouble, Father.'

> MAG *began chuckling silently — unnoticed by* JOE *— at the beginning of this interview. Now she can contain her laughter no longer. At the last line she screams her delight and throws herself at him, and they roll on the ground.*

MAG God forgive you!

JOE Stop! Stop! God's truth —

MAG God forgive you! Mocking's catching!

JOE Come on — quit the fooling.

MAG I'll give you a stammer. (*She tosses his hair and tickles him*)

JOE Mag — please — sorry — please — oooooh —

MAG I'll stammer you —

JOE You're hurting my —

MAG That'll teach you!

JOE You've ripped off a button —

MAG You're a right-looking sketch!

Exhausted after the wrestling they sit staring at one another. Suddenly he throws his arms around her and kisses her. As he does:

MAN On Saturday, June 25, at 11.00 a.m. an inquest was held.

WOMAN After various witnesses had given evidence about the movements of the deceased on the morning of Saturday, June 4, Dr Watson said that the State Pathologist's report bore out his initial opinion — that death was due to asphyxiation as a result of drowning.

MAN There was no evidence as to how the deceased got into the water. William Anthony Clerkin's boat was perfectly sound.

WOMAN Sergeant Finlay stated that the temperature on that afternoon was 77 degrees. And there was no wind.

MAN An open verdict was returned.

WOMAN On the following Sunday, June 5, at 12 noon, a solemn Requiem Mass was said by Father Kelly, president of St Kevin's, and a short panegyric was preached by him. The Mass was attended by a large turnout of the townspeople and also by pupils of the Convent of Mercy and St Kevin's.

MAN The bodies were buried in separate graves in the local cemetery, each in the family plot.

JOE *and* MAG *are now sitting with their arms around one another, looking down over the town. The boisterousness is all over; the mood is calm, content, replete.* MAG *lights a cigarette.*

JOE This day three weeks.

MAG Mrs Joseph Brennan.

JOE As long as you're not Big Bridie Brogan.

MAG Who?

JOE The one who died of pernicious something-or-other.

MAG I made it all up.

JOE Thought you did.

MAG The flat'll be lovely and cozy at night. But you'll have to stick a bit of cardboard under the table to keep it steady. And all the junk'll have to be thrown into the spare room.

JOE What junk?

MAG Your books and things and all that.

JOE The slide rule cost me thirty-seven and sixpence — It's staying in the kitchen. And you agreed that the dog sleeps inside.

MAG When do we get him?

JOE He's not pupped yet. I was only promised him.

MAG Maybe he'll be a she.

JOE It's a dog I'm promised — the pick of the litter.

MAG We'll call him . . . Austin!

JOE For God's sake —

MAG Austin's his name. Or else he sleeps out.

JOE Never heard of a bull terrier called that.

MAG And in the daytime he can sit at the door and guard the pram. Look —

JOE Where?

MAG The line of boarders.

JOE What are they up to now?

MAG Going to the chapel for a visit.

JOE (*Counting*) 14, 16, 18, 20 —

MAG It seems so remote — so long ago . . .

JOE — 26, 28, 30, 32 —

MAG And at home last week every time I heard the convent bell I cried: I felt so lost. I would have given anything to be part of them — to be in the middle of them.

JOE And three nuns.

MAG We were so safe . . . we had so much fun . . .

JOE Mm?

MAG But now I wouldn't go back for the world. I'm a woman at seventeen, and I wouldn't be a schoolgirl again, not for all the world.

JOE I suppose I'm a man, too.

MAG Would you go back?

JOE Where?

MAG To St Kevin's — to being a schoolboy?

JOE I never think of things like that.

MAG But if you could — if you had a chance.

JOE I like studying, Mag.

MAG Then you'd prefer to go back.

JOE No. Not there. I'm finished with all that.

MAG Then you wouldn't want to go back?

JOE Not to St Kevin's. No.

MAG Good.

JOE Know something, Mag?

MAG Mm?

JOE I think I should forget about studying and London University and all that.

MAG If that's what you want.

JOE It's maybe not what I want. But that's the way things have turned out. A married man with a family has more important things to occupy his mind besides bloody books.

She gives him a brief squeeze. But she has not heard what he has said. Pause.

Ballymore.

MAG Home.

JOE See the sun glinting on the headstones beside the chapel.

MAG Some day we'll be buried together.

JOE You're great company.

MAG I can't wait for the future, Joe.

JOE What's that supposed to mean?

MAGGIE *suddenly leaps to her feet. Her face is animated, her movements quick and vital, her voice ringing.*

MAG The past's over! And I hate this waiting time! I want the future to happen — I want to be in it — I want to be in it with you!

JOE You've got sunstroke.

She throws her belongings into her case.

MAG Come on, Joe! Let's begin the future now!

Not comprehending, but infected by her mood, he gets to his feet.

JOE You're nuts.

MAG Where'll we go? What'll we do? Let's do something crazy!

JOE Mad as a hatter.

MAG The lake! We'll dance on every island! We'll stay out all night and sing and shout at the moon!

JOE does a wolf howl up at the sky.

Come on, Joe! While the sun's still hot!

JOE O mad hot sun, thou breath of summer's being!

MAG Away to the farthest island.

JOE We've no boat.

MAG We'll take one.

JOE And get arrested.

MAG Coward. Then I'll take one.

JOE I'll visit you in jail.

MAG Quick! Quick!

JOE throws his books into his bag.

JOE Hold on there.

MAG Give me your hand. We'll run down the hill.

JOE You'll get those pains again.

MAG Your hand.

JOE You're not going to run down there.

MAG Come on! Come on! Come on!

JOE Have sense, Mag —

She catches his hand and begins to run.

MAG We're away!

JOE Easy — easy —

MAG Wheeeeeeeee —

JOE Aaaaaaaaah —

Lovers: Winners

They run down the hill, hand in hand. At the bottom
JOE *takes her bicycle. Their voices fade slowly. Pause.*
Then:

MAN   Beth Enright's health has improved greatly. She has
not had a relapse for almost seven months. And every
evening, if the weather is good, Walter and she go for
a walk together out the length of Whelan's Brae.

WOMAN   Mick Brennan never mentions his son's name. After the
funeral he took a tin trunk out to the waste ground
behind Railway Terrace and burned all the contents.
Nora Brennan has had to limit the amount of work she
does because her varicose veins turned septic and
Dr Watson ordered her to rest. She now works on afternoons only.

MAN   In the past eight months the population of Ballymore
has risen from 13,527 to 13,569.

WOMAN   Life there goes on as usual.

MAN   As if nothing had ever happened.

The MAN *and* WOMAN *close their texts, stand up, and*
exit, one left, one right.

LOSERS

The stage is divided into three equal areas: the portion right is the back-yard of a working-class terrace house; the centre portion is the kitchen/living room; the area left is the bedroom (left and right from the point of view of the audience). There should be no attempts at a realistic division of the stage areas, no dividing walls, no detailed furnishings: frames will indicate doors, etc.

The backyard is suggested by a dustbin and by two high stone walls (one backstage and one right). It is a grey, grimy, gloomy, sunless place.

The kitchen is furnished with a table and a few chairs and with a disproportionately large horsehair black couch. The couch sits along the imaginary wall between the kitchen and the backyard. There are three doors leading out of the kitchen: one to the yard, one to the scullery (unseen) and one to the hall/stairs (also unseen).

The bedroom area is raised on a shallow platform which is approached by two steps (because this room is supposed to be directly above the kitchen). It is furnished with a big iron double bed, a chest of drawers (the 'altar') and a few chairs. Except where indicated the bedroom will be hidden from the audience by a large draft screen.

When the curtain rises ANDY TRACEY *is sitting upright and motionless on a kitchen chair in the backyard. He is staring fixedly through a pair of binoculars at the grey stone wall which is only a few yards from where he is sitting. It becomes obvious that he is watching nothing: there is nothing to watch, and when he becomes aware of the audience he lowers the glasses slowly, looks at the audience, glances cautiously over his shoulder at the kitchen to make sure that no one in the house overhears him, and then speaks directly and confidentially down to the auditorium.*

He is a man of fifty, a joiner by trade, heavily built. His workmates look on him as a solid, decent, reliable, slightly dull man. Because his mind is simple, direct, unsubtle, he is unaware of the humour in a lot of the things that he says.

ANDY   I'll tell you something: I see damn-all through these things. Well, I mean, there's damn-all to see in a backyard. Now and again maybe a sparrow or something like that lands on top of the wall there but it's so close it's only a blur. Anyway, most of the time I sit with my eyes closed. And Hanna — she probably knows I do 'cos she's no dozer; but once I come out here — I'll say that for her — she leaves me alone. A gesture I make, and she — you know — she respects it. Maybe because her aul' fella used to do the same thing; for that's where I learned the dodge. As a matter of fact, these are his glasses. And this is where he was found dead, the poor bugger, just three years ago, slumped in a chair out here, and him all happed up in his cap and his top coat and his muffler and his woollen gloves. Wait — I'm telling you a lie. Four years ago — aye — that's more like it, 'cos he passed away that January Hanna and me started going, and we won't be married four years until next summer. Not that I knew the man, beyond bidding him the time of day there. Maybe he'd be inside in the kitchen, there or more likely sitting out here, and I'd say to him, 'Hello there, Mr Wilson' — you know the way, when you're going with a woman, you try to be affable to her aul' fella — and he'd say, 'Oh, hello there, Andy,' or something like that back. But you know yourself, a man that's looking through binoculars, you don't like interrupting him. Civil wee man he was, too. Fifty years a stoker out in the general hospital. And a funny thing — one of the male nurses out there was telling me — all his life he stuck to the night shift: worked all night and slept all day, up there in that room above the kitchen. Peculiar, eh? All his life. Never saw the wife except maybe for a couple of hours in the evening. Never saw Hanna, the daughter, except at the weekends. Funny, eh? And yet by all accounts the civilest and decentest wee man you could meet. Funny, too. And the way things turn out in life; when the mother-in-law found him out here about seven o'clock that evening she got such a bloody fright that she collapsed and took to the bed for good and hasn't risen since, not even the morning we got married. The heart. But that's another story. Anyway, Hanna and me, as I say, we were only started going at the time; and then with the aul' fella dying and the aul' woman taking to the bed, like we couldn't go out to the pictures nor dances nor nothing like any other couple; so I started coming here every evening. And this is where we done our courting, in there, on the couch. (*Chuckles briefly*) By God, we were lively enough, too. Eh? I mean to say, people think that when you're . . . well, when you're over the forty mark, that you're passified. But aul' Hanna, by God, I'll say that for her, she was keen as a terrier in those days. (*Chuckles at the memory*) If that couch could write a book — Shakespeare, how are you!

He rises from the chair.

Every evening, after I'd leave the workshop, I'd go home to my own place at Riverview and wash myself down and make a sup of tea and put on the good suit and call in at Boyce's paper shop and get a quarter of clove rock — that's the kind she liked — and come on over here and there she'd be, waiting for me, in a grey skirt and a blue jumper, and when she'd open the door to me, honest to God the aul' legs would damn near buckle under me.

> HANNA *comes into the kitchen from upstairs. She is dressed in a grey skirt and blue jumper.* ANDY *walks through the invisible walls, through the hall, and taps on the kitchen door.*
> HANNA *is in her late forties. She works in a local shirt factory, lives alone with her invalided mother, and until* ANDY *came on the scene has not been out*

*with a man for over twenty years. And this sudden
injection of romance into a life that seemed to be
rigidly and permanently patterned has transformed
a very plain spinster into an almost attractive
woman. With* ANDY *she is warm: with her mother
she reverts to waspishness.*

Because neither ANDY *nor* HANNA *is young there
is a curious and slightly dated diffidence between
them. And yet, when they begin courting, it is* HANNA
*who takes the initiative and caresses him with a
vigour and concentration that almost embarrass
him.*

ANDY Well, Hanna.

HANNA Hello, Andy.

ANDY Not a bad evening.

HANNA There's a cold wind, though.

ANDY It's sharp — sharp.

HANNA But it's nice all the same.

ANDY Oh, very nice — very fresh. (*Pause*) Nothing start-
ling at the factory?

HANNA Not a thing. Working away.

ANDY Suppose so.

HANNA Cutting out shirt collars this week. And you?

ANDY Still at the furniture for the new hotel. Going to cost
a fortune, yon place.

HANNA I'll bet you.

ANDY Only the very best of stuff going into it: maple and
pine and mahogany. Lovely to work with.

HANNA D'you see that now.

ANDY Lovely.

> *Pause. Then* ANDY *produces the small bag of sweets
> from his pocket.*

ANDY Here. Catch. (*He throws them to her*)

HANNA Oh, Andy . . .

ANDY They don't even ask me in the shop anymore. They
just say, 'Quarter pound of clove rock, Mr Tracey.

Right you are.'

HANNA You have me spoiled.

ANDY How's the mother?

HANNA (*Sharply*) Living. And praying.

ANDY Terrible sore thing, the heart, all the same.

HANNA I come home from my work beat out and before I get a bite in my mouth she says, 'Run out like a good child and get us a sprig of fresh flowers for St Philomena's altar.'

ANDY Did you go?

HANNA points to the flowers wrapped in paper lying on the kitchen table.

HANNA But she can wait for them.

ANDY She'll miss you when you leave, Hanna.

HANNA Hasn't she Cissy Cassidy next door? And if she hadn't a slavey like me to wait hand and foot on her her heart mightn't be just as fluttery! (*From behind the screen comes the sound of a bell — not a tinkling little bell, but a huge brass bell with a long wooden handle*) We're early at it the night! There's the paper. Have a look at it.

With a bad grace she goes to answer the summons. As she is about to exit:

ANDY The flowers.

She grabs them, grimaces and leaves. ANDY calls after her:

Tell St Philomena I was asking for her!

He chuckles at Hanna's bad humour. Then he comes downstage and addresses the audience:

That bloody bell! And nine times out of ten, you know, she didn't want a damn thing: Who's at the door? Is the fire safe? Did the Angelus ring? Is it time for the Rosary? Any excuse at all to keep Hanna on the hop, and at the same time making damn sure we weren't going to enjoy ourselves. But we got cute. You see, every sound down here carries straight up to her room; and we discovered that it was the long silences made her suspicious. That's the way with a lot of pious aul' women — they have wild dirty imaginations. And as soon as there was a silence down here she thought we were up to something and reached for the bloody bell. But if there was the sound of plenty of chatting down here she seldom bothered you. But I mean to say, if you're courting a woman there, you can't keep yapping about the weather all night. And it was the brave Hanna that hit on the poetry idea. Whenever we started the courting she made me recite the poetry — you know there, just to make a bit of a noise. And the only poetry I ever learned at school was a thing called 'Elegy Written in a Country Churchyard' by Thomas Gray, 1716 to 1771, if you ever heard tell of it. And I used to recite that over and over again. And Hanna, she would throw an odd word in there to make it sound natural. And, by God, we'd hammer away at it until we'd stop for breath or for a sup of tea or something; or else we'd get carried away and forget the aul' woman altogether — and then the bloody bell would go and the session would be destroyed. But they were good times . . . Funny thing about that poem, too: it had thirty-two verses, and as long as I could bull straight at it — you know, without thinking what I was saying — I could rattle it off like a man. But stop me in the middle of it or let me think of what I was saying and I had to go right back to the beginning and start all over again. Christ, they were rare times, too . . .

HANNA *returns*.

ANDY   Well?

HANNA 'Is that Andrew I hear?' 'No,' says I, 'it's Jack the Ripper.'

ANDY   And how's St Philomena?

HANNA You can laugh. 'The pair of you'll be up later for the Rosary, won't you?'

ANDY   (*Mock devotion*) With the help of God.

HANNA One of these days I'll do something desperate.

> *She sits dispiritedly beside him on the couch. He wants to say something tender and consoling to her but feels he is past the age for effusive, extravagant language.*

ANDY   You're looking nice, Hanna.

HANNA It's the jumper.

> *Pause. Then he takes her hand in his and strokes it. She raises his hand to her lips and kisses it gently again and again. He puts his arm round her shoulder. They sit like this for some time.*

We'd better keep talking.

ANDY   There's a nice smell of you.

HANNA Soap.

ANDY   Nice soap.

HANNA (*Dreamily*) Her bloody ear'll be twitching like a rabbit.

ANDY   Hanna . . .

> *Pause. They speak the next eight lines as if they were in a trance.*

HANNA Say something, Andy.

ANDY   I don't want to.

HANNA Please, Andy. She'll know.

ANDY   I don't give a damn.

HANNA Andy . . .

ANDY   Nice . . .

HANNA Please, Andy . . .
ANDY Very nice . . .

> *Very suddenly, almost violently,* HANNA *flings her-*
> *self on him so that he falls back, and she buries her*
> *face in his neck and kisses and caresses him with*
> *astonishing passion. He is momentarily at a loss. But*
> *this has happened before, many times, and he knows*
> *that this is his cue to begin his poem. His recitation*
> *is strained and too high and too loud — like a child*
> *in school memorizing meaningless facts. Throughout*
> *his recital, they court feverishly.*

'The curfew tolls the knell of parting day,
The lowing herd wind slowly o'er the lea,
The plowman homeward plods his weary way,
And leaves the world to darkness and to me.
Now fades the glimmering landscape on the sight —'
HANNA (*To ceiling*) It's a small world, isn't it?
ANDY 'Now fades the glimmering landscape on the sight,
And all the air a solemn stillness holds,
Save where the beetle wheels his droning flight,
And drowsy tinklings lull the distant folds —'
Oh, God, Hanna —
HANNA Just imagine. Fancy that. Keep going, man.
ANDY 'Save that from yonder ivy-mantled tower
The moping owl does to the moon complain
Of such as, wand'ring near her secret bower,
Molest her ancient solitary reign.'
HANNA Andy — Andy —
ANDY 'Beneath those rugged elms, that yew tree's
    shade —'

> HANNA *groans voluptuously.*

Steady on — steady on — say something —
HANNA Mm?
ANDY She'll be listening to —
HANNA I don't give a damn.

ANDY (*To ceiling*) Fine. Yes, indeed. Imagine that. Where in the name of God was I?

HANNA 'That yew-tree's shade —'

ANDY What, where?

HANNA 'Beneath those rugged elms.'

ANDY Oh. 'Beneath those rugged elms, that yew tree's shade,
Where heaves the turf in many a mouldering heap,
Each in his narrow cell for ever laid,
The rude forefathers of the hamlet sleep.'
Speak, woman!

She kisses him on the mouth.

Say something!

HANNA Kiss me.

ANDY For God's sake, woman —

HANNA Andy, kiss me.

He kisses her. They forget everything. The clanging of the bell shatters the silence — and HANNA breaks away roughly from him, jumps to her feet, and is almost trembling with fury. Her jumper and skirt are twisted.

Bitch! The aul' bitch!

ANDY Sure you're only after leaving her! What the hell can she want?

HANNA Stuffed!

ANDY Your jumper.

HANNA Agh! My . . . !

She pulls the jumper right up and then pulls it back into place. ANDY laughs at her anger.

ANDY Go on — go on — go on. A girl's best friend is her mother.

HANNA Shut up, will you.

*She adjusts her skirt and brushes back her hair
and charges out of the room.* ANDY *looks after her
and smiles contentedly. Then he addresses the
audience:*

ANDY By God, she had spunk in those days, eh? Suited
her, too: gave her face a bit of colour and made her
eyes dance. But whatever it was that happened to
her — well, I mean to say, I think I know what
happened . . . But, like, to see a woman that had
plenty of spark in her at one time and then to see
her turn before your very eyes into a younger
image of her mother, by God, it's strange, I tell you,
very peculiar . . .

But I was going to tell you about the aul' woman
and the altar and the Rosary and St Philomena and
Father Peyton and all that caper. The routine was
this. At the stroke of ten every night wee Cissy
Cassidy — her and the aul' woman's well met; two
lisping Lizzies — she came down and asked Hanna
and me to go up for the nightly Rosary. Fair enough.
Why not? And there's the aul' woman lying in the
bed, smiling like an angel, and there, smiling back
at her from the top of a chest of drawers, is this big
statue of St Philomena. And you know, you got this
feeling, with the flowers and the candles lit and
with all the smirking and smiling and nodding and
winking, you got the feeling by God that you were
up to the neck in some sort of a deep plot or other.
Like I knew damn well what the aul' woman was
up to: if she couldn't break it up between Hanna
and me at least she was going to make damn sure
that I wasn't going to take Hanna away from her.
And *she* knew that *I* knew what she was up to with
her wee sermons about Father Peyton and all the
stuff about the family that prays together stays together. And there was the pair of us, watching and
smiling, each of us knowing that the other knew,
and none of us giving away anything. By God, it

was strange. Eh? 'Cos she thought that every time I got down on my knees in that bedroom to join in the Rosary I was cutting my own throat. But because I knew what she was up to I was safe . . . or at least I thought I was. She's crafty, that aul' woman. You've got to hand it to her. By God she's crafty.

He goes upstage and casually lifts the newspaper to glance over it. HANNA *enters on her way through to the scullery. She is carrying her mother's soiled tray.*

HANNA Look at — the invalid tray! Not a crumb on it! Six rounds of a sliced-pan and a boiled egg! Thanks be to God she gets no fresh air or she'd eat up the town! (*Knock at the front door*) That'll be prissy Cissy.

She goes off to the scullery. ANDY *goes to open the door.* CISSY *and* ANDY *come back to the kitchen briefly before* CISSY *goes upstairs.*

CISSY *is a small, frail wisp of a woman in her late sixties. She lives next door, is a daily visitor and, because of the close friendship between herself and* MRS WILSON, *she has a proprietary air in the house. A lifetime spent lisping pious platitudes has robbed them of all meaning. The sickly piousity she exudes is patently false.*

ANDY Hello, Cissy.

CISSY Goodnight, Andrew. You're not alone, are you?

ANDY Hanna's inside. How's things, Cissy?

CISSY Struggling away, Andrew, thanks be to God. Sure as long as we have our health.

ANDY That's it, Cissy.

CISSY Thanks be to God, indeed. I'll go on up then, Andrew.

ANDY Right — right.

CISSY You'll be up later for the prayers?

ANDY Aye.

CISSY Thanks be to God.

> HANNA *enters from the scullery. She is abrupt with* CISSY.

Hello, Hanna. How's Mammy tonight?

HANNA As ever.

CISSY Sure that's grand.

ANDY (*Winking at* HANNA) Thanks be to God.

CISSY Just, Andrew — thanks be to God. Well . . . I'll see you both at ten.

ANDY Joyful Mysteries tonight, Cissy, isn't it?

CISSY Thursday — so it is! Oh, you're coming closer and closer to us, Andrew Tracey!

> *She leaves.* ANDY *laughs.*

HANNA Sweet wee wasp!

> HANNA *flops down on the couch.* ANDY *sits beside her. He sees she is in bad form and tries to coax her out of it.*

ANDY Tired?

HANNA Done out.

ANDY D'you think was Cissy ever courted?

HANNA Who cares?

ANDY Imagine a man putting a hand on her knee. 'Thanks be to God, mister.' (*She does not laugh*) You're in bad aul' form, Hanna.

> *He puts his arm round her. She jumps to her feet.*

HANNA Not now.

ANDY What's wrong? Is there something the matter?

HANNA Sick — sick — sick — sick of the whole thing; that's what's the matter! I can't stand it much longer!

ANDY Take a clove rock, Hanna.

HANNA What in the name of God are we going to do?

ANDY I've asked you half a dozen times to —

HANNA It's her I'm talking about! Her up there! What do we do with her?

ANDY When we're married she can come with us to Riverview. I've said that all —

HANNA Never! Never! The day I get married I'm getting shot of her for good!

> ANDY *spreads his hands: 'What can I reply to that?' the gesture says.*

And no matter what you say now you know fine well you don't want her hanging round your neck either.

ANDY I hear they took old Maggie Donaldson into St Patrick's.

HANNA She's not sick enough for hospital. And they've no spare beds for cranks.

ANDY The Nazareth nuns! Let her sell this place and go into the Nazareth House with the money.

HANNA She wouldn't go to them above all people.

ANDY What else is there?

HANNA I don't know, Andy. Honest to God, I just don't know.

> *Pause, and it dawns on* ANDY *that an offer is expected from him. He reacts strongly to the unspoken idea.*

ANDY Well, dammit all, you don't expect me to come in here, do you? I mean to say, I have a place and all of my own, ready and furnished and everything! And leaping sky-high every time you hear a bloody bell isn't my idea of married bliss! My God, you don't expect that of me, do you? Well, do you?

HANNA Bitch! That's what she is — an aul' bitch!

ANDY We're getting no younger, Hanna, you know.

HANNA Tomorrow — I'll tell her tomorrow that we're going

to clear out and she can damn well forage for herself!

ANDY You'll like it over at Riverview. It's — it's — (*He sees
that she is crying*) Hanna, Hanna — aw, God, you're
not away crying, are you —

> *He puts his arm round her and leads her to the
> couch. They sit. She blows her nose while he tries
> to console her.*

Come on, come on, there's no need for that. You
know I can't stand seeing you crying. And you
know I'd do anything to make you happy. We'll
solve it some way or other. Don't you worry about it
— we'll get some solution to it all.

HANNA No, we won't.

ANDY I'm telling you we will.

HANNA No, no. And only this morning I found myself
singing at my work. And sure I can't even sing in
tune.

ANDY I could listen to you all day.

HANNA But sure nobody goes through life singing all the
time.

ANDY We will, Hanna.

> *Very suddenly, almost violently — exactly as before
> — HANNA flings herself on him and smothers him
> with kisses. And, as before, he is taken unawares.
> Then he responds. But after a few seconds he real-
> izes that they are being silent and he launches into
> his poem.*

'The curfew tolls the knell of parting day,
The lowing herd wind slowly o'er the lea,
The plowman homeward plods his weary way,
And leaves the world to darkness and to me.'
Hanna . . . !

> *She does not hear him. Pause. Then he goes on:*

'Now fades the glimmering landscape on the sight,
And all the air a solemn stillness holds,
Save where the beetle wheels his droning flight,
And drowsy tinklings lull the distant folds.'
Say something, woman!

HANNA A loaf of bread costs one and threepence ha'penny
and a pound of tea six and eight pence.

ANDY 'Full many a gem of purest ray serene
The dark unfathomed caves of ocean bear:
E'en from the tomb the voice of Nature cries —'
I've bucked it!

HANNA 'Can storied urn or animated bust —'

ANDY What — what — what is it?

HANNA 'Back to its mansion call the fleeting breath?'

ANDY '... call the fleeting breath?
Can Honour's voice provoke the silent dust,
Or Flatt'ry soothe the dull cold ear of death?
Perhaps in this neglected spot is laid
Some heart once pregnant with celestial fire;
Hands that the rod of empire might have
swayed ...'

*But he fades out because he can no longer resist the
barrage of her passion. Their mouths meet. A long
kiss. Silence. Then — the bell.* HANNA *springs to her
feet. This time* ANDY *is angry too.*

HANNA Christ!

ANDY For God's sake!

HANNA Bitch! Bitch! Bitch! Bitch! Bitch!

ANDY It's your fault! You make no attempt at all.

HANNA I don't know no poems!

ANDY Well ... bloody shopping lists ... multiplication
tables ... anything! (*Again the bell*) What the hell
can she want? Isn't Cissy with her?

HANNA (*Evenly*) One of these days I'm going to strangle
that woman ... with her Rosary beads.

She marches off. ANDY *grabs a paper and tries to*

read it. We now see HANNA *enter the bedroom and
we hear* MRS WILSON*'s voice.*

MRS WILSON We're going to say the Rosary a bit earlier tonight,
dear. Cissy has a bit of a headache.

> HANNA *removes the screen and puts it to the side
> of the set. In the large iron bed, propped up against
> the pillows, lies* MRS WILSON. *Like* CISSY *she is a
> tiny woman with a sweet, patient, invalid's smile.
> Her voice is soft and commanding. Her silver hair
> is drawn back from her face and tied with a blue
> ribbon behind her head. She looks angelic.* CISSY,
> *her understudy, is sitting beside her, watching her
> with devotion.*
>
> *Directly facing* MRS WILSON *is a chest of drawers,
> on which are a white cloth, two candles, a large
> statue of a saint, and a vase of flowers — a minia-
> ture altar.* MRS WILSON *frequently nods and smiles
> to the statue and mouths 'Thank you, thank you'.*
> HANNA *clumps around the room doing her chores
> with an ungracious vigour and with obvious ill-
> will.*

HANNA Whatever suits Cissy suits me!

CISSY She's looking lovely tonight, Hanna, isn't she? It
must be the good care you're taking of her.

MRS WILSON I'm blessed, Cissy dear, and I know it. A good
daughter is a gift of God. (*To the statue*) Thank you.
(*To* HANNA *who is fixing the bedclothes too robustly*)
That's fine, dear, thank you. Just fine.

HANNA Pillows.

MRS WILSON What's that, dear?

HANNA D'you want me to beat up the pillows?

MRS WILSON No, I'm grand. A wee bit of discomfort's good for
me.

CISSY Invalids is all saints — that's what I say.

MRS WILSON Here's the matches, dear.

HANNA *goes and lights the candles.*

Cissy, could I trouble you to give Andrew a call?

CISSY Pleasure.

MRS WILSON (*To* HANNA) And maybe you'd be good enough to move St Philomena round a wee bit so that she's facing me . . . just a little to the left . . . so that we're looking at each other . . . That's it. Lovely. Thank you, dear.

CISSY (*Off and unseen*) Andrew!

MRS WILSON God be praised a thousand times. St Vibiana, Virgin and Martyr, protect us. St Hyacintha de Mariscotti, look after us this day and this night.

CISSY (*Off*) The Rosary!

ANDY (*Off*) Coming.

MRS WILSON (*To* HANNA) And my jewels, dear.

HANNA What are you saying?

MRS WILSON Could you hand me my beads, please? (HANNA *does this*) God bless you. Another day is nearly o'er. A journey closer to the heavenly shore.

Enter CISSY.

CISSY He's coming. Thanks be to God.

MRS WILSON Amen to that. Poor Hanna's run off her feet, isn't she?

CISSY A labour of love.

ANDY *enters. He tries to be brisk and matter-of-fact in this cloying feminine atmosphere.*

MRS WILSON Ah, Andrew!

ANDY How are you tonight, Mrs Wilson?

MRS WILSON Grand, Andrew, thanks. I have St Philomena during the day and I have you all at night.

ANDY Very nice.

MRS WILSON Are you going to join us in the prayers?

HANNA Didn't you send down for him!

MRS WILSON Thank you, Andrew. As Father Peyton says: the

family that prays together stays together.

HANNA Get started.

MRS WILSON And Father Peyton is right, isn't he, Andrew?

ANDY Right, Mrs Wilson.

MRS WILSON If you only knew the consolation it is for me to have you all kneeling round my bed.

CISSY It's what you deserve.

MRS WILSON Thank you, St Philomena. Thank you.

HANNA Who's giving it out?

MRS WILSON Aren't the flowers pretty, Andrew?

ANDY Very nice.

MRS WILSON Hanna got them for me. But then — why wouldn't she? Didn't she take the name Philomena for her Confirmation.

HANNA Lookat — are we going to say the prayers or are we not?

CISSY Hanna dear, you're talking to a sick woman.

MRS WILSON (*Laying a restraining hand on* CISSY) She's tired, Cissy. I know. I don't mind. Maybe you'd give it out to-night, Andrew, would you?

ANDY I — I — I —

HANNA He will not, then. I will.

> MRS WILSON *mouths her thanks to the statue.*
> HANNA *begins at top speed.*

In the name of the Father and of the Son and of the Holy Ghost. We fly to Thy protection, O holy mother of God. Despise not our prayers in our necessity, but deliver us from all dangers, O glorious and ever blessed virgin. Thou, O Lord, will open my lips.

OTHERS And my tongue shall announce Thy praise.

HANNA Incline unto my aid, O God.

OTHERS O Lord, make haste to help me.

HANNA Glory be to the Father and to the Son and to the Holy Ghost.

OTHERS As it was in the beginning, is now, and ever shall be, world without end, Amen.

They are all on their knees around the bed, facing the altar now. While the prayers continue ANDY *gets to his feet and places the screen in its opening position — that is, completely hiding the bedroom. He then goes behind the screen to continue the Rosary.*

The lights come down slowly and the prayers fade. Total black for about a minute.

When the lights go up ANDY *is sitting as we first saw him, in the backyard, with his binoculars. He leaves down the binoculars, glances cautiously over his shoulder at the kitchen to make sure that no one in the house overhears him and then speaks to the audience:*

ANDY The big mistake I made was to come back here after the honeymoon — *even* for the couple of weeks that it was supposed to be at the beginning. I should have put the foot down then. But, like, everything happened so sudden. One bright morning the firm turns round and says 'All the single men in the joinery room are being sent to Belfast on a contract job.' So there was nothing for it, like, but to get married. And that's what we done. And then when we got back from the three days in Dublin, there's the damn painters still hashing about in Riverview, and the aul' woman has a bit of 'flu, and Hanna's kind of worried about her, and dammit, between one thing and another we find ourselves back here. But it was to have been only for a couple of weeks — that was the arrangement — aw, no, there was no doubt about that. Two weeks, she said. And a funny thing, you know, looking back on it, there was a change in the tune even then. No, not so much with the aul' woman — she's too crafty — Christ, you've got to hand it to the aul' woman — but with Hanna. Like, you know, before we got married, she was full of fight, there: let the aul' woman step out of line or say something sharp to me and by God she jumped at her like a cock at a gooseberry. But somehow the spirit seemed to drain out of her from the very beginning. Of course, when the bloody bell would go she would still say, 'The aul' bitch!' But, you know, even the way she said it now, like kind of weary, and almost as if it wasn't anger at the aul' woman at all but more to please me. That sort of thing. And a funny thing about the bloody bell, too. You know, before, if there was no noise coming from downstairs that ringing would be enough to waken the dead. But *after* we got married it only went when Hanna and me started talking. Wasn't that perverse now, eh? Oh, a deep one; deep as a well. We could sit, by God, for a whole night and not say a word to each other, and there wouldn't be a cheep from upstairs. But let us start chatting and the clanging would damn near shake the house! You know there, that sort of thing.

And then there was the Rosary caper. Well, I mean to say, a man has to draw the line somewhere. Oh, no, says I; we may have to stay together of necess-ity, says I, but by God it won't be because we pray together; I'll say my own mouthful of prayers down here. And that settled that. I mean to say, a man has to take a stand sometime. No harm to Father USA Peyton, says I; but all things in their proper place, and the proper place for me and my missus is in Riverview. I'll manage rightly down here, says I; and Father Peyton and St Philomena and the three Sorrowful Mysteries can hammer away upstairs. She didn't like that, the aul' woman, I'll tell you. Didn't speak to me for weeks. And would you believe what she done on me to get her own back: it was Cissy told me with a wee toss of her head. 'She offered you up to St Philomena,' says she. Crafty? Oh, man! Hanna's thick — there's no deny-ing that; but she'll never have the craft of the aul' woman.

But I got her! By God I got her! . . . Or I damn near

got her. It was this day in the works — a Friday — I'll never forget it — and George Williamson comes sidling up to me with a newspaper in his hand and a great aul' smirk on his jaw, and says he, 'So the Pope's not infallible after all, Andy,' says he. Oh, a bad bitter Protestant, the same Williamson. 'What's that?' says I, you know there, very quiet. 'According to the paper here,' says he, 'even the Pope can make a mistake. What d'you make of that now, eh? Isn't that a surprise?' And he hands me the paper. So I pulls out the glasses, very calm, and puts them on, and takes the paper from him and looks at it. And true as Christ, when I seen it, you could have tipped me over I was that weak. Like, for five seconds I couldn't even speak with excitement; only the heart thumping like bloody hell in my chest. For there it was in black and white before my very eyes: THE SAINT THAT NEVER WAS. 'Official Vatican sources today announced' — I know it by heart —'that the devotion of all Roman Catholics to St Philomena must be discontinued at once because there is little or no evidence that such a person ever existed.' Like, I never knew I was a spiteful man until that minute; and then, by God, my only thought was to stick that paper down the aul' woman's throat. Poor Williamson — Christ, I shot past him like a scalded cat and out of the workshop like the hammers of hell.

What I should have done — like, I know now — my God, no need to tell me; instead of coopering the things up the way I done — but what I should have done was wait until after the tea and then go upstairs nice and calm, you know there, and sit down on the side of the bed very pleasant and say, 'Have a look through the paper there, Mrs Wilson,' and watch, by God, watch every wee flicker of her eye when she'd come to the big news . . . but I bollixed it. I know. I know. I bollixed it. Straight from the workshop into a pub. And when closing

time comes, there I am — blotto. And back to the
house singing and shouting like a madman.

> HANNA, *who has been in the bedroom, now removes
> the screen. And, as she does this,* ANDY *goes off.*
>
> MRS WILSON *is in bed.* CISSY *is sitting on the
> edge of the bed.* HANNA *has been crying for some
> time and shuffles around the room, vaguely touch-
> ing different things.*
>
> *The candles are lit. The atmosphere is subdued
> and doleful and expectant. Trite words of consol-
> ation are being spoken. And one gets the sense of
> feminine solidarity and of suffering womanhood.*

MRS WILSON I promise you, dear: he's all right. I know he is.

HANNA But where *is* he?

MRS WILSON Maybe he met some of his companions.

HANNA He has no companions.

MRS WILSON Maybe he's doing overtime.

HANNA There's no overtime this week.

MRS WILSON Or maybe he's gone to Confession.

CISSY Ah! Indeed!

HANNA At half-past-ten? For God's sake!

MRS WILSON Well, we'll say the Rosary; that's what we'll do; and
we'll ask God and St Philomena to look after us all.
And before we're finished you'll find he'll be home
safe and sound to us.

CISSY Thanks be to God.

MRS WILSON All down on your knees. God and His holy mother
guide all our thoughts and actions this day and this
night. In the name of the Father and of the Son and
of the Holy Ghost. The five Sorrowful Mysteries of
the most holy Rosary —

> *Remote sounds of* ANDY *singing.*

HANNA Sshhh!

MRS WILSON The first Sorrowful Mystery — the agony in the
garden —

HANNA Sh! Sh! Listen! Listen!

> *The women freeze. Downstairs* ANDY *staggers into*
> *the kitchen singing 'God Save Ireland'. The women*
> *are horrified.*

MRS WILSON Is it — ?
HANNA Shut up!
CISSY Singing! Andrew?
MRS WILSON He's not — ?
HANNA He is!
CISSY A drunk man!

> ANDY *flings his coat on the couch and reels to the*
> *bottom of the stairs. Calls up:*

ANDY Mrs Wilson! Hello there, Old Mammy Wilson! I've
got news for you . . . big, big news.

> HANNA *is terrified.* MRS WILSON *takes control.*

HANNA What in the name of God — ?
MRS WILSON Leave him to me.
ANDY Stay where you are till I come up . . . very import-
ant, Old Mammy . . . very important.
MRS WILSON Don't say a word. Leave everything to me.
CISSY Drunk — the dirty animal!
MRS WILSON Quiet.
HANNA But what if he — ?
MRS WILSON Don't worry. I'll settle him. And stop whingeing!

> ANDY *enters and surveys the three alarmed faces.*
> *He has the newspaper in his hand.*

ANDY By God if it's not the Dolly Sisters! (*He gives them a*
grand bow) And St Philomena! (*Grand bow to the*
statue) All we need now is Father Peyton . . .
Where's Father Peyton? . . . I'll tell you something:
the family that drinks together sinks together.

MRS WILSON   Andrew!

ANDY   'The cock's shrill clarion, or the echoing horn — '

CISSY   Dirty animal!

ANDY   'No more shall rouse them from their lowly bed.
For them no more the blazing hearth shall burn,
Or busy housewife ply her evening care — '
Thomas Gray, 1716 to 1771.

HANNA   Mother, please — !

MRS WILSON   Listen to me, Andrew!

ANDY   She (*Hanna*) knows what I'm talking about 'cos
she's my wife —

MRS WILSON   If you don't behave yourself —

ANDY   As for prissy Cissy here —

CISSY   All for Thee — all for Thee —

ANDY   You'll go down with the white bobbins. Know what
that means, prissy Cissy? The white bobbins? It
means you'll never know your ass from your elbow.

HANNA   Andy!

MRS WILSON   I'll give you one minute to get out of this house — !

ANDY   News for you, Old Mammy — here, in this paper.
(*To the statue*) And news for you, darling, too.

MRS WILSON   Get out!

ANDY   You've (*Philomena*) been sacked.

MRS WILSON   I said get out!

ANDY   (*To statue*) You and me — both sacked.

He comes over to the bed with the paper.

HANNA   Stop it, Andrew! Stop it!

ANDY   In black and white . . . Read it . . . It says: We don't
stay together — that's what it says. Father Peyton,
it says, your head's a marly. That's what it says.

CISSY   Dirty, dirty animal.

MRS WILSON   I warned you! I gave you ample warning! And if
you think you can profane in this room —

She breaks off and clutches her heart and cries out.

CISSY   What — what is it?

HANNA Mother! Mother?

> ANDY *staggers back to the altar. On his way he*
> *kicks over the bell. He laughs.*

ANDY 'The curfew tolls no more the knell of parting day.'

> *He lifts the statue and waltzes with it.*

Come on, darling; we know when we're not wanted.
MRS WILSON Don't — touch — that —
CISSY The statue!
HANNA Andrew!
CISSY Oh, my God!
MRS WILSON Stop him! Stop him!

> *Chaos and confusion as* HANNA *and* CISSY *rush at*
> ANDY *and wrest the statue from him. Everyone is*
> *shouting at the same time.* MRS WILSON *gets out*
> *of bed and* CISSY *puts a coat round her.*

CISSY Come on! Come on! Into my place!
HANNA Are you all right, Mother?
ANDY 'Large was his bounty, and his soul sincere,
Heaven did a recompense as largely send — '
MRS WILSON Take all — statue — candles — cloth —
CISSY Brute animal!
MRS WILSON Oh, my heart —
HANNA Out — quick —

> CISSY *and* HANNA *each take an arm of* MRS WILSON
> *and they support her out.* HANNA *also takes the*
> *altar things.* MRS WILSON *groans loudly and path-*
> *etically.* CISSY *consoles her.* ANDY *reels over to the*
> *bed and sits on it. He is muttering to himself.*
> HANNA *leaves the others, goes to him, and sticks*
> *her face into his, and hisses:*

You'll regret this day, Andrew Tracey! You'll regret

this day as long as you live!

She then pulls over the screen hiding ANDY *from view and joins* CISSY *and* MRS WILSON *who go off chattering hysterically.* ANDY *rises and watches them go.*

ANDY (*Shouts after them from behind the screen*) We're sacked, Philomena — both of us — both sacked! What the hell are we going to do now? What the hell are we going to do now?

The three women have struggled downstairs and pause in the kitchen before escaping to Cissy's house.

MRS WILSON Oh, my heart! Oh, my God!
HANNA How are you, Mother?
CISSY All men is animals — brute animals.
HANNA Come on, Mother. I'll look after you.
CISSY Brutes of the field.
MRS WILSON God have mercy on us this day and this night.
HANNA He'll pay for this. By God, he'll pay for this!

The three ladies go off. ANDY *appears, in cardigan and house slippers, and comes into the kitchen. He addresses the audience:*

ANDY I don't think I told you about the tenant I have over in Riverview. Retired accountant. Quiet couple. No kids. He pays me on the first Saturday of every month. Sometimes if the weather's good I take an odd walk over there and look at the outside of the house. He has rose trees in the front and vegetables in the back. Very nice. Very cozy. But by the time you get home from work and get washed you don't feel like going out much. So I usually sleep at the fire for a while and then come out here for a breath of air. Kills an hour or two. And then when the bell rings I go up to the aul' woman's room for the prayers. Well, I mean to say, anything for a quiet life. Hanna sleeps there now, as a matter of fact, just in case the aul' woman should get an attack during the night. Not that that's likely. The doctor says she'll go on forever.

And a funny thing, you know: nothing much has changed up there. Philomena's gone, of course. And she never mentions Father Peyton anymore. But she still has the altar and she still lights the candles and has the flowers in the middle and she still faces it when she's praying and mouths away to it. I asked Cissy about it one night when she came in — who the hell they were supposed to be praying to.

Enter CISSY *in coat and hat. She is about to go straight upstairs but sees* ANDY *and pauses. She is very formal with him.*

CISSY Goodnight, Andrew.

ANDY 'Night, Cissy.

CISSY The crowds for Confession! You should see them. The poor priests must be mortified.

ANDY Cissy —

CISSY You'll be up later for the prayers?

ANDY I will. I will. Cissy —

CISSY Well?

ANDY Cissy, you've no statue up there now.

CISSY I'm not blind.

ANDY Well, I mean to say, what does she think she's at?

CISSY We've no statue, true enough; but we have a saint in our mind even though we've no figure for it.

HANNA *enters.* ANDY *does not see her at first.*

ANDY What saint?

CISSY Aha, that's something you'll never know, Andrew Tracey! Wild horses wouldn't drag that out of us. You robbed us of St Philomena but you'll never rob us of this one, for you'll never be told who it is!

CISSY *marches upstairs and* ANDY *turns with embarrassment to* HANNA. *Her coldness to him is withering.*

ANDY   Dammit, she's fighting fit . . . isn't she? Hanna —
HANNA What?
ANDY   Hanna, things are . . . we're not making . . . you and me, Hanna, we're not . . . Here, have a clove rock, Hanna.

She moves toward him as if she were going to take one, hesitates, then says:

HANNA No. They'd put me off my supper.
ANDY   I suppose you're right.
HANNA You'll be up for the prayers?
ANDY   I will . . . I will . . .

HANNA *goes upstairs.* ANDY *turns to the audience and speaks with strained joviality:*

And that's the way things are now.

He goes slowly out toward the yard.

And when I go into the bedroom she smiles and nods at me and you can see her lips saying *Thank you, thank you* to the altar. And when we kneel down, she says, 'It's nice for me to have you all gathered round my bed. As a certain American cleric says: The family that prays together stays together.'

By God, you've got to admire the aul' bitch. She could handle a regiment.

He lifts the binoculars, puts them in front of his eyes, and stares at the wall in front of him.
   Slowly bring down the lights until the stage is totally black.

CRYSTAL
AND FOX

Characters

FOX MELARKEY
CRYSTAL MELARKEY, his wife
PAPA, her father
PEDRO
EL CID
TANYA, Cid's wife
GABRIEL, Fox's son
AN IRISH POLICEMAN
TWO ENGLISH DETECTIVES

FOX MELARKEY is the proprietor of the travelling show that carries his name. He is about fifty, a small man, narrow shouldered, lightly built, with a lean sallow face grooved by a few deep wrinkles, a face that has been stamped with age since early manhood.

CRYSTAL, his wife, is a few years younger. She is taller than the Fox and heavier. She has a well-structured peasant face, and on those rare occasions when she is groomed she has a fresh and honest attractiveness.

PAPA, Crystal's father, is in his late seventies. His voice is husky with age. He is almost totally deaf and shuffles around with his head down, doing his allotted chores with an almost desperate concentration. He is determined to be worthy of his keep.

EL CID and TANYA, a husband-and-wife team, are in their thirties. Their talent is limited, their self-confidence and optimism limitless.

PEDRO is sixty. A gentle and guileless man, untouched by the elations and depressions of his profession.

Crystal and Fox was first produced at the Gaiety Theatre, Dublin, on 12 November 1968, with the following cast:

FOX MELARKEY	Cyril Cusack
CRYSTAL MELARKEY	Maureen Toal
PAPA	John McDarby
PEDRO	Cecil Sheridan
EL CID	Robert Carrickford
TANYA	Yvonne Cooper
GABRIEL	Chris O'Neill
AN IRISH POLICEMAN	Tom Irwin
TWO ENGLISH DETECTIVES	Niall O'Briain/Brendan Sullivan

Directed by	Hilton Edwards
Setting by	Robert Heade

for Sean McMahon

ACT ONE
Episode One

The acting area is divided into two portions. The portion left (from the point of view of the audience) occupies about one-third of the area; the portion right two-thirds. The dividing line is a flimsy and transparent framework which runs at an angle upstage. The portion left of this division is the stage inside Fox's marquee; the portion right is the back-stage; the dividing framework is the back wall of the stage.

We join the Fox Melarkey Show during a brief interval before the final episode of their drama, The Doctor's Story.

CRYSTAL — *Mother Superior — is on her knees on the stage, her elbows resting on a chair. She is wearing a nun's white tropical habit that could do with a wash.*

EL CID — *Dr Giroux — is backstage. He is wearing a short white medical coat. He is helping* TANYA — *Sister Petita Sancta — out of a nun's habit and into a gaudy floral dress.*

PAPA, *their stage manager, is pumping a primus stove.*

FOX *is bustling around, trying to get his cast organized. He is on edge because from offstage left can be heard the slow clapping of an unseen audience and the chanting of 'We want Fox! We want Fox!' The audience is restless and not very respectful; they have long since grown tired of suspending their disbelief. In a circle around the primus stove are some upturned boxes and some props. Fox's piano accordion is in the wings.*

> FOX   Come on! Come on! They're getting tired. What the hell's up now? Cid? Tanya?
>
> TANYA   Just a minute, Fox.
>
> FOX   Jaysus, will you hurry!
>
> CID   Keep your hair on.
>
> CRYSTAL   A good house, my sweet. A few weeks of this and we'll be able to trade in the truck.
>
> FOX   (*Automatically*) Beautiful, my love. (*He kisses her on*

the forehead) Very moving. Gets me here (_heart_) . . .
every time.

CRYSTAL   My Fox.

FOX   (_To_ ALL) They're a noisy pack of bailiffs so belt it out
a bit more. Plenty of guts.

PAPA   (_To_ FOX) What's my name?

FOX   (_To_ CRYSTAL) What's Papa's name?

CRYSTAL   (_To_ FOX) Sean O'Sullivan.

FOX   (_To_ PAPA) Sean O'Sullivan.

PAPA   Sean O'Sullivan.

CRYSTAL   (_To_ FOX) From outside Dublin.

FOX   (_To_ PAPA) From outside Dublin.

PAPA   (_To_ FOX) What am I doing here?

FOX   Who the hell's going to ask you that! You — you —
you're training for the Olympics.

     PEDRO's _head appears._

PEDRO   What's the hold-up, Fox?

FOX   Our little missionary here (_Tanya_). Ready yet?

TANYA   One more second, Fox —

FOX   As far as I'm concerned you can take a week at it;
but there happen to be people out there —

CID   The lady asked for one second.

FOX   The who?

CID   Look, Melarkey, if you don't watch that tongue of
yours —

CRYSTAL   Fox, go out and quieten them. Tell them a story.

FOX   (_Surveys his_ COMPANY _with distaste_) If they're restless
tell them a story! Christ!

    _Then, switching on his professional smile, he swings
    out on to the stage and acknowledges his boisterous
    reception._

Thank you, thank you, thank you very much, ladies
and gentlemen. You have been a wonderful audience and it's a great pleasure for the Fox Melarkey
Show to be back again in Ballybeg —

VOICE Whose pleasure?

FOX Who let my mother-in-law in here? (*Laughter*) But it's wonderful to see you all again, and you've been very appreciative of our little show; and tomorrow night at the same time —

VOICE What about the raffle?

FOX Look at what's shouting about the raffle! Scrounged a penny from the child behind him so that he could go halves in his wife's twopenny ticket! (*Laughter*) Keep calm, spendthrift: the raffle's coming immediately after this last episode of our little drama.

VOICE Is it faked?

FOX Course it's faked! (*Laughter*) And the word's fixed. Can't even speak English, that fella. Must be one of those Gaelic speakers from the back of the hills. I didn't tell you, did I, about his brother, Seamus, the one that never heard a word of English until he left school? Got a job in a drapery shop in Killarney. And the boss said to him, 'Let's hear how you'd talk to the customers.' 'Musha, Sir, me English, Sir, sure it do be weak. Me jacket, Sir? Am I right? And me breeches — and me shirt? Ah sure don't worry, Sir; I do have all the right words up here (*indicating his head*) — in me ass.' (*Laughter*) And now, ladies and gentlemen, the final episode in our little drama, *The Doctor's Story*.

> *He bows briefly, retreats behind the curtain and has a quick look around.*

Bloody cowboys! Ready?

CRYSTAL Ready.

FOX Tanya?

TANYA Go ahead.

FOX Belt it out. And plenty of tears. All the hoors want is a happy ending. OK, Papa; take it up.

> PAPA *hoists up the curtain.* FOX *stands in the wings.*
> CRYSTAL *buries her face in her hands and prays.* TANYA

enters the set and knocks on the framework.

TANYA   Mother. (CRYSTAL *is lost in prayer*) Mother Superior.

CRYSTAL   Did someone call me?

TANYA   It's me, Mother. Sister Petita Sancta. (CRYSTAL *does not turn round*)

CRYSTAL   Ah, Petita, Petita, come in, my child.

TANYA   I'll come back later, Mother.

CRYSTAL   No, no, no. Come on in. I was just talking to God about all our little problems in our mission hospital here at Lakula in Eastern Zambia.

> *She blesses herself and rises. She now faces her visitor.*

But is it — ? Yes, it is my Petita! Heavens bless me, I didn't recognize you in those clothes. O, my child, you look so fresh and sweet.

TANYA   The wife of the vice-consul presented it (*dress*) to me gratuitously.

CRYSTAL   Dear Petita. We're going to miss you so much here. But then our loss is Dr Alan Giroux's gain.

TANYA   He is bidding —

> *She breaks off because the kettle on the stove has boiled and is whistling shrilly.* FOX *hisses at* PAPA *who does not hear him. So* FOX *dashes to the kettle and lifts it off.*

CRYSTAL   Indeed, our loss is Dr Alan Giroux's gain.

TANYA   He is bidding farewell to the other Sisters. Just reflect, Mother: this time tomorrow he and I shall be in Paris! Ah, here he comes!

> EL CID *enters. He is a professional magician: acting is not his most fluent talent.*

CID   I am here to say *adieu, mon mère superior.*

CRYSTAL   Dear, dear Dr Giroux.

CID I have just had a quick run round the children's, casualty, fever and maternity wards. All is shipshape and Bristol fashion for my replacement, Dr Karl Krauger, when he arrives at noon tomorrow. And just to forestall any emergency I gave every patient a double injection of streptomycin.

CRYSTAL May God reward you, my son.

CID You know I do not believe in your God, Mother.

CRYSTAL Some day you will, Doctor. I have my Sisters praying for you. (CID *laughs a sceptic's laugh*)

TANYA I shall pray too.

CRYSTAL And now would you mind if an old woman gave you both a blessing?

TANYA (*Looks appealingly to* CID) For my sake, Alan.

CID If it makes you happy, *mon amour*.

> *They kneel at* CRYSTAL's *feet. In the wings* FOX *has lifted his accordion and plays throbbing churchy chords as* CRYSTAL *prays.*

CRYSTAL May God reward you both for your years of dedication to our little mission hospital here in Lakula in Eastern Zambia. May you both find the joy and happiness and content you deserve so richly. And if ever you feel like coming back to us, singly or doubly, our arms will be open wide to hold you to my bosom. My children.

TANYA Thank you, Mother.

> CID *and* TANYA *rise. A long uneasy pause.*

CRYSTAL Listen — the river boat.

> PAPA *has missed his cue.* FOX *dashes over to one of the upturned boxes, grabs a whistle and pumps a whooping sound from it.*

Yes, I knew I heard the river boat. (*Arms out*) *Au revoir, mon enfants.* (*She embraces them both*)

CID (*Manfully brushes back a tear*) Someday, Mother, I'll
. . . I'll . . .

> *He cannot trust himself to speak. He grabs* TANYA
> *by the hand and together they run off.*

CRYSTAL Goodbye . . . goodbye . . .

> *She sinks to her knees, joins her hands and lifts her
> face up to heaven. It is a face of suffering and accept-
> ance.* PAPA *lowers the curtain. There is sporadic
> clapping.* FOX *moves around briskly, dispensing
> tired compliments while the* ARTISTS *change cos-
> tume for their final appearance.*

FOX Very nice . . . beautiful work . . . very moving . . .
lovely show.

TANYA The line is 'O, my child, you look so young and so
beautiful' but you're too damn bitchy to say that!

CRYSTAL Sorry, love; I meant to say that — I really did —
and —

CID That damned old fool (*Papa*) — he makes that kettle
whistle on purpose just to throw me!

FOX OK, OK, let's get changed, good work all round,
very convincing, very pathetic, where's Pedro?

> PEDRO *enters. In his arms he carries Gringo, his
> performing dog. She is dressed in a green skirt and
> green matching hat.*

PEDRO Here, boss.

FOX (*To* CRYSTAL, *with casual intimacy*) Exquisite, my love.
(*He kisses her*)

CRYSTAL My pet?

FOX My sweet. (*Aloud*) Everybody ready?

CID Just a minute, Fox — don't forget our agreement.

FOX Nice performance, Cid.

CID Me and Tanya take the last call. Agreed?

FOX Agreed. (*Aloud*) All set?

CID It's understood then, Fox? We're agreed on that?

FOX Anything you say. (*Aloud*) All standing by? Right. Up she goes, Papa.

CID Remember, Fox! I'm not asking you again!

> PAPA *hoists up the curtain. The others wait in the wings.* FOX *is wearing his accordion. He is greeted by the same uncertain enthusiasm.*

FOX Thank you, thank you, thank you. And now once more I'd ask you to show your appreciation of the top-rank artistes who performed on these boards tonight. Ireland's best known and best loved man of mystery and suspense — El Cid, and his beautiful assistant, Tanya!

> *He strikes a heralding chord. Thin clapping from the audience. Pause.*

CID Bastard!

> CID *catches* TANYA's *hand and assuming a radiant smile he runs on.*

FOX Thank you, Tanya; thank you, El Cid. And now that dashing Spaniard and his team of superhuman dogs — the ex-star of the Moscow Circus — Pedro!

> *Another chord. Applause.* PEDRO *enters. He takes the dog with him.*

And lastly and by no means least, the lady whose musical and Thespian arts held us all in thrall tonight — I give you — my charming and devoted wife — the gracious Crystal Melarkey!

> *Another chord. Applause.* CRYSTAL *skips on.*

And now for our raffle for the five pound note.

Would you, my love . . . ?

CRYSTAL My Fox. And thank you, ladies and gentlemen. If you have your tickets ready we'll get some little boy or girl to draw from this box. Have we a volunteer? Come on, children; don't be shy. What about that little lady down there?

FOX Nobody in Ballybeg needs a fiver!

This is greeted by hooting and laughter.

CRYSTAL If you're all too shy, perhaps Pedro would be kind enough to draw for us. Pedro?

PEDRO draws and hands her a ticket.

A pink ticket; and the number is eighty-seven — eight, seven. Would the lucky holder of ticket number eighty-seven please come up for his prize?

PAPA approaches from the audience. He is wearing a top coat and hat. FOX strikes a chord. Applause, led by CRYSTAL.

FOX Give him a big hand, friends.

CRYSTAL What is your name, sir?

PAPA (*By rote*) My name is Sean O'Sullivan and I come from outside Dublin.

FOX (*To audience*) Is he courting a Ballybeg girl? (*Laughter*)

CRYSTAL Can I see your ticket? (*After checking*) And he is absolutely correct! Mr Sean O'Sullivan from outside Dublin is the lucky winner!

FOX (*Hands over the money*) Don't sicken yourself with ice-pops, sonny.

CRYSTAL Congratulations, sir.

FOX strikes up an introduction to their theme song — 'A-Hunting We Will Go' — and the COMPANY link arms and do a simple dance routine as they sing.

ALL   'A-hunting we will go
      A-hunting we will go
      We'll catch a fox and put him in a box
      A-hunting we will go
      Tantiffy tantiffy tantiffy
      A-hunting we will go.'

FOX   Tomorrow's our last night in Ballybeg. Same time, same place, children under seven admitted free. A complete new variety show, another lucky raffle, and by popular demand a repeat of tonight's classical drama, *The Doctor's Story*. See you again tomorrow. God bless.

They strike up the chorus again. By now PAPA *has returned and lowers the curtain. The thin clapping dies away very quickly.*

CRYSTAL   The tide's turned! I told you, my love, didn't I?

FOX   (*Flat*) You did indeed.

CID   Melarkey!

FOX is fully aware of CID's *rage but completely ignores it. He goes very calmly, almost gently, to* PAPA *to recover the fiver. Then he changes into his ordinary clothes.*

FOX   Thanks, Papa. Nice performance.

CID   I'm talking to you, Melarkey!

TANYA   Easy, Cid.

CID   You promised! You said it was agreed!

TANYA   Don't lose control, Cid. Please don't.

CID   I gave you every warning! But that's OK! That suits me fine. I mean to say — money and conditions — I can rough it as good as the next. But when a man's professional standing is spit on by a weasel like that . . . !

FOX   Atta girl, Gringo. Worth your weight in gold. Eh?

CRYSTAL   My Fox . . .

TANYA   We'll talk about it after we've changed.

CID There's been enough talk. He promised me — it was agreed — we take the last call. But I know him — watched him since I joined this lousy fit-up — twisted, that's what he is — twisted as a bloody corkscrew! No wonder his own son cleared off to England!

TANYA Please, Cid —

CID And I'll tell you something more about him: he's not going to stop until he's ratted on everybody! I know that character!

TANYA (*To* FOX) He's upset, Fox. His stomach curdles on him. (*To* CRYSTAL) In the morning he'll be —

CID In the morning I'll be signed up with Dick Prospect's outfit! (*As he leaves*) And I'll tell you another thing about him: it won't be long before he's back where he began — touting round the fairs with a rickety wheel!

He rushes off. TANYA *knows she must go with him.*

TANYA I gave him bacon for his tea. It always gripes him . . .

She hesitates uncertainly — then rushes off.

CRYSTAL Tanya! (*To* OTHERS) He doesn't mean it, does he?

No one speaks. She turns to FOX. *On occasions like this* FOX's *eyes go flat and he hides behind a mask of bland simplicity and vagueness.*

You're not letting him go, are you?

FOX What's that?

CRYSTAL Cid and Tanya! You're not going to let them walk away like that?

PEDRO If it's only the calls, Fox, Gringo and me we don't give a damn; we'll come on first.

CRYSTAL Fox!

FOX My love?

CRYSTAL They're really leaving!

FOX Are they?

CRYSTAL Go after them! Speak to them!

FOX What about, my sweet?

CRYSTAL For God's sake, we can't afford to lose them! I know he's difficult — but he's a good act. And if they go that's twenty minutes out of the variety. And we've no play, Fox!

FOX No play?

CRYSTAL Without Cid! Without Tanya! What's got into you? Last month it was Billy Hercules. And before that it was the Fritter Twins. Fox, I'm asking you.

FOX What?

CRYSTAL Just speak to him.

PEDRO Maybe if I had word with Tanya —

CRYSTAL It has to be the Fox. (*Pleading*) My love —

FOX My sweet.

CRYSTAL Say you're sorry — say anything you like — blame me, I don't care; but we must hold on to him.

FOX No, no; couldn't blame you, my love.

CRYSTAL I'm asking you — for my sake — go after them.

FOX Couldn't do that, my love.

CRYSTAL But they'll leave if you don't.

FOX Will they?

CRYSTAL My Fox! We need them.

FOX That's true.

CRYSTAL Then do something. You don't want them to leave us too, do you?

FOX (*Gives her a most pleasant smile*) If I knew a simple answer to that, my Crystal, I'd go in for telling fortunes.

Bring down lights.

ACT ONE

Episode Two

When the lights go up CRYSTAL *and* PEDRO, *now out of costume, are sitting disconsolately on upturned boxes. They have been drinking tea.* CRYSTAL *is brooding over the departure of Cid and Tanya:* PEDRO *is trying to be cheerful.*

PEDRO   It was in a pub just outside Galway, in the middle of last summer. Cid was there and me and Billy Hercules and Tanya. And he comes in with this big red face of his and a tart with him and he says, 'The drinks are on Dick Prospect, the biggest travelling show in Ireland!' So we says nothing, and he sits himself beside me and he says, 'How's the Fox these times?' 'Fine,' I says. 'Haven't run into him for years. And Crystal? Give her my love,' he says, and he laughs and gives the tart a dig with his elbow. 'And the lad — what's this his name is?' 'Gabriel,' says I. 'That's it. How's he shaping in the business?' So I never says a word to that: what the bugger didn't know did him no harm. And the next thing, out of the blue: 'Pedro,' says he, 'I'll make you an offer: leave the Fox and come with me and you can name your own price.' And everybody stopped talking. And I just put down the glass and I says to him, 'Twenty years ago the Fox Melarkey gave me a job when no other show in the country would touch me,' I says. 'And the day I leave the Fox will be the day I'm not fit to do my piece.' And d'you know what he done, Crystal? He gave me a shove and he says, 'You're a fool — that's what you are, a fool,' and threw a big bull head back and laughed.

God, he's a cheeky bugger, isn't he?

CRYSTAL Mm?

PEDRO Dick Prospect — he's a cheeky bugger.

CRYSTAL That's right, Pedro.

> PAPA *enters. There are four untouched teacups on the ground. He points to them.*

PAPA What's keeping Cid and Tanya?

PEDRO They're gone.

PAPA (*To* CRYSTAL) What's he say?

PEDRO Left.

PAPA Left?

> PEDRO *nods.* PAPA *shrugs his shoulders, lifts one cup and sits sipping.*

PEDRO Good house tonight, wasn't it?

CRYSTAL That's the point — the same all last week — things were beginning to pick up! I told him that! Another month like this and we could have got a new truck. Now — ! Honest to God, Pedro, I can't see what's going to happen.

PEDRO He gets that way now and again. It passes.

CRYSTAL Things start to go well and you begin to make plans; and then he has to go and make trouble. And you know it's coming on him — you can see it — he goes all sort of quiet. And then you could shout at him and he doesn't even hear you.

PEDRO He has his ways — like the rest of us.

CRYSTAL You don't have to defend him to me, Pedro. And you know what I'm talking about. You've seen him.

PEDRO It's only in the past few years.

CRYSTAL Just before Gabriel went away; that's when it began.

PEDRO (*With genuine enthusiasm and pride*) Eight — ten years ago — my God he was on top of his form then! Cracking jokes, striding about, giving orders like a king; and everywhere he went, Gabby perched up there on top of his shoulders! My God, the Fox

Melarkey show was a real show then!

CRYSTAL Wasn't it, though?

PEDRO He had the country in the palm of his hand!

CRYSTAL That won't pay the bills now.

PEDRO If he put his mind to it he could build it up again. He could! Not a showman in the country to touch him!

CRYSTAL For God's sake, look around you, man. Holes in the roof. Broken seats. And when the truck falls apart what's going to pull the vans?

PEDRO I've got a couple of quid put by, Crystal . . . there's not much in it . . . and there's only me and Gringo to spend it . . . and if it's any use . . .

CRYSTAL Good, Pedro.

PEDRO Well, you know it's there and all you have to do is . . .

He breaks off because he hears FOX *approach.* FOX *swings on, singing, full of bounce and good spirits. He has a paper under his arm.*

FOX 'There is a happy land far, far away
Where we get bread and jam four times a day'
(*Speaks*) D'you believe that, Pedro, eh? Move over in the bed and let an honest man in at his work.

PEDRO You're looking very happy.

FOX Me? Oh, just a simple man's satisfaction at the end of a good day's work. Another step closer to paradise. Is there nothing for the Fox? (CRYSTAL *ungraciously thrusts a cup in front of him*) Thank you, my love. And then, of course, we've lost our young couple, Sir Cid and Dame Tanya, off to a pressing engagement in Stratford. 'This time tomorrow he and I shall be in Paris.' Jaysus, if I had to listen to that again I'd shoot myself.

PAPA (*To* FOX) They're gone.

FOX Gone but not forgotten, Papa.

PAPA That's the way — here today, gone tomorrow.

FOX Very true, Papa. (*Turns to* CRYSTAL) Your father's a

real sage, my sweet: nothing ruffles him anymore.
All clowns become sages when they grow old, and
when young sages grow old they turn into clowns.
I was an infant sage — did you know that, Pedro?

PEDRO Have they left — Cid and Tanya?

FOX *(With a bitter smile)* In this company you discuss a
thing — Jaysus — for half-an-hour, and then someone asks you what you're talking about. Round and
round in circles. Same conversations, same jokes,
same yahoo audiences; just like your Gringo, Pedro,
eh? — doing the same old tricks again and again,
and all you want is a little cube of sugar as a reward.
How many tons of sugar have you given to bloody
dogs over the past twenty, thirty years? Eh?

PEDRO I couldn't even —

FOX *(Still smiling)* And how do you know that one night
when there's a sudden moon that lights up the whole
countryside brilliantly for a second — it comes out
from behind a cloud and for that second everything's black and white — how do you know that
on a night like that Gringo wouldn't give you all the
sugar cubes in the world for just one little saucer of
arsenic? Answer me that, Pedro.

CRYSTAL Leave him alone.

FOX He loves the dog — he really does — and all I want
to know is does he love him that much that he'd —

CRYSTAL Leave Pedro alone!

FOX *(Making a florid gesture of obedience to her)* My queen.
(To PEDRO) Contentment lies in total obedience — St
Paul's epistle to the South Africans.

He opens the paper and looks through it. Pause.
CRYSTAL *rises and crosses to* PAPA. *She speaks into
his ear.*

CRYSTAL You should go to bed.

PAPA I'm not a baby.

CRYSTAL Do you want a hot-water bottle?

PAPA Hate them things.

FOX   (*Reads for general amusement*) 'The local Grand Opera
        Society held its annual meeting last Wednesday
        in Sweeney's Hotel in Drung. It was agreed to do
        Faust next April. There are four members in the
        Society.'

PEDRO   Where's Drung?

FOX   County Tyrone; not far from where I first met my
        Crystal. The month of May.

CRYSTAL June.

FOX   No, no, my love; it was the 12th day of a glorious
        May. And the Fox was cycling out to make his for-
        tune in the world with nothing but his accordion
        and his rickety wheel and his glib tongue, when
        what did he spy at the edge of the road but three
        snow-white horses and three golden vans.

CRYSTAL (*To* PEDRO) The vans were brown.

FOX   And there was no one in the first golden van. And
        there was no one in the second golden van. But be-
        side the third and last golden van there was Papa
        rubbing down a snow-white mare. And beside him
        a princess. And she had her hair tied up with a royal
        blue ribbon, and a blue blouse, and a navy skirt —

CRYSTAL (*Gruffly with embarrassment*) You're a blatherskite.

FOX   — and a brooch here with 'Mother' written across
        it.

CRYSTAL (*With sudden simplicity*) That's true!

FOX   And Papa was wearing puttees; and there was a
        smell of heather; and the mare's name was Alice.

CRYSTAL Alice it was!

FOX   (*Quietly*) And I got off my bicycle — I had no idea
        what I was going to say; and Papa went on rubbing
        the mare. And the princess looked at me.

        Pause.

PEDRO   What happened, Fox? By God, you weren't stuck for
        a word!

FOX   (*Briskly again*) And the Fox whipped off his cap and
        bowed low and said, 'What big eyes you've got.'

CRYSTAL I fell on my feet that day.

FOX Did you?

CRYSTAL Take your tea, you eejit you!

PEDRO (*To* CRYSTAL) And then you and him and Papa set up on your own — after you got married?

CRYSTAL We had more courage than sense.

FOX And more hope than courage, my love.

PEDRO By God, you were going great guns altogether when you took me on.

FOX And aren't we still, Pedro? (*Deliberately finishing off the conversation*) Listen to this — something I saw here — about the caves at Knockmore — we could make it in a day, couldn't we? Here we are: (*Reads*) 'Four young American students trapped in underground caves at Knockmore.'

PEDRO By God, those Americans are everywhere these times.

FOX 'So far rescue teams have been unable to get to the young people who have been cut off since the entrance to the largest cave became blocked by falling boulders.'

CRYSTAL Any crowds gathering?

FOX Doesn't say.

CRYSTAL I still think we should head towards Dublin.

PEDRO They don't flock to the tragedies the way they used to.

CRYSTAL Television has them spoiled. It needs to be something very big.

PEDRO A train crash or an explosion in a school.

FOX Has to be children. Remember the time that orphanage in the Midlands burned down?

PEDRO That sort of thing.

CRYSTAL For three solid weeks not an empty seat.

PEDRO Marvellous.

CRYSTAL And a matinee every other day.

PEDRO But your chance of being actually on the spot — once in a lifetime.

PAPA (*Rising*) I'd better put on the parking lights in the truck.

CRYSTAL I'll see to it, Papa.

PAPA What's that?

CRYSTAL I'll do it.

PAPA Don't forget. I'm away to bed, then. Goodnight all.

CRYSTAL Sleep well, Papa.

PEDRO 'Night, Papa.

FOX Goodnight, Papa. (*Suddenly*) Oh, Papa, Papa!

PAPA *stops.* FOX *fumbles in his pocket.*

The day before yesterday — remember when I was going into the town? — you gave me a shilling to put on a horse for you.

PAPA Did I?

FOX Planter's Delight in the 3.30. It romped home at nine-to-one. Here's your winnings.

PAPA (*Face lighting up with joy*) I forgot all about it . . . isn't that a good one, eh? . . . went clean out of my head . . . ten shillings eh? . . . good man, Fox.

PEDRO Maybe you're set for a lucky streak, Papa.

PAPA Clean out of my head . . . bloody good man, Fox.

FOX You can still pick them, Papa!

PAPA Bloody good . . .

PAPA *leaves.*

PEDRO That's the first win he's had in months. There'll be no stopping him now.

CRYSTAL You weren't in the town the day before yesterday.

FOX Papa got his winnings, didn't he? He's happy, isn't he? (*Changing the subject*) Here — look at that. (*He stares at* PEDRO's *hands*)

PEDRO What are you staring at?

FOX Just a thought.

PEDRO What does that mean? What sort of a thought?

FOX Look at those hands, my pet.

CRYSTAL Whose hands?

FOX Pedro's. (PEDRO *puts his hands behind his back like a child*) No — no — hold them out — let's look at them. (PEDRO *brings them out reluctantly*)

PEDRO What's wrong with them?

FOX That's it — turn them over — look at them.

CRYSTAL What, Fox?

FOX The long slender fingers — the strength of them.

PEDRO They're clean, aren't they?

FOX Never noticed it before.

PEDRO Now you're making them shake!

FOX There's your man. The problem's solved.

PEDRO Who? — what? — what are you talking about?

FOX The hands of a surgeon. There's your Dr Alan Giroux.

CRYSTAL Our Pedro?

FOX A natural.

PEDRO A natural what? — what problem?

CRYSTAL I don't know, Fox; he's —

FOX I do. I'm sure of it. Absolutely perfect.

CRYSTAL Would you, Pedro?

PEDRO Would I what?

FOX Course he would.

CRYSTAL Cid's part in the play — the young French doctor.

PEDRO Me?

CRYSTAL (*To* FOX) Maybe he's —

PEDRO Me? Me in the play? Christ, you're not serious! Me? Sure I can't even introduce my own act! Come on, Fox, cut it out — none of that sort of talk! Crystal, you know, Crystal, Christ Almighty, I couldn't! For God's sake, have a heart, man! Don't ask it of me!

CRYSTAL He doesn't want to, Fox. Anyway, we'd still have no Petita.

PEDRO I'd do anything to pull you out of a hole, Fox — anything — you know that — but, Christ, acting a part! Dogs is all I can handle — I'm nothing without a dog — you know that, Crystal.

FOX OK. Shut up. Stop bleating.

PEDRO If it was anything else, Fox —

FOX Forget it.

PEDRO You know, Crystal —

FOX Forget it! Stop whining about it! Papa'll play it!

FOX's *outburst creates an embarrassed silence. He*

goes back to his paper. PEDRO *looks appealingly to*
CRYSTAL *but she is not looking at him. Pause.*

CRYSTAL It's time we all went to bed.

*She begins to gather up the tea things. No one has
yet noticed the entrance of a motorcycle* POLICEMAN
*in helmet, goggles, gauntlets, riding breeches, leather
knee-boots. He stands motionless, slowly survey-
ing every detail. His silent presence generates an
immense threat. When he speaks his voice is soft
and controlled.* FOX *glances over his paper and sees
him first. Immediately he switches on his best manner but his garrulousness betrays his unease.*

FOX Goodnight, Sergeant! Visitors, my love! You're a bit
late for the show, Sergeant, but you're just in time
for a cup of tea. Tea for the gentleman, my love.

The POLICEMAN *moves silently around.*

Wait a minute — didn't I see you at the show tonight? In civvies — standing down at the back?
Amn't I right, boss? It was the goggles there that
threw me for a —
POLICEMAN Fox Melarkey?
FOX At your service, Sergeant. Have a pew. Take the
weight off your legs.

Silence. The POLICEMAN *stands before* PEDRO.

POLICEMAN Who are you?
FOX (*Before* PEDRO *can reply*) That's Pedro, boss. A wizard
with dogs. One of the top artists in the profession.
Been with the Fox Melarkey show for the best part
of —
POLICEMAN Can you speak? What's your name?
PEDRO Paddy Donnellan. Pedro's the name I use for the
show.

FOX And this is the better half — Crystal — Mrs Fox
Melarkey — or the vixen as I sometimes call her!

POLICEMAN (*Ignoring* FOX) Who else is there?

FOX You mean who else is there in the company, boss?
Well, there's Papa, that's Crystal's father — he's just
gone to bed — the old ticker's liable to jack up on
him without warning — as a matter of fact you just
missed him by a few seconds — great character —
was a clown all his days — toured with some of the
biggest outfits in Europe. And there's . . . and there's
. . . dammit, that's it! An hour ago we had another
pair, man and wife team; but they upped and offed
on me without as much as by your leave. You've no
idea, boss, what it's like trying to cater to top quality
artistes these days with competition from TV
and —

POLICEMAN Only four? No one else?

FOX That's it, Sergeant. Just four — for the time being.
We'll just have to say our prayers and tour the
agents again. No want of talent round the country,
boss, as a gentleman in your position knows well;
but when your audiences are made up of decent
country people and their little kiddies you just can't
sign up every cheapjack that wants to join you.

POLICEMAN No one else in the vans?

CRYSTAL If you don't take his word why don't you search
them?

FOX No one else, Sergeant. Not a soul. Just the four of
us: Crystal, Pedro, Papa and yours truly. As Shakespeare says 'We are a few and a happy few and a
band of brothers' —

POLICEMAN When are you moving out?

FOX When are we moving out? Isn't that a coincidence
— the very thing we were talking about when you
arrived! Right, my pet? I'll tell you our problem,
boss. We could do another week, ten days here
easy. Jaysus, if we turned away five the night we
must have turned away — what would you say, my
love? — fifty? sixty? On the other hand, if we don't

	keep to our schedule our advance agents start scream-

POLICEMAN When?

FOX When? As a matter of fact, Sergeant, it was . . . it was the consensus of opinion that . . . that we honour our previous commitments and . . . pull out tomorrow morning.

POLICEMAN Make it early in the morning so that you'll be outside my territory by noon.

CRYSTAL Why should we?

FOX Sure, boss, sure. Anything you say, Sergeant. Suits us fine. As a matter of fact we've got to be in Ardbeg by tomorrow afternoon. The new hall there's at our disposal any time we want it. That's what we were just saying — can we make it in time? But we'll make it, boss; don't you worry; that's where we'll be. The Fox Melarkey never let his public down yet. Leave it to me, Sergeant. I'll handle it.

The POLICEMAN *pauses before he leaves and looks at* CRYSTAL.

POLICEMAN I'm just giving you good advice, missus. Pay heed to it.

FOX And we're grateful for it, boss, very grateful. And now that you're here you're the very man that can advise me on the best route. Should we go up through the gap or should we go round by the foot of Glenmore? It's so long since I did that trip that I've forgotten which is the quickest road . . .

His voice fades away as he follows the POLICEMAN *off.*

CRYSTAL Gestapo!

PEDRO He's after something, whatever it is.

CRYSTAL The Fox is far too sweet to them fellas. I'd give them their answer.

PEDRO No point in crossing them.

CRYSTAL Out of his territory! You'd think he owned the place! You'd think we were criminals!

PEDRO He's doing his job.

CRYSTAL It's a dirty job, then. And I never could stomach them.

PEDRO So we're moving out tomorrow?

CRYSTAL Gestapo.

PEDRO I say — looks as if we're moving out in the morning.

CRYSTAL Why should we?

PEDRO It was Fox — he said it — he said we were going to —

CRYSTAL 'He said — he said.' If he had his way we'd keep moving all the time and never light anywhere. Near time he made up his mind to run the show right or pack it in altogether.

> CRYSTAL's *uncustomary sharpness embarrasses* PEDRO.

PEDRO Well I thought . . . maybe he only meant . . . Supper time for Gringo.

CRYSTAL I'd give them their answer.

PEDRO 'Night, Crystal.

> *She does not hear him. She gathers up the tea things, making a lot of noise in her agitation.*
> GABRIEL *appears right and stands watching them. He is in his early twenties. He has inherited a portion of Crystal's forthrightness and a portion of Fox's depth and they make an uneasy marriage in him. He gives a first impression of being weak — an impression that is not altogether accurate. He is wearing an anorak and an open-necked shirt. He carries a sailor's duffel bag over his shoulder.*

GABRIEL (*Quietly, without intonation*) Any chance of a bed for the night?

PEDRO Crystal! Look! It's Gabriel!

CRYSTAL *turns round and stares incredulously.*

CRYSTAL Gabriel? . . . Oh my God — Gabriel! It's Gabriel — Oh my God!

She runs to him and flings her arms round him.

GABRIEL Crystal!
CRYSTAL Son!
GABRIEL Great to see you.
CRYSTAL I heard Pedro — and I looked up — and whatever way the light was — !
GABRIEL I wanted to surprise you.
CRYSTAL And the size of him? Look at him, Pedro! A man big!
GABRIEL Pedro!

PEDRO *and* GABRIEL *embrace.*

PEDRO Welcome . . . Welcome back.
GABRIEL It's great to be back! How are you all? Where's Papa? Where's Fox? Where is everybody?
CRYSTAL Fox is about, and Papa's just gone to bed, and here's Pedro, and here's me! He's got so . . . so mannish looking! When did you come? How did you find us?
GABRIEL Crossed from Glasgow last night and hitched the rest of the way. Pedro! How's all the dogs, man?
PEDRO Only one now — Gringo —
GABRIEL One? Only one?
PEDRO — but she — she's — I'll show her to you — hold on —
CRYSTAL Not now. In the morning.
PEDRO Never had a dog like her. She's . . . she's like a wife.
CRYSTAL Papa'll be so excited. I'll tell him. No, I won't — he wouldn't sleep after.
GABRIEL How's he keeping?
CRYSTAL Not bad. Seventy-eight last month.
GABRIEL (*Diffidently*) And the Fox?

CRYSTAL Great. As ever. The same Fox. Fighting the world.

PEDRO My God, wait till he sees you!

GABRIEL Maybe I should . . . maybe you should tell him I'm here first in case —

CRYSTAL That was five years ago. It's all forgotten. He talks about you all the time — doesn't he?

PEDRO Every day, twice a day.

GABRIEL He threw me out, remember.

CRYSTAL I'm telling you — he'll be delighted. Are you hungry? When did you last eat?

> FOX *enters briskly. He doesn't see* GABRIEL.

FOX Trust you to put the big feet in it! The truck sitting there not taxed and no parking lights and you have to give lip to the peeler! Only that I kept talking bloody quick — (*Now he sees* GABRIEL) — It's not . . . ?

GABRIEL The prodigal son, Fox.

FOX Jaysus!

CRYSTAL I told him you'd be —

FOX Gabriel!

> FOX *moves first towards him. They meet and embrace.* FOX *holds his son very tightly. He is on the point of tears.*

GABRIEL Easy, Fox, easy.

CRYSTAL Isn't he looking great?

FOX He's looking . . . divine. A lad went away — remember, Pedro? — and look, my sweet, a man, a man. And the presence — the style! When did he come?

CRYSTAL Just now.

FOX How did he find us?

GABRIEL (*Deadpan*) Well, when I got off the ship this morning I bought an Irish paper and I looked to see were there any big catastrophes that would gather a crowd of sightseers; and I read that in County —

FOX The hoor! Still at his bloody monkey-tricks! (*To* PEDRO) You always said he'd make a great clown.

(*Softly*) Jaysus, but it's good to see you, son. After you went away, somehow we . . . we . . . But now you're back to us and suddenly life's . . . (*He breaks off; continues briskly*) How d'you think she's looking?

GABRIEL No change.

FOX No change at all. She is my constant enchantment. (*He kisses her*)

CRYSTAL My Fox.

FOX And without her I am nothing. And Pedro?

GABRIEL Not a day older.

PEDRO Haa!

FOX We survive.

CRYSTAL And your father?

GABRIEL The very same.

FOX No, no.

GABRIEL Maybe a bit heavier.

FOX And more perverse and more restless and more . . . You're the one that's put on weight.

GABRIEL Too much beer. Where's the rest of the gang?

FOX Crystal — Pedro — your humble servant — and Papa, of course; you haven't seen Papa yet? He'll be glad to see you. Well, that's about it. Things have changed since . . . since you left. Nowadays if you're not compact, streamlined, overheads cut to a minimum, you're out of business. Quick, slick, first-rate. TV finished the shoddy show. But we've been lucky; my sweet?

CRYSTAL Very lucky.

FOX Things have changed all right; audiences, artists. Strange. You'd be surprised. And a man changes, too. You'd be surprised. The years do strange things to a man. But I have my Crystal.

CRYSTAL And Pedro.

PEDRO I'll show you the dog later, Gabriel. She wears a green hat and a green skirt.

GABRIEL Can she count?

PEDRO And read. She's uncanny.

CRYSTAL She lies in the bed with him and eats at the table

with him!

FOX You're home to stay, aren't you?

Pause.

CRYSTAL Even for a while?

GABRIEL For a while — sure — why not.

PEDRO We'll have a celebration! I've a bottle of whiskey since Christmas that I haven't opened.

CRYSTAL What about something to eat?

PEDRO We'll drink first — then we'll eat. (*To* CRYSTAL) Have you any glasses?

CRYSTAL I'll get some.

PEDRO Come over to my van. Gringo'll want to be in on the fun. (*As he leaves*) It's like old times again.

PEDRO *goes off.*

CRYSTAL He's as excited as if you were his own child.

GABRIEL Great guy.

CRYSTAL We're all excited.

GABRIEL I remember that smell: wet fields and paraffin and turf.

CRYSTAL I knew the tide was turned — I said that — didn't I?

FOX My love — glasses.

CRYSTAL But we're round the corner now. I know we are.

She goes off. Now that FOX *and* GABRIEL *are alone there is a diffidence between them: they are both conscious of it.*

GABRIEL Same old stove.

FOX It goes for no one but Papa.

GABRIEL (*Avoiding conversation*) And that patch (*on the roof*) — I remember helping Pedro to sew it. Must have been only nine or ten at the time. He was up on top of a stepladder and I was trying to hold it steady and it kept sinking into the ground and I was sure he was going to fall on top of me . . . but he didn't

353

... How's business?

FOX Good. Fair.

GABRIEL Have things got rough?

FOX No rougher than usual.

GABRIEL But you're managing?

FOX We've always managed. Sometimes you get sick managing. Smoke?

GABRIEL Thanks.

FOX (*With his brittle smile*) And we're getting on, Gabby boy; maybe that's it. Not as much spirit now.

GABRIEL You're still a young man.

FOX (*Pleasantly; almost casually*) Weary of all this . . . this making-do, of conning people that know they're being conned. Sick of it all. Not sick so much as desperate; desperate for something that . . . that has nothing to do with all this. Restless, Gabby boy, restless. And a man with a restlessness is a savage bugger.

GABRIEL What do you want?

FOX What do I want? I want . . . I want a dream I think I've had to come true. I want to live like a child. I want to die and wake up in heaven with Crystal. What do I want? Jaysus, man, if I knew the answer to that I might be content with what I have. (*Without stopping*) I like your jacket.

GABRIEL I never had any talent for this business. I would have been no help.

FOX That row we had —

GABRIEL Which one? We fought every other day. I was a cocky bastard.

FOX You know the one I mean — the big one. I'm sorry about that . . . my fault. I would have written to you but I didn't know —

GABRIEL Forget it, Fox; for Christ's sake, forget it.

FOX Well, now I've said it.

GABRIEL If I had a pound for every fight I've been in since, I'd be a rich man . . . a bloody millionaire. Been here long?

FOX Just tonight.

GABRIEL How is it?

FOX Great — great.

GABRIEL You'll stay, then?

FOX Pulling out in the morning, as a matter of fact. Booking lined up in Ardmore. I tried to cancel it — phoned just before the show — but they're holding us to it.

GABRIEL That sounds good. I think I remember Ardmore.

FOX What have you been doing since?

GABRIEL Me? Everything . . . nothing much . . . a bit of a drifter.

FOX Were you at sea?

GABRIEL (*Touches the duffel bag with his foot*) For a while. And British Railways for a while. And dish-washing. And street photographer. Anything that came along. We're a restless breed, Fox.

FOX You're not home to stay at all.

GABRIEL Maybe. I don't know. Depends.

FOX You're in trouble — isn't that it?

GABRIEL Trouble?

FOX With the police. Isn't that it?

GABRIEL Takes a fox to know a fox. That's why we could never get on — we're too alike.

FOX What's the trouble?

GABRIEL When I was nabbed first — not long after I went over there — they sent me to one of those psychiatrist blokes. And do you know what he said, Fox? He said I was autistic — 'unable to respond emotionally to people'. Funny word — autistic — isn't it? Got me off the hook a couple of times.

FOX The trouble.

GABRIEL And this bloke kept asking me about the show and about you and Crystal and the travelling around. Dead serious. Make a good straight man.

FOX Why are the police after you?

GABRIEL He got everything all wrong: he worked it out that you were some sort of a softy and that Crystal was tough as nails.

FOX What did you do?

GABRIEL Me? I —

CRYSTAL (*Off*) Fox! Gabriel!

FOX She's to know nothing.

GABRIEL Do you think I'd tell her?

FOX Tell me.

GABRIEL I was in this digs. In Salford. And it was a Saturday night — last Saturday three weeks. And I had a bad day with the horses. And this bitch of a landlady she kept shouting up for her money. And the bloke that shared the room with me — I owed him money too. So I gathered my things and dropped them out the window and then I went out to the yard and over the wall.

CRYSTAL (*Off*) Come on, you two!

GABRIEL We're missing the fun.

FOX Go on.

GABRIEL Must have been nearly midnight by then. And about four streets away there was this newspaper shop and the old woman — she knew me — I used to go in there sometimes — she was closing up. And I asked her for a packet of fags and she said, 'Hold on, love, till I put up these shutters.' And when she went out to the front I saw the till was open. And there was no one about. And just as I reached my hand across, in she comes and starts clawing at me and screaming at me. I tried to shake her off and I couldn't. And she kept screaming and scratching at me. And I was terrified. And I caught this weight — I think it was on the scales — and I hit her. But that didn't stop her. So I hit her again. And again . . .

Pause.

FOX Did you kill her?

GABRIEL That's the point, Fox; I'm not sure.

FOX Jaysus.

Curtain.

356

ACT TWO

Episode One

Early evening, a week later. Backstage of the marquee: only now it is pitched on a different site — the backstage is left.

A rehearsal is in progress. FOX *is kneeling, his elbows on a chair. He is wearing the habit — but not the headdress — that* CRYSTAL *wore at the opening of Episode One. He is also wearing a large leather belt and hopes to look like a monk.*

FOX (*Roars*) I'm not staying on my bloody knees all day! Will you hurry up!

> CRYSTAL *appears at the door carrying a bucket of water.*

CRYSTAL (*Sharply*) Someone has to carry the water, you know!

FOX Surely! In the middle of a rehearsal? All right — all right; get a move on now.

CRYSTAL 'Cos if I don't go for it none of the gentlemen around here would think of carrying it.

FOX It's your entrance.

CRYSTAL So just cool down. (*Very sweetly*) Father. (FOX *is lost in prayer*) Father Superior.

FOX Did someone call me?

CRYSTAL It's me, Father, Sister Petita Sancta. (FOX *does not turn round*)

FOX Ah, Petita, Petita, come in, my child.

CRYSTAL I'll come back later, Father.

FOX No, no, no. Come on in. I was just talking to God about all our little problems in our mission hospital here at Lakula in Eastern Zambia.

FOX *now rises and faces his visitor.*

But is it — ? Yes, it is my Petita! Heavens bless me, I didn't recognize you in those clothes. O, my child, you look so young and so beautiful.

CRYSTAL The wife of the vice-consul presented it to me gratuitously.

FOX Dear Petita. We are going to miss you so much here. But then our loss is Dr Alan Giroux's gain.

CRYSTAL He is bidding farewell to the other sisters. Just reflect, Father: this time tomorrow he and I shall be in Paris! Ah, here he comes! Come on, Dr Giroux!

PEDRO *runs on. He is wearing a short white medical coat. He is absolutely wretched.*

PEDRO I have just had a quick run round —

FOX (*Prompts*) 'I am here to say *adieu*.'

PEDRO I am here to say *adieu, mon mère superior*.

FOX Dear, dear Dr Giroux.

PEDRO I have just had a quick run round the children's, casualty, fever and maternity wards. I gave every nun a double injection of streptomycin.

FOX (*Wryly*) Why not! They're all drug addicts!

CRYSTAL Let him go on, Fox. I'm late for the hospital as it is.

FOX OK, OK. May God reward you, my son.

PEDRO You know I do not believe in your God, Fox — Father.

FOX Some day you will, Doctor. I have my priests praying for you. (*Pause*) Laugh.

PEDRO I can't.

FOX Try. (PEDRO *produces a strange sound*) Cut the laugh.

CRYSTAL I shall pray, too.

FOX And now would you mind if an old man gave you both his blessing?

CRYSTAL For my sake, Alan.

PEDRO If it makes you happy, *mon amour*.

CRYSTAL *and* PEDRO *kneel.*

FOX May God reward you both for your years . . . and
so on and so on . . . our arms will be open wide to
hold you to our bosom — chest. My children.

GABRIEL *comes on and watches the rehearsal.*

CRYSTAL Thank you, Father.
FOX Toot-toot. Listen — the river boat.
PEDRO Some day, Father, I'll —
FOX Goodbye, goodbye. (*To* CRYSTAL) If you hurry you'll
still make it. (*To* PEDRO) Exquisite, Pedro. Very mov-
ing.
PEDRO Fox, for the love of God —
FOX A sincerity all his own; hasn't he, my love?

FOX *takes off his habit.* CRYSTAL *pulls on a coat.*

CRYSTAL There's a bus around six. We'll be back on it.
PEDRO I can't do it! And you know I can't do it!
FOX You'll be fine, man. Don't worry.
CRYSTAL Ready, Gabriel? Come on. Visiting time'll be over
and Papa'll think we've forgotten him.
GABRIEL Tell him I'll see him at the weekend.
CRYSTAL You're not coming?
GABRIEL Next Saturday — tell him next Saturday.
CRYSTAL That's what you said last Saturday. You said you
were coming today. You promised me, Gabriel.
GABRIEL It's not — it's just . . . I'm not feeling so well.
CRYSTAL And you're the only one he keeps asking for.
GABRIEL Next weekend — tell him that — next weekend for
sure.
CRYSTAL When did you get sick?
GABRIEL It's a headache. I often get them.

CRYSTAL *looks to* FOX *for an explanation.*

FOX (*Quickly*) You're going to miss the bus.
CRYSTAL I don't understand it; that's all. And neither will he.
PEDRO Tell him Gringo sent her love.

FOX Have you the clean pyjamas and the oranges? (CRYSTAL *nods*) And tell him we can't hold a raffle until he comes back.

CRYSTAL He (*Gabriel*) could do the raffle.

FOX *takes a packet of cigarettes from his pocket, shakes them, and throws them to* CRYSTAL.

FOX Here — give him these.

CRYSTAL I'll be back before seven.

She goes off.

FOX (*Calling*) And tell him to keep his hands off the nurses. (*To* GABRIEL) The least you could do is go and see him before he dies. (GABRIEL *ignores him*) I'm talking to you!

GABRIEL (*Completely calm; almost indifferent*) You know I can't walk about.

FOX She doesn't know that.

GABRIEL It's a wonder you didn't tell her.

FOX I didn't tell her — for her sake, not yours.

GABRIEL If there was money in it you wouldn't have kept so quiet, would you?

FOX I'm not much, sonny, but I'm no informer.

PEDRO Fox, I don't want to keep on about it —

FOX What-what-what?

PEDRO You don't know how miserable I am doing this stuff.

FOX Beautiful, Pedro. Exquisite.

PEDRO I can't even pronounce the words right. (*Absolutely miserable*) Gabriel, would you . . . ?

GABRIEL Ug-huh.

PEDRO You'd be great — a young man and all.

GABRIEL I won't be around much longer, Pedro.

PEDRO *shuffles off. As he goes:*

PEDRO All I know is if I could see myself up there (*on stage*) I'd never lift my head again.

FOX *busies himself gathering up the props.* GABRIEL
*and he are both conscious of the tension between
them.*

GABRIEL Do you want a hand?

FOX No.

Pause.

GABRIEL Isn't there a show tonight?

FOX Unlikely.

GABRIEL I thought you went around with handbills this
morning?

FOX I did.

GABRIEL Well, if you put out bills —

FOX *interrupts him sharply and stands poised,
listening.*

FOX Shh!

GABRIEL What is it?

Silence. FOX *relaxes and goes on working.*

FOX Nothing.

GABRIEL Crystal thinks there's a show. That's why she's rush-
ing back. (*Pause*) I didn't mean what I said — about
you and money.

FOX Doesn't matter.

GABRIEL Well, what do you expect me to do? Go to the hospital with her and be picked up there? Is that what
you want? All right then; I'll go. And I'll tell her
first —

FOX She's not to know.

GABRIEL She's going to know. If the old man dies and I
haven't gone to see him —

He breaks off because CRYSTAL *enters.*

FOX What's wrong?

CRYSTAL Missed it by a second. It went flying past just as I got to the road.

FOX Come on. There's enough petrol in the truck to take us there and back.

CRYSTAL And it not taxed? And all those peelers about the town?

FOX It's insured. Isn't that enough for them? Come on — the old man'll be waiting.

GABRIEL Crystal, I've something to tell you.

FOX If nobody else is going I'm going myself.

GABRIEL I can't go anywhere, Crystal, because the police are after me.

CRYSTAL Police?

FOX It's nothing — nothing at all —

GABRIEL I've been on the run for over a month.

CRYSTAL What did you do?

FOX He stole money from a shop — that's what he did —

GABRIEL And there was an old —

FOX He lifted a few shillings and bolted.

CRYSTAL Where?

GABRIEL Salford.

CRYSTAL Where's that?

GABRIEL Near Manchester.

CRYSTAL How much?

GABRIEL I don't know — £2 — maybe £3 — it's not the —

FOX And then he ran and that's the whole story. I told him not to tell you. Can't keep his bloody mouth shut.

GABRIEL I'll clear out in the morning — sign on with a tanker —

CRYSTAL *is very cool, very calm, very much in command.*

CRYSTAL Is it the English police that are after you?

GABRIEL I don't know. I think so.

CRYSTAL Were you seen?

GABRIEL I suppose so —

FOX. He was.

CRYSTAL Have they got your name?

GABRIEL I don't think so.

CRYSTAL How much money did you lift?

GABRIEL A few pounds —

CRYSTAL How much?

GABRIEL Four-ten.

CRYSTAL When did this happen?

GABRIEL About a month ago.

CRYSTAL Where were you since?

FOX Glasgow.

CRYSTAL And then you came straight here to us?

GABRIEL Yes.

CRYSTAL Did you hang about Dublin?

GABRIEL No. Look, I'll clear out tomorrow —

FOX If we got him the length of Cork or Belfast he could get a boat to —

CRYSTAL He's going nowhere! We've been in trouble before; and the way to get out of it is to sit still and say nothing — to nobody! Is that clear? You can help with the show. You'll get some money. And as long as we keep on the move and steer clear of the towns you're as safe as houses. Out of sight — out of mind — they'll soon forget about you. Is that clear? (GABRIEL *shrugs.* CRYSTAL *turns to* FOX) Is that clear?

FOX What if they come looking for him?

CRYSTAL D'you think they're going to search the country for the sake of four pounds ten shillings? (*To* GABRIEL) It's up to you: stick with the show and keep your mouth shut and that'll be the end of it. Anyway, we could do with the help . . . I suppose it's near tea-time.

GABRIEL I'm sorry, Crystal.

CRYSTAL Maybe this way you'll have to stay with us.

> *She wearily goes to the other end of the marquee and throws her coat across a seat. While she is out-side their range:*

FOX (*Viciously*) You're a louse to have told her!

GABRIEL She suspected.

FOX And what are you going to tell her if they come for you? Eh?

GABRIEL I would have told her the whole truth at the beginning.

FOX That you may be wanted for murder?

GABRIEL You leave me alone and I'll keep out of your way.

CRYSTAL *is back.*

CRYSTAL We need some methylated for the stove. That was one of Papa's jobs.

FOX He'll wonder nobody turned up.

CRYSTAL There's visiting tomorrow. I'll get the early bus and —

She breaks off because PEDRO has entered, carrying the lifeless body of Gringo in his arms. PEDRO is so stunned that he is beyond emotion.

PEDRO It's Gringo.

CRYSTAL Pedro —

GABRIEL Is she sick? She's not —

CRYSTAL What's wrong, Pedro? What's happened?

PEDRO Gringo.

GABRIEL Christ!

CRYSTAL I saw her this morning after breakfast — she was fine —

GABRIEL She's stiff.

CRYSTAL Oh God! (GABRIEL *touches the dog's mouth*) What — what's that stuff?

PEDRO My Gringo.

GABRIEL Must have been poisoned.

CRYSTAL How could she have been poisoned, you fool! She never leaves the van!

PEDRO And she's wise, very wise. And humorous, very humorous.

CRYSTAL Oh God, Pedro, Pedro!

PEDRO She'll be seven next birthday . . . 10th of March. I make a cake and put candles on it.

CRYSTAL Is there nothing — ? Brandy — ?

GABRIEL Dead a good while.

PEDRO I called her. 'Where are you?' I says. 'I know you're hiding,' I says. 'I've got liver for your supper,' I says. 'And if you don't come out I'll eat it all myself,' I says. 'Cos I know she likes liver.

> CRYSTAL *puts her arm around him. He moves very slowly off. She goes with him.*

And I put it on the pan. And I thought the smell would coax her. And all the time I kept talking to her the way I always do . . .

CRYSTAL Pedro.

PEDRO And when there was no sign of her I started looking for her. 'I'll give you a skelp,' I says. 'That's what you'll get — a right good skelp.' 'Cos she knows I'd never lay a finger on her . . . (*His voice fades away*)

GABRIEL Christ, that's awful . . . She's all he has . . . And at his age . . .

FOX That's the way.

GABRIEL How the hell could she have picked up poison around here? For Christ's sake, no one sets poison in the middle of a bog!

> FOX *shrugs his shoulders and moves away.* GABRIEL *glances at him, then looks at him, then stares at him.*

Fox . . .

FOX (*Quickly, defensively*) Well?

GABRIEL God, Fox . . . you didn't?

FOX What are you mouthing about?

GABRIEL You did?

FOX Did what?

GABRIEL Christ, man, how could you?

FOX Who are you to talk?

GABRIEL You might as well have killed Pedro himself.

FOX It's a dog, remember — not an old woman.

GABRIEL You did it ... deliberately ... to get rid of Pedro.

FOX Shut up.

GABRIEL Just as you got rid of the Fritter Twins and Cid and Tanya and all the others I heard about.

FOX You know nothing about it.

GABRIEL Why, man?

FOX You know nothing about it.

GABRIEL What are you at?

FOX Just leave me. I'm managing fine.

GABRIEL Fine? You call this fine? Wrecking the show? Killing an old man's dog? What are you doing?

Pause.

FOX Once, maybe twice in your life, the fog lifts, and you get a glimpse, an intuition; and suddenly you know that this can't be all there is to it — there has to be something better than this.

GABRIEL You're going mad! What fog?

FOX And afterwards all you're left with is a vague memory of what you thought you saw; and that's what you hold on to — the good thing you think you saw.

GABRIEL You planned it all! That's it. It's all deliberate!

FOX Because there must be something better than this.

GABRIEL It's some sort of crazy scheme!

FOX (*Wearily*) Go away, boy.

GABRIEL You're full of hate — that's what's wrong with you — you hate everybody!

FOX No.

GABRIEL Even Crystal.

FOX What about Crystal?

GABRIEL She'll be the next. You'll ditch her, too.

FOX How little you know, boy. My Crystal is the only good part of me.

Bring down lights.

ACT TWO
Episode Two

Night. The stage is empty and almost totally dark. Off right there are muffled sounds of excited voices. Then suddenly GABRIEL *enters right and races frantically across the stage. He is in his bare feet, vest and trousers. As he gets to extreme left a uniformed Irish* POLICEMAN *steps out of the shadows — and* GABRIEL *lands in his arms.*

POLICEMAN The running's over. Take it easy, Melarkey.

> *Two plainclothes English* DETECTIVES *enter right.*

DET. 1 Hold him, Sergeant!
DET. 2 The bastard bit my hand! (*Produces handcuffs*) Hold them out, Paddy. When I get you back I'll fix your teeth.

> GABRIEL *holds out his hands.* DETECTIVE 2 *hits him in the lower stomach.* GABRIEL *doubles up.*

POLICEMAN No need for that.
DET. 2 And that's only the beginning, Paddy. A warming up, you might say.
POLICEMAN Better get some clothes for him.
DET. 1 I'll get them.
POLICEMAN And shoes.

> DETECTIVE 1 *leaves.*

DET. 2 I'd take him as he is. (*Catches* GABRIEL *by the chin*) Might cool you off, Paddy, eh? And I want you to know me. My name's Coalstream. Been after you

367

for quite a while now, Paddy. And after I've finished
with you you'll be sorry you ever left your gypsy
encampment.

POLICEMAN You'll be charged in the station.

DET. 2 And in the morning we go to Manchester. By plane.
For speed, Paddy. Extradition papers — reservations — all in order. You're quite a big piece of dirt;
you know that, Paddy?

> *Enter* FOX *and* CRYSTAL, *wearing coats over their
> nightclothes.* FOX *is carrying a hurricane lamp.*

FOX What the hell's all the —

CRYSTAL Fox! It's Gabriel!

DET. 2 You two his parents?

CRYSTAL What's wrong? Who are you? (*Sees handcuffs*) Why
is he handcuffed?

DET. 2 He's under arrest, missus. And tomorrow afternoon
he'll be charged in Manchester with the attempted
manslaughter of an old lady two months ago.

CRYSTAL Manslaughter? . . . Gabriel?

DET. 2 He's lucky it's not murder.

CRYSTAL Oh my God . . .

> FOX *holds her arm to steady her.*

GABRIEL He (*Fox*) knew. I told him.

CRYSTAL It's lies! It's lies!

DET. 2 Why don't you ask him (*Gabriel*), missus? He knows
all about it.

CRYSTAL Why didn't you tell me, Fox? Why didn't you tell
me?

FOX Easy, my love. Shhhh.

> DETECTIVE 1 *returns with Gabriel's shoes and clothes.*
> *Because* GABRIEL *is handcuffed the jacket is draped*
> *over his shoulders. The* POLICEMAN *puts the shoes*
> *on his feet. While this is going on:*

CRYSTAL Manchester? . . . Why are you taking him there?

DET. 1 That's where he coshed the old lady. Twenty-nine stitches she got. You've a boy to be proud of, missus — a real gentleman.

CRYSTAL I'm going, too. Wherever you're taking him, I'm going too.

GABRIEL I'll be all right, Crystal.

DET. 1 You can't hold his hand in jail for ten years.

DET. 2 He'll do. I've a special heater in the car for him.

CRYSTAL Fox — !

FOX Easy, easy, easy.

DET. 2 Bloody gypsies. Same all over.

FOX Where are you taking him to?

POLICEMAN To the station. Then to Dublin . . .

CRYSTAL Stop them, Fox! Stop them!

DET. 1 He'll get a fair trial, missus.

DET. 2 He'll get his desserts. Come on.

CRYSTAL Give him back to me!

> *She breaks away from* FOX *and flings herself at the police. There is a brief scuffle. She is thrown to the ground.*

DET. 2 Stinking gypsies! Let's go.

> *The two* DETECTIVES *move off with* GABRIEL *between them.* CRYSTAL *does not hear the following:*

POLICEMAN I warned you to get out of my territory, Melarkey.

FOX How did you know he was here?

POLICEMAN The old man in hospital spilled the beans.

FOX Papa!

POLICEMAN The old doting man. Everyone that lights in his ward he tells them to tell Gabriel to come and see him.

FOX And some rat went and told you?

POLICEMAN He told me himself, Melarkey. And if the boy had gone to see him — even once — the old man would have been content and we might never have known.

He leaves. FOX *turns round, sees* CRYSTAL *sobbing. He sits beside her and puts his arms around her.*

CRYSTAL Gabriel . . .

FOX My love.

CRYSTAL My boy.

FOX It's all right . . . all right . . .

CRYSTAL My Gabriel.

FOX Easy . . . easy . . .

She sobs convulsively. FOX *holds her head to his shoulder.*
Bring down lights.

ACT TWO

Episode Three

When the lights come up dawn is breaking. FOX *and* CRYSTAL *are dressed as we left them.* CRYSTAL *is sitting on an upturned box staring at the dead stove. They have not been in bed all night and their conversation has an exhausted and ragged inconsequence.* FOX *has been watching the dawn break. He now moves over beside her.*

FOX   The sun's coming up. (*He sits beside her and takes her hand*) My sweet?

CRYSTAL   My Fox.

FOX   How do you feel?

CRYSTAL   Not bad.

FOX   You should lie down for a while now.

CRYSTAL   You know I couldn't sleep.

FOX   (*Briskly, the entertainer*) That's what I'll do, then. This very morning. 'Mr. Prospect,' I'll say, 'because of considerations of health the Fox Melarkey show is prepared to — to — to consider a takeover bid offered by you, provided, of course, the financial terms are acceptable to the joint shareholders of the Melarkey board.' Eh? No — 'provided the cash settlement is realistic in terms of our national reputation and all currently functioning equipment.' How about that?

CRYSTAL   What's that, Fox?

FOX   Is that all right?

CRYSTAL   (*Listless*) That's good. That's fine.

FOX   Everything except the accordion and the rickety wheel.

CRYSTAL   And this (*stove*) too.

FOX   What d'you think his offer'll be?

CRYSTAL Couldn't even make a guess, my pet.

FOX Well, I mean to say, there's the truck; and two vans — one in semi-mint condition; and the marquee and the stage; and the ornate proscenium and velour curtains; and — and — and of course the reputation and goodwill — if he offers me sixty quid for the lot, Jaysus, I'll take the arm off him.

CRYSTAL It's cold.

FOX You're tired.

CRYSTAL I'll get some solicitor to defend him, won't I?

FOX Flash the money, my love, and you'll get the Lord Chief Justice.

CRYSTAL I just can't get it out of my head . . . Not Gabriel somehow . . . he was never that kind . . . or maybe you never know anybody.

FOX They'll be in Dublin by now.

CRYSTAL If he'd been a rough boy or anything. But he's so . . . so soft . . . at least I thought he was.

FOX Probably he panicked.

CRYSTAL Those shoes (*Fox's*) are letting in.

FOX The ground's dry.

CRYSTAL 'There's no worse shod than a shoemaker's wife' — that was a great expression of Papa's. I never knew what it meant.

FOX I think we shouldn't tell him about Gabriel.

CRYSTAL Makes no difference now. He's past understanding.

FOX Maybe.

CRYSTAL Sure you know he's completely doting.

FOX I suppose so. (*He rises*) A strange time of day, this . . . Every time I see the sun coming up I think of the morning we — (*he breaks off and looks at her*) Do you remember the channel?

CRYSTAL What's that?

> He begins quietly, diffidently. But as he recalls the episode — and as she remembers it too — his warmth and obvious joy spread to her.

FOX A few miles north of Galway — along the coast

— a channel of water — a stream — just where it
entered the sea. We were only two weeks married
at the time.

CRYSTAL (*Listlessly*) Galway's nice.

FOX (*He sits beside her*) And you got a mad notion of
going for a swim at dawn. And this morning, just
about this time, you woke me up, and we slipped
out and raced across the wet fields in our bare feet.
And when we got to the sea we had to wade across
this stream to get to the beach.

CRYSTAL (*Suddenly remembering*) The channel!

FOX D'you remember? And you hoisted up your skirt
and you took my hand and we stepped into the —

CRYSTAL Fish! Flat fish!

FOX Hundreds of them! Every step you took! D'you remember?

CRYSTAL Oh my God!

FOX Every time you put a foot down!

CRYSTAL The wriggling of them! Under your bare feet!

FOX And you couldn't go forward! And you couldn't go
back!

CRYSTAL And you splitting your sides laughing!

FOX Trying to keep hopping so that you wouldn't touch
bottom!

CRYSTAL Squirming and wriggling!

FOX And then you lost your balance — and down you
went!

CRYSTAL And pulled you down too.

FOX And then you started to laugh!

CRYSTAL It was the sight of you spluttering!

FOX The water was freezing!

CRYSTAL We were soaked to the skin!

FOX And we staggered over to the beach.

CRYSTAL And you, you eejit, you began to leap about like a
monkey!

FOX The seagulls — remember? — they sat on the rocks,
staring at us.

CRYSTAL And you tied a plait of seaweed to my hair.

FOX And we danced on the sand.

CRYSTAL Wet clothes and all.

FOX And then the sun came out.

CRYSTAL The channel . . . Funny, I'd forgotten that altogether.

FOX Just the two of us.

Silence; each with his own thoughts.

CRYSTAL Fox, I was thinking —

FOX (*Eagerly*) What?

CRYSTAL Before you had this idea of selling out, I was thinking where we could raise the money for a solicitor.

FOX (*Flatly*) Oh.

CRYSTAL And Pedro was the only person I could think of. He offered me money before, you know.

FOX A good man.

CRYSTAL A great man. I wonder where he's disappeared to.

FOX God knows.

CRYSTAL He used to talk to that dog as if it was a baby.

FOX That's the way.

CRYSTAL Maybe he went to Dublin; he has a cousin there.

FOX She died years ago.

CRYSTAL I didn't know that. How long does it take to fly from Dublin to Manchester?

FOX About an hour.

CRYSTAL I don't think he was ever in an airplane before, was he?

FOX Not that I know of.

> FOX *is conscious that he should match* CRYSTAL's *sombre mood. But he is unable to suppress the strange excitement he feels. He moves closer to her.*

My sweet —

CRYSTAL My Fox.

FOX My sweet, when we get rid of this stuff to Prospect —

CRYSTAL Maybe he won't touch it.

FOX Don't you worry: I'll get rid of it. And when I do there'll just be you and me and the old accordion and the old rickety wheel — all we had thirty years

374

ago, remember? You and me. And we'll laugh again at silly things and I'll plait seaweed into your hair again. And we'll go only to the fairs we want to go to, and stop only at the towns we want to stop at, and eat when we want to eat, and lie down when we feel like it. And everywhere we go we'll know people and they'll know us — 'Crystal and Fox!' Jaysus, my love, if I weren't a superstitious man, I'd say — I'd say —

CRYSTAL What?

FOX I'd say that heaven's just round the corner.

Bring down lights.

ACT TWO

Episode Four

Two days later. A crossroads in the open country. A signpost pointing in four directions. It is a beautiful sunny day. From some distance off can be heard the sound of FOX *and* CRYSTAL *approaching. They make so much noise — chattering, laughing, whooping, singing — that one would expect to see a dozen happy children appear. Now they arrive at the crossroads.* FOX *is carrying the rickety wheel, the accordion, and the stove.* CRYSTAL *is carrying two shabby suitcases.* FOX *has a bottle of wine in his pocket, and when their hands are free, the bottle passes between them. Neither is drunk, nor even tipsy, but both are more than a little elated: all their immediate worries have been solved; and the afternoon is warm; and the wine is heady.* FOX *is particularly jaunty and vivacious, like a young man being flamboyant to entertain and impress his girl.*

FOX This is it! Here we are!

CRYSTAL Where?

FOX Here!

CRYSTAL You're pulling my leg!

FOX Anything that's going anywhere has to pass here. Dublin — Galway — Cork — Derry; you're at the hub of the country, girl.

CRYSTAL The hub of the country! Fox, you're an eejit!

FOX (*Sings*) 'A-hitching we will go
A-hitching we will go!'
Throw your stuff down there and leave everything to the Fox. Two single tickets to — where do you wish to go to, Madam?

CRYSTAL Manchester!

FOX Manchester it'll be!

CRYSTAL *drops down on the side of the road.*

CRYSTAL (*Giggling*) No one's ever going to stop, my Fox. They're all going to *swizzzzz* right past. And we're going to spend the rest of our lives in the middle of nowhere. God, I'm giddy!

FOX (*Toasting*) To a great day's work. To your lawyer, Mr King —

CRYSTAL Ring! Frederick Ashley Ring!

FOX — who'll see that our boy is well defended; and to Dick Prospect who parted with forty crisp notes for a load of rubbish and for a truck that won't go into reverse.

CRYSTAL You didn't tell him!

FOX D'you think I'm mad? He kept saying, 'She runs sweet enough, Fox, I can see that. Turn her at this gate and take me back.' 'No, no, Dick, a fair trial; we'll go right round the circuit. I want you to know what you're getting.'

CRYSTAL Too damn good for him!

FOX And when we got back to his place who d'you think I saw?

CRYSTAL Who?

FOX Cid.

CRYSTAL You did not!

FOX Eating a big feed of bacon and eggs — his van door was open; and she was standing outside, screaming in at him.

CRYSTAL What about?

FOX 'You've lost control! And don't blame me if your stomach curdles and gripes on you!'

CRYSTAL *rolls over with laughter.*

This is the life, girl; it should always have been like this. (*He hears a car approaching*) Transport! Transport! We're in business! This is it. We're away! Gather up your things!

He hides the bottle, straightens his tie, assumes a
pleasant face, does a brief jig for CRYSTAL's *enter-*
tainment, and then takes up his position at the
verge of the road.

CRYSTAL God, this is a scream!

FOX (*To car*) Come on, come on — that's it, me aul' darlin'
— a lift for the Crystal and the Fox — slow down —
that's it — decent fella — we'll go wherever you're
going — look at the wee narrow shoulders and the
wee sad face smiling in at you —

CRYSTAL (*Laughing*) You eejit, you!

FOX — sure you never saw anything as pathetic in all
your life — the honest Fox Melarkey depending on
charity for his transportation and edification —

CRYSTAL (*Laughing*) Quit it, Fox!

FOX Doesn't hear a word I'm saying. (*To car*) May God
reward you for your years of dedication to our
little mission hospital here in Lakula in Eastern
Tipperary — Jaysus, you couldn't say no to a pair
of innocent eyes like these — Jaysus, you could —
Jaysus, you're a hoor! (*The car has gone past. Peals of*
laughter from CRYSTAL. *To car*) And in the next bad
frost I hope they drop off you!

CRYSTAL He heard you, you clown you!

FOX *is moved by a strange elation; not so much joy*
as a controlled recklessness. The sun, the wine, the
release from responsibility. The desire to play up to
an easy audience like CRYSTAL — *these are all the*
obvious ingredients of his exultation. But he is
aware — and CRYSTAL *is not — that it has also a*
cold brittle quality, an edge of menace. He gives
the rickety wheel a sharp turn, and addresses an
imaginary crowd:

FOX Red-yellow-black or blue, whatever it is that tickles
your fancy, now's your chance to turn a bad penny
into a decent pound, there's a wee lassie out there

that looks as if she might, come on, my love, now's
your chance, if you wait till your mother tells you
the notion'll have gone off you.

CRYSTAL Take a swig before it's done.

FOX No more for me.

CRYSTAL All the better.

FOX (*Irritably*) Are there no bloody cars in the country?

CRYSTAL Lie back here beside me and relax.

FOX I have to be on the move. (*Eagerly*) My Crystal, let's
get married again!

CRYSTAL You're drunk.

FOX My love, marry me again. Please marry me again.

CRYSTAL Full as a pig!

FOX I'm asking you, my sweet.

CRYSTAL Here?

FOX Now.

CRYSTAL At this moment?

FOX Immediately.

CRYSTAL In these clothes?

FOX Just as you are.

CRYSTAL This is so sudden. But why not? You only die once?
(*Rises and sings*) 'Here comes the bride, small fat and
wide — ' (*She breaks off suddenly*) A car!

FOX (*Irritably*) Let it pass.

CRYSTAL A big swanky one! Come on, Fox; do your job!

FOX I hear no car.

CRYSTAL There it is. Quick! Hide that bottle!

FOX (*Vaguely*) Will I try it?

CRYSTAL What d'you mean — will you try it? You don't want
to be stuck in this godforsaken place, do you? Will
you try it! What's wrong with you, man?

FOX (*Very sharply*) OK. OK. Stop nagging!

CRYSTAL 'Will I try it'!

*He faces the approaching car and switches on his
professional smile.*

FOX That's it — take it easy — slow now — slower —

CRYSTAL We're away this time!

FOX Good day to you, ma'am — Fox and Crystal, a professional couple temporarily inconvenienced and maladjusted — Melarkey's the name — and who's to say, perhaps the first lay pope —

CRYSTAL Ha-ha-ha-ha!

FOX That'll be an entry for your diary: 'Today I gave a lift to the Supreme Pontiff and his missus outside the village of Slaughmanus —'

CRYSTAL She hears you, you fool you!

FOX Wait — wait — wait — wait — (*The car has gone*)

CRYSTAL She heard every word you said!

FOX (*Shouts*) With a face like that you'd need a Rolls! Elephant!

CRYSTAL The sun's roasting.

FOX We've got to move. We must keep moving.

CRYSTAL Honest to God, my sweet, I'm tipsy! Haven't seen Dickie Prospect for years. How's he looking?

FOX As usual.

CRYSTAL Was he asking for Crystal?

FOX You're plastered.

CRYSTAL Don't tell me my Fox is jealous!

FOX Of that animal? Jaysus!

CRYSTAL Don't worry, my sweet. It was a long, long, long, time ago, before I met my Fox.

FOX Animal.

CRYSTAL And he never, never, never crosses my mind.

FOX What the hell sort of a dead-end is this?

CRYSTAL Very pretty. And the sun's warm. And there's a smell of heather. And I feel . . . gorgeous. D'you think I'm gorgeous, my pet? (*No response from* FOX) My Fox.

FOX Mm?

CRYSTAL Sit down here beside me.

FOX Can't sit.

CRYSTAL We're all rotten, my sweet.

FOX You're drunk.

CRYSTAL I am not drunk, Fox. But I am rotten. Papa's dying in hospital. Gabriel's going to jail. The show's finished. We've no money. And I'm happy as a lark. Amn't I rotten, my Fox? (*He does not answer*) Fox.

FOX Maybe we should try the other road.

CRYSTAL You changed, my pet.

FOX Or go back to the village.

CRYSTAL You think I didn't notice. But I did. Crystal saw it all.

FOX Good for Crystal.

CRYSTAL Just when things were beginning to go well for the show too. And then you got . . . restless. That's what happened. My Fox got restless. Out go the Fritter Twins. Out goes Billy Hercules. And I was frightened 'cos I thought: He's going to wreck it all, break it all up. That's when it began. Am I right, my sweet?

FOX You shouldn't drink, woman.

CRYSTAL And then you began to skip the places that were good in the past. And when we could have done four nights you left after two. And then you poisoned Pedro's dog —

FOX You don't know what you're saying!

CRYSTAL You did, my love. I know you did. And I never understood why you did those things. I wondered, of course, 'cos I know you loved him. But I never understood. And maybe I didn't want to know, my Fox, because I was afraid — it was the only fear I had — I was terrified that you were going to shake me off too. And I really didn't give a damn about any of them, God forgive me, not even Pedro, not as long as you didn't turn on me. That's all I cared about. And now we're back at the start, my love; just as we began together. Fox and Crystal. To hell with everything else.

This revelation stuns FOX. *He stares at her in utter amazement and incredulity.*

FOX And Pedro?

CRYSTAL Crystal saw it all.

FOX You knew?

CRYSTAL I told you — I'm rotten.

FOX That I had killed the one good thing he had?

CRYSTAL God forgive me, Fox.

FOX Our friend, Pedro?

CRYSTAL What are you looking at me like that for? It was you that did it, remember; not me. Here, my love, sit down here beside me.

> *As if he were in a dream he goes to her and sits beside her. She catches his hand.*

I'd marry you a dozen — a hundred times again.

FOX Would you?

CRYSTAL Every day. Every hour. (*She closes her eyes and rests her head on his shoulders*) My sweet Fox ... This is all I want.

> *When* FOX *speaks his voice is very soft, almost comforting.* CRYSTAL's *replies are sun-drowsy.*

FOX My pet ...

CRYSTAL Mm?

FOX You love me, Crystal?

CRYSTAL Mm.

FOX You love me, don't you?

CRYSTAL Sweet Fox.

FOX A lot — a great lot?

CRYSTAL Mm.

FOX (*More slowly*) If you were asked to, would you go to hell with me?

CRYSTAL There and back, my love.

> *Pause.*

FOX Crystal.

CRYSTAL Can't keep awake.

FOX I have something to tell you.

CRYSTAL Tell me.

FOX About Gabriel.

CRYSTAL He was always such a gentle boy.

FOX You don't know how they found him.

CRYSTAL Who, my pet?

FOX How the police found him.

CRYSTAL What d'you mean, my Fox?

FOX Do you remember that night he came — just after Cid and Tanya had gone — remember that night?

CRYSTAL Yes.

FOX Well, he told me the whole story that night — about what happened, and how he hid in Glasgow and then slipped over on the boat.

CRYSTAL I know.

FOX And then he told me about the reward.

CRYSTAL The what?

FOX The English police offered a reward of £100 for him: or £50 for any information about him. (CRYSTAL *sits up*) I did nothing for a while, couldn't make up my mind. And then one day when we were passing through Ballymore I went into the police station there, the white building at the end of the town, and the motorcycle policeman — remember him? — he was there, and I — I — I told him that Gabriel was travelling with us.

CRYSTAL *rises.*

CRYSTAL You?

FOX So they asked me a few questions. And then they made me wait until they phoned Dublin. And Dublin phoned Manchester. And that was it. That's how he was caught.

CRYSTAL Fox . . . ?

FOX So whenever we get to Dublin next there's £100 waiting there for us.

CRYSTAL You're lying —

FOX I don't think Gabriel knows; they probably didn't tell him.

CRYSTAL You're lying, Fox! — you're lying! — lying!

She leaps at him, catches his shirt and puts her face into his.

Jesus, man, deny it!

FOX It's the truth.

CRYSTAL It's a lie! Not your own son! Not Gabriel!

FOX We need the money. It'll start us off again.

She lets him go. She stares at him.

CRYSTAL Your own son? . . . To the police? . . .

FOX It's a lot of money.

CRYSTAL steps back from him.

CRYSTAL What . . . are . . . you?

He puts out a hand to touch her. She recoils. She screams.

Don't — don't — don't touch me!

She backs away from him.

Get away from me! Don't come near me! Don't touch me! Don't speak to me! Don't even look at me! Must get away from you — evil . . . a bad man . . . It's too much . . . I don't know you . . . Don't know you at all. . . Never knew . . . never . . .

Now she breaks away from him in a frenzy. She lifts her coat and a case and all the time she is sobbing and mumbling incoherently. We hear 'Gabriel . . . Never — never . . . Pedro . . . My boy . . . Evil . . .'

FOX I needn't have told you. You need never have known.

She has her belongings. She hesitates and looks at him with total bewilderment.

CRYSTAL I don't know who you are.

She runs off. FOX *takes a few steps after her.*

FOX Crystal! Crystal! (*Quietly, tensely*) It's a lie, Crystal,
all a lie, my love, I made it all up, never entered my
head until a few minutes ago and then I tried to
stop myself but I couldn't. It was poor Papa that
told the police and he didn't know what he was
saying, I don't know why I said it, I said it just to
— to — to — (*Roars*) Crystal! (*Again quiet, rapid*)
Lies, lies, yes, I wanted rid of the Fritters and Billy
Hercules, yes, I wanted rid of Cid and Tanya, and I
wanted rid of the whole show, everything, even
good Pedro, because that's what I saw, that's the
glimpse I got for the moment the fog lifted, that's
what I remember, that's what I think I remember,
just you and me as we were, but we were young
then, and even though our clothes were wet and
even though the sun was only rising, there were
hopes — there were warm hopes; and love alone
isn't enough now, my Crystal, it's not, my love, not
enough at all, not nearly enough. (*Viciously turns the
rickety wheel*) Red-yellow-black or blue, whatever it
is that tickles your fancy, now's your chance to turn
a bad penny into a decent pound, I love you, my
Crystal, and you are the best part of me, and I don't
know where I'm going or what will become of me,
I might have stumbled on as I did once, but I got an
inkling, my Crystal, and I had to hold on to that;
Crystal, my Crystal, where am I now, my Crystal?

Turns the rickety wheel listlessly and sings lamely:

'A-hunting you will go.
A-hunting you will go
You'll catch no fox and put him in a box
A-hunting you will go.'
(*Fairground voice*) Red-yellow-black or blue, what-
ever it is that tickles your fancy, the Fox knows all
the answers — what it's all about, that's why he's

dressed in velvets and drives about in a swank car, you're looking straight at the man that sleeps content at night because he's learned the secrets of the universe, strike me dead if I'm telling a lie and you wipe that grin off your jaw, lady, when you're at a wake, red-yellow-black or blue, you pays your money and you takes your choice, not that it makes a damn bit of difference because the whole thing's fixed, my love, fixed-fixed-fixed; (*almost gently*) but who am I to cloud your bright eyes or kill your belief that love is all. A penny a time and you think you'll be happy for life.

> *A car passes. He does not hear it. He closes his eyes, puts his arm over the rickety wheel, and quickly buries his face in his arm.*
> *Curtain.*

THE
GENTLE
ISLAND

Characters

MANUS SWEENEY
JOE, his son
PHILLY, his elder son
SARAH, Philly's wife
PETER QUINN
SHANE HARRISON
BOSCO
TOM
CON
ANNA, Con's daughter
NEIL ⎫
        ⎬ Sarah's parents
MARY ⎭
MARTIN
PADDY, his son

Time and place

The present. The action takes place on the island of Inishkeen,
off the west coast of County Donegal.

The Gentle Island was first produced at the Olympia Theatre, Dublin, on 30 November 1971, with the following cast:

MANUS SWEENEY	Liam Redmond
SARAH	Sheelagh Cullen
JOE SWEENEY	Eamon Morrissey
TOM	Eamonn Draper
BOSCO	Niall O'Brien
ANNA	Virginia Cole
CON	Seamus Healy
PADDY	Joe Conway
MARTIN	David Herlihy
MARY	Maureen Toal
NEIL	Paul Farrell
PHILLY SWEENEY	Bosco Hogan
PETER QUINN	Edward Byrne
SHANE HARRISON	Shane Connaughton
Directed by	Vincent Dowling

for David Hammond

ACT ONE

Scene One

About one third of the stage area, the portion upstage right from the viewpoint of the audience, is occupied by the kitchen of Manus Sweeney's cottage. The rest of the stage area is the street around the house. Against the gable wall are a currach, fishing nets, lobster pots, farming equipment.

There are two doors leading off the kitchen, one on each side of the fireplace. One leads to Manus/Joe bedroom, one to Sarah/Philly bedroom. There are no walls separating the kitchen area from the street.

A morning in the month of June. The inhabitants of Inishkeen, an island off the west coast of County Donegal, are leaving for good — all except MANUS SWEENEY *and his family. Most of the islanders are already in the boats. The last few hurry past Sweeney's house on their way down to the harbour. They are dressed in their best clothes.*

When the play opens MANUS *is sitting in an airplane seat in the kitchen, his back to the audience, staring resolutely into the fire. He is in his sixties, well made, still enormously powerful even though the muscles are now muted with flesh.*

SARAH, *his daughter-in-law, is sewing at the kitchen table. Occasionally she glances quickly out the window and down towards the harbour. She is dressed in men's boots, long skirt, coarse knitted jumper.*

Silence. Then JOE *rushes in from the left. He is carrying a spade — he has been splicing the handle. He is in his twenties. Like his father he has a big physique, but his strength is more brutal, not as precise, not as economical.*

JOE Father! Father! Come here quick! Sarah! Sarah! You're missing it all! There's four in one boat and six in the other and they're trying to get aul' Nora Dan to change over but they can't get a budge out of her. (*Shouting*) Good on you, Nora! She's sitting there in the stern, Father, clutching the box of hens on her knee and she's not going to move for man or beast. By God, are they — ? My God, they're going to lift her, hens and all! Sarah, Father, come here till you see! Eamonn and Big Anthony have her by the arms — they're pulling at her — the boat's rocking — Jaysus, she's in the water! — no, no, only the hens. Oh Christ, she's going mad! She's caught Eamonn by the hair of the head and she's kicking the shins off Big Anthony. They're all pulling and tearing at her now. God, she's biting and spitting and butting and flinging! Father, come here till you see!

> *Two young men enter in a great hurry from up left.*
> BOSCO *is carrying a mattress on his back.* TOM *has two*
> *huge cases.*

TOM   Yes, Joe.

JOE   Yes, men.

TOM   Great hooley last night, wasn't it?

JOE   Powerful. What the hell's the mattress for, Bosco?

BOSCO   Get the knickers off, all you Glasgow women! The Inishkeen stallions is coming!

JOE   Go on, you bastard you.

TOM   No chance of him changing his mind?

JOE   Who?

TOM   Who d'you think? — Your aul' fella.

JOE   For Christ's sake — no one left here but us — we own the whole island now.

BOSCO   And welcome to it.

TOM   I didn't see Philly at the do last night. Where was he?

BOSCO   Where is he always?

JOE   Started the salmon. Single-handed. He's not in yet.

BOSCO   It's a buck like me Sarah should have got. Jaysus, I'd never rise out of the bed except to eat.

TOM   Say goodbye to him, will you?

BOSCO   And to Sarah.

JOE   Right. Right. You'd better hurry.

TOM   Is your father about, Joe?

BOSCO (*Calls*) So long, Manus!

JOE He's up the hill. He wouldn't hear you.

TOM Goodbye, Joe.

JOE Good luck, lads.

BOSCO Get them off! Get them off! The Donegal bulls is coming for you!

They go off down left.

JOE Bloody madmen. You should see them, Father; you'd think they were going to a bloody dance. Bloody madmen . . . Dammit the first boat's pulling out. She's lying very low in the water. Someone's standing up and waving — (*he waves back*) — it looks like Barney Pat — God, aul' Barney — (*Softly*) Good luck, aul' Barney. Dammit he's got his fists clenched above his head and he's shaking them. What the hell's he at?

Sound of drunken singing. CON *enters upstage left. He has a bottle of whiskey in his hand. He has been drinking for days and is almost inarticulate. He is being steered and prodded along by his daughter* ANNA. *When she appears* JOE *becomes embarrassed.*

Yes, Con. Yes, Anna.

ANNA Are we the last?

JOE Almost.

ANNA Here's the key to the door. Maybe you'd light an odd fire — you know, to keep the place aired.

JOE Surely.

ANNA Might as well have it cosy for the fieldmice.

CON (*Calls into house*) She's bringing me to a place called Kilburn, Manus.

JOE I'll write you every Sunday night, Anna. Sarah'll do it for me. She's smarter with the pen than me.

CON (*Calls*) In London.

ANNA (*To* CON) We'll miss the boat.

JOE And Philly'll post it every Monday when he goes out to the fish auction. I'll — I'll — I'll tell you all the news

395

about here.

ANNA They'll be long letters.

CON (*Calls*) Goddamn you, Manus Sweeney, you won't always be as well set up as you are now.

ANNA Come on, Father, come on.

JOE Anna, I'll —

ANNA The boat's going to leave without us.

CON (*To* JOE) One bloody room in bloody Kilburn, son.

ANNA I'm going without you.

CON D'you think was the Flight of the Earls anything like this?

ANNA Come on! Come on! There's only one boat left.

CON bursts into song and plunges off.

CON 'My name is O'Donnell, the name of a king
And I come from Tirconnell whose beauty I sing.'

He goes off down left. ANNA, *afraid he'll fall, moves after him.*

JOE Anna, I will write to you, Anna.

ANNA You hadn't that much to say to me when I was here.

She goes off down left.

JOE Honest to God I will. Sarah will. (*Shouts*) Anna! Anna, I . . .

He breaks off suddenly and glances back in embarrassment at the kitchen.

Did you see Con, Father? Full as a bloody skin, the bastard. Jaysus, he hasn't sobered for nine days, that fella. Wants his head kicked in. That's what he wants. His bloody head kicked in.

Enter PADDY *and* MARTIN. PADDY, *a strong, determined man in his late thirties, walking towards the harbour*

as if he were in a daze, looking neither left nor right.
His son, MARTIN, *aged about ten, acting very manly,*
trots beside him.

MARTIN Yes, Joe.

JOE Yes, Martin. Look after yourself, boy. Good luck, Paddy.

PADDY *hesitates, then goes on.*

MARTIN Shake the aul' fella's hand for me, Joe.

JOE I'll do that. Paddy, I hope you have the best of luck
over there. I hope you . . .

But PADDY *has gone, as has* MARTIN. JOE *looks after*
them.

MARY (*Off*) Hold on! Hold on! We're coming! We're coming!

Enter up left MARY *and* NEIL — *Sarah's parents.* MARY
is a brisk, efficient woman. She has decided that by
keeping talking this situation can best be handled.
NEIL *is smiling — and on the point of breaking down.*
He is in his bare feet and carries his shoes in his hand.

(*Shouting towards harbour*) Hold on! Hold on! We're
coming! We're coming!

On hearing her mother's voice SARAH *comes out to the*
street.

I'm at that fool of a father of yours for the past month
to throw the dog into the tide but he has to leave it to
the last minute. And then what happens? The rope
breaks and the dog bites his hand and he falls into the
water himself and destroys his Sunday shoes. (*To* JOE)
He's bound to come about looking for food. Put a shot
in him, will you, Joe?

JOE Right, Mary.

MARY (*To* SARAH) Now. I've left all the blankets and sheets on the kitchen table. Take what you want. Leave what you want. There's a bag of meal up in the loft that'll do the hens and there's three sacks of seed potatoes inside the byre door. Where's Philly?

SARAH He's out at the salmon, Mother.

Pause.

MARY Thank God you got a sensible man — not like the fools I seen drinking themselves stupid last night. (*To* NEIL) Have you got the key? Mother of God, would you look at that! Put on your shoes, man!

NEIL They're —

MARY I know they're wet! But I'm not leading you into Manchester like an early Christian pilgrim!

NEIL *hands the key to* SARAH.

NEIL It was the dog. He thought I was going to drown him.

MARY And what were you trying to do? — Teach it to swim? My God, I married a fool. Come on. Move. Move. Say goodbye to Philly for us. And your father, Joe. We'll be back for the whole of July and August next year — or sooner, if needs be. (*Softly*, to SARAH) Any news to tell your sister beyond?

SARAH What sort of news?

MARY You're not throwing up your food or putting on weight, are you?

SARAH *turns aside.*

All in good time. Although when I was your length married I had Josephine talking and Christy crawling and Paddy in the cradle and I was six months gone with you and still that disciple was grinning at me like a sick sheep every time I bent over to put a turf on the fire. Lazy men are a constant burden to their wives. Thank your God you got an active one. By the time I get back you'll have your hands full. I left the cradle in the room down. Are we right? Goodbye, Joe.

JOE Goodbye, Mary. Good luck. Goodbye, Neil.

MARY Goodbye, *a thaisce*, see you next summer. Maybe before — if I'm needed.

NEIL shakes SARAH's hand formally.

NEIL They'll be dry before I get to Derry.

Suddenly he throws his arms around her. They embrace.

SARAH Father . . . Father . . .

NEIL If you were coming too it'd be nothing, nothing at all.

MARY Lookat — you're holding them all up. Mother of God, now the fool's going to cry!

SARAH I'll go down to the harbour with —

MARY You'll do no such thing. We're away! We're off! Send for me if you want me. I can be back in a day. Come on! Come on!

She catches NEIL's arm and takes him with her off down left. SARAH goes into the kitchen. JOE moves downstage. Now MANUS rises slowly from his seat, comes to the door, comes out on to the street. His left arm is missing. The empty sleeve is tucked into the pocket of his jacket. JOE glances back and sees his father. They stand silently looking down at the harbour.

JOE That's everybody. That's the last of them.

Pause.

Look at Bosco sitting up on top of his mattress. Playing the aul' mouth organ . . . if you could hear him.

Pause.

Whatever wind there is is with them.

Pause.

MANUS When Philly gets back tell him I'm away over to the meadow to look at the sheep. I might shift them up to the far hill. The grazing on it might be better.

JOE You're king of the whole island now, Father. King of the whole bloody island.

MANUS The well needs to be cleaned out. If this weather keeps up we'll have to carry to the cattle.

JOE There'll always be bloody cattle.

MANUS I'll not be long.

JOE King of Inishkeen, King of nothing.

MANUS We haven't much. But we have enough.

JOE They don't think so.

MANUS They're doing a wrong thing.

JOE They're doing what they want to do.

MANUS This is where they belong.

JOE There was a vote taken.

MANUS They'll regret it.

JOE So they'll be back tomorrow — is that what you're saying? You're saying they'll be back tomorrow, next week, the week after? Is that what you're saying?

MANUS No.

JOE Damned right they won't. There should never have been anyone here in the first place.

MANUS Fifty years ago there were two hundred people on this island; our own school, our own church, our own doctor. No one ever wanted.

JOE Scrabbing a mouthful of spuds from the sand — d'you call that living?

MANUS And by God there'll be life here again.

JOE When? When they all come flocking back?

MANUS You could take up on them in that currach if you want to.

Pause.

JOE You — you — you haven't even the guts to bid them goodbye.

MANUS They belong here and they'll never belong anywhere
else! Never! D'you know where they're going to? I do.
I know. To back rooms in the backstreets of London
and Manchester and Glasgow. I've lived in them. I
know. And that's where they'll die, long before their
time — Eamonn and Con and Big Anthony and Nora
Dan that never had a coat on her back until this day.
And cocky Bosco with his mouth organ — this day
week if he's lucky he'll be another Irish Paddy slaving
his guts out in a tunnel all day and crawling home to
a bothy at night with his hands two sizes and his head
throbbing and his arms and legs trembling all night
with exhaustion. That's what they voted for. And if
that's what you want it's there for the taking.

*JOE goes off left with his broken spade. MANUS goes
into the kitchen.*

Sarah, where's my stick?

She hands it to him.

Guts! Talking to me about guts!

SARAH He's not much more than a boy. Couldn't you see he
was going to cry?

MANUS What would he cry for?

SARAH For himself. For Anna.

MANUS Takes no guts to run away.

SARAH You're the man would know that.

MANUS You're turning into a sour woman.

SARAH It would be a comfort to him to know you did your
share of running away, wouldn't it?

MANUS And a sour woman never made a home.

*She goes into her bedroom. He goes out to the street.
PHILLY enters right. He is wearing thigh-boots and
carries an outboard engine across his shoulder. Unlike
his father and his brother he is lightly built. And unlike all the other islanders, he talks quietly.*

Well? How was it?

PHILLY All right.

MANUS There was too little wind.

PHILLY There was enough.

MANUS Where did you go?

PHILLY North-east of the Stags.

MANUS The moon was bright.

PHILLY At times.

MANUS And that aul' net — you could put your head through it in places.

PHILLY It'll do.

MANUS Was it no good at all?

PHILLY They're down at the slip. I'll need a hand. Is Joe about?

MANUS (*Roars*) Joe! How many?

PHILLY A hundred and thirty.

MANUS Salmon?

PHILLY I would have shot again but she (*outboard*) started missing.

MANUS You're taking a hand at me!

PHILLY Nothing under five pounds.

MANUS God, Philly man, you're a prince! Joe! Sarah! They haven't come like that, sir, since I was a boy. And how did you haul them by yourself?

JOE *enters left.*

A hundred and thirty he got! One shot! And not a fish under five pounds!

JOE How many?

PHILLY They were that thick in the water you could have walked on them.

MANUS Twelve dozen — damn near. Twelve dozen on his first night. And him alone. We never began a season like that before. Never. Not even in the old days.

JOE How did you haul them?

MANUS He hauled them, boy! He hauled them!

JOE One shot?

MANUS With a bad net!

JOE Christ, Philly, that's fierce altogether. Good on you, man.

PHILLY   They were in it. Anyone could have lifted them.

MANUS   A mouthful of spuds from the sand, eh? And I told them too. But they wouldn't listen to me. Rocks, dead, barren, they said. And their hearth fires aren't right dead when Philly proves me right and proves them liars.

PHILLY   Are they gone?

MANUS   And all our bad luck go with them. We'll manage better without them. Fetch the barrow, Joe, and we'll bring home the first harvest.

> *He goes off right.* PHILLY *takes the plug out of the out-board and cleans it carefully with a rag.*

JOE   Jaysus, you made great work all the same. I'll go with you the night, Philly. All right?

PHILLY   Right.

JOE   I'm not as awkward in a boat as he says.

PHILLY   Him! He's a blether.

JOE   Wasn't much blether from him last night. Felt a pity for the aul' bastard sitting in there by the fire, talking about the old days and about Mother and all.

PHILLY   Mouth. I couldn't listen to him.

JOE   He was telling me a good one about the first night he arrived in the States. He said when he got off the boat this wee Chinaman ran up to him and threw his arms about him and started shouting, 'Nephew! Nephew! Welcome, nephew, welcome!' And Father, Jaysus, he thought, maybe for all he knew this was the man Auntie Kate had married out there and she'd sent him to meet him, and Father he said, 'Thank you very much, Uncle Barney!' Jaysus!

PHILLY   What did he say about Mother?

JOE   She had long fair hair. I never knew that, Philly, did you? And I says to him sure her name was Rosie Dubh. And he said that was just a family name; but she was fair, he said. And his job was to plait it every night before she went to bed. And you should have seen his face when he was telling me.

PHILLY With one hand?

JOE One hand what?

PHILLY How did he plait it with one hand?

JOE Be God I never thought of that. With his mouth — that's it — with his mouth too.

PHILLY Did he not go up to the do in Big Anthony's?

JOE No, he couldn't face it.

PHILLY Was it any good?

JOE I didn't go up until he went to bed.

PHILLY More fool you.

JOE And by that time all the aul' ones were stupid drunk and the young ones were going wild. About two in the morning Bosco and the boys built a haystack in the middle of the kitchen floor and then began wrestling on top of it.

PHILLY Eejits.

JOE And when they got tired of that they tied two cats together and went chasing after them through the house, throwing hot water over them.

PHILLY A hard man, Bosco.

JOE Bloody savage. This day week if he's lucky he'll be just another Paddy slaving his guts out in a tunnel in Scotland. That'll knock some of the bully out of him.

PHILLY You'd think you'd been there.

JOE Is Glasgow nice, Philly?

PHILLY All right. What I saw of it.

JOE I'd like to see Glasgow. I'd like to see London. Jaysus, I'll be lucky if I ever see Dublin. (*Looking around the island*) It's like a Sunday when they're all out at Mass. Only the doors are shut and there's no smoke from the chimneys. (*Pause*) He says he's leaving me the lower fields and whatever beasts he has — if I'm here when he dies.

PHILLY With a ranch like that you'll be a gentleman farmer.

JOE Funny listening to him saying it all the same. And he's leaving you and Sarah the upper fields and the bog and the two boats and any other stuff there is about the place.

PHILLY That's big of him — I made the boats myself.

JOE And the house too, for this is where he wants his grandchildren reared.

PHILLY He's waiting for the wheelbarrow.

JOE Be God I forgot.

He goes towards right, stops, takes Anna's key from his pocket and holds it up.

Anna left me the key of her house. To light the odd fire in it. To have it nice for the fieldmice.

He looks at the key, then at PHILLY. *Then he pockets the key and goes off quickly.* PHILLY *takes off the big boots and goes into the house. He fills a basin with water and is washing when* SARAH *comes in from the bedroom.*

SARAH You're back.

PHILLY Aye.

SARAH Tired?

PHILLY A bit.

SARAH D'you want something to eat?

PHILLY I'll have a sleep first.

Pause.

SARAH How was the salmon?

PHILLY Good.

SARAH That'll please your father.

PHILLY How are you?

SARAH They're all away.

PHILLY So. (*Pause*) How did the father and mother go off?

SARAH She talked a lot.

PHILLY I thought I would have been back in time but the tide didn't favour me.

SARAH She left us blankets and meal and stuff. And a cradle, if you don't mind.

PHILLY What sort of form was he in?

SARAH She sent him out to drown the dog this morning and

he came back and said the rope broke. Couldn't even make up a good lie, the fool. And whatever messing he was at, he got his good shoes wet, and there he was, standing on the street in his bare feet and him going off to England and the wet socks sticking out of his pocket and not a sensible word out of his head and she says they'll be back next summer for two full months or sooner she says any time at all she's needed she says . . .

She almost cries but recovers. He watches her closely but makes no move towards her; she goes on almost formally, choosing her words with care.

Philly, I don't want to stay here. I want to go with them; not with my father and mother, but with all of them and with you, all of us together. I'll go out of my head with loneliness, I know I will.

PHILLY Easy.

SARAH It's nothing against your father or Joe. But the loneliness, Philly, the loneliness — I won't be able to thole it, Philly, I know I won't.

PHILLY You'll be all right.

SARAH We belong with the others. We should be with them.

PHILLY But they won't be together. As soon as they get to Derry they'll split up and they'll never see each other again. And when tonight comes there won't be a man of them that isn't wishing he was back here. D'you think your father's ever going to be content over there?

She shakes her head.

Or Con? Or Big Anthony? Or Nora Dan?

SARAH Because they're too old to change. But we're not.

PHILLY You know my plan. Stick it out until the end of the summer. I'll have made the most of £200 then. Then we'll pack up and off and bugger the lot.

SARAH That's what you said last year.

PHILLY I made nothing last year on account of the storms.

SARAH Your father'll never shift.

PHILLY He'll have his choice.

SARAH And you wouldn't leave him behind. You couldn't leave him alone.

PHILLY He'll have Joe, won't he? And when Joe gets sense and clears out he can talk his big talk to the rabbits for all I care.

SARAH And you wouldn't leave the sea.

PHILLY 'When Philly's on a boat he needs neither man nor food' — that's the way he rants.

SARAH Is he wrong?

PHILLY Any hard cash that comes into this house comes from the sea, not from his footering about the scraps of fields. And as long as I make money from it I'll fish it.

SARAH Maybe if you spent less time on it we might be better off.

PHILLY Farming? Here?

SARAH You and me.

Pause.

PHILLY I'm tired.

SARAH You're always tired when you're at home.

PHILLY I was up all night, woman. When you and the rest of them were away drinking and dancing I was working.

SARAH So you were.

> *He looks at her, uncertain what she means. He opens his mouth to say something more, decides against it, goes into the bedroom. She takes an empty bucket and goes off right.*
>
> PETER *enters left. A plump, balding, middle-aged man. He is slightly out of breath from the climb up the hill. He is joined by* SHANE, *twenty years younger, peeling an orange. Both men are dressed in summer slacks and open shirts.*

PETER My God, it's heavenly. Look, Shane, everywhere you

turn, look at the view; you can see for a hundred miles. And the clarity. Look — there's the river where we camped the night before last and the lake where the lorry picked us up and the old railway station and the plantation where the men were cutting the spruce. And the sea, Shane, look at the sea. And there's not a sound — listen — not a sound. My God, this is heaven.

SHANE *has been examining a stick he has picked up.*
He whispers nervously to PETER.

SHANE Apache.
PETER What?
SHANE Five-pointed star and the rising sun. Shhhh.

He grips PETER's *elbow and gives two low whistles.*

You think that's the cleft-palate whippoorwill?

He shakes his head slowly.

PETER Shane, let's forget about trying to make Galway. Let's spend the last few days here. What do you say?
SHANE Has it a name?
PETER Inishkeen.
SHANE Apache name. Means scalping island.
PETER We'll put the tent up on that meadow down there — no, on that green above the beach.
SHANE And sell pop to the kiddies.
PETER And for the rest of the holiday we'll just eat and sleep and sunbathe and laze about. What about that? Maybe we'll stay for a month — two months — maybe we'll never leave! What do you say? Do you agree?

SHANE *is prowling about with exaggerated stealth.*

For the last few days we have then. I don't really want to go to Galway. I'd rather stay here. I'm tired of hitching lifts and moving all the time. What about you?

Will you, Shane?

SHANE   Sinister.

PETER   I want to.

SHANE   Too quiet.

PETER   Please.

SHANE   What are the facts, Sergeant? A dozen furnished houses, all recently occupied. Crops in the fields. Some cattle. But no people. Now. There is no evidence of a hurried evacuation, so we can rule out plagues and fiery dragons. And yet the atmosphere reminds me of . . . Got it! Germany — Lower Saxony — 1940 — parachuted in to join the Resistance. Saw this column of Hitler Youth marching along country road leading to mountain. Chap in strange uniform up front playing recorder. Young people all laughing and singing. They reach the mountain. A door opens. They all march through. Disappear. Door shuts. Then silence. Not a sound. Just like here.

PETER   Shane, please be sensible, will you?

SHANE   Hamelin. That's the name of the place. Hamelin.

PETER   Stop fooling for a second.

SHANE   Why?

PETER   The boat's coming back for us. I want a decision made.

SHANE   You're wearing your *sincere* look.

PETER   Do we stay here or do you want to stick to the original plan and head for Galway?

SHANE   (*Sings*) 'And watch the sun go down on . . . '

PETER   Which is it to be?

SHANE   I've forgotten the question.

PETER   Stay here or head on.

SHANE   A choice.

PETER   Whatever you want.

SHANE   Yes.

Pause.

PETER   Well?

SHANE   I hate choices, Peter.

PETER   I want to stay. What do you want to do?

SHANE   In the circumstances, M'Lord, I'm torn between emotion and intellect, between the old heart and the old head, and the trouble is —

PETER   The trouble is you've damn little of either. OK. Fine. Right. We'll go. That's settled. Let's get away.

SHANE   Here!

PETER   Of course had I said I wanted to keep on the move, then wild horses wouldn't drag you away. But just because I said the damn place was pretty and that we could have a peaceful few days here, oh then Master Shane assumes his clown's costume and indulges in his juvenile jokes — the great protection. Fine, fine, fine, we'll go. We'll keep moving, talking, laughing, providing vast entertainment for every damn lorry driver that picks us up. What a jolly young man he is!

SHANE   You're perspiring.

PETER   Isn't it about time you dropped that façade of yours?

SARAH enters right carrying a bucket of water. They are not aware of her until she speaks.

SARAH   Good day to you.

PETER   Oh — hello — good day.

SHANE   (*To* PETER) Hiawatha.

SARAH   How did yous get in?

They stare at her.

How did yous get in to the island?

PETER   A young man took us out — in — in his motor boat, a young man called Doherty from the mainland. He's to come back for us within an hour. (*Pause*) We thought all the houses were empty. (*Pause*) A very lovely place you have here. (*Pause*) I hope — I hope — we're not trespassing?

SARAH   Are yous Yanks?

SHANE   (*To* PETER) Christ!

PETER   No, no, we're from Dublin.

SARAH   Are yous touring about?

PETER Making our way down along the coast. Hitch-hiking.

SARAH There's nothing to see here.

PETER We visited four other islands further north. And then we saw this one on the map. And this one's the fifth. Inishkeen — what does the Irish name mean?

SARAH 'The gentle island'.

PETER Lovely — the gentle island. Beautiful name, Shane, isn't it?

SARAH There's nothing here then.

PETER Perhaps you're used to it.

SARAH Were yous ever on the Isle of Man?

PETER No.

SARAH I was there. Six summers ago. I was a chambermaid in the Arcadia Hotel in Douglas. It was great.

PETER Quite a change from here.

SARAH We worked from seven in the morning till ten at night and we got every Sunday off and a half-day every second Thursday. And every night when the house-keeper went to bed we slipped down the fire escape and went to a dance. It was great.

PETER Every night? Weren't you exhausted?

SARAH In the eight weeks I was in Douglas I was at fifty-one dances. I wore out three pair of shoes. I never had a time like it.

PETER Why didn't you go back again?

SARAH You would like it.

PETER I prefer a less hectic holiday at my time —

SARAH Him (*Shane*).

PETER Oh, I thought you meant —

SARAH It's all young ones. He would have crack. What's your name?

PETER Peter Quinn. Shane Harrison.

SARAH What do you work at?

PETER We're teachers. Shane teaches engineering. I'm a music teacher.

SARAH You wouldn't be overworked here. Does he (*Shane*) say nothing?

PETER *turns to him.*

PETER Shane?

SHANE (*Accented English*) Eet ees most gratifying to our persons to be on thee Gentle Island.

SARAH What's he saying?

PETER Nonsense as usual. Pay no attention to him.

Enter MANUS *right.*

MANUS *Cad é mar atá sibh? Tá fáilte romhaibh.*

PETER Good day.

MANUS How do you do, gentlemen?

PETER We're well.

MANUS Having a look over our island?

PETER Very briefly, I'm afraid. There's a boat coming back for us.

MANUS You've been down at the harbour and the beach?

PETER Yes, that's where we arrived.

MANUS And have you seen the cliffs on the east side?

PETER I'm afraid this is as far as we've got.

MANUS Oh you must see the cliffs — and the caves. No one leaves Inishkeen without seeing them. Come in and have a rest and then I'll show you where to go. You've come to a very beautiful place, gentlemen.

PETER I can see that.

MANUS What boat took you in?

SARAH Red Doherty. Said he'd be back for them in an hour.

MANUS Hah! You'll be lucky if he remembers you next month. Come in. Come in. I could do with a cup of tea myself.

PETER No, we can't trouble you with —

MANUS What trouble is there in making a cup of tea?

JOE *enters right.*

And it's seldom enough we have company. This is my son, Joe. And I'm Manus Sweeney. I'm the — hah! — I'm the King of Inishkeen.

The men shake hands.

412

Tea, woman. Come in — come in — it's a tight climb
up that hill.

> *All enter kitchen except* SHANE *and* SARAH.

PETER (*To* JOE) I see you've been out fishing.

JOE I wasn't. My brother Philly was. Last night.

MANUS And he got fifteen dozen salmon, sir. Single-handed.
You'll have to meet Philly. The best fisherman on this
coast. And Joe here's our farmer. And I'm the — what's
the word for it? — I'm the coordinator. That's it. We're
a self-contained community here.

SARAH Are you coming, engineer?

SHANE Why not?

SARAH No one going to eat you.

PETER That's an unusual chair.

> *Aware that* SHANE *and* SARAH *are not in the kitchen
> he calls out to* SHANE.

Shane, come and see this chair.

> SHANE *and* SARAH *enter.*

MANUS That's a comfortable chair. Sit down on it. I'll tell you
about that chair. It came out of a German airplane that
crashed into the side of this hill.

PETER (*Sitting*) Lovely.

JOE It was flung out in the explosion and the pilot was still
in it.

MANUS And not a mark on him. Isn't that strange, sir? Not a
scratch. We buried him in the old cemetery alongside
the British sailors that were washed in.

PETER This was during the war years?

MANUS Rough times, gentlemen. We couldn't go away to work
and there was no money coming in. Only we're a tough
people there wouldn't be a trace of us now.

PETER Were you in the war yourself?

MANUS This (*arm*)? No, I lost it in a mine in Butte, Montana.

But that's another story.

JOE That clock came off a Dutch freighter that broke up on the Stags; and that table came off a submarine; and those lamps came off a British tanker; and these binoculars came off a French minesweeper. My father used to sit up all night waiting for the wreckage. All the men did. And they got bales of rubber and butter and tins of cigarettes and timber and whiskey and whatnot. Tell them about the night the Norwegian lifeboat floundered below the cliffs, Father, when the men were screaming and the —

MANUS The gentlemen'll think we're a race of scavengers. They were bad times. We had to live.

PHILLY *enters from bedroom.*

The fisherman himself!

PETER Your father tells me you got a big catch last night.

PHILLY It was all right.

MANUS (*To* PHILLY) Red Doherty brought them in. Told them he'd be back for them in an hour!

PETER We almost had an accident too — didn't we? He was talking so much that he wasn't watching where he was going.

MANUS Red Doherty all right!

PETER And the next thing we brushed against a huge rock just off the harbour there.

JOE Them's the Monks.

PETER The what?

MANUS There's three rocks in it, two big ones and a wee one. We call them the Monks. There's a name for every stone about here, sir, and a story too.

JOE Tell them about the Monks, Father.

MANUS I will not then. Night's the time for stories.

PETER What's the story?

MANUS It's a long one. I'll give it to you some other time.

PETER Is it a local legend?

JOE Go on and tell them. Go on.

PETER Do, please.

MANUS   Some night I'll tell you. No man can tell a story right in the middle of the day.

JOE   There used to be a monastery here hundreds of years ago — the ruins are still up there on our land; and the old monk in charge of it was very stern and very powerful.

MANUS   He'll only destroy it.

JOE   And one summer his niece came to visit him.

PHILLY   So beautiful was she that the fish came up from the sea and the birds down from the trees to watch her walk along the roads.

Pause. Everyone looks at PHILLY.

Isn't that the way it goes?

MANUS   He has it.

JOE   Jaysus, we all know it! And two of the young monks fell for her and wanted to go away with her but she couldn't choose between them so she took the two of them off in a currach with her one black night. And the old monk seen them skiting off and he turned the three of them into three rocks below.

MANUS   He's ruined it.

JOE   But they knew if they could ever reach the mainland they'd be free from under his curse. So every night when it gets dark them three rocks begin creeping away from the island. But daylight always nabs them before they make the shore and back they have to come.

MANUS   Now you've told it. And that's the Monks.

PETER   It's a good story, Joe.

JOE   I can't put a right skin on it though.

MANUS   Anyhow you're here, gentlemen, despite the Monks.

PETER   And Red Doherty.

MANUS   Will you remain for a while?

PETER   Just before you came along we were talking about staying here for three or four days — we have a tent and stuff down at the harbour — that's if you'd have no objection.

MANUS   Stay. Surely stay. Put your tent anywhere you want. You're welcome. And there's milk and vegetables for the taking. All you need.

PETER   We hadn't quite made up our mind.

JOE   When the weather's good strangers all say it's nice here.

PETER   (*To* SHANE) What about it?

JOE   They could use Anna's house, Father. She wouldn't mind.

SARAH   She didn't say it was for letting.

MANUS   Your friend's a quiet man. What's he for doing?

PETER   We'll stay, Shane. Please.

Pause.

SHANE   Why not? OK. Sure. We'll stay. We'll stay — why not?

Quick blackout.

ACT ONE

Scene Two

A few days later. Forenoon. Brilliant sunshine. SARAH *is setting the kitchen table. She is more attractively dressed and sings as she works.* SHANE *is out on the street. An ancient gramophone is sitting on an upturned creel and he is working at it.*

SHANE Is there a pair of pliers in there, Sarah?

She does not hear him. He goes to the door and as soon as she sees him he acts an old black Southern slave.

You got pliers about here, Missy Sarah Ma'am?
SARAH What are you saying, you eejit you?
SHANE Ah's lookin' foh pliers, Ma'am.

She gives him pliers from the large press.

SARAH Is that what you want?
SHANE Bless you, li'l lady. Ole Joshua he sure fix you' music box real good now. Bl-ess you.

He shuffles off, humming.

Ba-ba-be-do-be-da-boo-boo-boo-boo-boo-boo-dah.

She laughs at him and follows him to the door.

SARAH You made a good job of the radio, engineer. It's going stronger now than when it was bought.

He bows gallantly.

These nights when Philly's out fishing I lie in bed listening to it till almost daybreak. Sometimes I do listen to the music and sometimes to people talking in strange tongues and wonder what it is they do be talking about.

She comes out to the street.

I must call the men for the dinner.

She does not move.

You're a funny one too.

SHANE I'm hilarious.

SARAH You're like the ones on the radio: half the time I don't know what you be talking about.

SHANE His ideas are trivial; pay little attention to what he says. But watch his hands — that's where his genius lies. He could open the vaults of the Bank of England with a gimlet. He could make a computer with a handful of tacks. But give him a hairpin, and with a hairpin he could create an electronic brain that would solve the problems of the world.

SARAH What age are you?

SHANE What age am I? 'You are old, Father William, the young man said, / And your hair has become very white; / And yet you increasingly stand on your head . . . ' Thirty-two.

SARAH Are your father and mother alive?

SHANE Father's a drummer in a beer cellar in Hamburg called The Vicarage; and Mother's in Lapland. Every Christmas she's principal boy in the Lap National Pantomime. Last year they did *Humpty Dumpty*. They flew Father over to play the glockenspiel. No. I'm boasting again. I never knew either of them.

SARAH Have you any brothers?

SHANE Not that I know of.

SARAH Sisters?

SHANE No.

SARAH Were you born in Dublin?

SHANE So they tell me.

SARAH Have you got a house?

SHANE No.

SARAH Where do you live?

SHANE A flat.

SARAH In the town?

SHANE In the town.

SARAH Who cooks your food?

SHANE I live on pieces of string and rusted hair clips.

SARAH Have you any other friends besides Peter?

SHANE Millions.

SARAH Do you know him for long?

SHANE Centuries.

SARAH How long?

SHANE He taught me.

SARAH Peter?

SHANE The same.

SARAH He taught *you*?

SHANE Correct.

SARAH That's funny. What age is he?

SHANE Seventeen or eighteen.

SARAH He's sixty if he's a day! And he taught you!

SHANE *stops working at the gramophone.*

SHANE Yes. I was one of the orphanage children. There were
ten of us went out to Peter's school every day. And because I was talented with gimlets and hairpins he took
an interest in me. Bought me raincoats and fur-lined
boots and leather helmets with flaps that came down
over my ears and buttoned under my chin and kept me
snug and dry. And when the Christian Brothers released
me into the world he got me a job with an electrical
contractor and sent me to a technical college at night
and encouraged me in every possible way to get my
diploma. And when I got it he arranged a job for me in
his school. And for these endless and tireless kind-

nesses I have always been grateful, most grateful, to Peter. And here I now am. And there the story ends. And that's the truth, so help me God. If one admits that there is no absolute truth, would the panel agree that the melodramatic Victorian novelists reveal a concept of reality that does indeed have a kind of bizarre authenticity? Doctor Heimerstammer?

Pause.

SARAH Are yous definitely leaving tomorrow?
SHANE At full tide, lass, with a fresh wind and God willing.
SARAH Do you like living in Dublin?
SHANE No.
SARAH Why don't you leave it then?
SHANE I may. Soon.
SARAH There's nothing to stop you, is there?
SHANE I'm not sure.
SARAH A girl, maybe?
SHANE If it's anything, it's a spook. A spook called Obligation, sired by Duty out of Liability. Daughter, may he niver cross your gintle path. Do you believe in ghosts?

She smiles.

SARAH Philly does laugh at me.
SHANE Why?
SARAH He says I be only imagining things.
SHANE Have you seen 'things'?
SARAH Maybe I have.
SHANE What have you seen?
SARAH You'll laugh too.
SHANE Never when I'm working.
SARAH Well . . .
SHANE Go on!
SARAH Once I went into the byre. It was evening. It was just getting dark.
SHANE And?
SARAH And there the cow was, chained to the post; and I had

the bucket and the milking stool in my hand; and
when I went round to the far side of the cow, sitting
there milking into a pandy was this wee fat, bald man,
with a checked shirt and an ugly, sweaty face.

SHANE Peter!

*She bursts out laughing at the accuracy of the
description.*

SARAH God forgive you!

SHANE Who else!

SARAH Now I don't know where I was at.

SHANE He was milking into a pan.

SARAH A pandy, you clown you! Not a pan. And anyway I
went screaming into the house and dragged Philly out
and pushed him into the byre before me. And there
was nobody there but the cow. But —

SHANE But the air was still heavy with the bald man's aftershave lotion!

SARAH But the cow had been milked. There wasn't a drop in
her.

SHANE Never!

SARAH Honest to God.

SHANE What did Philly say?

SARAH He blamed the calf.

SHANE What calf?

SARAH There was a young calf in the byre too.

SHANE In a checked shirt?

She laughs. They both laugh.

SARAH I knew you wouldn't believe me.

Pause. He goes on working.

This place will be wild dead again when you leave.

SHANE A little less hectic maybe.

SARAH I'll miss you.

SHANE People always warm to me after I've told them I'm a

bastard.

SARAH   When you're not about the house here, when you're down below at the tent, I do watch you all the time through the French binoculars.

Pause.

Peter goes for a walk at ten o'clock every night along the white strand. When he goes out tonight I'll go down to the tent to you.

SHANE   Sorry. Rotary meeting tonight, luv.

SARAH   I want to lie with you, engineer.

He stops working.

SHANE   I snore in my sleep. And my elbows are like daggers.

SARAH   Will you lie with me?

SHANE   Philly.

SARAH   He's no good to me.

SHANE   He's your husband.

SARAH   Will you lie with me?

SHANE   No, Sarah.

SARAH   Why not? Tell me why not?

PETER *enters left.*

PETER   You still at that thing? Hello, Sarah. Is the dinner ready? I'm just ravenous. (*As she runs off right*) The men are on their way down. (*To* SHANE) Not got it fixed yet?

SHANE   Not yet.

PETER   Can it be done?

SHANE   I think so.

PETER   What's wrong with it anyhow?

SHANE   Age.

PETER   Looks like a collector's item to me.

PETER *sits on the ground and relaxes.*

If you think teaching's tiring, spend a morning cutting turf. My shoulders and the backs of my legs are just aching. No job for an old codger like me. Ahhhhh. That's good.

SHANE Where's the bog?

PETER Beyond the ruins of the old monastery. I showed it to you yesterday — just beyond where we had the picnic. My God, it's beautiful up there, Shane: the sun and the fresh wind from the sea and the sky alive with larks and the smell of heather.

SHANE Heaven.

PETER What's that?

SHANE Heavenly.

PETER It is. Really.

SHANE Divine.

PETER Are you being flippant?

SHANE Deadly earnest.

PETER Interesting the difference between Joe and Philly up there. Joe's all lather and earnestness; grunting and heaving and so obviously labouring. And Philly — he doesn't make a sound; but you should see him cutting that turf out of the bank — swift, clean, not a superfluous gesture. Sheer delight to watch him. Poor old Manus and myself messing along behind him. Lord, how I'd love a swim before we eat but I'm too damn lazy to walk down and up again. Did you have a bathe?

SHANE Not yet.

PETER We'll go after lunch. Fantastic weather. Never had a holiday like this in my life. Ever. And never saw a holiday fly as quickly. (*He sits up*) Manus was talking to me up there. Wants us to come back at Christmas. Spend the Christmas holidays here with him. He was very pressing. (*Pause*) I think it's a nice idea — Christmas on an island.

> SHANE *suddenly stops working at the gramophone. He slips his left arm out of his sleeve and tucks it into his belt.*

SHANE   Be Jaysus, Shane boy, you're a quare comedian. You should be on the stage. Like me. Look at the act I have — the simple, upright, hardworking island peasant holding on manfully to the *real* values in life, sustained by a thousand-year-old culture, preserving for my people a really worthwhile inheritance.

PETER *looks around nervously.*

PETER   Shhh!

SHANE   (*Recklessly*) D'you see that bed you're lying on, sir? Three hundred and forty-seven sailors went down with the ship that bed came off. And that ring on your finger was on the finger of a young airman when his plane plunged down on the very spot you're standing on. We're poor people, sir. We survive only because of other people's disasters — musha, God help them.

PETER   That's very mean, very rotten!

SHANE   And now, as a di-varsion, I'll tell yous the old tale of the white-headed harper from the townland of Bally-maglin in the barony of Kildare.

PETER   He couldn't have been kinder to us.

SHANE   True. So we're grateful, most grateful.

PETER   And he genuinely wants us back.

SHANE   Of course he does. Because we give support to his illusion that the place isn't a cemetery. But it is. And he knows it. The place and his way of life and every-thing he believes in and all he touches — dead, finished, spent. And when he finally faces that he's liable to be-come dangerous. You sympathize with him because you're a romantic, too. Where was I this summer? As a matter of fact I spent four days in a war museum. Fascinating place.

PETER   I thought you enjoyed it.

SHANE   You never listen to me.

PETER   You do like it here. I know you do.

SHANE   You see?

PETER   And they like you. They all like you.

SHANE   Which of me?

PETER   All I know is that they've been consistently kind, that they've made these few days memorable, and that they've asked us back. And I want to come back.

SHANE   Then come.

PETER   With you.

SHANE   I've stopped making plans.

PETER   I'm not asking much — a week at Christmas, that's all.

SHANE   You have the gauche subtlety of an insurance man: only tuppence a week — for a million years.

PETER   Is a week so precious to you?

SHANE   Christmas is six months away. Does our lease extend to that?

PETER   Shane, I'm not like you —

SHANE   Peter the Sincere.

PETER   — I can't live casually anymore; I'm too old for that. I've got to the stage when I need a — a — a modest permanence.

SHANE   Six months ahead is greedy.

PETER   Not at my time of day. And I'm not looking for a commitment. I've never asked you for a commitment, have I? Just a reasonable expectation.

SHANE   The ledgers say we've had ten years. That's quite a stretch. When are obligations fully satisfied?

PETER   Don't make me grovel, Shane.

SHANE   I couldn't stop you.

PETER   Please say you'll come. I'm asking you.

SHANE   (*Steps back from gramophone*) Ah! That's it! Fixed!

PETER   You owe it to me, Shane.

SHANE   I owe it to *you*?

PETER   You do. You know you do.

> SHANE *goes towards the kitchen.*

I don't mean money — material things — but in loyalty, devotion, dedication, concern, kindness —

SHANE   Love?

PETER   Goddammit, yes! Love, Shane, love, love — all I have is invested in you — everything — for the best years of my life. There must be some return. It's not extravagant to expect something.

SHANE It is.

PETER Not from someone who isn't as callous as you! But then your affections have always been as uncertain as your origins!

> SHANE *dashes into the kitchen, searches feverishly in presses for a record.* PETER, *genuinely shocked at himself, follows him.*

Shane, I'm sorry — my God, I'm sorry — I'm sorry, Shane — I didn't mean a word of it — I'm tired — I'm jittery — I'm jealous of Sarah, of Philly, of everyone — forgive me, Shane, please forgive me.

> SHANE *has found a record. He speaks at an almost hysterical speed and pitch.*

SHANE If you were going to end your days on a barren island, Sir Peter, what record would you choose?

> *He runs out to the street.* PETER *follows him.*

What record would I choose? Well, I think my first choice would be an ancient Gaelic folk song that I first heard sung by an old man on an island off the west coast of County Donegal, a song called — (*Reading record*) — 'Oh! Susanna', arranged and played by Harry Dudley and his band. And why would you choose that record, Sir Peter?

PETER I'm genuinely sorry.

SHANE Because it reminds me of a memorable holiday I once had on a heavenly island one divine summer.

> *He has wound up the gramophone. He puts the record on. The band plays an introductory line. Enter* PHILLY *and* JOE *left.*

Marvellous! Let's have 'Oh! Susanna' to bring back happy memories of that divine summer.

PHILLY You have it going, engineer?

JOE Good man, Seán.

> PHILLY *is wearing a straw hat. As* SHANE *begins to sing and dance to the music he picks up a stick from the ground and snatches the straw hat and puts it on the back of his head. Now he does a song-and-dance routine.*

SHANE (*Sings*) 'I come from Alabama
       With my banjo on my knee.
       I'm going to Louisiana
       My true love for to see!'

> PHILLY *claps in time with the music.* JOE *joins him.*

JOE Good on you, boy!

PHILLY Get up there, Peter!

SHANE 'It rained all night
       The day I left,
       The weather it was dry — '

> *He dances across to* PETER, *holds out his hands in invitation.*

Sir Peter?

JOE Ya-hoooooooooo!

SHANE '— the sun so hot I froze to death,
       Susanna, don't you cry.'

> *Hands out to* JOE.

Come on, Joe.

JOE You're doing great by yourself.

SHANE 'Oh! Susanna,
       Don't you cry for me,
       I come from Alabama

With my banjo on my knee.'

As the band plays a link passage between verses
SHANE *catches* PHILLY's *hand.*

Come on, Philly. Dance with me.
JOE Go on, Philly boy! Give us a buck-lep!

PHILLY *releases his hand roughly.*

PHILLY Go to hell!

SARAH *enters right as the second verse begins.* SHANE
sings and dances.

SHANE 'I had a dream
The other night
When everything was still,
I thought I saw Susanna
A-coming down the hill.
The buckwheat cake was in her mouth,
A tear was in her eye,
Says I'm coming from the south,
Susanna, don't you cry.
Oh! Susanna,
Don't you cry for me . . . '

When she enters SHANE *dances across to her, catches
her and swings her round. She slaps his face viciously
— howls of laughter from* JOE *and* PHILLY.

JOE Jaysus, that's a quare uppercut, Seán!
PHILLY Give him another! Another! Another!
JOE Beat the head off him, girl!
PETER Stop it! Stop it!

SHANE *pretends the slap has sent him reeling. He recovers. He goes after* SARAH *again as she goes into the
kitchen and then into her bedroom. As he pretends to*

follow her into the kitchen PHILLY *trips him at the door. He falls. The laughter rises. He gets up — without breaking his song — and pretends to stagger after her.* PHILLY *shoves him roughly back. He falls against* JOE. JOE *pushes him away. He falls against* PETER. PETER *shies away from him and looks around in rising panic. He lurches towards* PHILLY. PHILLY *punches him. He falls heavily. He makes no effort to rise. He just lies there, singing.* PHILLY *punches him again and again.*

PHILLY Dance, you bastard! Dance! Dance!
JOE Yip-eeeeeeeeee!

> PETER *can endure no more. He goes to the gramophone, stops it, takes off the record. Silence.*

What did you do that for, Peter?

> SHANE *rises, finds his hat and cane, strikes an exit attitude.*

SHANE Ta-ra-rah.

> PETER *smashes the record.*

JOE What in the name of God did you want to go and break the good record for, man?
PETER I thought he — I was afraid he'd hurt himself.
JOE Seán? Jaysus, it'd take more than that to hurt aul' Seán. Yes, boy?

> *He ruffles his hair as he passes him.*

Should be on the stage, man. A buck like you would make a fortune going round the halls. (*Now in the kitchen*) Any sign of the dinner, Sarah? Sarah!

> SHANE *is looking at his hand.* PHILLY *stands watching.*

PETER Are you hurt?

SHANE I'm fine.

PETER Show me.

SHANE I'm all right.

PETER Let me see.

SHANE I'm telling you — I'm fine, fine.

PHILLY We were only beginning to warm up there, weren't we? (*To* PETER) You should see us when we get going full steam.

He goes towards the kitchen, stops at the door.

What are you doing this evening?

PETER We're going —

PHILLY Shane.

SHANE What?

PHILLY I'll be shooting lobster pots on the east side later on. Come out for the run. I'll show you the caves the aul' fella was telling you about.

PETER We're going for a swim this afternoon.

PHILLY (*To* SHANE) About five o'clock. As soon as we finish in the bog. (*Laughs*) We're making a farmer out of your nanny — aren't we, Peter?

He laughs again and goes into the kitchen.

PETER Let me see.

SHANE It's nothing.

PETER It looks deep. Is it sore?

SHANE A bit.

PETER Put this (*handkerchief*) round it in the meantime.

SHANE Stop fussing.

PETER Come down to the tent. I've got iodine in my rucksack. Where's your jacket?

SHANE Did I have it?

PETER You had it this morning.

SHANE Yes — it's behind the kitchen door.

Pause.

PETER We'll get it later. Come on. That could turn nasty.

They go off left. JOE, *who has been setting the table, sees them go.*

JOE Where's the two off to?

PHILLY To the tent.

JOE Sure the dinner's ready. (*Calls*) Peter! Seán! The dinner's ready!

PHILLY They'll be back.

JOE A handy man all the same, the engineer. I thought the machine was finished. Did he fix the outboard?

PHILLY Aye.

JOE What was wrong with it?

PHILLY Something about the belt. I didn't understand it.

JOE A handy fella to have about a place. Must have a right head on him.

PHILLY What did you make of Peter at the turf?

JOE You're a bugger too.

PHILLY Me?

JOE Don't think I didn't see you — plunging the spade down within half an inch of his hand every time.

PHILLY Quarter of an inch.

JOE Mercy to God you didn't take the hand off him.

PHILLY But I didn't.

JOE And him killing himself trying to keep up with you.

PHILLY I knew what I was at.

JOE Just as well.

PHILLY I think he knew too.

MANUS *enters quickly from the left.*

MANUS That mongrel they tried to drown — he's outside at the henhouse. Give me my stick.

JOE Did he kill any?

MANUS He's still outside — trying to scratch his way under the door.

PHILLY *lifts a hay fork.*

PHILLY I'll settle him.

MANUS Give it to me. I'll get him. I'll wait till he's cornered inside.

He goes off with the fork.

JOE Mind he doesn't turn on you, Father! (*To* PHILLY) I seen him at the gable last night. Sarah throws him an odd crust of bread; that's what brings him about.

PHILLY She feeds him?

JOE She leaves an odd scrap for him.

PHILLY He damn near killed a lamb the day before yesterday!

JOE A dog's something we could do with ourselves. I was thinking, Philly, maybe if Sarah fed him regular —

PHILLY He was never a working dog.

JOE He was a nice dog.

PHILLY Good for nothing. Unless it's a pet you want! (*Yelping, off*) That's him anyway.

SARAH *enters from bedroom.*

SARAH What's that? What's the noise?

PHILLY We're waiting for the dinner. When you're ready.

SARAH Is it the dog that's yelping?

PHILLY Did you think it was the bucks below in the tent? Your friends?

SARAH No friends of mine.

PHILLY A fine long morning alone with the engineer, hadn't you?

SARAH It didn't bring you running back to the house.

MANUS *enters.*

JOE Did you get him?

MANUS I got one lunge at him.

PHILLY Did you kill him?

SARAH Kill who? My father's dog?

MANUS He made a jump for the window. I got him in the neck.

PHILLY He got away?

MANUS Dragging himself by the front paws.

PHILLY You botch everything!

MANUS He made over the wall and up the hill. I didn't get a second go. He'll not last long, though.

SARAH There's no harm in that dog.

MANUS He was at the hens. Where's the strangers?

JOE (*To* SARAH) The engineer fixed the outboard too.

PHILLY And her radio.

MANUS I don't understand a word that young lad says. Peter has more sense to him. He was asking me up there could they come back at Christmas.

JOE Here in a tent in December? Bloody mad!

MANUS That's what I said to him. What I think he was angling for was for me to ask them to stay here in the house.

JOE That's more sensible.

SARAH There's no room for them in this house or in any other house here either.

JOE Jaysus, you're in a bad twist.

PHILLY (*To* MANUS) What did you say? What did you say?

MANUS Well, I told him that —

> *Sound of dog baying. Silence in the kitchen.* SHANE *runs on to the street. The dog bays again.* SHANE *lifts his head and bays back.*

JOE That's no dog!

SARAH It's him.

MANUS Who?

> JOE *goes to the door.*

JOE It's Seán! Christ, would you look at him! Yes, Seán! Watch out or you'll get the fork in you too.

> SHANE *comes into the kitchen.*

SHANE Single yelp shatters fragile peace. Acute unease on paradise island. War thought imminent. All men over seventeen report for military service. Gentlemen — and

433

good lady — my friend is detained but will join us presently. He asks you not to wait for him. Is luncheon served? Bless us, O Lord, for these and all Thy other gifts which from Thy bounty we are about to receive.

PHILLY (*Laughing*) Amen to that, engineer! Amen to that!

Blackout.

ACT TWO

Scene One

Later that same evening. SARAH, JOE, MANUS *and* PETER *are playing Solo.* MANUS *has his cards on a breadboard on his knee.* JOE *is playing a hand.*

JOE   Come on, Father. Your lead. Play, man, play. Go down like a soldier.

MANUS   How many have you got?

PETER   He needs one more.

JOE   I'm home and dry. Yous might as well pack it in — yous are beat.

     MANUS *leads.*

MANUS   That's the best I can do.

JOE   And it's not much good. Yes, Sarah?

     SARAH *plays a card.* JOE *looks into her hand.*

The Jack's better than that.

SARAH   Is it?

JOE   Is it! What d'you think's trump? Take that up and play the Jack.

     She obeys.

Peter?

PETER   I'm afraid he's through.

     He plays a card.

JOE   Covered by a darling wee ace of trump! And that gives
      me nine! And game! And you're welcome to the rest
      of them. Pay up! Pay up!
MANUS The cards are that old he knows every scratch on the
      back of them.

SARAH *rises from the table.*

SARAH That's me out.
PETER (*To* JOE) You owed me a penny from the last hand.
      That's us quits.

JOE *pushes a handful of coins across the table to* SARAH.

JOE   Here, Sarah. That'll stake you for a couple of hands
      more.
SARAH I'm not playing.
JOE   You can't break up the game.
SARAH Finished.
JOE   Come on. Be a sport.
SARAH Are you deaf as well as thick!
JOE   Jaysus, you're in quare humour. (*To* OTHERS) What's
      biting her all day? Like a bag of bloody weasels.

MANUS *rises.*

MANUS It's getting dark anyway.
JOE   Three more hands — that's all. Two more.
MANUS We've had enough for one night.
JOE   A couple of hands of poker to finish up. Right, Peter?
PETER I'm agreeable.
JOE   Be a sport, Father. Sit down.
MANUS No, no more tonight. You get stiff sitting too long.
JOE   Damn poor losers, the lot of you.

PETER *rises.*

PETER It's hard to be a good loser when the cards are marked.
JOE   Sticks and stones will break my bones. But the truth is

it's the skill that counts in the end. And you haven't got it, boys.

SARAH *lights the lamp.*

MANUS Is the milking not going to be done?

JOE Is the bucket scalded?

SARAH There.

JOE It's hardly worthwhile milking these nights.

PETER You can't lift lobster pots in the dark, can you?

MANUS Not unless you have to.

PETER What I'm thinking is — Philly and Shane should be back, shouldn't they?

MANUS There'll be no hurry on Philly. He doesn't know what time means when he's out in a boat.

PETER He's going fishing again tonight, isn't he? I mean he'll come home first and then go out again?

JOE He'll probably leave Seán off at the far slip and head out again by himself. He'll hardly come up here. (*To* SARAH) Did he take a piece with him?

SARAH He did.

JOE You'll not see him till morning then. (*As he leaves with the bucket*) What about another wee hand later?

PETER The next game we'll have will be at Christmas — and then we'll play with *my* marked cards.

JOE *laughs and leaves.*

MANUS (*To* SARAH) Are you making supper?

No answer.

Sarah!

SARAH What?

MANUS Are you making no supper?

SARAH If you want it.

MANUS Surely we want it. Isn't it supper time? (*To* PETER) When are you leaving tomorrow?

PETER Before lunch. We'll need to be on the road early to get lifts.

MANUS Joe'll take you out. He's hoping there'll be a letter for him at the post office.

PETER *stands at the door looking out over the sea.*

PETER I imagine, if you could see them, they're trying to escape now.

MANUS Who?

PETER The monks and the girl.

MANUS Them. Hah! They're wasting their time. They'll make nothing of it.

PETER I can't tell you how I hate going, Manus.

MANUS You were lucky in the weather.

PETER Absolutely lovely (*view*).

MANUS The man in the radio says it's the warmest June since the turn of the century.

PETER It's not the weather; it's the . . . the calm, the stability, the self-possession. Everything has its own good pace. No panics, no feverish gropings. A dependable routine — that's what you have.

MANUS The weather makes all the difference.

PETER I envy you, Manus: the sea, the land, fishing, turf-cutting, milking, a house built by your great-grand-father, two strong sons to succeed you — everything's so damned constant. You're part of a permanence. You're a fortunate man.

MANUS You wouldn't live here all the same.

PETER I could.

MANUS Why would you want to be wrestling with the elements here and you with your clean indoor job and your good salary? And in another while you'll be sitting back and drawing your pension. Is it sixty or sixty-five you retire at?

PETER No pension for me, Manus.

MANUS Why's that?

PETER I gave up the clean, indoor, pensionable job years ago.

SARAH The engineer's a liar then!

PETER Shane?

438

SARAH He said you taught in the same school as him.

PETER I did. For a while. Then the principal and I had a row —

SARAH About the engineer?

PETER — and I haven't taught in a school since.

SARAH Why couldn't you get into another school? Why?

PETER Oh I work. Every Wednesday I play the piano in the lounge of the Imperial Hotel during afternoon teas. And I take pupils — I have a few pupils. And when times are really thin, d'you know what I do, Manus? You'd never guess. I tune pianos. Yes. I have a very efficient bicycle that takes me round the whole of Dublin. And in the spring and summer I venture as far afield as Wicklow. Tuning pianos . . .

MANUS As long as you make a living.

PETER Between us we manage. We have enough.

> MANUS *goes to the dresser. Embarrassment makes him formal.*

MANUS Peter, it has been a good thing for us to have you here with us. You came at a time when we were hungry for new voices.

PETER If anyone's grateful —

> MANUS *holds up his hand.*

MANUS Your educated company was my pleasure, and Shane himself was more entertainment for the young people than the instruments he set going again. As a token of my pleasure and gratitude I want you to accept this clock. There's a bit of a dent on the top but she's a damn fine time-keeper.

PETER I couldn't, Manus. I really couldn't —

MANUS Take it. Don't offend me. No more to be said.

PETER It's — gosh, it's — it's too much. It really is. We ate here, we took your milk and vegetables and —

MANUS No more. No more. She came off a Dutch freighter in '43. And if I hadn't got it some other man would.

PETER　I'm most grateful. Thank you very much.

MANUS　You're welcome. That's it now — we'll talk no more about it. I'll tell you something now, Peter, that I've always had in my heart: man, it's a thing I'd love to be able to do — play the piano. You haven't any pupils with one hand, have you?

PETER　One would be enough for most of them. What happened to it?

MANUS　Butte, Montana; in the copper mines there. We were working on our backs in a three-foot tunnel and the mine-face came down on us. And that was it. (*To* SARAH) I'll take more tea.

PETER　Was it painful?

MANUS　It was sorer getting used to being without it. Lucky I was a healthy buck or I mightn't be here today.

PETER　Were you alone at the time?

MANUS　There were six of us. Working a fourteen-hour shift. We earned our money hard. And damn little sense we had for holding on to it. I went away with fifteen dollars in my pocket, sir, and I came back with fifteen dollars. You could say I held my own.

PETER　You manage wonderfully.

SARAH　Tell him the truth.

MANUS　More tea, I said.

SARAH　When he came back from America he had his two arms.

MANUS　That'll do you.

SARAH　Two arms and a glib tongue and a roving eye he had.

MANUS　Shut up.

SARAH　And at the back of the hill there was a gentle young girl called Rosie Dubh — Rosie Duffy — living with two aul' uncles that never spoke and never washed and never lit a fire.

MANUS　Shut your mouth, woman!

SARAH　They were backward people. They never went to the shop, never mixed with the neighbours, and young Rosie was never out of the island in her life. And when the buck came home from the States he went smelling about the back of the hill. Oh, they all say he was a

smart buck, able with the tongue. And he got Rosie
Dubh pregnant.

MANUS   I'll break your neck!

SARAH   And as soon as she told him, off he skited to England.
And that's where Philly was born, back there, deliv-
ered by two filthy aul' men that kicked her about as
soon as she was fit to be on her feet. And after twelve
months he came home — God knows why — maybe
he was running away from some English girl. And the
night he arrived down at the harbour there the two
uncles were waiting for him with knives they use here
for gutting herring. And that's how the arm was lost
— in that fight. And he married Rosie then because
he had to — he was stuck here; there's no living in
England for one-armed labourers. But by that time
Rosie was past caring. And a month after her second
son was born she went out for a walk along the cliffs
on the east side and was never seen since.

MANUS   You're a foul-mouthed —

SARAH   Joe doesn't know the truth. But Philly does. And he'll
never forgive you for it. And if he can't father a family
you're the cause of it.

MANUS   Bitch!

SARAH *runs out and off right. Pause.*

There's ways and ways of telling every story. Every
story has seven faces. And there's things shouldn't be
said before a stranger.

In case the word offends PETER *he touches him on the
shoulder.*

When I came home from Montana, after all the whores
that lived in the camp, she was that — that — that —
she called me Mister Manus! Jesus, me that was born
and reared not three miles from her own doorstep!

PETER   It's none of my business, Manus.

MANUS   I came home to marry her. That's what brought me

back. And before I left London I had a place ready to bring her and the boy back to. It wasn't much of a place but it was better than the uncles' hovel.

PETER   No need to talk about it.

MANUS   When they jumped me below at the harbour I had the wedding ring in my pocket. That's what brought me back — I'd gathered a couple of pounds to start us off. It might have been better to leave her be. She'd got used to being alone in the twelve months. And she had the baby. And this (*arm*), somehow it made her uneasy with me.

PETER   The body was never found?

MANUS   Many's the thing the sea gave me but it held on to her. But she's lying about Philly. He knows the story but he knows the whole story. He holds nothing against me. Not Philly.

PETER   She's been upset all day.

MANUS   Damned right he doesn't. He knows the whole story.

JOE *enters left.*

JOE   Christ, Father, you'd get more milk from a billy goat than that aul' heifer. Look at that. It's this drought. If we don't get rain soon we'll be drinking black tea. Sarah! The strainer!

PETER   Is this it?

JOE   The boys is back: I could hear Seán singing over at the far slip. Jaysus, he's a jolly sailor. I wonder how the pots were. D'you know what lobsters are making now? Twenty shillings a pound! That's what you Dublin fellas are paying! Twenty shillings! And if poor aul' Philly gets half that from the dealer out, he thinks he's doing great.

PETER   I think I'll go for my walk and then get some things packed up. See you both in the morning.

JOE   What about your milk?

PETER   Shane'll take it. All we need is a cupful for breakfast.

JOE   There'll be a canful. We're not that hard pressed.

PETER   See you tomorrow, Manus.

MANUS Goodnight. Goodnight.

> PETER *goes off left.* JOE *picks up teapot.*

JOE Is it cold?

MANUS It shouldn't be.

JOE Was the clock stopped?

MANUS What?

JOE The clock — were you working at it?

MANUS I gave it to Peter. He must have forgotten it.

JOE I'll bring it down when I drink this.

MANUS Shane can take it.

> JOE *pours tea and sits.*

JOE It's not going to be as lively after tomorrow. (*Pause*) You'll miss the antics of the engineer about the place. Jaysus, he's as good as a concert, that fella. (*Pause*) Aye, it'll not be as lively after they go.

MANUS Did you write to Anna yet?

JOE To Anna? To Anna Con? Where would I get the time? Sunday, maybe, when Sarah's doing nothing.

MANUS Have you got her address?

> JOE *takes a scrap of paper from his pocket.*

JOE She wrote it out for me. It's 17 . . . 17 . . . (*He hands it to* MANUS) Christ, she's an awkward fist.

MANUS Get me the pen and paper.

JOE You? Dammit I'm at my supper, man.

MANUS Hurry up. You can post it tomorrow when you go out.

JOE Jaysus, Father, there's no news, unless the heifer going dry —

MANUS Now.

> JOE *gets the pen and paper.* MANUS *settles himself at the kitchen table.*

JOE You need to be in a humour for writing letters. I'm in

no humour, I can tell you.

MANUS What date's this?

JOE Saturday.

MANUS Date.

JOE I don't know the date. Jaysus, the date! How would I know the date! Jaysus.

MANUS Doesn't matter. Go ahead. (*Pause*) Well?

JOE Well what?

MANUS Tell me what you want me to say.

JOE How would I know! It's you that's writing it.

MANUS 'Dear Anna, my father is writing this letter for me.'

JOE That's smart. She'll know it's not me, won't she?

MANUS 'The weather has not broken since you left and for the past three days we have been carrying water from Big Anthony's well.' What else?

JOE The turf's all cut.

MANUS 'The turf's all cut.'

JOE And Philly's hammering away at the salmon and lobster. Two strangers from Dublin were here. They had a tent below at the green. They are leaving tomorrow. Every day since you left I go into your house and look about it. Sometimes I sit down for a while. Yesterday I was sitting at your fireplace and I thought I heard you . . . What in the name of God is there to write about in this place!

MANUS 'Anna, I want you to come back and marry me.'

JOE What are you at?

MANUS 'I will call on the priest tomorrow.'

JOE Jaysus.

MANUS 'We will make out all right. Bring Con back with you.'

JOE Jaysus, Father.

MANUS 'I am enclosing the fare for the two of you.'

JOE Fare? I haven't twenty pounds! I haven't twenty pence!

MANUS 'I mean this, Anna. Please come home and marry me. As soon as possible. Please.' How do I sign it?

JOE What do you mean?

MANUS How do I finish off?

JOE Manus.

MANUS It's from you!

JOE Joe, then.

MANUS Is that all?

JOE In haste, Joe. Kindly excuse writing and spelling. They are not mine.

MANUS *takes money from his pocket, puts it into the envelope, addresses envelope.*

MANUS That'll take them home.

JOE Christ, Father, she'll fall down with the shock. Christ, what'll she say? Rub out that bit about the hot weather — Christ, she'll think I've sunstroke. Holy Christ, Father, d'you think she'd ever have me? Oh my God, Sarah could never have written as powerful a letter as that.

MANUS *puts the letter on the mantelpiece.*

MANUS Tell the priest tomorrow that you want it fixed up next month at the latest.

JOE Father, if she takes me, Father, there'll be no happier man in Ireland.

SARAH *enters from the right.*

Sarah, I've written to Anna. I've asked her to marry me.

SARAH *addresses* MANUS *only. She speaks very softly.*

SARAH Would you like to have a look at your son? Would you like to see the bull that's going to sire your grand-children and bring back life to this graveyard?

MANUS What's this?

SARAH No, you don't want to see. Philly's the prince. Philly's the hero. Philly's the apple of your blind eye. And it's easier to blame me, isn't it? I'm the barren one. My womb bears no crop. Like the lower field good seed's wasted on me. The worst mistake your Philly could have made, wasn't it, to marry a sterile woman?

MANUS What are you trying to say?

SARAH That he's down there in the boathouse at the far slip, your Philly, my husband. That he's down there with that Dublin tramp, Shane. That they're stripped naked. That he's doing for the tramp what he couldn't do for me. That's what I'm trying to say. And that if you're the great King of Inishkeen you'll kill them both — that's what I'm saying.

Quick blackout.

ACT TWO

Scene Two

A short time later. JOE *is sitting at the kitchen table, his head in his hands.* MANUS *is in the airplane seat, facing upstage, as he was in the opening scene.* SARAH *is looking out the window. The lamp is turned down low. The kitchen is almost dark. The street outside is bright with moonlight.*

SARAH He's coming. He's alone. He has his jacket across his shoulder and his shoes in his left hand. He's stopped now. He's looking about him at everything clear in the moonlight. He's saying to himself, 'My God, it's heavenly.'

JOE What are you going to do, Father?

SARAH He's stooping down. He's picking up something. A stone. He's skimming it across the top of the water. He's moving again. He's coming.

JOE Tell me what you're going to do.

SARAH What are you going to do, Manus?

JOE No one's going to lay a finger on him.

SARAH What about the herring knives, Manus?

JOE *jumps up.*

JOE No one's using no knives here. Two's to blame or no one's to blame.

SARAH This is none of your business, boy.

JOE I'm warning you, woman. Put none of your poison into my father's head.

SARAH Manus knows his own mind. He knows what he'll do. Shhh! Quiet! I think — aye, he's singing! Listen and you'll hear him singing. He's a happy buck, the engineer.

447

Do you hear him singing, Manus?

MANUS People have lived here for hundreds of years, thousands of years.

SARAH He's in the hollow. I've lost him now.

MANUS There were people here before Christ was born.

JOE (*To* SARAH) You could have made a mistake.

SARAH I could have made a mistake, Manus.

JOE Maybe their clothes were wet. Philly wouldn't walk the length of himself in wet socks.

SARAH Maybe they were wet, Manus.

JOE And it's black dark in the boathouse. How could you see in the dark?

SARAH He's talking sense, Manus. How could I be sure in the dark? What do you think, Manus? Is there doubt in your mind?

In the distance right we can hear SHANE *singing 'Oh! Susanna' very faintly, getting louder slowly.*

MANUS The gun.

SARAH He's on the path. He's coming. He's coming. Listen. He's coming.

MANUS Give me the gun.

SARAH *gets the gun and gives it to him. He leaves it beside him on the ground.*

JOE Jaysus, he can't use that!

SARAH He's here, Manus.

JOE (*To* MANUS) They're going in the morning. They'll be gone this time tomorrow and —

SARAH Stay out of it!

JOE And you'll never see them again.

SARAH (*To* MANUS) Mind — if you haven't the stomach, I have!

JOE You can't use the gun, Father. For God's sake. You —

MANUS Shut up!

JOE I'll — I'll — I'll get Peter. Peter'll stop you.

JOE *dashes out and off left.*

SARAH 'Peter'll stop you.' For a while there he didn't know how he was going to escape, did he? But he's only a boy. This time you'll be a man, Manus. This time.

> SHANE *enters right.* SARAH *goes to the fireplace and pretends to be busy.* SHANE *goes into the kitchen.*

SHANE *Oíche mhaith daoibh agus bail ó Dhia ar an obair agus go n'éirí an bóthar libh.* How's that then? Philly taught me. Isn't that pretty good? Yes?

SARAH Very good.

SHANE I'm not finished yet. *Bíonn adharca fada ar na buaibh thar lear!* There are long horns on cows far away. Which means far away hills look green. Purest Donegal Irish, untouched by human hand. (*Softly, to* SARAH) Is he asleep?

SARAH Are you asleep, Manus?

MANUS No.

SARAH He's wide awake. What did you think of the caves?

SHANE Never saw them. By the time we got the pots lifted the skipper decided the tide was too far in. He said a fool can row into a cave in low water but it takes a wise man to get out when the tide's full. I'm sure there's an Irish equivalent for that. Something like: The widow-woman with three old hens makes potato bread more quickly than the grey seal grows feathers.

SARAH So what did you do?

SHANE After we lifted the pots? Your worthy husband brought me on a wonderful carefree cruise and pointed out the precise location of all the wartime disasters. We cunningly sidestepped the Monks below and headed for the Stags where the Dutch freighter went down and the point where the British tanker broke up and the beach where the sailors were washed in. It was a jolly, jolly trip, complete with gruesome details. When curt Captain Philly starts talking there's no stopping him. There must be an idiom for that, too: When the silent snipe flies high on a midsummer's night the beggarman with the red whiskers cries into the water at the broken ford. No. Obviously spurious. Too ornate. Too wordy — (*after a quick look round*) just like me.

SARAH Did you go for a swim?

SHANE Yes.

SARAH Where?

SHANE At the far slip.

SARAH Before you went out?

SHANE When we came back.

SARAH In the dark?

SHANE In the moonlight.

SARAH Just a while ago?

He looks at her for a second, then turns to MANUS.

SHANE You're quiet, Manus. What did they do to you up in the bog?

SARAH Half-an-hour ago?

MANUS There was a niggerman came to this island once when I was a boy. He arrived on a December morning, this niggerman, and he was carrying a caseful of holy pictures that he was selling round the country.

SHANE That's what Peter and I may end up doing.

MANUS And the day he came in a storm broke and he was stranded here. And there lived at that time in a bothy of a place down behind the harbour an old couple by the name of Boyle, Andy Boyle and Susan Boyle, and they were both reduced to half their size with the pains of rheumatism.

SHANE And he laid hands on their bent heads and —

SARAH Listen!

SHANE Sorry.

MANUS And that's where the niggerman shacked up, in the bothy with the Boyles. And one morning my father was gathering kelp on the beach and he heard the shouts and the roars coming from the bothy, and out hobbled old Andy, and behind him Susan, and they roared to my father, 'Seize the niggerman! He's a thief. He's robbed us of all our money! He stole our five golden sovereigns!' And with that, out of the bothy leaped the niggerman and off with him over the hill.

SHANE   All niggers is thieves, man.

SARAH   Quicker, Manus.

MANUS   Well, sir, the men of the place soon caught him, and they bound his hands and his feet, and they wrapped a net about him, and they carried him above to the schoolhouse, and true enough they found the five golden sovereigns in his pocket. And then they had to settle on his punishment. And the punishment they settled on was this —

SHANE   I'm breathless.

MANUS   Bound as he was, they harnessed him by a long rope to an old donkey. Then they pumped linseed oil down into the donkey's ears. And for a full day, sir, until it dropped dead, the mad donkey dragged that niggerman across the length and breadth of this island. Then they rowed that niggerman out to the mainland and dumped him there. And them that dumped him said all he was fit to do was inch away from them on all fours, sideways like a crab.

SARAH   That's what happened. What do you make of that story, engineer?

MANUS   All he took was five sovereigns.

SHANE   An obscene story.

SARAH   And he was only a travelling man.

SHANE   So what's the moral? Don't attempt to peddle religion to savages?

SARAH   (*To* MANUS) Savages! Listen!

MANUS   I'm looking for no moral, sir. But I'm thinking the men above in the schoolhouse estimated that it was a fair punishment for a thief.

SHANE   And no doubt they had their reasons. Did Peter collect the milk?

MANUS   And I'm thinking you did a worse thing than the niggerman.

SHANE   Me?

MANUS   I'm thinking, indeed, five golden sovereigns was a small enough thing, sir.

SHANE *stares at* MANUS, *then at* SARAH, *then back to*
MANUS.

SHANE Ah's ain't no black niggerman, Boss. Ah's just pu-ah
white trash, Ah's just nuthin', suh, Ah's just nuthin' at
all. (*Dances and sings*) 'Oh, dem golden sovereigns, Oh,
dem golden sovereigns — '

MANUS *lifts the gun and points it at him.*

MANUS Silence!
SHANE I have no idea what you're talking about, Manus.
MANUS You came in here. And I made you welcome. And in
return you robbed me, sir.
SHANE Robbed?
MANUS You stole my son.
SARAH I seen you — in the boathouse — you and Philly
stripped — I seen you — I watched it all — with my own
eyes — you and him, you dirty bastard — I seen it all
— you dirty, dancing bastard!
SHANE She's hysterical.
SARAH I seen you! I seen you!
SHANE (*To* MANUS) For God's sake, you don't heed her, do you?
SARAH (*To* MANUS) Ask him is it true? Ask him! Ask him!
SHANE *She* wanted to sleep with me.
SARAH With that thing, Manus! Is it the truth or is it a lie?
SHANE I wouldn't have her. That's what's eating her.
SARAH Deny it! Deny it! Deny it! Look at the face! Look at the
slippery eyes! He can't! He can't! 'Cos I seen him! I
seen him!
MANUS Is it the truth?
SHANE What? Is what the truth?
SARAH It is or it isn't? It is or it isn't?
SHANE Look at her, for Christ's sake! She's insane!
SARAH It is or it isn't? Yes or no. Which is it?
SHANE I'll get Philly. He'll —
MANUS Back!
SARAH You've had enough with Philly, engineer. He robbed
you, Manus. He robbed me. Shoot him! Shoot him!

SHANE   Manus, please, Manus, listen, listen to me —

SARAH   Shoot him! Shoot him!

SHANE   Manus, I swear to God —

SARAH   Shoot him!

> MANUS *brings the gun up.* SHANE *crouches before him.*

SHANE   Manus, Manus, Manus, please, please, Manus, please, please.

SARAH   Shooooot!

MANUS   I — I — I — I —

SARAH   Give it to me! I'll kill the tramp.

> *She rushes to* MANUS *and grabs the gun. In that moment* SHANE *bolts for the door.*

SHANE   (*As he dashes away*) Peter! Save me, Peter! Save me!

> *He gets halfway across the street.* SARAH *fires. He falls on his knees.*

Peter . . .

> *He falls on his face.* SARAH *stares at him. All passion is gone. Her mouth is open. Her whole body limp. The gun drops from her hands. Very softly she begins to lament — an almost animal noise.*
> *Blackout.*

ACT TWO

Scene Three

The beginning of dawn the following morning. MANUS *is huddled over a dead fire. He is mumbling inarticulately: but his voice is so modulated that we know he is talking to himself — posing questions and answering them. He rises from the fire and shuffles around the kitchen. He has aged a lot — the assurance has gone from his bearing. He goes to the door and looks out. With his hand he massages his chest and shoulders for heat. As he shuffles around he mumbles to himself.*

MANUS   Where's my stick, Rosie? Rosie? Rosie — my stick! (*He finds it*) Why do you hide it on me? The baby? The baby? It's always the baby. I'll never get used to carrying this thing, woman; never. (*Suddenly he comes alert*) He's back, Sarah! He's back!

> *He goes out to the street to meet* JOE *who enters left.*

Well?

> JOE *walks briskly past him and goes into the kitchen.* MANUS *trots after him.*

Well, boy?

> *During the following conversation* JOE *shaves busily.*

How is he?

JOE   Ill.

MANUS   I know he's ill. What happened? Where did you take him?

JOE   To the Ballybeg hospital.

MANUS Well?

JOE They patched him up as best they could.

MANUS But he'll live?

JOE Maybe.

MANUS How bad is he?

JOE I thought he was for death in the boat. He came round a bit in the hospital.

MANUS He lost a power of blood. What did they say?

JOE Even if he lives he'll never walk again. His spine's shattered.

MANUS He's lying there in Ballybeg?

JOE They could do nothing for him. They sent him away in an ambulance.

MANUS Away? Away where to?

JOE Dublin. He wasn't fit to travel but he'd die if he was left there. He looked like a ghost lying on the stretcher. Still trying to act the clown though.

MANUS Did he say anything about the law?

JOE Who?

MANUS Peter. The engineer.

JOE No.

MANUS Didn't the doctor ask?

JOE He told them he was out after rabbits and tripped going across a ditch.

Pause.

MANUS It was a bad do. It was a sorry day Red Doherty brought them in among us.

JOE Was it you or her?

MANUS What?

JOE Shot him.

MANUS Her. When the time came I — I — I — (*He sits at the fire*) Their stuff's still below.

JOE Peter says throw it in the tide.

MANUS What are you shaving for?

JOE It's morning.

MANUS That's true. It's morning. And he'll never walk again.

JOE If he lives. You should go to bed for a while.

MANUS I'll wait till Philly gets back.

JOE To use the gun on him too?

> JOE *goes into his bedroom. He returns with a case and an armful of clothes.*

MANUS Philly had nothing to do with — What's that?

JOE What does it look like?

MANUS You're not thinking of leaving, are you?

JOE The thinking's done.

MANUS Put that away, boy. You're going no place.

> *He grabs* JOE's *arm.* JOE *stands rigid. The grip is relaxed.* JOE *begins to pack.*

You're making a mistake, Joe. This is your home, this is where you belong. Don't go now. Wait a month. Wait a week. Wait till you know what you're at. You're all throughother. Wait till you're settled. You'll think different when your head's settled.

> JOE *closes the case.*

What's going to happen to us? How are we going to manage? You don't give a curse, do you? It doesn't matter to you that your father's handicapped, does it? Not as long as you're taking care of yourself. That's all you ever thought of — yourself. Go ahead. Go ahead. Think of yourself. You owe me nothing, nothing at all. I deserve no better — me that lost a limb away slaving for you. Go ahead. Clear out. I'll not starve. I can always scrape a hole and grow enough spuds to fill me.

JOE Come with me if you want.

MANUS You're going to London! To Anna! You're going to marry her. That's it. You're going to marry her and come back and raise your family here. That's it, man, that's it.

> *He goes to the mantelpiece, opens the envelope, thrusts*

the money at JOE.

Here you are — money and all. And you'll live here, in this house, this house'll be yours and the upper field and the far bog and the two boats — all yours — and this is where your family'll grow up — here — their grandfather's, their great-grandfather's house.

JOE I'm not taking that.

MANUS You'll need it, man. You'll need it and more.

He produces more notes from his pocket.

That's not near enough. Here — here — you'll need that too — your fare over and back — a wedding — digs — new clothes. Here — take it all. What use have I for it? Take it all.

JOE *lifts one note.*

JOE That'll pay my way to Glasgow.

MANUS Glasgow? She's in London!

JOE I'm going to Glasgow. To Bosco and the boys.

JOE *takes the letter, the proposal, tears it up, and tosses it into the fire.*

MANUS And what about Anna Con? What about the wedding?

JOE *goes into his bedroom.*

(*Shouts*) It's them — them queers! I should have killed the two of them when I had them! What we had wasn't much but what there was was decent and wholesome! And they blighted us! They cankered us! They blackened the bud that was beginning to grow again! My curse on them! My curse of hell on the two of them! *Agus marbhfháisc orthu* — an early shroud on them!

SARAH *enters from her bedroom. She is dressed in the clothes she was wearing yesterday evening. Because of the morning cold she has a shawl thrown over her shoulders. She does not look at* MANUS. *She shuffles around the kitchen listlessly.*

You didn't kill him.

SARAH I know.

MANUS All you did was maim him.

SARAH I heard.

MANUS If I had my two hands that wouldn't have been the story. And now he's going.

SARAH So.

MANUS Not to London — to Glasgow — to link up with the hooligans.

SARAH He'll have a bit of life there.

MANUS Life? What life is there working another man's land for a handful of money? What life is it fifteen men living and sleeping in a hovel no bigger than this kitchen?

SARAH He'll find out for himself. Maybe that's the thing'll please him.

MANUS A man that never saw a town bigger than Ballybeg.

SARAH I never seen anything as lovely as the Isle of Man. That'll do me. Many's the one lives and dies and doesn't see even that.

JOE enters, ready for departure.

JOE I'm off to Scotland, Sarah.

SARAH You're right too.

JOE Bosco'll write for me, let you know where I am, what's happening. Tell Philly I'll leave the boat tied up at the harbour out.

SARAH Goodbye, Joe.

He goes to MANUS *who has turned away.*

JOE I'm away, Father. (*Pause*) Father.

MANUS *does not turn.* JOE *goes to the door, remembers the key in his pocket, stops.*

(*To* SARAH) Anna's key. Maybe you'd light an odd . . . No. Let the fieldmice look after themselves.

He tosses the key on the table and leaves. SARAH *follows him out to the street.*

SARAH Good luck, Joe. Good luck.
JOE Good luck, amen.

Pause. MANUS *goes to the door and watches his son leave.*

MANUS Not a bad lump of a man. He'll not go under.

Pause.

All the same there isn't the same tidiness about him as there is about Philly.

Pause.

Philly'll miss him. Man but Philly'll miss him.
SARAH He'll get over it.

MANUS *joins her on the street.*

MANUS Will you do something for me, Sarah?
SARAH What?
MANUS Don't tell him about what happened here last night. The sooner it's forgotten the better. Will you do that for me?

She shrugs indifferently.

And sure maybe Joe was right. Maybe they only went into the boathouse to change their clothes because they were wet.

SARAH They didn't have a change of clothes.

MANUS Maybe so. Maybe so. But it's that dark in yon place you could imagine anything. One night when I went into it there was a sail hanging from the roof and as sure as God I thought it was a sheep making for me. I could have sworn it was a sheep making for me . . . It's that dark in yon place you could imagine anything. Maybe you . . .

SARAH has walked off left. He goes into the kitchen, looks around aimlessly, picks up the shaving things JOE *left behind.* PHILLY *enters right. He leaves the outboard at the door and enters the kitchen.*

You're early back.

PHILLY Aye.

MANUS I didn't expect you for a while yet. Was it no good?

PHILLY It wasn't much.

MANUS How many?

PHILLY Seven.

MANUS Seven? Well. That itself. Even seven. It's this damned weather. Going to destroy everything.

He gets a notebook and writes in the latest score.

Seven and two's nine . . . that makes two hundred and nine so far. With a bit of luck you could still tip the thousand before the season ends. No trouble with the engine?

PHILLY No. But I think I split the keel on the rocks coming in. I'll have to haul her up and have a look at her. Is Joe up yet?

MANUS I'll help you. I can do it.

PHILLY Joe and me'll manage.

MANUS Joe's away out.

PHILLY What for?

MANUS Joe's away altogether.

PHILLY Gone?

MANUS To Glasgow.

>   PHILLY *laughs heartily.*

PHILLY The bold Joe! Well, that's a good one! I thought he'd never try it!

MANUS To Bosco and the boys.

PHILLY That's the best yet. Joe's left the nest, eh? Man, he'll break his heart to be away from home. It must have been a sudden notion?

MANUS You wouldn't know with that fella. Maybe he had it all planned before the others pulled out.

PHILLY Last night?

MANUS This morning. The strangers went with him.

PHILLY They're away?

MANUS When they got the chance of the boat out.

PHILLY Their stuff's still there. I seen it coming in.

MANUS They left in a hurry. Joe — you know Joe — he was fussing and complaining about missing the Derry bus — wouldn't give them time to pack right. Damn little they had anyway apart from what they stood up in.

PHILLY There's the tent and the gear inside.

MANUS They're gone anyway.

PHILLY And Joe! God, that's a good one! (*Laughs*) Himself and the boys'll do some damage in Glasgow when they get going.

MANUS I think I'll go and lie down for a while. I didn't sleep too well last night.

>   SARAH *comes in with an armful of turf.*

PHILLY He tells me the young brother's away!

SARAH So.

PHILLY The best I've heard yet. Whoever he works to is getting a real bull. Not that he'll stick it long.

SARAH He'll stick it.

PHILLY Joe? Three weeks'll do him and he'll come creeping back. Joe couldn't live anywhere but here. I know Joe. And the strangers are gone too. A real red-out.

SARAH   Will you eat now or will you sleep first?
PHILLY   I'll eat.
MANUS   Give me a call in an hour.
PHILLY   Father.

> MANUS *stops at the bedroom door.*

Hadn't they a wee cooker below in the tent, a yoke
that worked on paraffin oil?
MANUS   They had.
PHILLY   I'll go down and fetch it. A right handy wee gadget
that. Useful in the morning when the fire's not lit.
MANUS   I don't want it. I couldn't work it.
PHILLY   There's nothing to it. Strike a match and away it goes.
And the tent — the best of good canvas that. Put that
over a haystack and it would be as dry as snuff.
MANUS   It wouldn't be healthy.
PHILLY   Healthy? Sure you wouldn't see a haystack out that
hasn't a covering. What d'you want to do? Let the stuff
lie there till the next high tide takes it? I doubt you're
getting old!

> MANUS *goes into his bedroom.*

Healthy! What's wrong with him?

> SARAH *kneels at his feet and pulls off his thigh-boots.*

SARAH   How was the salmon?
PHILLY   Bad.
SARAH   He's keeping a score in a wee notebook.
PHILLY   I seen him.

> *Pause.*

SARAH   You'll never make £200 now.
PHILLY   It might pick up.
SARAH   That means you're stuck for another year.
PHILLY   Maybe.

Pause.

The place'll be quiet without Joe thumping about. But he'll be back. I'll give him three weeks.

SARAH We'll get used to it.

PHILLY The wonder is he made the mainland even.

Fade to black.

Acknowledgements

The editor thanks Jean Fallon and Suella Holland for their invaluable contributions to the preparation of this edition. Acknowledgements are also due to Anne Friel and family, Leah Schmidt and Dinah Wood.

The Enemy Within was published first in *The Journal of Irish Literature* (Delaware) in 1975 and first published by The Gallery Press in 1979.

Philadelphia, Here I Come! was first published by Faber and Faber Limited in 1965.

The Loves of Cass McGuire was first published by Faber and Faber Limited in 1967 and published by The Gallery Press in 1984.

Lovers (*Winners* and *Losers*) was first published by Faber and Faber Limited in 1969 and published by The Gallery Press in 1984.

Crystal and Fox was first published by Faber and Faber Limited in 1970 and published by The Gallery Press in 1984.

The Gentle Island was first published by Davis-Poynter (London) in 1973 and published by The Gallery Press in 1993.